PRESENTED TO

_____

BY

_____

ON THE OCCASION OF

_____

DATE

_____

The grass withers
and the flowers fade,
but the word of our
God stands forever.

ISAIAH 40:8

*In this space, write or illustrate the story of how you met Jesus so that you will remember it and can share it with others.*

filament
ENABLED

EVERY
WOMAN'S™
BIBLE

NLT.

TYNDALE HOUSE PUBLISHERS
CAROL STREAM, ILLINOIS

Visit Tyndale online at newlivingtranslation.com and tyndale.com.

Visit the Every Woman's Bible online at EveryWomansBible.com.

Filament-enabled Bibles and the Filament Bible app are protected by US Patent 10,896,235.

Designed and typeset using Bible Serif and Bible Sans Next by 2k/denmark, Højbjerg, Denmark

For information about special discounts for bulk purchases, please contact Tyndale House Publishers at csresponse@tyndale.com, or call 1-855-277-9400.

ISBN 978-1-4964-5299-3    Hardcover
ISBN 978-1-4964-5300-6    Hardcover Indexed
ISBN 978-1-4964-5301-3    LeatherLike Soft Gold
ISBN 978-1-4964-5302-0    LeatherLike Soft Gold Indexed
ISBN 978-1-4964-8438-3    LeatherLike Sky Blue
ISBN 978-1-4964-8439-0    LeatherLike Sky Blue Indexed

Printed in China

30    29    28    27    26    25    24
8     7     6     5     4     3     2

# CONTENTS

Welcome to Your Filament-Enabled Bible! . . . . . . . . . . . . . . . . . . . . . . . . . . . . A6

Canonical Listing of Bible Books . . . . . . . . . . . . . . . . . . . . . . . . . . . . . . . . . . A7

Alphabetical Listing of Bible Books . . . . . . . . . . . . . . . . . . . . . . . . . . . . . . . . A8

Welcome to the *Every Woman's Bible* . . . . . . . . . . . . . . . . . . . . . . . . . . . . . . A9

*Every Woman's Bible* User's Guide . . . . . . . . . . . . . . . . . . . . . . . . . . . . . . . . A10

How to Explore a Relationship with God . . . . . . . . . . . . . . . . . . . . . . . . . . . A14

Where to Start Reading the Bible . . . . . . . . . . . . . . . . . . . . . . . . . . . . . . . . . A16

Basic Bible Helps . . . . . . . . . . . . . . . . . . . . . . . . . . . . . . . . . . . . . . . . . . . . . A17

Bible Reading Worksheet . . . . . . . . . . . . . . . . . . . . . . . . . . . . . . . . . . . . . . . A18

Meet Our Contributors . . . . . . . . . . . . . . . . . . . . . . . . . . . . . . . . . . . . . . . . A19

A Note to Readers . . . . . . . . . . . . . . . . . . . . . . . . . . . . . . . . . . . . . . . . . . . . A25

New Living Translation: Our Choice for You . . . . . . . . . . . . . . . . . . . . . . . . A26

Introduction to the New Living Translation . . . . . . . . . . . . . . . . . . . . . . . . A27

THE OLD TESTAMENT . . . . . . . . . . . . . . . . . . . . . . . . . . . . . . . . . . . . . . . . .1

What Is My Purpose? . . . . . . . . . . . . . . . . . . . . . . . . . . . . . . . . . . . . . . . . . .1170

THE NEW TESTAMENT . . . . . . . . . . . . . . . . . . . . . . . . . . . . . . . . . . . . . . .1187

The One Year Bible Reading Plan . . . . . . . . . . . . . . . . . . . . . . . . . . . . . . . . 1655

What Do We Learn About God's Mission and Ours? . . . . . . . . . . . . . . . . . 1669

Image Index . . . . . . . . . . . . . . . . . . . . . . . . . . . . . . . . . . . . . . . . . . . . . . . . . 1672

Identity Index . . . . . . . . . . . . . . . . . . . . . . . . . . . . . . . . . . . . . . . . . . . . . . . . 1675

Come Close Index . . . . . . . . . . . . . . . . . . . . . . . . . . . . . . . . . . . . . . . . . . . . 1678

Perspective Index . . . . . . . . . . . . . . . . . . . . . . . . . . . . . . . . . . . . . . . . . . . . .1680

What the Bible Says About . . . Index . . . . . . . . . . . . . . . . . . . . . . . . . . . . . .1682

Insight Index . . . . . . . . . . . . . . . . . . . . . . . . . . . . . . . . . . . . . . . . . . . . . . . . .1683

She Says Index . . . . . . . . . . . . . . . . . . . . . . . . . . . . . . . . . . . . . . . . . . . . . . . 1685

Scripture Pause Index . . . . . . . . . . . . . . . . . . . . . . . . . . . . . . . . . . . . . . . . . 1689

Contributors Index . . . . . . . . . . . . . . . . . . . . . . . . . . . . . . . . . . . . . . . . . . . .1690

NLT Dictionary/Concordance . . . . . . . . . . . . . . . . . . . . . . . . . . . . . . . . . . 1693

Image Credits . . . . . . . . . . . . . . . . . . . . . . . . . . . . . . . . . . . . . . . . . . . . . . . .1777

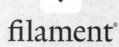

# filament®

**WELCOME TO YOUR FILAMENT-ENABLED BIBLE!**

This Bible works with the Filament Bible app, which uses your phone or tablet to enhance this Bible with even more powerful study and devotional content.

**WHY USE THE FILAMENT BIBLE APP?**

The Filament Bible app illuminates and amplifies this Bible. By simply scanning Filament-enabled page numbers, it instantly delivers helpful, in-depth content centered on the passage you are reading. Study notes, devotionals, videos, profiles, interactive maps, and more enable you to get the most out of your time in God's Word.

**HOW TO GET STARTED WITH FILAMENT:**

1. Grab your device, and open the App Store or Google Play.

2. Search for "Filament Bible," and install the app.

3. Follow the prompts to learn how it works, and enjoy exploring!

**TO LEARN MORE ABOUT FILAMENT, GO TO
FILAMENTBIBLES.COM**

# CANONICAL LISTING OF BIBLE BOOKS

## OLD TESTAMENT

| | | |
|---|---|---|
| Genesis . . . . . . . . . . . . . . .3 | 2 Chronicles . . . . . . . . . 515 | Daniel . . . . . . . . . . . . .1033 |
| Exodus . . . . . . . . . . . . . .79 | Ezra . . . . . . . . . . . . . . . .557 | Hosea . . . . . . . . . . . . .1057 |
| Leviticus . . . . . . . . . . . .131 | Nehemiah . . . . . . . . . .573 | Joel . . . . . . . . . . . . . . 1071 |
| Numbers . . . . . . . . . . 167 | Esther . . . . . . . . . . . . .593 | Amos . . . . . . . . . . . . . .1079 |
| Deuteronomy . . . . . . . 217 | Job . . . . . . . . . . . . . . . 607 | Obadiah . . . . . . . . . . .1093 |
| Joshua . . . . . . . . . . . . .257 | Psalms . . . . . . . . . . . . 649 | Jonah . . . . . . . . . . . . .1097 |
| Judges . . . . . . . . . . . . 289 | Proverbs . . . . . . . . . . . .753 | Micah . . . . . . . . . . . . . 1105 |
| Ruth . . . . . . . . . . . . . .323 | Ecclesiastes . . . . . . . . .793 | Nahum . . . . . . . . . . . . . 1117 |
| 1 Samuel . . . . . . . . . . .333 | Song of Songs . . . . . . 809 | Habakkuk . . . . . . . . . . 1125 |
| 2 Samuel . . . . . . . . . . 371 | Isaiah . . . . . . . . . . . . . 821 | Zephaniah . . . . . . . . . .1131 |
| 1 Kings . . . . . . . . . . . . 407 | Jeremiah . . . . . . . . . . . 895 | Haggai . . . . . . . . . . . . 1139 |
| 2 Kings . . . . . . . . . . . . 441 | Lamentations . . . . . . . 961 | Zechariah . . . . . . . . . . 1145 |
| 1 Chronicles . . . . . . . .477 | Ezekiel . . . . . . . . . . . .973 | Malachi . . . . . . . . . . . .1161 |

## NEW TESTAMENT

| | | |
|---|---|---|
| Matthew . . . . . . . . . . . 1189 | Ephesians . . . . . . . . . .1489 | Hebrews . . . . . . . . . . . .1559 |
| Mark . . . . . . . . . . . . . .1239 | Philippians . . . . . . . . . 1501 | James . . . . . . . . . . . . . 1579 |
| Luke . . . . . . . . . . . . . . .1271 | Colossians . . . . . . . . . .1511 | 1 Peter . . . . . . . . . . . . .1587 |
| John . . . . . . . . . . . . . . 1319 | 1 Thessalonians . . . . . 1519 | 2 Peter . . . . . . . . . . . . 1597 |
| Acts . . . . . . . . . . . . . . 1357 | 2 Thessalonians . . . . . 1527 | 1 John . . . . . . . . . . . . .1605 |
| Romans . . . . . . . . . . .1407 | 1 Timothy . . . . . . . . . .1533 | 2 John . . . . . . . . . . . . . 1615 |
| 1 Corinthians . . . . . . .1435 | 2 Timothy . . . . . . . . . 1541 | 3 John . . . . . . . . . . . . . 1619 |
| 2 Corinthians . . . . . . . 1461 | Titus . . . . . . . . . . . . . .1549 | Jude . . . . . . . . . . . . . .1623 |
| Galatians . . . . . . . . . .1479 | Philemon . . . . . . . . . . 1555 | Revelation . . . . . . . . . 1627 |

# ALPHABETICAL LISTING OF BIBLE BOOKS

| | | |
|---|---|---|
| Acts . . . . . . . . . . . . . . . 1357 | James . . . . . . . . . . . . . 1579 | Nehemiah . . . . . . . . . .573 |
| Amos . . . . . . . . . . . . . .1079 | Jeremiah . . . . . . . . . . . 895 | Numbers . . . . . . . . . . . 167 |
| 1 Chronicles . . . . . . . . 477 | Job . . . . . . . . . . . . . . . 607 | Obadiah . . . . . . . . . . .1093 |
| 2 Chronicles . . . . . . . . 515 | Joel . . . . . . . . . . . . . . 1071 | 1 Peter . . . . . . . . . . . . . 1587 |
| Colossians . . . . . . . . . . 1511 | John . . . . . . . . . . . . . . 1319 | 2 Peter . . . . . . . . . . . . 1597 |
| 1 Corinthians . . . . . . . 1435 | 1 John . . . . . . . . . . . . .1605 | Philemon . . . . . . . . . . 1555 |
| 2 Corinthians . . . . . . . 1461 | 2 John . . . . . . . . . . . . . 1615 | Philippians . . . . . . . . . 1501 |
| Daniel . . . . . . . . . . . . .1033 | 3 John . . . . . . . . . . . . . 1619 | Proverbs . . . . . . . . . . . .753 |
| Deuteronomy . . . . . . . 217 | Jonah . . . . . . . . . . . . .1097 | Psalms . . . . . . . . . . . . 649 |
| Ecclesiastes . . . . . . . . .793 | Joshua . . . . . . . . . . . . .257 | Revelation . . . . . . . . . 1627 |
| Ephesians . . . . . . . . . .1489 | Jude . . . . . . . . . . . . . .1623 | Romans . . . . . . . . . . .1407 |
| Esther . . . . . . . . . . . . .593 | Judges . . . . . . . . . . . . . 289 | Ruth . . . . . . . . . . . . . .323 |
| Exodus . . . . . . . . . . . . .79 | 1 Kings . . . . . . . . . . . . . 407 | 1 Samuel . . . . . . . . . . . .333 |
| Ezekiel . . . . . . . . . . . .973 | 2 Kings . . . . . . . . . . . . 441 | 2 Samuel . . . . . . . . . . . 371 |
| Ezra . . . . . . . . . . . . . .557 | Lamentations . . . . . . . . 961 | Song of Songs . . . . . . 809 |
| Galatians . . . . . . . . . .1479 | Leviticus . . . . . . . . . . . .131 | 1 Thessalonians . . . . . 1519 |
| Genesis . . . . . . . . . . . . .3 | Luke . . . . . . . . . . . . . .1271 | 2 Thessalonians . . . . . 1527 |
| Habakkuk . . . . . . . . . . 1125 | Malachi . . . . . . . . . . . .1161 | 1 Timothy . . . . . . . . . . 1533 |
| Haggai . . . . . . . . . . . . 1139 | Mark . . . . . . . . . . . . . .1239 | 2 Timothy . . . . . . . . . . 1541 |
| Hebrews . . . . . . . . . . .1559 | Matthew . . . . . . . . . . . 1189 | Titus . . . . . . . . . . . . . .1549 |
| Hosea . . . . . . . . . . . . .1057 | Micah . . . . . . . . . . . . . 1105 | Zechariah . . . . . . . . . . 1145 |
| Isaiah . . . . . . . . . . . . . . 821 | Nahum . . . . . . . . . . . . . 1117 | Zephaniah . . . . . . . . . .1131 |

# Every Woman's Bible

*Welcome. You belong here.*

I am so glad you opened these pages to see what we have prepared for you, a Bible that invites every woman to explore her story through God's story. Here, in this Bible, I hope you can shed every expectation, role, and fear and hear God's deep, authentic call to extraordinary purpose.

You may be wondering, "How will this Bible live up to the name, *Every Woman's Bible*?" What you hold in your hands is an answer the Lord gave me in prayer: "By having as many women as possible tell their own stories and inviting you to tell your story too." In this Bible, you'll meet a global sisterhood of more than one hundred voices (see the contributors' map, page A19). Each woman tells her story alongside God's story, and these women reflect the diversity of God's creation in their cultures, faces, races, ages, gifts, and vocations. Each book benefits from globally respected women Bible scholars who wrote study notes adding women's perspectives.

When it comes to living our stories, some days we soar toward a great, life-giving mission. On other days we struggle to get off the ground, fighting against our burdens. Sometimes we struggle with our faith or just with ourselves, and other times we feel sure, confident. In many, many ways, each of us is "every woman." We are all these women, just on different days.

As we open this Bible, we might fear we'll meet women who are nothing like us. We fear feeling different, divided by political convictions, social issues, bank accounts, facial lines, or body sizes. But God's love letter for us, the Bible, speaks life to our social-media-airbrushed anxieties. God's love letter is for every woman. When we open this Bible, we hear God through his story and through others' stories.

I pray the Bible's story and these women's stories cheer you on to live abundantly and serve extravagantly. I pray they help you go deeper in God's story—available to all of us, new every day, no matter what our stories have been before.

Additionally, in the middle of this Bible (page 1170), you'll find a unique section that walks you through a proven journey to find your purpose in God's purpose, your story in God's story.

As you journey through these pages, we want to be right alongside so you come to say, "I'm living what God made me for, alongside other women who make me strong." We want you to feel guided toward action! We want you to feel rooted in God, strengthened in your relationships, and activated in God's calling, his world-renewing cause.

Sister, you have a story. A story that matters. I can't wait to hear your voice.

---

*With my ordinary and God's extraordinary,*
DR. NAOMI CRAMER OVERTON
GENERAL EDITOR

# Every Woman's Bible

The *Every Woman's Bible* focuses on what hundreds of women say they desire from a Bible: great study notes and information from maps and charts, clarity on their calling, insights from others' stories, and help for their needs. This begins with the clear and trusted New Living Translation, which communicates the Bible's message in language that meets us where we are today.

Globally respected Bible scholars, who also happen to be women, provide the study notes and walk alongside you on your journey through God's story and your story. This Bible contains an array of illustrations and charts, including original ones written by women. This Bible also offers writings by women from many places, stages, and walks of life.

*For a full list of each of these writings, see the indexes beginning on page 1669.*

## INTRODUCTION

*Before each of the Bible's sixty-six books you will find:*

**BEAUTY** To help you prepare visually for what you'll read, a full-page image draws on the themes and feel of each book.

**MISSION** To help you consider what each book has to say about God's purposes and your own, look for a key takeaway on *God's mission and ours*.

**HISTORY** *Who, When,* and *How* questions orient you to each book. Timelines give you further historical context, showing what events were happening at the time.

**ESTIMATED READING TIMES** To show you how much time to budget, these estimates are divided into thirty-minute segments.

**FEATURE HIGHLIGHTS** A sampling of articles on purpose and calling, identity, needs, and wonderings. They spotlight topics you've told us you care about, illuminating the Bible's story through the lens of women scholars and writers who make Scripture more relatable.

## STUDY NOTES

Each respected Bible scholar—all of whom are women—applied her research and cultural understanding of the ancient world to craft these notes. The scholars particularly focused the notes and additional commentary on portions of Scripture which address topics women might find relevant, fascinating, and helpful and zeroed in on aspects that women might silently struggle with but that are rarely addressed. These notes clarify the cultural, historical, and literary context we all need so we can read the Bible with greater understanding.

## IMAGE
Discover your purpose and how to make the most of God's designs for your four core relationships. We find our purpose and calling as we relate to (1) God; (2) our family and friends; (3) our communities, including our workplaces, neighborhoods, schools, and churches; and (4) the unique ways God has made each of us to bring more goodness to God's world. *Learn more on page 13.*

## IDENTITY
These articles showcase both stories of Bible people and stories of God's character to shed light on who they were, their role in God's mission, and what their lives can teach us. Many of these explore stories through imaginative, first-person narrative based on what the Bible suggests the woman might tell us herself if she could. Learning about these women's hopes, struggles, failures, and victories can help us grow in our own God-given identities.

## COME CLOSE
These devotionals address real-life emotions and needs that invite us to draw near to God. For some, it's pain or a problem. For others, it's a life season or a startling opportunity. Each includes a quote from someone who has faced a similar need, a relevant Bible quote, and a prayer.

## PERSPECTIVE
Have you ever encountered something in the Bible and thought, "Wait, what?" Here, we dig into questions we'd like to ask but may not have thought we could. The Perspective articles take a deep look at these passages rather than giving us pat answers. They highlight each passage's language, meaning, and context to provide deeper wisdom from God's Word. These focus especially on aspects of the Bible that may unsettle us.

# WHAT THE BIBLE SAYS ABOUT...

Sometimes it helps to look at the big picture. This feature illuminates key themes throughout the Bible, especially themes of interest to women, by gathering key verses all in one place. Consider these pages to be a starting place for your study of each topic.

# INSIGHT

These charts, maps, graphs, and illustrations help us understand the Bible beyond what words alone may offer. You'll find these where an illustration, more information, or a cultural insight can help you see beyond the pages themselves to the real world of the Bible.

# SHE SAYS

Throughout the Bible, you'll find powerful quotes that capture the voices of Christian women across history. These quotes show us how they lived out their faith across many cultures and places. We gain inspiration from their words as we hear from leaders of movements and church denominations, singers and writers and artists, and missionaries and theologians. We find strength from the variety of voices, reminding us that women throughout history and from many walks of life have much to say about how God is with us today, where we are.

# SCRIPTURE PAUSE

Throughout this Bible, you'll find full-page script lettering of Bible verses that inspire us. We hope these pages give you space to take a breath, spend a moment reflecting on a brief Bible verse, and experience the peace God's Word gives.

# WORDS TO REMEMBER

You will find highlighted portions of Scripture throughout the Bible. We've spotlighted these frequently cited passages so you can see what verses draw the most interest from other readers. And you may want to take some of these with you into your days by committing them to memory.

# DIGGING DEEPER INTO IMAGE

## LIVING GOD'S MISSION THROUGH OUR FOUR CORE RELATIONSHIPS

We are made for relationships—with God, our family and friends, our communities, and our own place of unique influence. Our relationships form us at least as much as we shape them! Understanding these relationships, and how we can invest in their health and purpose, allows us to thrive and live out our God-given callings. Through these relationships, we see how those around us and we ourselves are made in the image of God and how to share that with the world.

### THEOS MY STORY WITH GOD

The Greek word *Theos* means "God," and in this sphere we can discover our extraordinary purpose in the God whose faithful love defines each of us. This place of relationship is just for you and God. One central way we get to know God is through his Word, the Bible—and he invites us to join his mission.

### OIKOS MY STORY WITH FAMILY & FRIENDS

The Greek word *Oikos* means "home" or "household." But this sphere, so dear to many of us, can consume us, bringing us comfort and life or struggle and grief (often both). The Bible shows us complicated family and friend dynamics, where God can reveal how he wants us to relate to each other in ways that yield life.

### KOINONIA MY STORY WITH COMMUNITY, WORKPLACE & CHURCH

The Greek word *Koinonia* means "fellowship," and this sphere comes naturally to some. It's a place we can find fulfillment. And yet, these relationships can also develop places of deep hurt, burnout, and avoidance. God can show us how to develop this sphere intentionally so that our neighborhoods, workplaces or schools, and churches thrive. And we thrive, too.

### SHALOM MY STORY OF MY UNIQUE INFLUENCE

The Hebrew word *Shalom*, at its simplest, means "peace." However, this word carries an even greater depth of meaning beyond our language. This sphere relates to our contentment, completeness, wholeness, well-being, and harmony, which come from expressing our unique calling in God's mission.

# A RELATIONSHIP WITH GOD

When I (Naomi) was a little girl, I wanted to know God. So I grabbed the little Bible someone at church had handed me, and at night, I'd open it up and read it all alone. One time, I remember praying one enormously powerful prayer in my dark room: "God, if you're real, I am desperate to know you. Will you help me?" He did by showing me in the Bible how I didn't live up to the good ways God asked me to live, particularly that part about loving others as myself.

Thankfully, in college, my friend Beth invited me to a group where I heard about how to know God in a way I never had before. I told Beth, "I'm a Christian, but I don't understand why so many people always talk about Jesus." Beth explained that the gap between how I wanted to live and the way I really did live was a gap Jesus came to fill.

The diagram below shows how Jesus and his death on the cross bridges the gap between our problem with sin and being with God. God's greatest act of drawing close to us is in his Son, Jesus. Sin, or falling short of living and loving perfectly, separates us from God (Genesis 3:1-24; Romans 5:12), but Jesus came to earth and lived a perfectly loving and just life so he could draw us to God.

Jesus paid for our wrongdoing by dying in our place on the cross, but he did not stay dead! He returned to life forever and now offers us forgiveness for our sins and new life, too. Jesus is alive today and wants to give us a new life:

*"This means that anyone who belongs to Christ has become a new person. The old life is gone; a new life has begun!"*
2 CORINTHIANS 5:17

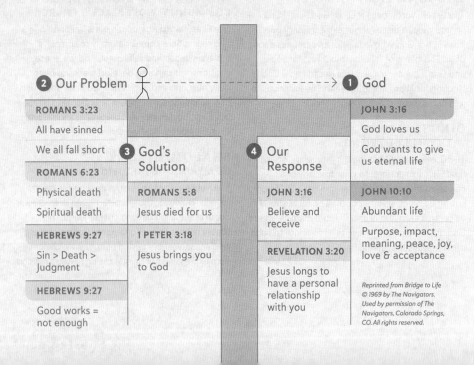

| ② Our Problem | | ④ Our | ① God |
|---|---|---|---|
| **ROMANS 3:23** | ③ God's | Response | **JOHN 3:16** |
| All have sinned | Solution | | God loves us |
| We all fall short | | | God wants to give us eternal life |
| **ROMANS 6:23** | **ROMANS 5:8** | **JOHN 3:16** | **JOHN 10:10** |
| Physical death | Jesus died for us | Believe and receive | Abundant life |
| Spiritual death | | | Purpose, impact, meaning, peace, joy, love & acceptance |
| **HEBREWS 9:27** | **1 PETER 3:18** | **REVELATION 3:20** | |
| Sin > Death > Judgment | Jesus brings you to God | Jesus longs to have a personal relationship with you | |
| **HEBREWS 9:27** | | | |
| Good works = not enough | | | |

Reprinted from Bridge to Life © 1969 by The Navigators. Used by permission of The Navigators, Colorado Springs, CO. All rights reserved.

Do you ever feel like I felt, like you long to be close to God but don't know how that can happen? What will you do with the God who pursues you, covers your wrongs, heals your heart, and invites you to new life now and forever? How do we begin this new life he offers? By trusting Jesus. If you're ready to believe in God's good purpose for you and your story, you can begin by telling him so in prayer. Here's a simple and memorable way to pray:

**CONFESS:** We confess that we have fallen short of living a perfectly loving and just life. We tell God that we cannot earn his forgiveness, cannot be good enough on our own, and are ready to stop trying. We accept the free gift of our new life and ask God to give us the Holy Spirit to lead our life. ROMANS 10:9-13, PAGE 1422

**BELIEVE:** We believe that God loves us so much that he gave what he loved most—his Son, Jesus—to pay the life sentence for our sin. JOHN 3:16, PAGE 1324 We agree that he saves us not because of good things we have done but because of his undeserved kindness. Because of God's kindness and love, we have confidence that God makes us new from the inside out in this life and gives us everlasting life with him after we die. TITUS 3:4-7, PAGE 1552

**ACCEPT:** We accept that God forgave us and brought us close when we confessed and believed. We accept that we can't take credit for it. We accept that we are God's masterpiece, now living with new life thanks to Jesus. And we embrace the good things God has planned for us to do. EPHESIANS 2:8-10, PAGE 1490

When we believe in and trust Jesus, he pens new stories for us. God retitled mine from "She Is Striving and Stuck" to "She Is Accepted and Free." Do you want to begin this new story, this new life? You might pray something like this:

*Father, I confess I fall short of being perfectly loving and just, as you are. I believe you sent your Son, Jesus, to die on the cross and pay entirely for all my sin. I call on Jesus as Lord and accept your gift of life now, with your Spirit living in me, and life with you forever in your Kingdom. I pray this in your Son's name, Jesus. Amen (an affirmation that means "So be it!").*

So, sister, I don't want you to do what I did—read this book alone in the dark. Don't wait to feel close to the Author of the story and the Creator of you. You can know God now by asking him to forgive you and give you new life. If you've done so, then you are a child of God (1 John 3:1) and you have become a new person. You are never alone because God is always with you.

*Turn to page A16 for more help getting started reading your Bible!*

# READING THE BIBLE

*Opening the Bible can be intimidating or confusing. It's hard to know exactly where to start! And not every way of reading the Bible works for everyone in every life season. It's good to try different ways, and it's okay to try a new one if you get stuck. Below are some ideas for how to get started.*

## START WITH A SIMPLE READING PLAN

We've provided a daily Bible reading plan that helps you read the whole Bible in one year (see page 1655). Each day offers portions from the Old Testament, the New Testament, Psalms, and Proverbs. If you'd like to follow along, the readings might take you about ten to twenty minutes a day.

## START WITH JESUS

Each of the four Gospels—Matthew, Mark, Luke, and John—tells the story of the life of Jesus from a different perspective. These books are a good place to start because they show us who Jesus is and what his plans are for the world. Choose any one and get started: Matthew begins on page 1189; Mark begins on page 1239; Luke begins on page 1271; and John begins on page 1319.

## START WITH WHERE YOU ARE AND WHERE YOU WANT TO GO

Turn to "What Is My Purpose?" on page 1170. This is a guide to help you know where you are right now in your story with God and discover where you want to go next. This guide focuses especially on your four core relationships (see page A13): your relationship with God, your relationship with family and friends, your relationship with community, workplace, and church, and your unique influence.

 ## START WITH CORE RELATIONSHIPS AND WHAT YOU HOPE FOR

If you want to see how the Bible can guide your relationships, check out the Image articles and use the Scripture passages they cover and their devotionals as a place to begin reading. You can explore the topics within each sphere by turning to page 1672.

 ## START WITH A BIBLE WOMAN YOU'D LIKE TO KNOW MORE ABOUT

The Identity articles help you learn from others' stories. Each Identity article pairs with the Bible references where that woman is mentioned or her story is told. See page 1675 for a full list of these women and where you can find their features.

 ## START WITH HOW YOU ARE FEELING RIGHT NOW

The Come Close articles tend to your heart. Those times we feel uncomfortable can offer us good opportunities for God to make us stronger. Turn to page 1678 and look for a topic or theme that speaks to you.

 ## START WITH YOUR TOUGH QUESTIONS

God is not afraid of your most challenging questions, and the Perspective articles show how the Bible can answer them too. Go to page 1680 for a list of these questions and the Bible verses they cover, and take on some of the big ones you wonder about. We didn't shy away from hard passages. We purposely asked knowledgeable scholars and writers to dive into every bit that could put a woman off from reading the Bible.

# BASIC BIBLE HELPS

## THE DIFFERENCE BETWEEN THE OLD TESTAMENT AND THE NEW TESTAMENT

The Old Testament and the New Testament are separated by time, and each focuses on different eras in God's story. See page A7 for a list of which books are in each group.

The Old Testament takes place between Creation and 445 BC. It includes historical narratives like the creation account, the Flood account, the origin of the Israelites (God's chosen people group), chronologies of Israel's rulers and records of political changes. It also includes poetry and wise sayings in books like Psalms and Proverbs. God's encouragements and warnings to his people from his prophets also appear in the Old Testament.

Between the Old Testament and New Testament, there is a gap in the Biblical record of about four hundred years.

The New Testament takes place between approximately 7 BC and AD 100. It includes books about the life of Jesus, the historical account of the beginning of the Christian church, letters to early churches about their new life in Jesus Christ, and the apocalyptic book of Revelation, describing John's vision about Jesus' final return.

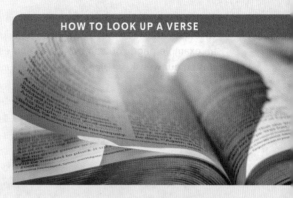

## HOW TO LOOK UP A VERSE

Bible verse references are a human-made system for navigating the Bible. The first part is the Bible book name (either from the Old Testament or the New Testament). The second part is the chapter number (the number before the colon). And the third part is the verse number or span (the number[s] after the colon).

## JOHN 3:16

| BOOK JOHN | New Testament book, found toward the back of the Bible |
| --- | --- |
| CHAPTER 3 | The third chapter of the Gospel of John |
| VERSE 16 | The verse labeled 16 within that chapter |

See page A7 for a list of the Bible books in the order they appear and the page numbers they start on.

See page A8 for an alphabetical list of the Bible books and the page numbers they start on. Once you've found the book, then turn to the chapter, and finally the verse.

# BIBLE READING WORKSHEET

Taking notes while reading the Bible can help us remember what we've learned, come back to it later, and see how we are growing in knowing—and living from—God's story. Here is an example page you can use to take notes. You can also find a downloadable version of this on our website  EveryWomansBible.com  that you can use time and again.

**DATE**

**BIBLE PASSAGE**

**WHO IS THIS ABOUT?**

**WHEN & WHERE IS THIS HAPPENING?**

**WHAT DO I UNDERSTAND?**

**WHAT DO I NOT UNDERSTAND?**

Is there a study note or article that helps me? *See indexes on page 1669.*

**WHAT CAN I ACT ON TODAY?**

# MEET OUR CONTRIBUTORS

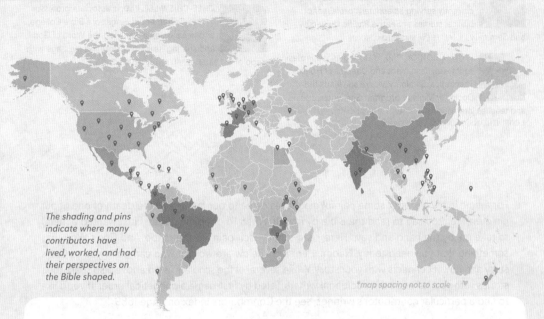

The shading and pins indicate where many contributors have lived, worked, and had their perspectives on the Bible shaped.

*map spacing not to scale

I (Naomi) am most excited about inviting you to discover God's story and your story alongside others who help you know you're not alone. Let's begin by meeting the scholars who wrote the study notes and some of the other articles (especially Perspective articles, see page 1680 for a full list) to help answer our difficult questions.

**CARMEN JOY IMES, PhD,** is an author, speaker, blogger, YouTuber, and serves as associate professor of Old Testament at Biola University in California. ◆ GENESIS, EXODUS

**JENNIFER BROWN JONES, PhD,** is an author, speaker, and instructor of Old Testament for Liberty University's PhD of Bible Exposition program. She loves helping others see how God speaks to them through the Bible today. ◆ LEVITICUS, NUMBERS, DEUTERONOMY, JOB, PSALMS, PROVERBS

**SHIRLEY SIONG SHU HO, PhD,** is assistant professor of Old Testament at China Evangelical School of Theology in Taiwan. She loves teaching and mentoring students. She is a Langham scholar. ◆ JOSHUA

**HAVILAH DHARAMRAJ, PhD,** serves at South Asia Institute of Advanced Christian Studies, Bangalore, India. Her research interests include biblical narrative and comparative literature.

She encourages her students to retrieve traditional story-telling methods for ministry. ◆ JUDGES, OBADIAH, JONAH, ZEPHANIAH, HAGGAI, ZECHARIAH, MALACHI

**ALEXIANA FRY, MDiv, PhD,** is a devoted academic in the Hebrew Bible. She is a professor, wife, and pug mom who is working on her first book post-dissertation. ◆ RUTH, 1 SAMUEL 2 SAMUEL

**JENNIFER M. MATHENY, PhD,** is associate professor of Old Testament at Nazarene Theological Seminary, Missouri, and director of the Wynkoop Center for Women in Leadership. She enjoys speaking engagements and research. ◆ 1 KINGS, 2 KINGS, 1 CHRONICLES, 2 CHRONICLES, EZRA, NEHEMIAH, ESTHER, ECCLESIASTES, SONG OF SONGS, ISAIAH, JEREMIAH

**CATHERINE L. McDOWELL, PhD,** is associate professor of Old Testament at Gordon-Conwell Theological Seminary. She has authored several books and articles on Bible backgrounds, Genesis, Isaiah, and Biblical Hebrew. ◆ LAMENTATIONS, HOSEA, JOEL, AMOS, NAHUM, HABAKKUK, MALACHI

**CHRISTINE WALKER, MDiv,** is a spiritual director who facilitates spiritual formation sessions for people desiring to grow their relationship with Christ. She loves ancient languages and teaches Biblical Hebrew and Koine Greek. ◆ EZEKIEL, DANIEL, MICAH

**ESTHER G. CEN, MDiv, PhD,** is a follower of Christ and multilingual writer and teacher, currently serving as assistant professor of biblical studies at Seattle Pacific University and Seminary. ◆ MATTHEW, MARK, LUKE, JOHN

**LYNN H. COHICK, PhD,** is Distinguished Professor of New Testament and Director of Houston Theological Seminary, where she leads the Doctor of Ministry program. She writes, speaks, and teaches internationally. ◆ ACTS, ROMANS, 1 CORINTHIANS, 2 CORINTHIANS, GALATIANS, EPHESIANS

**SARAH HARRIS, PhD,** lectures in New Testament at Carey Baptist College, Auckland, New Zealand. She is a scholar who specializes in the Gospel of Luke. She loves to teach, preach, and encourage women in their callings. ◆ PHILIPPIANS, COLOSSIANS, 1 THESSALONIANS, 2 THESSALONIANS, 1 TIMOTHY, 2 TIMOTHY, TITUS, PHILEMON, HEBREWS, JAMES, 1 JOHN, 2 JOHN, 3 JOHN

**CHEE-CHIEW LEE, PhD,** is associate professor in New Testament at Singapore Bible College, and her passion is studying the Word of God and sharing its life-transforming message with people. ◆ 1 PETER, 2 PETER, JUDE, REVELATION

For a time in my life, after some painful diagnoses came to our family and the death of one of our children, I felt too sad to read the Bible by myself. When I'd open the pages, I just wanted a friend to take me by the hand and say, "Here, read this. I've felt pain like yours too. And God's Word has something that you need today, Naomi. Here it is." Below are women who can point you to God's story and how it connects with your story. While several of the scholars listed above also share their stories with you, here are the additional writers, listed by first-name alphabetical order. If you'd like to find a particular contributor's writings, see the Contributors Index on page 1689.

**ADELAIDE MANYARA MUCHETU** shares true life experiences with many women and believes in relational evangelism. Discipleship is her mantra with exhortation being her greatest strength.

**ALEXANDRA KUYKENDALL** is a cofounder of The Open Door Sisterhood and author of several books, including *Seeking Out Goodness: Finding the True and Beautiful All around You.*

**ALICE PATTERSON, JD,** is an associate court attorney in New York who has a fondness for teaching the Old Testament. She encourages everyone to put down the world's lies and put on God's truth.

**AMANDA AZADIAN** is a Christ follower on a mission to bridge traditional medicine and modern innovation. She is a doctoral student of acupuncture, a senior product manager in digital health strategy, and a lover of adventure.

**AMY SIMPSON, MBA,** is the Bible publisher at Tyndale House Publishers, and she can't think of a better job than making God's Word available and accessible around the world.

**ANDREA GIBSON** is a certified coach and trainer. She and her husband spent seventeen years church planting. Her deepest desire now is to mentor and train women in the art of wise, godly leadership.

**ANGELA TKACHENKO** is an evangelist, worshiper, and leader of Steiger Ukraine mission. She is passionate to see this generation love the Bible.

NO PHOTO **AVA JAMES** is an editor who advocates for living with compassion and respect.

**BELÉN PETERS** is a mobilizer with Scatter Global. Since 2002, she has been mobilizing mission-minded Latinos to take their passion and profession to places where Christ is unknown.

**BRENDA GARCIA de BRIZENDINE** is the former communications manager for Compassion International's Guatemala office. She works with Iron Rose Sister Ministries and also interprets Spanish for CPCD-Head Start in Colorado Springs, CO.

**BRENDA L. YODER, MA, LMHC,** is a licensed mental health counselor and school counselor whose passion is encouraging others when life doesn't fit the storybook image.

CARA DAY is a writer and illustrator. She has served with Stonecroft Ministries helping women live "extraordinary."

CATHY SCRIVNER has twenty-five years of experience as a diversity, equity, and inclusion consultant. She is a devoted Christian who believes in loving people to Christ.

DAISY ASIIMWE BYARUGABA is a learning and development professional passionate about empowering people to become the most productive version of themselves that God intended. She and her husband minister at Church of the Resurrection, Bugolobi, in Kampala, Uganda.

DEBORA DA SILVA is from Brazil and found release from poverty through Compassion International. She works with Facebook in Colombia and lives to serve as she tries to be a channel—not only a recipient—of God's goodness.

DELANEY OVERTON develops programs and business strategies for impact-oriented organizations in education, food access, environmentalism, and other sectors. She experiences God's love and glory through creation, especially the seemingly unending ocean.

DONNA LEE LAMOTHE, MA, is executive director and founder of inSPIRE Channels at RSVP Ministries. She teaches and guides all to find wholeness through faith in Jesus.

ELISA MORGAN, MDiv, speaks, writes, and cohosts podcasts for Our Daily Bread Ministries. For twenty years, she served as president of MOPS International, now as president emerita. Her motto is "Living really ... Really living."

ELISABETH SELZER ROGERS, MDiv, MA, PhD, is a passionate believer and follower of Christ, bringing his love to the secular world through mentoring, coaching, and modeling his unconditional love.

ELIZA CORTÉS BAST, DEd candidate, is senior director of programs with Stonecroft. She is a pastor, professor, wife, mom, and mentor. She believes in passionately pursuing God and people by developing talent, asking strategic questions, and amplifying the good.

ELIZABETH GLANVILLE, PhD, is retired faculty from Fuller Theological Seminary, School of Mission and Theology. She is an international teacher on missions and leadership and chaplain for a local police department and her retirement community.

ELLEN RICHARD VOSBURG, MA, is a Bible editor for Tyndale House Publishers. She studied Greek and Hebrew and lives to lead others into God's deep love by getting to know him through his Word.

EMILY SARMIENTO is a wife and mom of two school-aged children and serves as president and CEO of Tearfund USA, based in Denver, CO.

ESTHER FLEECE ALLEN is an international speaker and bestselling author of *No More Faking Fine: Ending the Pretending* and *Your New Name: Saying Goodbye to the Labels That Limit.*

EVIE POLSLEY, MS, loves stories of how God uses everyday people. A digital communications manager at Tyndale, her favorite roles are wife to the good doctor and mom to two girls who will one day change the world.

GABRIELA MAGAÑA BANKS, PhD, is an author, teacher, and certified HeartSync inner healing prayer minister who facilitates freedom. Biblical principles and powerful moves of the Holy Spirit are her passion.

HÉLÈNE M. DALLAIRE, PhD, serves as Earl S. Kalland Professor of Old Testament and Semitic Languages at Denver Seminary. She is deeply involved in the Messianic movement, serving in worship, prayer, teaching, and preaching.

IRENE PACE trusts the Lord Jesus Christ and believes his life-changing message of salvation. She writes about God's lessons learned through adversity; she speaks with gratitude and joy.

JANICE MAYO MATHERS is author of multiple books and Bible studies, including *Every Season: Embracing a Forever Kind of Purpose* (Stonecroft) and *Mothers-in-Law vs. Daughters-in-Law: Let There Be Peace.* She helps women see adverse circumstances as godly challenges.

JENNIFER KELLER, MA Min, is a pastor at a multisite church in Central Indiana and has self-published three Bible studies. She is a devoted Christ-follower, wife, and mom of four.

JENNIFER ROSNER, PhD, is a writer and Messianic Jewish theologian currently serving as Affiliate Assistant Professor at Fuller Theological Seminary. Much of her work focuses on the relationship between Judaism and Christianity.

JULIE WRIGHT is author of *Redeeming Eve: When a Woman Lives Loved* and founder of Live Loved Ministry. Her passion is for women to embrace God's love and cultivate an authentic relationship with Jesus.

KARA POWELL, PhD, is the executive director of the Fuller Youth Institute and chief of leadership formation at Fuller Theological Seminary. Kara speaks and has authored numerous books, including *3 Big Questions That Change Every Teenager.*

KAT ARMSTRONG, MA, is a Bible teacher, preacher, coach, and ministry leader. She cofounded the Polished Network and authored *No More Holding Back*, *The In-Between Place*, and the Storyline Bible Studies series.

KATHERINE LEARY ALSDORF founded and directed Redeemer Church's Center for Faith & Work. She co-authored *Every Good Endeavor: Connecting Your Work to God's Work* with Timothy Keller.

KATHERINE WOLF is a communicator, author, and advocate. She leverages her redemptive story to encourage those with broken bodies, broken brains, and broken hearts.

KATRIEL OVERTON is a Christian with autism who experiences and believes all people can feel and know God's love if they choose. She sees God helping her love people, including herself.

KRISTIN CARY, CPSAS, cofounded Living Truth with her husband. She guides women toward hope and healing after the devastating impact of sexual betrayal in their marriage.

LILLIAN GITAU is a lifelong learner and an advocate for the marginalized. She finds satisfaction from seeing others realize their full potential. She is the author of *You Are Special* and *Pia Was Different*.

LISA D. EDMONDS is mother of two daughters, a Stonecroft Ministries speaker and speaker trainer, worship leader, and constituent care director for The Dr. James Dobson Family Institute.

LISA WHITTLE is a sought-out Bible teacher, podcast host, and bestselling author whose works include *Jesus Over Everything*. She is the founder of the online communities Ministry Strong and Called Creatives. She's a wife, mom, and a self-professed feisty work in progress.

LOIS NANGUDI, MA, studied spiritual formation and discipleship at Moody Seminary. She served as an advocate with Compassion International, founded Awaken To Follow, and is currently serving in the Pastors Discipleship Network.

LORINA AVENIDO, BEEd with CAR, has served for thirty-seven years as a full-time pastor/missionary of Philippine Good News International Inc. She is a licensed minister of Worldwide Impact Group, preaching the gospel and empowering women leaders.

LYNN LONG has studied at National Louis University and is completing her doctorate at Wheaton College. Lynn is a Native American writer and speaker with Stonecroft Ministries.

MANDY ARIOTO is the president and CEO of MOPS International, influencing millions of moms around the world every year. She is a scholar of Greek, author, and speaker who believes in the transformational power of Scripture.

MARGARET FITZWATER, MS, MBA, is a Navigator and life and leadership coach. Her passion is helping others live and lead from the Word to thrive in their lives and ministries.

MARY SCHALLER, MDiv, is the former president of Q Place and coauthor of *The 9 Arts of Spiritual Conversations*. Her life mission is to build and nurture Christ-centered communities.

MAY YOUNG, MDiv, PhD, is an associate professor of biblical studies at Taylor University, with a passion for discipleship, teaching, and writing.

MEGAN C. ROBERTS, PhD, teaches Old Testament at Prairie College in Three Hills, Alberta, Canada. She loves mountains, music, and the unending joy of discovering the depths of the gospel in Scripture and the church.

MELISSA HOUDMANN is the cofounder of GotQuestions Ministries, a website dedicated to answering Bible questions. She also wrote Stonecroft Ministries' *Why Believe* study.

MENCHIT WONG, MBA, is a Gallup-certified Strengths Coach and leadership consultant. She also serves on the leadership of global mission movements that enable children to be disciples of Jesus.

MILLIE SERRANO is a faithful follower of Jesus Christ devoted to supporting women in their pursuit of growing a biblical, strong, and fruitful relationship with God through his Son, Jesus.

MINDY CALIGUIRE is founder and president of Soul Care, dedicated to increasing soul health in the Body of Christ. Her books include *Discovering Soul Care* and *Spiritual Friendships*.

MISTY ARTERBURN is an author and speaker, contributing to Bible projects, devotionals, and recovery materials for over twenty years. Wife and mom to five, Misty is the founder of Recovery Girls and the general editor of *The One Year Bible for Women*.

NANCY CHAMBERLIN SPROWLS is a devotional writer, mother, and grandmother. She encourages women to have a passion for God's Word and to leave a spiritual legacy for their families.

 NAOMI CRAMER OVERTON, MBA, DIS, lives to realize beauty-filled visions that lift us to flourishing, with our families and beyond. Naomi has been CEO for Stonecroft and MOPS, director with Compassion International and World Vision, and General Editor for this Bible.

 PATRICIA RAYBON is an award-winning Colorado author, essayist, and novelist who writes top-rated books and stories at the daring intersection of faith, race, and mystery—including the Annalee Spain mystery series.

 QUANTRILLA ARD, PhD, is a faith-based personal and spiritual development author, speaker, Bible teacher, and literary agent who believes in the power of collective strength, community, and fellowship.

 RACHEL LINDSAY McCANTS is an author, speaker, and founder of R. Lindsay Unlimited, which encourages, inspires, and challenges ladies to raise their self-worth and standards and to walk in God's will, in Jesus' name.

 ROBIN REESE is a volunteer leader with Stonecroft Ministries. She and her husband, Terry, love to travel, enjoy the company of their son and two corgis, and live life to the fullest!

 SARA HALL is a professional marathon runner and cofounder of the Hall Steps Foundation. She has been competing professionally for seventeen years in various distances and using her platform to bring aid to orphaned children in Ethiopia.

 SARAH OVERTON, MA, is a researcher specializing in refugee and asylum policy. She has worked in the UK Parliament, public-policy think tanks, and at Lambeth Palace.

 SHARON WILHARM is the host of the *All God's Women* podcast and internationally syndicated radio show. She loves bringing to life stories of Bible women and providing takeaways for modern women.

 STEPHANIE THOMAS is a follower of Jesus Christ. She is the coordinator and a contributing author at Pruned Life. She is also a gospel singer.

 SUSAN I. BUBBERS, MDiv, DMin, PhD, is the Dean of the Center for Anglican Theology in Orlando, FL. She is a professor, Anglican priest, spiritual director, and a Fellow of the Oxford Centre for Animal Ethics.

 SUSAN M. JONES is a US Army veteran, native Alaskan, wife, mother, and follower of Jesus Christ. She shares her testimony with Stonecroft Ministries. Sprinkling the love of Jesus is her joy.

 SUSIE GAMEZ, MA, is a teaching pastor at Midtown Covenant Church in Sacramento, CA, and preaches across the country, making the reconciling love of Jesus come alive through the Scriptures.

 SUZY SHEPHERD is the founder of SHINE, creator of Stonecroft's Where Love Lives outreach experience, and mom to a blended tribe of nine. She finds great joy in creating experiences for people to know God's love.

 TAMI HEIM is president and CEO of Christian Leadership Alliance and serves on many non-profit boards. She and her husband lead mission teams to Haiti to love and disciple orphans.

 TONI J. COLLIER is a speaker, the founder of Broken Crayons Still Color, the host of the *Still Coloring* podcast, and the author of *Brave Enough to Be Broken: How to Embrace Your Pain and Discover Hope and Healing*.

 TRACI CROWDER is a joyful, energetic, Jesus-following wife, mom, and pastor. She serves with Stonecroft and deeply longs for every person to experience God's extraordinary in their ordinary, together in community.

 VALERIE BELL is an author of several books on children, including *RESILIENT: Child Discipleship and the Fearless Future of the Church*. Valerie serves as Awana's CEO emerita and 2050 vision caster.

 VANEETHA RENDALL RISNER is the author of *Walking Through Fire*. She and her family live in North Carolina, where she writes and speaks about how God meets us in suffering.

 VIRGINIA WARD, MA, DMin, serves as the Dean of the Boston Campus for Gordon-Conwell Theological Seminary. She is a wife, a mother, and an associate pastor at Abundant Life Church in Cambridge, MA.

 VIVIAN MABUNI is a national speaker, author of *Open Hands, Willing Heart*, and podcast host of *Someday Is Here* for AAPI Christians, with over thirty years of ministry experience.

 WHITNEY PUTNAM is the senior director of women's events and marketing at New Life Ministries. She is an overall joy-chaser and is often found dancing in her kitchen.

# ADDITIONAL CONTRIBUTORS

**GENERAL EDITOR**
Dr. Naomi Cramer Overton

**ASSOCIATE EDITOR**
Misty Arterburn

**PROJECT DEVELOPER &
EDITORIAL CONSULTANT**
Stephen Arterburn

**PUBLISHER**
Amy Simpson

**TYNDALE HOUSE EDITOR**
Ellen Richard Vosburg

**DEVELOPMENTAL EDITORS**
Mark R. Norton
Jonathan Bryant

**COPY EDITORS**
Ava James
Leanne F. Rolland
Susan F. Tristano
Charles E. Cruise

**PROOFREADING**
Peachtree Publishing Services

**DESIGNER**
Jennifer L. Phelps

**TYPESETTING**
Laura Cruise

# A NOTE TO READERS

The *Holy Bible,* New Living Translation, was first published in 1996. It quickly became one of the most popular Bible translations in the English-speaking world. While the NLT's influence was rapidly growing, the Bible Translation Committee determined that an additional investment in scholarly review and text refinement could make it even better. So shortly after its initial publication, the committee began an eight-year process with the purpose of increasing the level of the NLT's precision without sacrificing its easy-to-understand quality. This second-generation text was completed in 2004, with minor changes subsequently introduced in 2007, 2013, and 2015.

The goal of any Bible translation is to convey the meaning and content of the ancient Hebrew, Aramaic, and Greek texts as accurately as possible to contemporary readers. The challenge for our translators was to create a text that would communicate as clearly and powerfully to today's readers as the original texts did to readers and listeners in the ancient biblical world. The resulting translation is easy to read and understand, while also accurately communicating the meaning and content of the original biblical texts. The NLT is a general-purpose text especially good for study, devotional reading, and reading aloud in worship services.

We believe that the New Living Translation—which combines the latest biblical scholarship with a clear, dynamic writing style—will communicate God's word powerfully to all who read it. We publish it with the prayer that God will use it to speak his timeless truth to the church and the world in a fresh, new way.

**THE PUBLISHERS**

*A complete list of the translators can be found at tyndale.com/nlt/scholars.*

# NEW LIVING TRANSLATION:
# OUR CHOICE FOR YOU

I (Naomi) love the New Living Translation because the brilliant people who translated it used simple, understandable words that we use in our everyday lives. Have you ever found that writing a simple sentence is harder than a long, complicated one? I love this translation because it serves *you*—the woman we most want to help find her story in God's story. I want the language to be an invitation—not a barrier—for you. It's easy to read, and the language draws us in.

*Here is one of my favorites:*

> Don't be afraid, for I am with you.
> Don't be discouraged, for I am your God.
>
> I will strengthen you and help you.
> I will hold you up with my victorious right hand.
>
> ISAIAH 41:10

I prayed this verse while in labor with my twins, one of whom I knew I would deliver stillborn. The other, I wasn't sure how she would be when I finally saw her after such a stressful, high-risk pregnancy. I held these simple words on a 3x5 index card and sensed God's victorious right hand strengthening me to breathe, bear the pain, and set aside my fear of the future.

Isaiah is a big book with lofty ideas. It's also full of gems like this one that feel like God is speaking straight to us amid our everyday lives, full of stresses and anxieties. And the New Living Translation reads in a way our hearts can hear.

We believe you will experience this, too, as you move through the Bible with the help of our sisterhood of contributors. We all experience times when we read the Bible and need a little help understanding, but the more straightforward the language, the more our hearts and minds can absorb the words.

*For more about this translation, see the Introduction to the New Living Translation on the following page.*

# NEW LIVING TRANSLATION

## TRANSLATION PHILOSOPHY AND METHODOLOGY

English Bible translations tend to be governed by one of two general translation theories. The first theory has been called "formal-equivalence," "literal," or "word-for-word" translation. According to this theory, the translator attempts to render each word of the original language into English and seeks to preserve the original syntax and sentence structure as much as possible in translation. The second theory has been called "dynamic-equivalence," "functional-equivalence," or "thought-for-thought" translation. The goal of this translation theory is to produce in English the closest natural equivalent of the message expressed by the original-language text, both in meaning and in style.

Both of these translation theories have their strengths. A formal-equivalence translation preserves aspects of the original text—including ancient idioms, term consistency, and original-language syntax—that are valuable for scholars and professional study. It allows a reader to trace formal elements of the original-language text through the English translation. A dynamic-equivalence translation, on the other hand, focuses on translating the message of the original-language text. It ensures that the meaning of the text is readily apparent to the contemporary reader. This allows the message to come through with immediacy, without requiring the reader to struggle with foreign idioms and awkward syntax.

The pure application of either of these translation philosophies would create translations at opposite ends of the translation spectrum. But in reality, all translations contain a mixture of these two philosophies. A purely formal-equivalence translation would be unintelligible in English, and a purely dynamic-equivalence translation would risk being unfaithful to the original. That is why translations shaped by dynamic-equivalence theory are usually quite literal when the original text is relatively clear, and the translations shaped by formal-equivalence theory are sometimes quite dynamic when the original text is obscure.

The translators of the New Living Translation set out to render the message of the original texts of Scripture into clear, contemporary English. As they did so, they kept the concerns of both formal-equivalence and dynamic-equivalence in mind. On the one hand, they translated as simply and literally as possible when that approach yielded an accurate, clear, and natural English text. Many words and phrases were rendered literally and consistently into English, preserving essential literary and rhetorical devices, ancient metaphors, and word choices that give structure to the text and provide echoes of meaning from one passage to the next.

On the other hand, the translators rendered the message more dynamically when the literal rendering was hard to understand, was misleading, or yielded archaic or foreign wording. They clarified difficult metaphors and terms to aid in the reader's understanding. The translators first struggled with the meaning of the words and phrases in the ancient context; then they rendered the message into clear, natural English. Their goal was to be both faithful to the ancient texts and eminently readable.

## TRANSLATION PROCESS AND TEAM

To produce an accurate translation of the Bible into contemporary English, the translation team needed the skills necessary to enter into the thought patterns of the ancient authors and then to render their ideas, connotations, and effects into clear, contemporary English. To begin this process, qualified biblical scholars were needed to interpret the meaning of the original text and to check it against our base English translation. In order to guard against personal and theological biases, the scholars needed to represent a diverse group of evangelicals who would employ the best exegetical tools. Then to work alongside the scholars, skilled English stylists were needed to shape the text into clear, contemporary English.

With these concerns in mind, the Bible Translation Committee recruited teams of scholars that represented a broad spectrum of denominations, theological perspectives, and backgrounds within the worldwide evangelical community. (A list of these scholars can be found online.) Each book of the Bible was assigned to three different scholars with proven expertise in the book or group of books to be reviewed. Each of these scholars made a thorough review of a base translation and submitted suggested revisions to the appropriate Senior Translator. The Senior Translator then reviewed and summarized these suggestions and proposed a first-draft revision of the base text. This draft served as the basis for several additional phases of exegetical and stylistic committee review. Then the Bible Translation Committee jointly reviewed and approved every verse of the final translation.

Throughout the translation and editing process, the Senior Translators and their scholar teams were given a chance to review the editing done by the team of stylists. This ensured that exegetical errors would not be introduced late in the process and that the entire Bible Translation Committee was happy with the final result. By choosing a team of qualified scholars and skilled stylists and by setting up a process that allowed their interaction throughout the process, the New Living Translation has been refined to preserve the essential formal elements of the original biblical texts, while also creating a clear, understandable English text.

The New Living Translation was first published in 1996. Shortly after its initial publication, the Bible Translation Committee began a process of further committee review and translation refinement. The purpose of this continued revision was to increase the level of precision without sacrificing the text's easy-to-understand quality. This second-edition text was completed in 2004, with minor changes subsequently introduced in 2007, 2013, and 2015.

## WRITTEN TO BE READ ALOUD

It is evident in Scripture that the biblical documents were written to be read aloud, often in public worship (see Nehemiah 8; Luke 4:16-20; 1 Timothy 4:13; Revelation 1:3). It is still the case today that more people will hear the Bible read aloud in church than are likely to read it for themselves. Therefore, a new translation must communicate with clarity and power when it is read publicly. Clarity was a primary goal for the NLT translators, not only to facilitate private reading and understanding, but also to ensure that it would be excellent for public reading and make an immediate and powerful impact on any listener.

## THE TEXTS BEHIND THE NEW LIVING TRANSLATION

The Old Testament translators used the Masoretic Text of the Hebrew Bible as represented in *Biblia Hebraica Stuttgartensia* (1977), with its extensive system of textual notes. The translators also further compared the Dead Sea Scrolls, the Septuagint and other Greek manuscripts, the Samaritan Pentateuch, the Syriac Peshitta, the Latin Vulgate, and any other versions or manuscripts that shed light on the meaning of difficult passages.

The New Testament translators used the two standard editions of the Greek New Testament: the *Greek New Testament,* published by the United Bible Societies (UBS, fourth revised edition, 1993), and *Novum Testamentum Graece,* edited by Nestle and Aland (NA, twenty-seventh edition, 1993). These two editions, which have the same text but differ in punctuation and textual notes, represent, for the most part, the best in modern textual scholarship. However, in cases where strong textual or other scholarly evidence supported the decision, the translators sometimes chose to differ from the UBS and NA Greek texts and followed variant readings found in other ancient witnesses. Significant textual variants of this sort are always noted in the textual notes of the New Living Translation.

## TRANSLATION ISSUES

The translators have made a conscious effort to provide a text that can be easily understood by the typical reader of modern English. To this end, we sought to use only vocabulary and language structures in common use today. We avoided using language likely to become quickly dated or that reflects only a narrow subdialect of English, with the goal of making the New Living Translation as broadly useful and timeless as possible.

But our concern for readability goes beyond the concerns of vocabulary and sentence structure. We are also concerned about historical and cultural barriers to understanding the Bible, and we have sought to translate terms shrouded in history and culture in ways that can be immediately understood. To this end:

- We have converted ancient weights and measures (for example, "ephah" [a unit of dry volume] or "cubit" [a unit of length]) to modern English (American) equivalents, since the ancient measures are not generally meaningful to today's readers. Then in the textual footnotes we offer the literal Hebrew, Aramaic, or Greek measures, along with modern metric equivalents.
- Instead of translating ancient currency values literally, we have expressed them in common terms that communicate the message. For example, in the Old Testament,

"ten shekels of silver" becomes "ten pieces of silver" to convey the intended message.

- Since the names of Hebrew months are unknown to most contemporary readers, and since the Hebrew lunar calendar fluctuates from year to year in relation to the solar calendar used today, we have looked for clear ways to communicate the time of year the Hebrew months (such as Abib) refer to. Where it is possible to define a specific ancient date in terms of our modern calendar, we use modern dates in the text. A textual footnote then gives the literal Hebrew date and states the rationale for our rendering.
- Since ancient references to the time of day differ from our modern methods of denoting time, we have used renderings that are instantly understandable to the modern reader. Accordingly, we have rendered specific times of day by using approximate equivalents in terms of our common "o'clock" system.
- When the meaning of a proper name (or a wordplay inherent in a proper name) is relevant to the message of the text, its meaning is often illuminated with a textual footnote. For example, in Exodus 2:10 the text reads: "The princess named him Moses, for she explained, 'I lifted him out of the water.'"

Sometimes, when the actual meaning of a name is clear, that meaning is included in parentheses within the text itself. For example, the text at Genesis 16:11 reads: "You are to name him Ishmael *(which means 'God hears'),* for the LORD has heard your cry of distress." Since the original hearers and readers would have instantly understood the meaning of the name "Ishmael," we have provided modern readers with the same information so they can experience the text in a similar way.

- Many words and phrases carry a great deal of cultural meaning that was obvious to the original readers but needs explanation in our own culture. For example, the phrase "they beat their breasts" (Luke 23:48) in ancient times meant that people were very upset, often in mourning. In our translation we chose to translate this phrase dynamically for clarity: "They went home *in deep sorrow.*"

- Metaphorical language is sometimes difficult for contemporary readers to understand, so at times we have chosen to translate or illuminate the meaning of a metaphor. For example, the ancient poet writes, "Your neck is *like* the tower of David" (Song of Songs 4:4). We have rendered it "Your neck is *as beautiful as* the tower of David" to clarify the intended positive meaning of the simile.

- When the content of the original language text is poetic in character, we have rendered it in English poetic form. Hebrew poetry often uses parallelism, a literary form where a second phrase (or in some instances a third or fourth) echoes the initial phrase in some way. Whenever possible, we sought to represent these parallel phrases in natural poetic English.

- The Greek term *hoi Ioudaioi* is literally translated "the Jews" in many English translations. In the Gospel of John, however, this term doesn't always refer to the Jewish people generally. In some contexts, it refers more particularly to the Jewish religious leaders. We have attempted to capture the meaning in these different contexts by using terms such as "the people" (with a footnote: Greek *the Jewish people*) or "the Jewish leaders," where appropriate.

- One challenge we faced was how to translate accurately the ancient biblical text that was originally written in a context where male-oriented terms were used to refer to humanity generally. We needed to respect the nature of the ancient context while also trying to make the translation clear to a modern audience that tends to read male-oriented language as applying only to males. Often the original text, though using masculine nouns and pronouns, clearly intends that the message be applied to both men and women. A typical example is found in the New Testament letters, where the believers are called "brothers" (*adelphoi*). Yet it is clear

from the content of these letters that they were addressed to all the believers—male and female. Thus, we have usually translated this Greek word as "brothers and sisters" in order to represent the historical situation more accurately.

We have also been sensitive to passages where the text applies generally to human beings or to the human condition. In some instances we have used plural pronouns (they, them) in place of the masculine singular (he, him). For example, a traditional rendering of Proverbs 22:6 is: "Train up a child in the way he should go, and when he is old he will not turn from it." We have rendered it: "Direct your children onto the right path, and when they are older, they will not leave it." At times, we have also replaced third person pronouns with the second person to ensure clarity. A traditional rendering of Proverbs 26:27 is: "He who digs a pit will fall into it, and he who rolls a stone, it will come back on him." We have rendered it: "If you set a trap for others, you will get caught in it yourself. If you roll a boulder down on others, it will crush you instead."

We should emphasize that all masculine nouns and pronouns used to represent God (for example, "Father") have been maintained without exception. All decisions of this kind have been driven by the concern to reflect accurately the intended meaning of the original texts of Scripture.

## LEXICAL CONSISTENCY IN TERMINOLOGY

For the sake of clarity, we have translated certain original-language terms consistently, especially within synoptic passages and for commonly repeated rhetorical phrases, and within certain word categories such as divine names and non-theological technical terminology (e.g., liturgical, legal, cultural, zoological, and botanical terms). For theological terms, we have allowed a greater semantic range of acceptable English words or phrases for a single Hebrew or Greek word. We have avoided some theological terms that are not readily understood by many

modern readers. For example, we avoided using words such as "justification" and "sanctification," which are carryovers from Latin translations. In place of these words, we have provided renderings such as "made right with God" and "made holy."

## THE SPELLING OF PROPER NAMES

Many individuals in the Bible, especially the Old Testament, are known by more than one name (e.g., Uzziah/Azariah). For the sake of clarity, we have tried to use a single spelling for any one individual, footnoting the literal spelling whenever we differ from it. This is especially helpful in delineating the kings of Israel and Judah. King Joash/Jehoash of Israel has been consistently called Jehoash, while King Joash/Jehoash of Judah is called Joash. A similar distinction has been used to distinguish between Joram/Jehoram of Israel and Joram/Jehoram of Judah. All such decisions were made with the goal of clarifying the text for the reader. When the ancient biblical writers clearly had a theological purpose in their choice of a variant name (e.g., Esh-baal/Ishbosheth), the different names have been maintained with an explanatory footnote.

For the names Jacob and Israel, which are used interchangeably for both the individual patriarch and the nation, we generally render it "Israel" when it refers to the nation and "Jacob" when it refers to the individual. When our rendering of the name differs from the underlying Hebrew text, we provide a textual footnote, which includes this explanation: "The names 'Jacob' and 'Israel' are often interchanged throughout the Old Testament, referring sometimes to the individual patriarch and sometimes to the nation."

## THE RENDERING OF DIVINE NAMES

In the Old Testament, all appearances of *'el, 'elohim,* or *'eloah* have been translated "God," except where the context demands the translation "god(s)." We have generally rendered the tetragrammaton (*YHWH*) consistently as "the Lord," utilizing a form with small capitals that is common among English translations. This will distinguish it from the name *'adonai,* which we render "Lord." When *'adonai* and *YHWH* appear together, we have rendered it "Sovereign LORD." This also distinguishes *'adonai YHWH* from cases where *YHWH* appears with *'elohim,* which is rendered "LORD God." When *YH* (the short form of *YHWH*) and *YHWH* appear together, we have rendered it "LORD GOD." When *YHWH* appears with the term *tseba'oth,* we have rendered it "LORD of Heaven's Armies" to translate the meaning of the name. In a few cases, we have utilized the transliteration, *Yahweh,* when the personal character of the name is being invoked in contrast to another divine name or the name of some other god (for example, see Exodus 3:15; 6:2-3).

In the Gospels and Acts, the Greek word *christos* has normally been translated as "Messiah" when the context assumes a Jewish audience. When a Gentile audience can be assumed (which is consistently the case in the Epistles and Revelation), *christos* has been translated as "Christ." The Greek word *kurios* is consistently translated "Lord," except that it is translated "LORD" wherever the New Testament text explicitly quotes from the Old Testament, and the text there has it in small capitals.

## TEXTUAL FOOTNOTES

The New Living Translation provides several kinds of textual footnotes, all designated in the text with an asterisk:

- When for the sake of clarity the NLT renders a difficult or potentially confusing phrase dynamically, we generally give the literal rendering in a textual footnote. This allows the reader to see the literal source of our dynamic rendering and how our translation relates to other more literal translations. These notes are prefaced with "Hebrew," "Aramaic," or "Greek," identifying the language of the underlying source text. For example, in Acts 2:42 we translated the literal "breaking of bread" (from the Greek) as "the Lord's Supper" to clarify that this verse refers to the ceremonial practice of the church rather than just an ordinary meal. Then we attached a footnote to "the Lord's Supper," which reads: "Greek the breaking of bread."
- Textual footnotes are also used to show alternative renderings,

prefaced with the word "Or." These normally occur for passages where an aspect of the meaning is debated. On occasion, we also provide notes on words or phrases that represent a departure from long-standing tradition. These notes are prefaced with "Traditionally rendered." For example, the footnote to the translation "serious skin disease" at Leviticus 13:2 says: "Traditionally rendered *leprosy.* The Hebrew word used throughout this passage is used to describe various skin diseases."

- When our translators follow a textual variant that differs significantly from our standard Hebrew or Greek texts (listed earlier), we document that difference with a footnote. We also footnote cases when the NLT excludes a passage that is included in the Greek text known as the *Textus Receptus* (and familiar to readers through its translation in the King James Version). In such cases, we offer a translation of the excluded text in a footnote, even though it is generally recognized as a later addition to the Greek text and not part of the original Greek New Testament.
- All Old Testament passages that are quoted in the New Testament are identified by a textual footnote at the New Testament location. When the New Testament clearly quotes from the Greek translation of the Old Testament, and when it differs significantly in wording from the Hebrew text, we also place a textual footnote at the Old Testament location. This note includes a rendering of the Greek version, along with a cross-reference to the New Testament passage(s) where it is cited (for example, see notes on Psalms 8:2; 53:3; Proverbs 3:12).
- Some textual footnotes provide cultural and historical information on places, things, and people in the Bible that are probably obscure to modern readers. Such notes should aid the reader in understanding the message of the text. For example, in Acts 12:1, "King Herod" is named in this translation as "King Herod Agrippa" and is identified in a footnote as being "the nephew of Herod Antipas and a grandson of Herod the Great."

- When the meaning of a proper name (or a wordplay inherent in a proper name) is relevant to the meaning of the text, it is either illuminated with a textual footnote or included within parentheses in the text itself. For example, the footnote concerning the name "Eve" at Genesis 3:20 reads: "*Eve* sounds like a Hebrew term that means 'to give life.'" This wordplay in the Hebrew illuminates the meaning of the text, which goes on to say that Eve "would be the mother of all who live."

AS WE SUBMIT this translation for publication, we recognize that any translation of the Scriptures is subject to limitations and imperfections. Anyone who has attempted to communicate the richness of God's word into another language will realize it is impossible to make a perfect translation. Recognizing these limitations, we sought God's guidance and wisdom throughout this project. Now we pray that he will accept our efforts and use this translation for the benefit of the church and of all people.

We pray that the New Living Translation will overcome some of the barriers of history, culture, and language that have kept people from reading and understanding God's word. We hope that readers unfamiliar with the Bible will find the words clear and easy to understand and that readers well versed in the Scriptures will gain a fresh perspective. We pray that readers will gain insight and wisdom for living, but most of all that they will meet the God of the Bible and be forever changed by knowing him.

**THE BIBLE TRANSLATION COMMITTEE**

OLD
TESTAMENT

# Genesis

**WHAT DO WE LEARN ABOUT GOD'S MISSION AND OURS?**
God made women and men in God's image, to be like God, and reign over creation.

**WHO WROTE IT?** Moses, according to Jewish and Christian traditions.

**WHEN DID IT HAPPEN?** The events of Genesis stretch from the beginning of time through the 1800s BC.

**HOW IS IT ORGANIZED?**

1–5: God creates the world; humans sin

6–11: Flood destroys the world; Noah's family rebuilds

12–25: God provides for Abraham and Sarah and for Hagar and Ishmael

25–35: Isaac and Rebekah's lives; Jacob meets Leah and Rachel and builds their family

36: Esau's many descendants

37–50: Jacob's family suffers betrayal and famine and moves to Egypt

**FEATURE HIGHLIGHTS**

+ *Being God's Image (5)*
+ *Days of Creation (6)*
+ *Why Would God Punish Eve Like That? (8)*
+ *Eve: Ruined to Redeemed (9)*
+ *Needing Favor: Finding God's Gift (13)*
+ *Image (43)*

*Words to Remember are highlighted throughout this book*

**HOW LONG DOES IT TAKE TO READ?**

| | | | | | 3:00 | |
|---|---|---|---|---|---|---|
| :30 | 1:00 | 1:30 | 2:00 | 2:30 | 3:00 | 3:30 |

## Timeline

**BC**

| | |
|---|---|
| | **CREATION** — Adam and Eve made by God — Eve bears Cain and Abel, then Seth |
| **NOT DATED** | **FLOOD** — Noah's wife, sons, and daughters-in-law survive |
| 2166 | **ABRAM BORN** |
| 2156 | **SARAI BORN** |
| c. 2100 | **HAGAR BORN** |
| 2091 | **ABRAM AND SARAI ENTER CANAAN** |
| 2066 | **SARAH GIVES BIRTH TO ISAAC** |
| c. 2069 | **HAGAR AND ISHMAEL RESCUED BY "THE GOD WHO SEES"** |
| c. 2050 | **REBEKAH BORN** |
| 2006 | **REBEKAH GIVES BIRTH TO JACOB AND ESAU** |
| c. 1940 | **LEAH BORN, RACHEL BORN** |
| 1929 | **JACOB FLEES TO HARAN** |
| c. 1918 | **LEAH GIVES BIRTH TO JUDAH** |
| 1915 | **RACHEL GIVES BIRTH TO JOSEPH** |
| 1898 | **JOSEPH SOLD INTO SLAVERY** |
| c. 1890 | **TAMAR BECOMES PREGNANT BY JUDAH** |
| 1885 | **JOSEPH RULES EGYPT** |
| 1805 | **JOSEPH DIES** |

## The Account of Creation

1 In the beginning God created the heavens and the earth.* ²The earth was formless and empty, and darkness covered the deep waters. And the Spirit of God was hovering over the surface of the waters.

³Then God said, "Let there be light," and there was light. ⁴And God saw that the light was good. Then he separated the light from the darkness. ⁵God called the light "day" and the darkness "night."

And evening passed and morning came, marking the first day.

⁶Then God said, "Let there be a space between the waters, to separate the waters of the heavens from the waters of the earth." ⁷And that is what happened. God made this space to separate the waters of the earth from the waters of the heavens. ⁸God called the space "sky."

And evening passed and morning came, marking the second day.

⁹Then God said, "Let the waters beneath the sky flow together into one place, so dry ground may appear." And that is what happened. ¹⁰God called the dry ground "land" and the waters "seas." And God saw that it was good. ¹¹Then God said, "Let the land sprout with vegetation—every sort of seed-bearing plant, and trees that grow seed-bearing fruit. These seeds will then produce the kinds of plants and trees from which they came." And that is what happened. ¹²The land produced vegetation—all sorts of seed-bearing plants, and trees with seed-bearing fruit. Their seeds produced plants and trees of the same kind. And God saw that it was good.

¹³And evening passed and morning came, marking the third day.

¹⁴Then God said, "Let lights appear in the sky to separate the day from the night. Let them be signs to mark the seasons, days, and years. ¹⁵Let these lights in the sky shine down on the earth." And that is what happened. ¹⁶God made two great lights—the larger one to govern the day, and the smaller one to govern the night. He also made the stars. ¹⁷God set these lights in the sky to light the earth, ¹⁸to govern the day and night, and to separate the light from the darkness. And God saw that it was good.

¹⁹And evening passed and morning came, marking the fourth day.

²⁰Then God said, "Let the waters swarm with fish and other life. Let the skies be filled with birds of every kind." ²¹So God created great sea creatures and every living thing that scurries and swarms in the water, and every sort of bird—each producing offspring of the same kind. And God saw that it was good. ²²Then God blessed them, saying, "Be fruitful and multiply. Let the fish fill the seas, and let the birds multiply on the earth."

²³And evening passed and morning came, marking the fifth day.

²⁴Then God said, "Let the earth produce every sort of animal, each producing offspring of the same kind—livestock, small animals that scurry along the ground, and wild animals." And that is what happened. ²⁵God made all sorts of wild animals, livestock, and small animals, each able to produce offspring of the same kind. And God saw that it was good.

²⁶Then God said, "Let us make human beings* in our image, to be like us. They will reign over the fish in the sea, the birds in the sky, the livestock, all the wild animals on the earth,* and the small animals that scurry along the ground."

²⁷ So God created human beings* in his own
    image.
  In the image of God he created them;
  male and female he created them.

1:1 Or *In the beginning when God created the heavens and the earth,* ... Or *When God began to create the heavens and the earth,* ...
1:26a Or *man;* Hebrew reads *adam.* 1:26b As in Syriac version; Hebrew reads *all the earth.* 1:27 Or *the man;* Hebrew reads *ha-adam.*

**1:1** Some Christians read Genesis as a description of how God made the world. Other Christians see it as a poetic celebration of creation that unveils God's intentions without revealing his methods. Whatever you conclude about the way God made the world, Genesis leaves no room to see our world as an accident. Other biblical accounts of creation agree (for example, Job 38; Psalm 104).
**1:11-12** The focus of the creation week is fertility. God told the residents of creation to "be fruitful and multiply" and to "fill the earth" (1:22, 28). He repeatedly emphasized the fruitfulness of plants (1:11-12, 29-30) and made each living thing "able to produce offspring of the same kind" (1:11-12, 21, 25). Like animals, people are residents of the world God made, but unlike animals, people were made in God's likeness, according to his image.

**1:22** In the context of his creative work, God blessed a few specific things: fish and birds (1:21-22), animals and humans (1:25-28), and the seventh day (2:3)—later called the Sabbath. This trilogy of blessings highlights the Creator's plan: God made humankind in his image to exercise stewardship over the creatures of the earth and to participate in God's Sabbath rest.
**1:26-27** Humans are not divine, but we share kinship with our creator as the only creature made in his image. "Image of God" is our human identity, expressed through the loving rule of creation on God's behalf (see Psalm 8:5-8). Men and women share this role. Together we participate in the human task of creating culture, maintaining order, and ensuring the flourishing of the natural world. Male and female sexuality is central to what it means to be human because the perpetuation of the human race depends on it.

# Being God's Image—
# Finding Our Human Identity and Vocation

**SCRIPTURE CONNECTION: GENESIS 1:1-31**

When I was twenty, I had my first chance to teach in a college classroom under the supervision of my professor. I was hooked. I knew instantly that this is what I was born to do.

You and I are different people. We each possess unique talents and interests and participate in a unique sphere of relationships. The fact that humans have been created as God's image-bearers means that every life is precious—yours, mine, our neighbors, even our enemies (see 9:6). And because we reflect God's image, each of us is needed for the world to be what God intended.

Genesis 1 is a beautifully structured account of God's creative work. At the beginning of the chapter, the earth was "formless and empty" (1:2). Step by step, God created the framework in which life could flourish. On days one to three, God formed three domains, preparing each for inhabitants—light and darkness, water and sky, and dry land. On days four to six, God populated those domains with residents—heavenly lights, fish and birds, and animals and humans. By the end of creation week, the earth was no longer "formless and empty," but organized and filled with life.

The Bible imagines creation as a cosmic temple in which all creatures worship God. Unlike other ancient temples, the Israelite temple lacked a statue or idol of God as a symbol of divine presence in the central sanctuary. God prohibited such images because, as we see in the creation account, humans fill the role of representing him. This mission to represent him,

> Our mission is to represent God on earth.

which arises from this crucial chapter, requires every one of us—in a wide variety of ways, in every corner of the globe. Both men and women are essential workers in this task.

Genesis 1:28-30 hints at one particular task envisioned by God. We represent the Creator by being responsible stewards of the world he made. Edible plants are to be food for both humans and animals. This human stewardship does not imply unlimited resources for people or free and unlimited enterprise. Part of our job is to ensure equitable access to the world's resources for both humans and animals. If we pollute the natural world and endanger animal or human habitats, then we are not fulfilling our God-given roles. If each of us leans into our roles as God's image-bearers, his glory will be evident over the whole earth.

## IMAGINE

How does it feel to know you are God's appointed representative?

In what ways might God be calling you to care for some part of the earth?

*"My mom and I have very different gifts. While I teach in a college classroom, my mom works in her sewing room, using her skills to make feminine hygiene products to ensure that teenage girls in Africa can stay in school."*

CARMEN JOY IMES, PhD, is an author, speaker, blogger, YouTuber, and serves as associate professor of Old Testament at Biola University in California.

# Insight

## DAYS OF CREATION

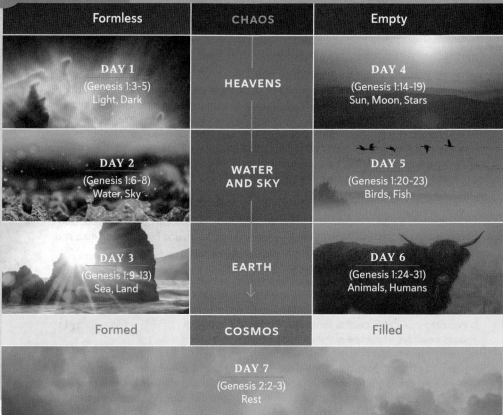

| Formless | CHAOS | Empty |
|---|---|---|
| **DAY 1**<br>(Genesis 1:3-5)<br>Light, Dark | **HEAVENS** | **DAY 4**<br>(Genesis 1:14-19)<br>Sun, Moon, Stars |
| **DAY 2**<br>(Genesis 1:6-8)<br>Water, Sky | **WATER AND SKY** | **DAY 5**<br>(Genesis 1:20-23)<br>Birds, Fish |
| **DAY 3**<br>(Genesis 1:9-13)<br>Sea, Land | **EARTH** | **DAY 6**<br>(Genesis 1:24-31)<br>Animals, Humans |
| Formed | COSMOS | Filled |

**DAY 7**
(Genesis 2:2-3)
Rest

²⁸Then God blessed them and said, "Be fruitful and multiply. Fill the earth and govern it. Reign over the fish in the sea, the birds in the sky, and all the animals that scurry along the ground."

²⁹Then God said, "Look! I have given you every seed-bearing plant throughout the earth and all the fruit trees for your food. ³⁰And I have given every green plant as food for all the wild animals, the birds in the sky, and the small animals that scurry along the ground—everything that has life." And that is what happened.

³¹Then God looked over all he had made, and he saw that it was very good!

And evening passed and morning came, marking the sixth day.

2 So the creation of the heavens and the earth and everything in them was completed. ²On the seventh day God had finished his work of creation, so he rested* from all his work. ³And God blessed the seventh day and declared it holy, because it was the day when he rested from all his work of creation.

⁴This is the account of the creation of the heavens and the earth.

## The Man and Woman in Eden

When the LORD God made the earth and the heavens, ⁵neither wild plants nor grains were growing on the earth. For the LORD God had not yet sent rain to water the earth, and there were no people to cultivate the soil. ⁶Instead, springs* came up from the

2:2 Or *ceased;* also in 2:3. 2:6 Or *mist.*

2:2 God did not rest because he was tired. He rested because his creative work was finished. He rested the way a king rests on his throne when his dominion is at peace. The creation week is a model for us to emulate. None of us can work nonstop. We need regular periods of rest. Genesis 1:1–2:3 invites us to pattern our work week after God's.

ground and watered all the land. ⁷Then the LORD God formed the man from the dust of the ground. He breathed the breath of life into the man's nostrils, and the man became a living person.

⁸Then the LORD God planted a garden in Eden in the east, and there he placed the man he had made. ⁹The LORD God made all sorts of trees grow up from the ground—trees that were beautiful and that produced delicious fruit. In the middle of the garden he placed the tree of life and the tree of the knowledge of good and evil.

¹⁰A river flowed from the land of Eden, watering the garden and then dividing into four branches. ¹¹The first branch, called the Pishon, flowed around the entire land of Havilah, where gold is found. ¹²The gold of that land is exceptionally pure; aromatic resin and onyx stone are also found there. ¹³The second branch, called the Gihon, flowed around the entire land of Cush. ¹⁴The third branch, called the Tigris, flowed east of the land of Asshur. The fourth branch is called the Euphrates.

¹⁵The LORD God placed the man in the Garden of Eden to tend and watch over it. ¹⁶But the LORD God warned him, "You may freely eat the fruit of every tree in the garden—¹⁷except the tree of the knowledge of good and evil. If you eat its fruit, you are sure to die."

¹⁸Then the LORD God said, "It is not good for the man to be alone. I will make a helper who is just right for him." ¹⁹So the LORD God formed from the ground all the wild animals and all the birds of the sky. He brought them to the man* to see what he would call them, and the man chose a name for each one. ²⁰He gave names to all the livestock, all the birds of the sky, and all the wild animals. But still there was no helper just right for him.

²¹So the LORD God caused the man to fall into a deep sleep. While the man slept, the LORD God took out one of the man's ribs* and closed up the opening. ²²Then the LORD God made a woman from the rib, and he brought her to the man.

²³"At last!" the man exclaimed.

"This one is bone from my bone,
    and flesh from my flesh!
She will be called 'woman,'
    because she was taken from 'man.'"

²⁴This explains why a man leaves his father and mother and is joined to his wife, and the two are united into one.

²⁵Now the man and his wife were both naked, but they felt no shame.

## The Man and Woman Sin

**3** The serpent was the shrewdest of all the wild animals the LORD God had made. One day he asked the woman, "Did God really say you must not eat the fruit from any of the trees in the garden?"

²"Of course we may eat fruit from the trees in the garden," the woman replied. ³"It's only the fruit from the tree in the middle of the garden that we are not allowed to eat. God said, 'You must not eat it or even touch it; if you do, you will die.'"

⁴"You won't die!" the serpent replied to the woman. ⁵"God knows that your eyes will be opened as soon as you eat it, and you will be like God, knowing both good and evil."

⁶The woman was convinced. She saw that the tree

---

2:19 Or *Adam,* and so throughout the chapter.   2:21 Or *took a part of the man's side.*

**2:7** God personally formed the first human (*adam* in Hebrew) from the dust of the ground (*adamah* in Hebrew) and brought him to life with divine breath. This description emphasizes God's personal attention, and it reinforces the representative role of humans as God's image. In ancient Mesopotamia, artisans would craft an idol (or "image") and wash the statue's mouth in a garden ritual, preparing it to be inhabited by the divine presence. Similarly, God placed the first human in a garden and breathed life into him so that he could carry out his role as God's representative (2:15), a fitting role for someone made in God's image (1:27).

**2:18-20** For the first time, something in creation was "not good," namely, the lack of a partner for the human. The man could not carry out all his work alone. He needed "a helper . . . just right for him." The Hebrew word *ezer,* translated "helper" here, is not a term of subservience, as though the man needed a servant. In fact, the term *ezer* most often describes God as Israel's helper (see Genesis 49:25; Exodus 18:4; Deuteronomy 33:7; Psalm 146:5). The human needed a true partner who would be just like him.

**2:21-22** While the first human came from the ground, the second human came from the first. This origin emphasizes their essential unity. They are "of the same kind." The word "rib"

may be misleading. The Hebrew term (*tsela*) denotes the "side" of something or a "supporting beam" (see Exodus 25:12). The verbal form of the word (*tsala*) means "to limp" (Genesis 32:31). One might even imagine that God divided the first human in half, making each half into a whole.

**2:23-25** Woman (*ishah* in Hebrew) was from man (*ish*) just like human (*adam*) was from the ground (*adamah*). The wordplays in Hebrew underscore the connectedness of humans to the earth and to each other. Unity in marriage is possible because man and woman share the essential characteristics of humanity, including the status as God's image-bearer and representative (1:27). Their relationship began in mutual trust and honor.

**3:1-7** Did the serpent ask the woman because she would be more easily deceived? She was not present when God instructed Adam. This may explain Paul's instruction in 1 Timothy 2:11-14 that women be allowed to learn so that they will not be easily deceived. But even though the woman is the first to appear in this scene, the man was clearly present and culpable as well. Neither resisted the temptation to define good and evil for themselves. Every temptation begins with casting doubt on the goodness of God. Cultivating trust in him is the surest defense against temptation.

# Perspective

## Why would God punish Eve like that?

SCRIPTURE CONNECTION: GENESIS 3:1-19

Why would God impose such consequences for Eve's one wayward choice? After all, when she decided to take and eat, she did not yet know good and evil. Though adult in form, Eve was young in creation and unwise to the serpent's shrewdness.

When a toddler plays with fire, will the parent discipline for spite? Or to protect? Banning Adam and Eve was God's rescue. In their fallen state, eating of the tree of life would tragically seal them in sin's aftermath.

Eve bore some of God's own torment. Her pain in bringing forth life would compel her toward the Creator, and she would begin to understand how a loving parent chooses pain to give life. Eve's love for Adam would also bear pain, requiring a lifetime of learning what it means to partner in the mystery of marriage.

Our pain compels our outreach for God, and therein lies the gift.

Eve's consequences led to another sacred tree, the Cross, from which we now partake. This time, the body and blood of Christ and the pain he bore delivers us into life everlasting, restoring our perfect communion with God. As Paul says,

Yes, Adam's one sin brings condemnation for everyone, but Christ's one act of righteousness brings a right relationship with God and new life for everyone. (Romans 5:18)

## VIEWPOINTS

HERS: *Perhaps unaware of what her choice would mean, how was Eve's perspective limited? How did Eve's understanding grow?*
MINE: *"We do not get to choose results, only our actions. We can practice choosing wisely and entrusting results to God."*
YOURS: *Even in pain, how might we trust God as a loving parent?*

MISTY ARTERBURN is an author and speaker, contributing to Bible projects, devotionals, and recovery materials for over twenty years. Wife and mom to five, Misty is the founder of Recovery Girls and the general editor of *The One Year Bible for Women.*

was beautiful and its fruit looked delicious, and she wanted the wisdom it would give her. So she took some of the fruit and ate it. Then she gave some to her husband, who was with her, and he ate it, too. 7At that moment their eyes were opened, and they suddenly felt shame at their nakedness. So they sewed fig leaves together to cover themselves.

8When the cool evening breezes were blowing, the man* and his wife heard the LORD God walking about in the garden. So they hid from the LORD God among the trees. 9Then the LORD God called to the man, "Where are you?"

10He replied, "I heard you walking in the garden, so I hid. I was afraid because I was naked."

11"Who told you that you were naked?" the LORD God asked. "Have you eaten from the tree whose fruit I commanded you not to eat?"

12The man replied, "It was the woman you gave me who gave me the fruit, and I ate it."

13Then the LORD God asked the woman, "What have you done?"

"The serpent deceived me," she replied. "That's why I ate it."

14Then the LORD God said to the serpent,

"Because you have done this, you are cursed
    more than all animals, domestic and wild.
You will crawl on your belly,
    groveling in the dust as long as you live.
15 And I will cause hostility between you and the
    woman,
    and between your offspring and her
        offspring.
He will strike* your head,
    and you will strike his heel."

16Then he said to the woman,

"I will sharpen the pain of your pregnancy,
    and in pain you will give birth.
And you will desire to control your husband,
    but he will rule over you.*"

3:8 Or *Adam,* and so throughout the chapter. 3:15 Or *bruise;* also in 3:15b. 3:16 Or *And though you will have desire for your husband, / he will rule over you.*

3:11-13 Rather than confessing, the man blamed the woman for giving him the fruit and God for giving him the woman. The woman followed suit, accusing the serpent. The serpent played a role and would be punished (3:14), but that did not release the woman or the man from their guilt.
3:16-19 The consequences of human rebellion complicated human vocation. Pain in childbirth would make it more difficult to fill the earth. The partnership God intended between man and woman would become antagonistic, so that rather than ruling the earth, they would seek to dominate each other. Fruitful cultivation of the land would prove difficult. Although humans do far more than have babies and plant crops, these activities bear the brunt of the consequences of sin because they are essential to the fulfillment of the creation blessing (1:26-28).

## Eve

**IDENTITY** — Ruined to Redeemed

*Eve remembers...*

The fruit looked *so* good. It was so beautiful I could almost taste it before I bit into it. The serpent promised that good things would come from it: I would be wise and know everything. That first bite was so sweet...

And then everything changed, dramatically.

If I had only known. I didn't really understand the consequences. Adam was right there, and he didn't stop me either. In fact, he later blamed me. Wasn't he to blame too? Oh, God, now what?

The consequences: pain in childbirth, desire to control my husband. What does that even mean?

A promise: A descendant of mine will one day crush the head of the serpent? When? How?

Life became painful. We were driven out of the Garden, never to reenter. God gave us clothes, but we had to learn how to survive. We lost two sons—Cain killed Abel, then Cain was banished from our presence. Oh, the pain of loss!

Yet in the pain, God provided. He gave us Seth, a son to carry on life. We learned to trust that God is still in charge.

EVE'S STORY IS TOLD IN GENESIS 2:19–4:26.

> God is bigger than our missteps and our pain. He is always ready to restore and provide.

### IDENTIFY

What life-changing events have you experienced?

Where do you find God in them?

*"I miscarried my second child, propelling me into early menopause. Then, God opened doors to counsel grieving women and to a new career in academia, which I may not have pursued if I had a small child at home."*

ELIZABETH GLANVILLE, PhD, is retired faculty from Fuller Theological Seminary, School of Mission and Theology. She is an international teacher on missions and leadership and chaplain for a local police department and her retirement community.

[17]And to the man he said,

"Since you listened to your wife and ate from
　　the tree
　　whose fruit I commanded you not to eat,
the ground is cursed because of you.
　All your life you will struggle to scratch a
　　living from it.
[18] It will grow thorns and thistles for you,
　　though you will eat of its grains.
[19] By the sweat of your brow
　　will you have food to eat
until you return to the ground
　　from which you were made.
For you were made from dust,
　　and to dust you will return."

## Paradise Lost: God's Judgment

[20]Then the man—Adam—named his wife Eve, because she would be the mother of all who live.* [21]And
the LORD God made clothing from animal skins for
Adam and his wife.

[22]Then the LORD God said, "Look, the human beings* have become like us, knowing both good and
evil. What if they reach out, take fruit from the tree
of life, and eat it? Then they will live forever!" [23]So the
LORD God banished them from the Garden of Eden,
and he sent Adam out to cultivate the ground from
which he had been made. [24]After sending them out,
the LORD God stationed mighty cherubim to the east
of the Garden of Eden. And he placed a flaming sword
that flashed back and forth to guard the way to the
tree of life.

## Cain and Abel

4 Now Adam* had sexual relations with his wife,
Eve, and she became pregnant. When she gave
birth to Cain, she said, "With the LORD's help, I have
produced* a man!" [2]Later she gave birth to his
brother and named him Abel.

When they grew up, Abel became a shepherd,
while Cain cultivated the ground. [3]When it was time
for the harvest, Cain presented some of his crops as
a gift to the LORD. [4]Abel also brought a gift—the best

portions of the firstborn lambs from his flock. The
LORD accepted Abel and his gift, [5]but he did not accept Cain and his gift. This made Cain very angry, and
he looked dejected.

[6]"Why are you so angry?" the LORD asked Cain.
"Why do you look so dejected? [7]You will be accepted
if you do what is right. But if you refuse to do what
is right, then watch out! Sin is crouching at the door,
eager to control you. But you must subdue it and be
its master."

[8]One day Cain suggested to his brother, "Let's go
out into the fields."* And while they were in the
field, Cain attacked his brother, Abel, and killed him.

[9]Afterward the LORD asked Cain, "Where is your
brother? Where is Abel?"

"I don't know," Cain responded. "Am I my brother's
guardian?"

[10]But the LORD said, "What have you done? Listen! Your brother's blood cries out to me from the
ground! [11]Now you are cursed and banished from
the ground, which has swallowed your brother's
blood. [12]No longer will the ground yield good
crops for you, no matter how hard you work!
From now on you will be a homeless wanderer on
the earth."

[13]Cain replied to the LORD, "My punishment* is
too great for me to bear! [14]You have banished me
from the land and from your presence; you have
made me a homeless wanderer. Anyone who finds
me will kill me!"

[15]The LORD replied, "No, for I will give a sevenfold
punishment to anyone who kills you." Then the LORD
put a mark on Cain to warn anyone who might try
to kill him. [16]So Cain left the LORD's presence and
settled in the land of Nod,* east of Eden.

## The Descendants of Cain

[17]Cain had sexual relations with his wife, and she
became pregnant and gave birth to Enoch. Then
Cain founded a city, which he named Enoch, after
his son. [18]Enoch had a son named Irad. Irad became
the father of* Mehujael. Mehujael became the father of Methushael. Methushael became the father
of Lamech.

---

3:20 Eve sounds like a Hebrew term that means "to give life." 3:22 Or the man; Hebrew reads ha-adam. 4:1a Or the man; also
in 4:25. 4:1b Or I have acquired. Cain sounds like a Hebrew term that can mean "produce" or "acquire." 4:8 As in Samaritan
Pentateuch, Greek and Syriac versions, and Latin Vulgate; Masoretic Text lacks "Let's go out into the fields." 4:13 Or My sin.
4:16 Nod means "wandering." 4:18 Or the ancestor of, and so throughout the verse.

---

**3:20-24** God graciously clothed Adam and Eve since they
had become ashamed of their nakedness. In his mercy, God
prevented them from eating of the tree of life, so that they
would not live forever in their state of alienation from God
and each other.

**4:1** Eve recognized God's blessing in the gift of children.
The birth of a son ensured the continuation of the family line.
However, the tragic consequences of sin threatened her family's survival. Cain did not offer God his best, and his jealousy
toward Abel drove him to kill his own brother.

**4:17** Where did Cain find a wife? If Adam and Eve were the
only people, then he would have to have married his sister.
However, Genesis does not specifically claim that Adam and
Eve were the only humans created. It's possible that their
story is an archetype of the human experience. The existence
of other humans seems to be implied in Cain's fear that others
would kill him if he wandered alone (4:14-15). In 1 Corinthians
15:22, the apostle Paul speaks of Adam's representative role
for humanity. Some believe Adam's role requires him to be the
genetic parent of all humans, while others do not.

¹⁹Lamech married two women. The first was named Adah, and the second was Zillah. ²⁰Adah gave birth to Jabal, who was the first of those who raise livestock and live in tents. ²¹His brother's name was Jubal, the first of all who play the harp and flute. ²²Lamech's other wife, Zillah, gave birth to a son named Tubal-cain. He became an expert in forging tools of bronze and iron. Tubal-cain had a sister named Naamah. ²³One day Lamech said to his wives,

"Adah and Zillah, hear my voice;
    listen to me, you wives of Lamech.
I have killed a man who attacked me,
    a young man who wounded me.
²⁴ If someone who kills Cain is punished
        seven times,
    then the one who kills me will be punished
        seventy-seven times!"

**4:19** Lamech was the first polygamist mentioned in the Bible. Marrying two women is contrary to God's pattern for marriage (2:24) and might have been a manifestation of the rebellion of Cain's descendants. Lamech later boasted to his wives about his vengeful spirit, revealing his violent nature. Genesis certainly does not present him as a role model. For other negative examples related to polygamy, see 28:6-9; 29:14–30:24.

## Oikos

IMAGE · MY STORY WITH FAMILY & FRIENDS

## Seeing Our Families Shine

**SCRIPTURE CONNECTION: GENESIS 4:1-12**

Have you ever had a rock hit your windshield while driving? The sound may startle you, and at first you might not see any damage. Then a few days later, you notice a tiny chip. Then the chip becomes a crack, and soon there's a line across the windshield you can no longer ignore.

Isn't that how brokenness works in our families? Cain's sin starts so small—unjustified anger—and only he knows about it. In the end, his selfishness and jealousy break the entire family.

Abel loses life.

Cain loses community.

Eve and Adam lose two sons.

Has your family experienced loss because sin caused a fracture? Divorce was ours. As we meet families in the Bible and consider our own families, we see that every family member has flaws. And our failures hurt us and others.

But that's not the end of the story.

Family is God's idea. He longs to see whole, healthy, joy-filled homes that display his love. Just as an intact windshield helps us see and protects those in the car, asking God to show us what's broken can make us a blessing to our families—and make our families a blessing to others.

Through divorce, I lost much. But God restored. He redeemed. He also stretched my previously limited view of family. When we come to the end of denial and invite God's intervention, he responds. For every crack, his love restores.

> God's love brings blessings, sparkling through our family's shattered places.

### IMAGINE

Consider your best and highest dream for your family. How has God positioned you to help lead them there?

What conversations or actions of love need to happen?

*"I pray God helps me see my own faults and be courageous enough to address them before they splinter and grow."*

**SUZY SHEPHERD** is the founder of SHINE, creator of Stonecroft's Where Love Lives outreach experience, and mom to a blended tribe of nine. She finds great joy in creating experiences for people to know God's love.

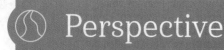

# Perspective

## Does God okay the "forcible taking" of women?

**SCRIPTURE CONNECTION: GENESIS 6:1-8**

What "sons of God" would forcibly take any women they wanted to be their wives? This doesn't sound very godly at all.

Many scholars resolve this by concluding that the "sons of God" phrasing refers to spiritual or angelic beings who had rebelled against God. Others suggest that it refers to human rulers who married commoners. Still others argue that it refers to descendants of Seth who married the female descendants of Cain.

Regardless, we recognize that the sexual arena has been a favorite playground for the enemy from the time man and woman first knew their nakedness (3:7). At the birth of their shame, they covered their sexual bodies with fig leaves.

This passage from Genesis 6 conceals whether the human women were consenting to these unions or were taken against their will. But one thing is clear: This sexual deviancy wreaked havoc.

---

### VIEWPOINTS

---

**HERS:** *What does the phrase "took any they wanted" suggest about how these "sons of God" esteemed women and interacted with them?*
**MINE:** *"I am not a fan of the word victim—at least with respect to many of my own experiences. While I acknowledge its appropriate use when I have been deceived, used, or harmed, I don't want to downplay any part of choice I may have had in a matter: how I show up, how I respond, what resources I turn to, whether an incident defines or grows me, whether I reach for God or reject him. I am not responsible for others' choices, and sometimes I may not have a choice, but when I do, I can ask, What choices will I make today?"*
**YOURS:** *How might you guard against sexual trouble and champion sexual responsibility today?*

---

MISTY ARTERBURN is an author and speaker, contributing to Bible projects, devotionals, and recovery materials for over twenty years. Wife and mom to five, Misty is the founder of Recovery Girls and the general editor of *The One Year Bible for Women*.

## The Birth of Seth

[25] Adam had sexual relations with his wife again, and she gave birth to another son. She named him Seth,* for she said, "God has granted me another son in place of Abel, whom Cain killed." [26] When Seth grew up, he had a son and named him Enosh. At that time people first began to worship the LORD by name.

## The Descendants of Adam

5 This is the written account of the descendants of Adam. When God created human beings,* he made them to be like himself. [2] He created them male and female, and he blessed them and called them "human."

[3] When Adam was 130 years old, he became the father of a son who was just like him—in his very image. He named his son Seth. [4] After the birth of Seth, Adam lived another 800 years, and he had other sons and daughters. [5] Adam lived 930 years, and then he died.

[6] When Seth was 105 years old, he became the father of* Enosh. [7] After the birth of* Enosh, Seth lived another 807 years, and he had other sons and daughters. [8] Seth lived 912 years, and then he died.

[9] When Enosh was 90 years old, he became the father of Kenan. [10] After the birth of Kenan, Enosh lived another 815 years, and he had other sons and daughters. [11] Enosh lived 905 years, and then he died.

[12] When Kenan was 70 years old, he became the father of Mahalalel. [13] After the birth of Mahalalel, Kenan lived another 840 years, and he had other sons and daughters. [14] Kenan lived 910 years, and then he died.

[15] When Mahalalel was 65 years old, he became the father of Jared. [16] After the birth of Jared, Mahalalel lived another 830 years, and he had other sons and daughters. [17] Mahalalel lived 895 years, and then he died.

[18] When Jared was 162 years old, he became the father of Enoch. [19] After the birth of Enoch, Jared lived another 800 years, and he had other sons and daughters. [20] Jared lived 962 years, and then he died.

[21] When Enoch was 65 years old, he became the father of Methuselah. [22] After the birth of Methuselah, Enoch lived in close fellowship with God for another 300 years, and he had other

**4:25** *Seth* probably means "granted"; the name may also mean "appointed." **5:1** Or *man;* Hebrew reads *adam;* similarly in 5:2. **5:6** Or *the ancestor of;* also in 5:9, 12, 15, 18, 21, 25. **5:7** Or *the birth of this ancestor of;* also in 5:10, 13, 16, 19, 22, 26.

**5:1-3** This second biblical mention of the image of God helps to define it. God made humans to be like him. Similarly, Adam fathered a son who was just like him—in his very image. Our identity as God's image implies kinship. We are related to God in a way analogous to a human family. This passage also affirms that the human status as God's image was not lost when Adam and Eve sinned.

sons and daughters. ²³Enoch lived 365 years, ²⁴walking in close fellowship with God. Then one day he disappeared, because God took him.

²⁵When Methuselah was 187 years old, he became the father of Lamech. ²⁶After the birth of Lamech, Methuselah lived another 782 years, and he had other sons and daughters. ²⁷Methuselah lived 969 years, and then he died.

²⁸When Lamech was 182 years old, he became the father of a son. ²⁹Lamech named his son Noah, for he said, "May he bring us relief* from our work and the painful labor of farming this ground that the LORD has cursed." ³⁰After the birth of Noah, Lamech lived another 595 years, and he had other sons and daughters. ³¹Lamech lived 777 years, and then he died.

³²After Noah was 500 years old, he became the father of Shem, Ham, and Japheth.

## A World Gone Wrong

6 Then the people began to multiply on the earth, and daughters were born to them. ²The sons of God saw the beautiful women* and took any they wanted as their wives. ³Then the LORD said, "My Spirit will not put up with* humans for such a long time, for they are only mortal flesh. In the future, their normal lifespan will be no more than 120 years."

⁴In those days, and for some time after, giant Nephilites lived on the earth, for whenever the sons of God had intercourse with women, they gave birth to children who became the heroes and famous warriors of ancient times.

5:29 *Noah* sounds like a Hebrew term that can mean "relief" or "comfort."   6:2 Hebrew *daughters of men;* also in 6:4.   6:3 Greek version reads *will not remain in.*

---

**6:1-4** Obviously the birth of daughters was nothing new, but in this passage, the daughters take center stage. Their stunning beauty attracted some unlikely suitors. Scholars have suggested three possibilities for the identity of the "sons of God" in this passage: angelic beings who left their stations to cohabit with women, royalty who intermarried with commoners, or members of Seth's family who married women from Cain's family. Language reminiscent of 3:6 ("saw . . . took") shows the rebellious nature of this act. The result of these unions was a warrior race known for its wickedness.

---

# Come Close   NEEDING FAVOR: FINDING GOD'S GIFT

### SCRIPTURE CONNECTION: GENESIS 6:5-9

Favor. It's something we pray for often. Favor in our jobs. Favor in our relationships. Favor in our personal endeavors. We read about the lives of women and men in the Bible such as Abel, Abraham, Noah, Hannah, and Jesus' mother, Mary, who all experienced the favor of God in one way or another. Whether it was for a season or a lifetime, the blessing of God's favor truly changed the lives of these individuals. God's favor still has the power to do so for us today.

There are quite a few mentions of God's favor (or "grace," depending on the translation) in the Bible. In a famous proverb, quoted multiple times in the New Testament, favor is attached to the character trait of humility (Proverbs 3:34; see James 4:6; 1 Peter 5:5). Could it be that our humility moves God to grant us favor? When we think of others who lost God's favor, such as Cain or King Saul, could a lack of humility have contributed?

Favor is a gift; we can't work ourselves into it. We accept and receive it by faith through our relationship with God. As we learn to love the Giver more than the gift, we will begin to see strands of his favor weaving throughout our lives.

**REFLECT** "For you bless the godly, O LORD; you surround them with your shield of love." PSALM 5:12

*Lord, thank you for the gift of your gracious favor. May I walk humbly before you all the days of my life. Amen.*

**CONSIDER** "Humility is the gateway into the grace and the favor of God." HAROLD WARNER

## God's favor is a gift; greater still is knowing the gift-Giver.

**QUANTRILLA ARD, PhD,** is a faith-based personal and spiritual development author, speaker, Bible teacher, and literary agent who believes in the power of collective strength, community, and fellowship.

⁵The LORD observed the extent of human wickedness on the earth, and he saw that everything they thought or imagined was consistently and totally evil. ⁶So the LORD was sorry he had ever made them and put them on the earth. It broke his heart. ⁷And the LORD said, "I will wipe this human race I have created from the face of the earth. Yes, and I will destroy every living thing—all the people, the large animals, the small animals that scurry along the ground, and even the birds of the sky. I am sorry I ever made them." ⁸But Noah found favor with the LORD.

### The Story of Noah

⁹This is the account of Noah and his family. Noah was a righteous man, the only blameless person living on earth at the time, and he walked in close fellowship with God. ¹⁰Noah was the father of three sons: Shem, Ham, and Japheth.

¹¹Now God saw that the earth had become corrupt and was filled with violence. ¹²God observed all this corruption in the world, for everyone on earth was corrupt. ¹³So God said to Noah, "I have decided to destroy all living creatures, for they have filled the earth with violence. Yes, I will wipe them all out along with the earth!

¹⁴"Build a large boat* from cypress wood* and waterproof it with tar, inside and out. Then construct decks and stalls throughout its interior. ¹⁵Make the boat 450 feet long, 75 feet wide, and 45 feet high.* ¹⁶Leave an 18-inch opening* below the roof all the way

6:14a Traditionally rendered *an ark.*   6:14b Or *gopher wood.*   6:15 Hebrew *300 cubits* [138 meters] *long, 50 cubits* [23 meters] *wide, and 30 cubits* [13.8 meters] *high.*   6:16 Hebrew *an opening of 1 cubit* [46 centimeters].

## Insight  NOAH'S ARK

These illustrations depict what the ark might have looked like based on the descriptions we read in 6:14-16. Noah and his wife, and their sons and daughters-in-law, and all the creatures they brought on board survived the Flood in a boat like this.

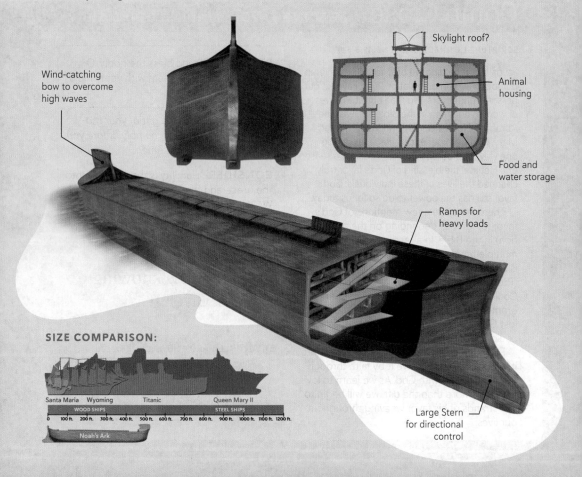

Skylight roof?

Wind-catching bow to overcome high waves

Animal housing

Food and water storage

Ramps for heavy loads

**SIZE COMPARISON:**

Santa Maria   Wyoming          Titanic          Queen Mary II
WOOD SHIPS                      STEEL SHIPS
0   100 ft.   200 ft.   300 ft.   400 ft.   500 ft.   600 ft.   700 ft.   800 ft.   900 ft.   1000 ft.   1100 ft.   1200 ft.

Noah's Ark

Large Stern for directional control

around the boat. Put the door on the side, and build three decks inside the boat—lower, middle, and upper.

¹⁷"Look! I am about to cover the earth with a flood that will destroy every living thing that breathes. Everything on earth will die. ¹⁸But I will confirm my covenant with you. So enter the boat—you and your wife and your sons and their wives. ¹⁹Bring a pair of every kind of animal—a male and a female—into the boat with you to keep them alive during the flood. ²⁰Pairs of every kind of bird, and every kind of animal, and every kind of small animal that scurries along the ground, will come to you to be kept alive. ²¹And be sure to take on board enough food for your family and for all the animals."

²²So Noah did everything exactly as God had commanded him.

## The Flood Covers the Earth

7 When everything was ready, the LORD said to Noah, "Go into the boat with all your family, for among all the people of the earth, I can see that you alone are righteous. ²Take with you seven pairs—male and female—of each animal I have approved for eating and for sacrifice,* and take one pair of each of the others. ³Also take seven pairs of every kind of bird. There must be a male and a female in each pair to ensure that all life will survive on the earth after the flood. ⁴Seven days from now I will make the rains pour down on the earth. And it will rain for forty days and forty nights, until I have wiped from the earth all the living things I have created."

⁵So Noah did everything as the LORD commanded him.

⁶Noah was 600 years old when the flood covered the earth. ⁷He went on board the boat to escape the flood—he and his wife and his sons and their wives. ⁸With them were all the various kinds of animals—those approved for eating and for sacrifice and those that were not—along with all the birds and the small animals that scurry along the ground. ⁹They entered the boat in pairs, male and female, just as God had commanded Noah. ¹⁰After seven days, the waters of the flood came and covered the earth.

¹¹When Noah was 600 years old, on the seventeenth day of the second month, all the underground waters erupted from the earth, and the rain fell in mighty torrents from the sky. ¹²The rain continued to fall for forty days and forty nights.

¹³That very day Noah had gone into the boat with his wife and his sons—Shem, Ham, and Japheth—and their wives. ¹⁴With them in the boat were pairs of every kind of animal—domestic and wild, large and small—along with birds of every kind. ¹⁵Two by two they came into the boat, representing every living thing that breathes. ¹⁶A male and female of each kind entered, just as God had commanded Noah. Then the LORD closed the door behind them.

¹⁷For forty days the floodwaters grew deeper, covering the ground and lifting the boat high above the earth. ¹⁸As the waters rose higher and higher above the ground, the boat floated safely on the surface. ¹⁹Finally, the water covered even the highest mountains on the earth, ²⁰rising more than twenty-two feet* above the highest peaks. ²¹All the living things on earth died—birds, domestic animals, wild animals, small animals that scurry along the ground, and all the people. ²²Everything that breathed and lived on dry land died. ²³God wiped out every living thing on the earth—people, livestock, small animals that scurry along the ground, and the birds of the sky. All were destroyed. The only people who survived were Noah and those with him in the boat. ²⁴And the floodwaters covered the earth for 150 days.

## The Flood Recedes

8 But God remembered Noah and all the wild animals and livestock with him in the boat. He sent a wind to blow across the earth, and the floodwaters began to recede. ²The underground waters stopped flowing, and the torrential rains from the sky were stopped. ³So the floodwaters gradually receded from the earth. After 150 days, ⁴exactly five months from the time the flood began,* the boat came to rest on the mountains of Ararat. ⁵Two and a half months later,* as the waters continued to go down, other mountain peaks became visible.

⁶After another forty days, Noah opened the window he had made in the boat ⁷and released a raven. The bird flew back and forth until the floodwaters on the earth had dried up. ⁸He also released a dove to see if the water had receded and it could find dry ground. ⁹But the dove could find no place to land because the water still covered the ground. So it returned to the boat, and Noah held out his hand and drew the dove back inside. ¹⁰After waiting another seven days, Noah released the dove again. ¹¹This time

---

7:2 Hebrew *of each clean animal;* similarly in 7:8.   7:20 Hebrew *15 cubits* [6.9 meters].   8:4 Hebrew *on the seventeenth day of the seventh month;* see 7:11.   8:5 Hebrew *On the first day of the tenth month;* see 7:11 and note on 8:4.

---

**6:11–7:24** Human wickedness had reached the point that God decided to start over with Noah, the only godly person alive. The Flood would return the world to its pre-created state—formless and empty, with water covering everything. Therefore, Noah and his family needed to preserve a pair of every animal to repopulate the earth after the Flood (see 8:17).
**8:1** This verse is the center of a massive chiasm (or literary sandwich). What precedes this verse is a description of the building and boarding of the ark and the rising of the waters for 150 days. What follows is a description of the receding of the waters for 150 days and the disembarking of the animals. God's *remembering* Noah does not suggest that he forgot about him but marks the moment in which God took action to keep his promise.

the dove returned to him in the evening with a fresh olive leaf in its beak. Then Noah knew that the flood-waters were almost gone. [12]He waited another seven days and then released the dove again. This time it did not come back.

[13]Noah was now 601 years old. On the first day of the new year, ten and a half months after the flood began,* the floodwaters had almost dried up from the earth. Noah lifted back the covering of the boat and saw that the surface of the ground was drying. [14]Two more months went by,* and at last the earth was dry!

[15]Then God said to Noah, [16]"Leave the boat, all of you—you and your wife, and your sons and their wives. [17]Release all the animals—the birds, the livestock, and the small animals that scurry along the ground—so they can be fruitful and multiply throughout the earth."

[18]So Noah, his wife, and his sons and their wives left the boat. [19]And all of the large and small animals and birds came out of the boat, pair by pair.

[20]Then Noah built an altar to the LORD, and there he sacrificed as burnt offerings the animals and birds that had been approved for that purpose.* [21]And the LORD was pleased with the aroma of the sacrifice and said to himself, "I will never again curse the ground because of the human race, even though everything they think or imagine is bent toward evil from childhood. I will never again destroy all living things. [22]As long as the earth remains, there will be planting and harvest, cold and heat, summer and winter, day and night."

## God Confirms His Covenant

**9** Then God blessed Noah and his sons and told them, "Be fruitful and multiply. Fill the earth. [2]All the animals of the earth, all the birds of the sky, all the small animals that scurry along the ground, and all the fish in the sea will look on you with fear and terror. I have placed them in your power. [3]I have given them to you for food, just as I have given you grain and vegetables. [4]But you must never eat any meat that still has the lifeblood in it.

[5]"And I will require the blood of anyone who takes another person's life. If a wild animal kills a person,

it must die. And anyone who murders a fellow human must die. [6]If anyone takes a human life, that person's life will also be taken by human hands. For God made human beings* in his own image. [7]Now be fruitful and multiply, and repopulate the earth."

[8]Then God told Noah and his sons, [9]"I hereby confirm my covenant with you and your descendants, [10]and with all the animals that were on the boat with you—the birds, the livestock, and all the wild animals—every living creature on earth. [11]Yes, I am confirming my covenant with you. Never again will floodwaters kill all living creatures; never again will a flood destroy the earth."

[12]Then God said, "I am giving you a sign of my covenant with you and with all living creatures, for all generations to come. [13]I have placed my rainbow in the clouds. It is the sign of my covenant with you and with all the earth. [14]When I send clouds over the earth, the rainbow will appear in the clouds, [15]and I will remember my covenant with you and with all living creatures. Never again will the flood-waters destroy all life. [16]When I see the rainbow in the clouds, I will remember the eternal covenant between God and every living creature on earth." [17]Then God said to Noah, "Yes, this rainbow is the sign of the covenant I am confirming with all the creatures on earth."

## Noah's Sons

[18]The sons of Noah who came out of the boat with their father were Shem, Ham, and Japheth. (Ham is the father of Canaan.) [19]From these three sons of Noah came all the people who now populate the earth.

[20]After the flood, Noah began to cultivate the ground, and he planted a vineyard. [21]One day he drank some wine he had made, and he became drunk and lay naked inside his tent. [22]Ham, the father of Canaan, saw that his father was naked and went outside and told his brothers. [23]Then Shem and Japheth took a robe, held it over their shoulders, and backed into the tent to cover their father. As they did this, they looked the other way so they would not see him naked.

---

8:13 Hebrew *On the first day of the first month;* see 7:11. 8:14 Hebrew *The twenty-seventh day of the second month arrived;* see note on 8:13. 8:20 Hebrew *every clean animal and every clean bird.* 9:6 Or *man;* Hebrew reads *ha-adam.*

---

**9:1-3** The blessing first given to Adam (1:28) was reissued to Noah, the "Adam" of the newly cleansed world in need of repopulation and cultural expansion. God introduced two modifications to the created order: Now animals would live in terror of humans, and humans were allowed to eat meat along with seed-bearing plants (see 1:29)—a change in diet related to the animals' terror.
**9:5-6** Violence, including murder, was a major factor in bringing about God's judgment in the form of the Flood (4:8; 6:11, 13). At this new beginning for humans, God affirmed the sanctity of human life and established a system of retributive justice for the taking of human life. Being created in God's image gives humans

a unique status and authority within creation. Since murder destroys a person made in God's image, a murderer incurred the ultimate penalty.
**9:20-25** The significance of Ham's shameful behavior is not fully clear. He may have engaged sexually with his father or with his mother (this type of act is elsewhere referred to literally in the original language as "uncovering the nakedness of one's father," Leviticus 20:11). It is possible that he merely gazed upon his naked father and, rather than covering him and keeping the matter secret, dishonored him by mocking him to his brothers. The curse likely fell on Ham's son Canaan to emphasize the shameful father-son dynamic of Ham's sin.

<sup>24</sup>When Noah woke up from his stupor, he learned what Ham, his youngest son, had done. <sup>25</sup>Then he cursed Canaan, the son of Ham:

"May Canaan be cursed!
    May he be the lowest of servants to his
      relatives."

<sup>26</sup>Then Noah said,

"May the LORD, the God of Shem, be blessed,
    and may Canaan be his servant!
<sup>27</sup> May God expand the territory of Japheth!
May Japheth share the prosperity of Shem,*
    and may Canaan be his servant."

<sup>28</sup>Noah lived another 350 years after the great flood. <sup>29</sup>He lived 950 years, and then he died.

**10** This is the account of the families of Shem, Ham, and Japheth, the three sons of Noah. Many children were born to them after the great flood.

## Descendants of Japheth

<sup>2</sup>The descendants of Japheth were Gomer, Magog, Madai, Javan, Tubal, Meshech, and Tiras. <sup>3</sup>The descendants of Gomer were Ashkenaz, Riphath, and Togarmah. <sup>4</sup>The descendants of Javan were Elishah, Tarshish, Kittim, and Rodanim.* <sup>5</sup>Their descendants became the seafaring peoples that spread out to various lands, each identified by its own language, clan, and national identity.

## Descendants of Ham

<sup>6</sup>The descendants of Ham were Cush, Mizraim, Put, and Canaan. <sup>7</sup>The descendants of Cush were Seba, Havilah, Sabtah, Raamah, and Sabteca. The descendants of Raamah were Sheba and Dedan.

<sup>8</sup>Cush was also the ancestor of Nimrod, who was the first heroic warrior on earth. <sup>9</sup>Since he was the greatest hunter in the world,* his name became proverbial. People would say, "This man is like Nimrod, the greatest hunter in the world." <sup>10</sup>He built his kingdom in the land of Babylonia,* with the cities of Babylon, Erech,

9:27 Hebrew *May he live in the tents of Shem.* 10:4 As in some Hebrew manuscripts and Greek version (see also 1 Chr 1:7); most Hebrew manuscripts read *Dodanim.* 10:9 Hebrew *a great hunter before the LORD;* also in 10:9b. 10:10 Hebrew *Shinar.*

10:1-32 The birth of many children after the Flood began to fulfill God's purposes for the renewed creation (9:1; see 1:26-28). This chapter, often called the Table of Nations, lists seventy nations descending from Noah's sons. The total of seventy names indicates completeness and symbolizes the totality of the world, which would later be blessed by the descendants of Abraham (12:3; 18:18). Women are not named because male heirs were the basis for genealogical records.

# Perspective

## Where are the women?

SCRIPTURE CONNECTION: GENESIS 10:1-32

Genesis 10 ranks among the most boring parts of the Bible. So many hard-to-pronounce names!

Are you bothered by how few women appear in these lists?

The ancient Israelites usually recorded only male heirs in their genealogies. A genealogy traced the transfer of wealth from one generation to another and identified tribal membership through fathers and sons. Without a complex chart, marriage alliances between clans were much more difficult to trace. Women were remembered through stories and songs, rather than through genealogies. And they took pride in the social standing of their fathers, husbands, and sons.

God revealed himself in ways that made sense to ancient cultures, and he engages with us in ways that make sense today. Our task is to read the Bible well in its ancient context, discern how it reveals God's character, and then ask how we can live out its principles in our contexts today.

### VIEWPOINTS

**HERS:** *How would an ancient Israelite woman have felt hearing her husband's name read aloud in a list such as this?*
**MINE:** *"I love finding women's names in Bible genealogies. It is rare, so when one does appear, it means she is notable in some way. I love to be a detective and find out why!"*
**YOURS:** *Can you imagine life as an ancient Israelite woman? Would you have been glad to stay in the shadows? Or would you have longed to play a bigger role in public life?*

CARMEN JOY IMES, PhD, is an author, speaker, blogger, YouTuber, and serves as associate professor of Old Testament at Biola University in California.

# Insight NATIONS OF THE ANCIENT WORLD

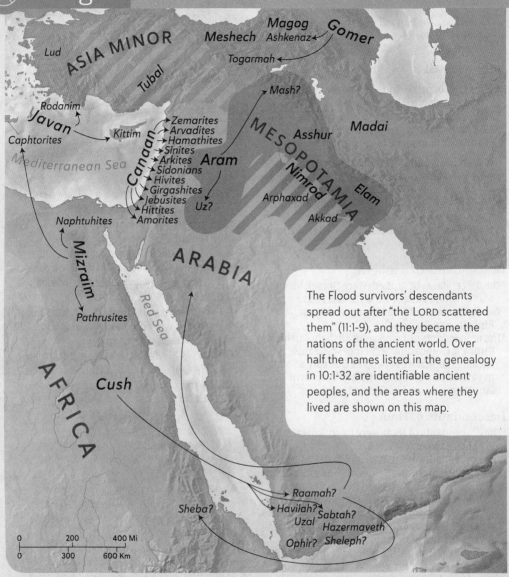

Lud

ASIA MINOR

Magog
Meshech  Ashkenaz  Gomer

Togarmah

Tubal

Mash?

Rodanim
Javan
Caphtorites  Kittim

Zemarites
Arvadites
Hamathites
Sinites
Arkites
Sidonians
Hivites
Girgashites
Jebusites
Hittites
Amorites

Canaan

Aram

MESOPOTAMIA

Asshur      Madai

Nimrod      Elam

Arphaxad

Uz?

Akkad

Mediterranean Sea

Naphtuhites

Mizraim

Pathrusites

ARABIA

Red Sea

AFRICA

Cush

> The Flood survivors' descendants spread out after "the LORD scattered them" (11:1-9), and they became the nations of the ancient world. Over half the names listed in the genealogy in 10:1-32 are identifiable ancient peoples, and the areas where they lived are shown on this map.

Raamah?
Havilah?  Sabtah?
Sheba?    Uzal    Hazermaveth
          Ophir?  Sheleph?

0     200     400 Mi
0   300    600 Km

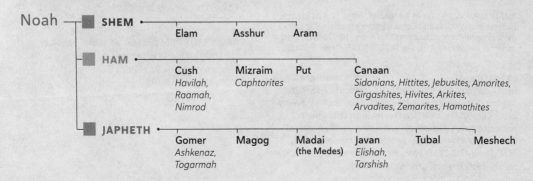

Noah — **SHEM**
Elam      Asshur      Aram

**HAM**
Cush          Mizraim      Put      Canaan
*Havilah,*    *Caphtorites*          *Sidonians, Hittites, Jebusites, Amorites,*
*Raamah,*                            *Girgashites, Hivites, Arkites,*
*Nimrod*                             *Arvadites, Zemarites, Hamathites*

**JAPHETH**
Gomer      Magog      Madai      Javan      Tubal      Meshech
*Ashkenaz,*            (the Medes) *Elishah,*
*Togarmah*                        *Tarshish*

Akkad, and Calneh. ¹¹From there he expanded his territory to Assyria,* building the cities of Nineveh, Rehoboth-ir, Calah, ¹²and Resen (the great city located between Nineveh and Calah).
¹³Mizraim was the ancestor of the Ludites, Anamites, Lehabites, Naphtuhites, ¹⁴Pathrusites, Casluhites, and the Caphtorites, from whom the Philistines came.*
¹⁵Canaan's oldest son was Sidon, the ancestor of the Sidonians. Canaan was also the ancestor of the Hittites,* ¹⁶Jebusites, Amorites, Girgashites, ¹⁷Hivites, Arkites, Sinites, ¹⁸Arvadites, Zemarites, and Hamathites. The Canaanite clans eventually spread out, ¹⁹and the territory of Canaan extended from Sidon in the north to Gerar and Gaza in the south, and east as far as Sodom, Gomorrah, Admah, and Zeboiim, near Lasha.
²⁰These were the descendants of Ham, identified by clan, language, territory, and national identity.

## Descendants of Shem

²¹Sons were also born to Shem, the older brother of Japheth.* Shem was the ancestor of all the descendants of Eber.
²²The descendants of Shem were Elam, Asshur, Arphaxad, Lud, and Aram.
²³The descendants of Aram were Uz, Hul, Gether, and Mash.
²⁴Arphaxad was the father of Shelah,* and Shelah was the father of Eber.
²⁵Eber had two sons. The first was named Peleg (which means "division"), for during his lifetime the people of the world were divided into different language groups. His brother's name was Joktan.
²⁶Joktan was the ancestor of Almodad, Sheleph, Hazarmaveth, Jerah, ²⁷Hadoram, Uzal, Diklah, ²⁸Obal, Abimael, Sheba, ²⁹Ophir, Havilah, and Jobab. All these were descendants of Joktan.
³⁰The territory they occupied extended from Mesha all the way to Sephar in the eastern mountains.
³¹These were the descendants of Shem, identified by clan, language, territory, and national identity.

## Conclusion

³²These are the clans that descended from Noah's sons, arranged by nation according to their lines of descent. All the nations of the earth descended from these clans after the great flood.

## The Tower of Babel

**11** At one time all the people of the world spoke the same language and used the same words. ²As the people migrated to the east, they found a plain in the land of Babylonia* and settled there.

³They began saying to each other, "Let's make bricks and harden them with fire." (In this region bricks were used instead of stone, and tar was used for mortar.) ⁴Then they said, "Come, let's build a great city for ourselves with a tower that reaches into the sky. This will make us famous and keep us from being scattered all over the world."

⁵But the LORD came down to look at the city and the tower the people were building. ⁶"Look!" he said. "The people are united, and they all speak the same language. After this, nothing they set out to do will be impossible for them! ⁷Come, let's go down and confuse the people with different languages. Then they won't be able to understand each other."

⁸In that way, the LORD scattered them all over the world, and they stopped building the city. ⁹That is why the city was called Babel,* because that is where the LORD confused the people with different languages. In this way he scattered them all over the world.

## The Line of Descent from Shem to Abram

¹⁰This is the account of Shem's family.

Two years after the great flood, when Shem was 100 years old, he became the father of* Arphaxad. ¹¹After the birth of* Arphaxad, Shem lived another 500 years and had other sons and daughters.
¹²When Arphaxad was 35 years old, he became the father of Shelah. ¹³After the birth of Shelah, Arphaxad lived another 403 years and had other sons and daughters.*

---

10:11 Or *From that land Assyria went out.* 10:14 Hebrew *Casluhites, from whom the Philistines came, and Caphtorites.* Compare Jer 47:4; Amos 9:7. 10:15 Hebrew *ancestor of Heth.* 10:21 Or *Shem, whose older brother was Japheth.* 10:24 Greek version reads *Arphaxad was the father of Cainan, Cainan was the father of Shelah.* Compare Luke 3:36. 11:2 Hebrew *Shinar.* 11:9 Or *Babylon. Babel* sounds like a Hebrew term that means "confusion." 11:10 Or *the ancestor of;* also in 11:12, 14, 16, 18, 20, 22, 24. 11:11 Or *the birth of this ancestor of;* also in 11:13, 15, 17, 19, 21, 23, 25. 11:12-13 Greek version reads *¹²When Arphaxad was 135 years old, he became the father of Cainan. ¹³After the birth of Cainan, Arphaxad lived another 430 years and had other sons and daughters, and then he died. When Cainan was 130 years old, he became the father of Shelah. After the birth of Shelah, Cainan lived another 330 years and had other sons and daughters, and then he died.* Compare Luke 3:35-36.

---

**11:1-9** After the Flood, human civilization spread far and wide in fulfillment of God's purposes (9:1). Babel represented a vain attempt to avoid scattering. The tower was likely a ziggurat, a massive stepped tower built to support a staircase near a temple garden, likely intended to facilitate the descent of the gods to earth. Without divine instruction to build, the project represented a human attempt to dictate the terms of acceptable worship. The people's desire for fame and security apart from God prompted the Lord's response to confuse their building efforts.

¹⁴When Shelah was 30 years old, he became the father of Eber. ¹⁵After the birth of Eber, Shelah lived another 403 years and had other sons and daughters.

¹⁶When Eber was 34 years old, he became the father of Peleg. ¹⁷After the birth of Peleg, Eber lived another 430 years and had other sons and daughters.

¹⁸When Peleg was 30 years old, he became the father of Reu. ¹⁹After the birth of Reu, Peleg lived another 209 years and had other sons and daughters.

²⁰When Reu was 32 years old, he became the father of Serug. ²¹After the birth of Serug, Reu lived another 207 years and had other sons and daughters.

²²When Serug was 30 years old, he became the father of Nahor. ²³After the birth of Nahor, Serug lived another 200 years and had other sons and daughters.

²⁴When Nahor was 29 years old, he became the father of Terah. ²⁵After the birth of Terah, Nahor lived another 119 years and had other sons and daughters.

## Shalom

**IMAGE** — MY STORY OF MY UNIQUE INFLUENCE

# God's Call and Mine

**SCRIPTURE CONNECTION: GENESIS 12:2-3**

"What is my purpose?" I pleaded, scrambling down New Mexico's tallest mountain. A lightning storm above me, with no trees to protect me, I hurtled down the boulder field. For months, I'd asked God for my calling. Now, intensified by visions of a life cut short, I yelled it. Maybe you cry out for purpose too. As with Abram, God's calling comes:

- before we bless—Abram didn't earn God's blessing;
- to bless others—God empowered Abram to do good;
- to bless near and far—Abram gave life to family, nation, and ultimately, God's redemption plan.

Abram's calling fit within God's mission to reconcile his creation to himself, a mission God actively pursues throughout the Bible. God's purpose begins with God himself, not us; is empowered by him, not us; and comes through those he chooses, not by our choice alone.

> Knowing my calling comes from God, not me, gives me confidence to press on.

As with Abram, God made his call clear for me, too. As I scuttled down, avoiding the lightning strikes, I sensed it. It came as though a whisper from God, "*I am your purpose.*"

"Ow," I yelped, as I caught a tree and hugged it, glad even for its rough bark that stopped my descent. Like the tree, this answer protected me from exposure to any lesser calling. My calling begins with, is empowered by, and is guided by God; no other source will do.

## IMAGINE

How might seeing God as your chief purpose guide you?

*"In seminary, I learned to see the entire Bible reflecting God's mission to restore. Knowing my calling comes from God, not me, gives me confidence to live on purpose for a lifetime."*

**NAOMI CRAMER OVERTON, MBA, DIS,** lives to realize beauty-filled visions that lift us to flourishing, with our families and beyond. Naomi has been CEO for Stonecroft and MOPS, director with Compassion International and World Vision, and General Editor for this Bible.

²⁶After Terah was 70 years old, he became the father of Abram, Nahor, and Haran.

## The Family of Terah

²⁷This is the account of Terah's family. Terah was the father of Abram, Nahor, and Haran; and Haran was the father of Lot. ²⁸But Haran died in Ur of the Chaldeans, the land of his birth, while his father, Terah, was still living. ²⁹Meanwhile, Abram and Nahor both married. The name of Abram's wife was Sarai, and the name of Nahor's wife was Milcah. (Milcah and her sister Iscah were daughters of Nahor's brother Haran.) ³⁰But Sarai was unable to become pregnant and had no children.

³¹One day Terah took his son Abram, his daughter-in-law Sarai (his son Abram's wife), and his grandson Lot (his son Haran's child) and moved away from Ur of the Chaldeans. He was headed for the land of Canaan, but they stopped at Haran and settled there. ³²Terah lived for 205 years* and died while still in Haran.

## The Call of Abram

**12** The LORD had said to Abram, "Leave your native country, your relatives, and your father's family, and go to the land that I will show you. ²I will make you into a great nation. I will bless you and make you famous, and you will be a blessing to others. ³I will bless those who bless you and curse those who treat you with contempt. All the families on earth will be blessed through you."

⁴So Abram departed as the LORD had instructed, and Lot went with him. Abram was seventy-five years old when he left Haran. ⁵He took his wife, Sarai, his nephew Lot, and all his wealth—his livestock and all the people he had taken into his household at Haran—and headed for the land of Canaan. When they arrived in Canaan, ⁶Abram traveled through the land as far as Shechem. There he set up camp beside the oak of Moreh. At that time, the area was inhabited by Canaanites.

⁷Then the LORD appeared to Abram and said, "I will give this land to your descendants.*" And Abram built an altar there and dedicated it to the LORD, who

had appeared to him. ⁸After that, Abram traveled south and set up camp in the hill country, with Bethel to the west and Ai to the east. There he built another altar and dedicated it to the LORD, and he worshiped the LORD. ⁹Then Abram continued traveling south by stages toward the Negev.

## Abram and Sarai in Egypt

¹⁰At that time a severe famine struck the land of Canaan, forcing Abram to go down to Egypt, where he lived as a foreigner. ¹¹As he was approaching the border of Egypt, Abram said to his wife, Sarai, "Look, you are a very beautiful woman. ¹²When the Egyptians see you, they will say, 'This is his wife. Let's kill him; then we can have her!' ¹³So please tell them you are my sister. Then they will spare my life and treat me well because of their interest in you."

¹⁴And sure enough, when Abram arrived in Egypt, everyone noticed Sarai's beauty. ¹⁵When the palace officials saw her, they sang her praises to Pharaoh, their king, and Sarai was taken into his palace. ¹⁶Then Pharaoh gave Abram many gifts because of her—sheep, goats, cattle, male and female donkeys, male and female servants, and camels.

¹⁷But the LORD sent terrible plagues upon Pharaoh and his household because of Sarai, Abram's wife. ¹⁸So Pharaoh summoned Abram and accused him sharply. "What have you done to me?" he demanded. "Why didn't you tell me she was your wife? ¹⁹Why did you say, 'She is my sister,' and allow me to take her as my wife? Now then, here is your wife. Take her and get out of here!" ²⁰Pharaoh ordered some of his men to escort them, and he sent Abram out of the country, along with his wife and all his possessions.

## Abram and Lot Separate

**13** So Abram left Egypt and traveled north into the Negev, along with his wife and Lot and all that they owned. ²(Abram was very rich in livestock, silver, and gold.) ³From the Negev, they continued traveling by stages toward Bethel, and they pitched their tents between Bethel and Ai, where they had camped before. ⁴This was the same place where

---

**11:32** Some ancient versions read *145 years;* compare 11:26 and 12:4. **12:7** Hebrew *seed.*

---

**11:30** Sarai, Rebekah, and Rachel all experienced infertility (25:21; 29:31). Sarai's infertility introduced a paradox between her experience and God's promise of many descendants (12:2). Frequently in the Old Testament, God demonstrated his sovereignty by miraculously giving children to women who had previously been unable to have children (Judges 13:3; 1 Samuel 1:2; 2:5; see also Psalm 113:9; Isaiah 54:1).

**12:1-3** Before Abram could experience God's blessing, he had to step out in obedience by setting out on a journey of unknown length and destination. The exclusivity of God's covenant with Abram may seem troubling at first, but God blessed his family so that they could bless all the other families on earth. Abram's blessing was God's solution for

the brokenness and violence of the post-Flood world (see Psalm 67).

**12:10-20** Abram deceived Pharaoh regarding his wife's identity rather than trusting God's protection, putting both her and Pharaoh's household at risk (see 20:1-18; 26:1-11). Sarai was in fact his half sister (20:12), but Abram's deception resulted in their expulsion from Egypt.

**13:1-18** God had asked Abram to leave his father's family (12:1), but he took his nephew Lot with him. Lot's company became problematic when the two households grew so large that the land could not support them both. Abram gave Lot first choice of land because he believed in God's promise. After they parted ways, God reaffirmed his plan to bless Abram (13:14-17).

# Insight

## SARAI AND ABRAM'S TRAVELS

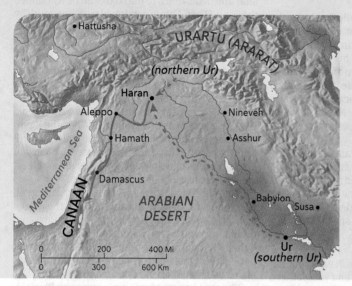

Hattusha

URARTU (ARARAT)

(northern Ur)

Haran

Aleppo

Nineveh

Hamath

Asshur

Mediterranean Sea

CANAAN

Damascus

ARABIAN
DESERT

Babylon
Susa

Ur
(southern Ur)

0     200     400 Mi
0     300     600 Km

Abram, Sarai, their extended family, and their servants walked from Ur to Haran (600 miles), on to Canaan (400 miles), then down to Egypt (325 miles), and back to Canaan again. How many steps do you walk a day? Women worldwide walk 5,000 steps daily. If Sarai had done that, it would have taken her 660 days to complete this route.

5,000
steps
per day

660
days

---

Abram had built the altar, and there he worshiped the LORD again.

⁵Lot, who was traveling with Abram, had also become very wealthy with flocks of sheep and goats, herds of cattle, and many tents. ⁶But the land could not support both Abram and Lot with all their flocks and herds living so close together. ⁷So disputes broke out between the herdsmen of Abram and Lot. (At that time Canaanites and Perizzites were also living in the land.)

⁸Finally Abram said to Lot, "Let's not allow this conflict to come between us or our herdsmen. After all, we are close relatives! ⁹The whole countryside is open to you. Take your choice of any section of the land you want, and we will separate. If you want the land to the left, then I'll take the land on the right. If you prefer the land on the right, then I'll go to the left."

¹⁰Lot took a long look at the fertile plains of the Jordan Valley in the direction of Zoar. The whole area was well watered everywhere, like the garden of the LORD or the beautiful land of Egypt. (This was before the LORD destroyed Sodom and Gomorrah.) ¹¹Lot chose for himself the whole Jordan Valley to the east of them. He went there with his flocks and servants and parted company with his uncle Abram. ¹²So Abram settled in the land of Canaan, and Lot moved his tents to a place near Sodom and settled among the cities of the plain. ¹³But the people of this area were extremely wicked and constantly sinned against the LORD.

¹⁴After Lot had gone, the LORD said to Abram, "Look as far as you can see in every direction—north and south, east and west. ¹⁵I am giving all this land, as far as you can see, to you and your descendants* as a permanent possession. ¹⁶And I will give you so many descendants that, like the dust of the earth, they cannot be counted! ¹⁷Go and walk through the land in every direction, for I am giving it to you."

¹⁸So Abram moved his camp to Hebron and settled near the oak grove belonging to Mamre. There he built another altar to the LORD.

## Abram Rescues Lot

**14** About this time war broke out in the region. King Amraphel of Babylonia,* King Arioch of Ellasar, King Kedorlaomer of Elam, and King Tidal of Goiim ²fought against King Bera of Sodom, King Birsha of Gomorrah, King Shinab of Admah, King Shemeber of Zeboiim, and the king of Bela (also called Zoar).

³This second group of kings joined forces in Siddim Valley (that is, the valley of the Dead Sea*). ⁴For twelve years they had been subject to King Kedorlaomer, but in the thirteenth year they rebelled against him.

⁵One year later Kedorlaomer and his allies arrived and defeated the Rephaites at Ashteroth-karnaim, the Zuzites at Ham, the Emites at Shaveh-kiriathaim, ⁶and the Horites at Mount Seir, as far as El-paran at the edge of the wilderness. ⁷Then they turned back and came to En-mishpat (now called Kadesh) and conquered all the territory of the Amalekites, and also the Amorites living in Hazazon-tamar.

⁸Then the rebel kings of Sodom, Gomorrah, Admah, Zeboiim, and Bela (also called Zoar) prepared for battle in the valley of the Dead Sea.* ⁹They fought

---

**13:15** Hebrew *seed;* also in 13:16. **14:1** Hebrew *Shinar;* also in 14:9. **14:3** Hebrew *Salt Sea.* **14:8** Hebrew *Siddim Valley* (see 14:3); also in 14:10.

against King Kedorlaomer of Elam, King Tidal of Goiim, King Amraphel of Babylonia, and King Arioch of Ellasar—four kings against five. [10]As it happened, the valley of the Dead Sea was filled with tar pits. And as the army of the kings of Sodom and Gomorrah fled, some fell into the tar pits, while the rest escaped into the mountains. [11]The victorious invaders then plundered Sodom and Gomorrah and headed for home, taking with them all the spoils of war and the food supplies. [12]They also captured Lot—Abram's nephew who lived in Sodom—and carried off everything he owned.

[13]But one of Lot's men escaped and reported everything to Abram the Hebrew, who was living near the oak grove belonging to Mamre the Amorite. Mamre and his relatives, Eshcol and Aner, were Abram's allies.

[14]When Abram heard that his nephew Lot had been captured, he mobilized the 318 trained men who had been born into his household. Then he pursued Kedorlaomer's army until he caught up with them at Dan. [15]There he divided his men and attacked during the night. Kedorlaomer's army fled, but Abram chased them as far as Hobah, north of Damascus. [16]Abram recovered all the goods that had been taken, and he brought back his nephew Lot with his possessions and all the women and other captives.

## Melchizedek Blesses Abram

[17]After Abram returned from his victory over Kedorlaomer and all his allies, the king of Sodom went out to meet him in the valley of Shaveh (that is, the King's Valley).
[18]And Melchizedek, the king of Salem and a priest of God Most High,* brought Abram some bread and wine. [19]Melchizedek blessed Abram with this blessing:

> "Blessed be Abram by God Most High,
>     Creator of heaven and earth.
> [20]  And blessed be God Most High,
>     who has defeated your enemies for you."

Then Abram gave Melchizedek a tenth of all the goods he had recovered.
[21]The king of Sodom said to Abram, "Give back my

14:18 Hebrew *El-Elyon;* also in 14:19, 20, 22.

14:11-16  Lot's unfortunate choice to live near Sodom resulted in trouble for himself and for Abram. Lot had chosen land that looked fruitful, but the violent and corrupt residents would ruin him (19:1-38).
14:18-20  The story of Melchizedek portrays the initial fulfillment of 12:1-3, where God declared that nations who blessed Abram would be blessed. Abram shared with Melchizedek the spoils of his victory. Melchizedek was a non-Israelite priest who feared God, pointing to the future expansion of the Kingdom of God among non-Israelites. The author of Hebrews saw justification for Christ's priesthood here. Like Melchizedek, Jesus was not from Israel's priestly line (see Hebrews 7).

# Perspective

## God's ideal or our real?

SCRIPTURE CONNECTION: GENESIS 14:11-16

Is ancient Hebrew culture an ideal to emulate? Or is it incidental to the message?

In some cases, God gives instructions about how to live based on universal truths. For example, every human being is made in the image of God, so every human life is precious and worth protecting (9:6). But other times the Bible describes practices that do not easily transfer to our context today.

Abraham and Sarah lived as semi-nomadic tent dwellers who kept herds of animals. And in that day, the men would often fight battles and take women as plunder. But God is not asking us to move into tents, keep sheep, and carry swords. Does that mean these stories have nothing to teach us?

Ancient Hebrew culture does not provide a template for us to replicate. We are not called to re-create culture-specific elements in our own lives, and many times the characters are not models for emulation. But we can still learn a great deal about God through these stories, including the ways he shows himself to be faithful, even to flawed people—just like us.

### VIEWPOINTS

HERS: *Sarah might shudder to think women would read her stories and think of her as a role model. She had her fair share of failures and likely felt she was often just muddling through.*
MINE: *"Seeing how God communicated to ancient cultures inspires me. God works in and through flawed people in less-than-ideal societies. That means he can work through me, too, even though I have a long way to go!"*
YOURS: *Can you think of aspects of our culture that are less than ideal? And can you see ways that God works in and through us anyway?*

CARMEN JOY IMES, PhD, is an author, speaker, blogger, YouTuber, and serves as associate professor of Old Testament at Biola University in California.

people who were captured. But you may keep for yourself all the goods you have recovered."

²²Abram replied to the king of Sodom, "I solemnly swear to the LORD, God Most High, Creator of heaven and earth, ²³that I will not take so much as a single thread or sandal thong from what belongs to you. Otherwise you might say, 'I am the one who made Abram rich.' ²⁴I will accept only what my young warriors have already eaten, and I request that you give a fair share of the goods to my allies—Aner, Eshcol, and Mamre."

## The LORD's Covenant Promise to Abram

**15** Some time later, the LORD spoke to Abram in a vision and said to him, "Do not be afraid, Abram, for I will protect you, and your reward will be great."

²But Abram replied, "O Sovereign LORD, what good are all your blessings when I don't even have a son? Since you've given me no children, Eliezer of Damascus, a servant in my household, will inherit all my wealth. ³You have given me no descendants of my own, so one of my servants will be my heir."

⁴Then the LORD said to him, "No, your servant will not be your heir, for you will have a son of your own who will be your heir." ⁵Then the LORD took Abram outside and said to him, "Look up into the sky and count the stars if you can. That's how many descendants you will have!"

⁶And Abram believed the LORD, and the LORD counted him as righteous because of his faith.

⁷Then the LORD told him, "I am the LORD who brought you out of Ur of the Chaldeans to give you this land as your possession."

⁸But Abram replied, "O Sovereign LORD, how can I be sure that I will actually possess it?"

⁹The LORD told him, "Bring me a three-year-old heifer, a three-year-old female goat, a three-year-old ram, a turtledove, and a young pigeon." ¹⁰So Abram presented all these to him and killed them. Then he cut each animal down the middle and laid the halves side by side; he did not, however, cut the birds in half. ¹¹Some vultures swooped down to eat the carcasses, but Abram chased them away.

¹²As the sun was going down, Abram fell into a deep sleep, and a terrifying darkness came down over him. ¹³Then the LORD said to Abram, "You can be sure that your descendants will be strangers in a foreign land, where they will be oppressed as slaves for 400 years. ¹⁴But I will punish the nation that enslaves them, and in the end they will come away with great wealth. ¹⁵(As for you, you will die in peace and be buried at a ripe old age.) ¹⁶After four generations your descendants will return here to this land, for the sins of the Amorites do not yet warrant their destruction."

¹⁷After the sun went down and darkness fell, Abram saw a smoking firepot and a flaming torch pass between the halves of the carcasses. ¹⁸So the LORD made a covenant with Abram that day and said, "I have given this land to your descendants, all the way from the border of Egypt* to the great Euphrates River—¹⁹the land now occupied by the Kenites, Kenizzites, Kadmonites, ²⁰Hittites, Perizzites, Rephaites, ²¹Amorites, Canaanites, Girgashites, and Jebusites."

## The Birth of Ishmael

**16** Now Sarai, Abram's wife, had not been able to bear children for him. But she had an Egyptian servant named Hagar. ²So Sarai said to Abram, "The LORD has prevented me from having children. Go and sleep with my servant. Perhaps I can have children through her." And Abram agreed with Sarai's proposal. ³So Sarai, Abram's wife, took Hagar the Egyptian servant and gave her to Abram as a wife. (This happened ten years after Abram had settled in the land of Canaan.)

⁴So Abram had sexual relations with Hagar, and she became pregnant. But when Hagar knew she was pregnant, she began to treat her mistress, Sarai, with contempt. ⁵Then Sarai said to Abram, "This is all your fault! I put my servant into your arms, but now that she's pregnant she treats me with contempt. The LORD will show who's wrong—you or me!"

⁶Abram replied, "Look, she is your servant, so deal with her as you see fit." Then Sarai treated Hagar so harshly that she finally ran away.

**15:18** Hebrew *the river of Egypt,* referring either to an eastern branch of the Nile River or to the Brook of Egypt in the Sinai (see Num 34:5).

**15:1-6** Abram and Sarai's infertility was a source of consternation because it cast doubt on God's promise of many descendants. Abram freely expressed his doubts to God, and God reaffirmed the promise.

**15:7-21** With a solemn ceremony, God made a binding covenant with Abram that guaranteed the fulfillment of his promises. Normally, in such a ceremony both parties would walk between the cut animals to symbolize the severity of the oath, staking their lives on their mutual commitment. However, Abram merely observed as a torch and firepot passed through the pieces, indicating God's unilateral commitment. The flame and smoke may have anticipated the pillars of

fire and cloud that would lead Israel out of Egypt (Exodus 13:21-22).

**16:1-3** Infertility is always painful, but in the case of Abram and Sarai, the lack of a child presented a theological crisis as God had promised Abram a son (15:1-6). Sarai resorted to the customary Mesopotamian strategy for dealing with childlessness by offering her servant to her husband as a surrogate. The child would be Abram's official heir.

**16:4-6** After Hagar conceived, tension arose with Sarai. Hagar's air of superiority provoked mistreatment from Sarai. Ironically, Sarai's mistreatment of her Egyptian servant anticipated the Egyptians' mistreatment of Sarai's descendants (Exodus 1:11-12).

# Hagar

## Honored by Names

"What's in a name? That which we call a rose by any other name would smell as sweet." Shakespeare penned these words spoken by Juliet, pondering the significance of names. For Hagar, being called by name and being allowed to name bring her honor.

Sarai was unable to get pregnant, despite God's promise, so she took matters into her own hands and arranged for Hagar, an enslaved Egyptian woman, to sleep with Abram. Hagar conceived, and her relationship with Sarai turned awful. Hagar was treated so harshly by Sarai that she decided to run away.

God went looking for Hagar and called her by name (16:8). Throughout the story, Abram and Sarai had never called Hagar by her name. But God knew her and her situation intimately. And they had a one-on-one conversation. Hagar, a Gentile who was considered property, enjoyed a powerful and tender exchange with the God of the universe.

When they had finished, Hagar gave God a name (16:13). She is the only one in Scripture to have this honor. She called him El-roi, which translates to "the God who sees me."

Hagar was seen and known by God and was allowed to know God right back. Through Hagar's story, God showed he values and honors women, even when others might not.

> When I feel invisible, I find hope in El-roi, the God who sees me and knows my name.

HAGAR'S STORY IS TOLD IN GENESIS 16; 21; SHE IS ALSO MENTIONED IN GALATIANS 4:21-31.

## IDENTIFY

Have you ever felt overlooked or invisible?

What was that like?

Have you experienced God looking and calling for you?

What happened and how did you respond?

*"When I feel invisible or overlooked, I find hope in El-roi, the God who sees me and knows my name and circumstances. He is near to you and me as we look to him."*

**VIVIAN MABUNI** is a national speaker, author of *Open Hands, Willing Heart*, and podcast host of *Someday Is Here* for AAPI Christians, with over thirty years of ministry experience.

# Perspective

## Are concubines God's plan?

SCRIPTURE CONNECTION: GENESIS 16:1-10

Today, when we read about concubines, feelings of confusion or even disgust might tempt us to skip over these Scriptures. But each story of a marginalized woman in the Bible is another reminder that things are not the way they are supposed to be. No woman should be owned by someone else.

In ancient culture, concubines helped landowners build their households by increasing their offspring. The Old Testament doesn't explicitly condemn polygamy, but it repeatedly demonstrates its perils.

While some societies and individuals value women only as property, God elevates women to image-bearing status, marked by his love and reflecting his glory. Amid a worldly system that oppresses, God is at work to redeem, and his people can be a part of that redemption work.

### VIEWPOINTS

HERS: *How do we see God care for Hagar, who was marginalized in this way?*
MINE: *"How can I trust that God sees me in circumstances where I am not valued?"*
YOURS: *When you feel unseen or devalued, how can you trust God to redeem those parts of your life?*

KAT ARMSTRONG, MA, is a Bible teacher, preacher, coach, and ministry leader. She cofounded the Polished Network and authored *No More Holding Back*, *The In-Between Place*, and the Storyline Bible Studies series.

⁷The angel of the LORD found Hagar beside a spring of water in the wilderness, along the road to Shur. ⁸The angel said to her, "Hagar, Sarai's servant, where have you come from, and where are you going?"

"I'm running away from my mistress, Sarai," she replied.

⁹The angel of the LORD said to her, "Return to your mistress, and submit to her authority." ¹⁰Then he added, "I will give you more descendants than you can count."

¹¹And the angel also said, "You are now pregnant and will give birth to a son. You are to name him Ishmael (which means 'God hears'), for the LORD has heard your cry of distress. ¹²This son of yours will be a wild man, as untamed as a wild donkey! He will raise his fist against everyone, and everyone will be against him. Yes, he will live in open hostility against all his relatives."

¹³Thereafter, Hagar used another name to refer to the LORD, who had spoken to her. She said, "You are the God who sees me."* She also said, "Have I truly seen the One who sees me?" ¹⁴So that well was named Beer-lahai-roi (which means "well of the Living One who sees me"). It can still be found between Kadesh and Bered.

¹⁵So Hagar gave Abram a son, and Abram named him Ishmael. ¹⁶Abram was eighty-six years old when Ishmael was born.

## Abram Is Named Abraham

**17** When Abram was ninety-nine years old, the LORD appeared to him and said, "I am El-Shaddai—'God Almighty.' Serve me faithfully and live a blameless life. ²I will make a covenant with you, by which I will guarantee to give you countless descendants."

³At this, Abram fell face down on the ground. Then God said to him, ⁴"This is my covenant with you: I will make you the father of a multitude of nations! ⁵What's more, I am changing your name. It will no longer be Abram. Instead, you will be called Abraham,* for you will be the father of many nations. ⁶I will make you extremely fruitful. Your descendants will become many nations, and kings will be among them!

⁷"I will confirm my covenant with you and your descendants* after you, from generation to generation. This is the everlasting covenant: I will always be your God and the God of your descendants after you. ⁸And I will give the entire land of Canaan, where you now live as a foreigner, to you and your descendants. It will be their possession forever, and I will be their God."

---

16:13 Hebrew *El-roi.*   17:5 *Abram* means "exalted father"; *Abraham* sounds like a Hebrew term that means "father of many." 17:7 Hebrew *seed;* also in 17:7b, 8, 9, 10, 19.

---

**16:7-12** Hagar's distress did not go unnoticed. Even though her son would not be heir of God's covenant promises to Abram, God gave Ishmael promises of his own. God's instruction for Hagar to return to Sarai was not a universal call for submission to abuse. Later, God would allow Hagar to leave (21:8-21).
**16:13** Hagar was the first person in the Bible to give God a name: "the God who sees me." Although she lacked power, wealth, and status in her household, she was not invisible to God. And although her son was not the heir of God's covenant promise, she was not outside God's care. God's promise to bless all nations through Abram's family would include the nations that descended from Ishmael.

## The Mark of the Covenant

⁹Then God said to Abraham, "Your responsibility is to obey the terms of the covenant. You and all your descendants have this continual responsibility. ¹⁰This is the covenant that you and your descendants must keep: Each male among you must be circumcised. ¹¹You must cut off the flesh of your foreskin as a sign of the covenant between me and you. ¹²From generation to generation, every male child must be circumcised on the eighth day after his birth. This applies not only to members of your family but also to the servants born in your household and the foreign-born servants whom you have purchased. ¹³All must be circumcised. Your bodies will bear the mark of my everlasting covenant. ¹⁴Any male who fails to be circumcised will be cut off from the covenant family for breaking the covenant."

## Sarai Is Named Sarah

¹⁵Then God said to Abraham, "Regarding Sarai, your wife—her name will no longer be Sarai. From now on her name will be Sarah.* ¹⁶And I will bless her and give you a son from her! Yes, I will bless her richly, and she will become the mother of many nations. Kings of nations will be among her descendants."

¹⁷Then Abraham bowed down to the ground, but he laughed to himself in disbelief. "How could I become a father at the age of 100?" he thought. "And how can Sarah have a baby when she is ninety years old?" ¹⁸So Abraham said to God, "May Ishmael live under your special blessing!"

¹⁹But God replied, "No—Sarah, your wife, will give birth to a son for you. You will name him Isaac,* and I will confirm my covenant with him and his descendants as an everlasting covenant. ²⁰As for Ishmael, I will bless him also, just as you have asked. I will make him extremely fruitful and multiply his descendants. He will become the father of twelve princes, and I will make him a great nation. ²¹But my covenant will be confirmed with Isaac, who will be born to you and Sarah about this time next year." ²²When God had finished speaking, he left Abraham.

²³On that very day Abraham took his son, Ishmael, and every male in his household, including those born there and those he had bought. Then he circumcised them, cutting off their foreskins, just as God had told him. ²⁴Abraham was ninety-nine years old when he was circumcised, ²⁵and Ishmael, his son, was thirteen. ²⁶Both Abraham and his son, Ishmael, were circumcised on that same day, ²⁷along with all the other men and boys of the household, whether they were born there or bought as servants. All were circumcised with him.

## A Son Is Promised to Sarah

**18** The LORD appeared again to Abraham near the oak grove belonging to Mamre. One day Abraham was sitting at the entrance to his tent during the hottest part of the day. ²He looked up and noticed three men standing nearby. When he saw them, he ran to meet them and welcomed them, bowing low to the ground.

³"My lord," he said, "if it pleases you, stop here for a while. ⁴Rest in the shade of this tree while water is brought to wash your feet. ⁵And since you've honored your servant with this visit, let me prepare some food to refresh you before you continue on your journey."

"All right," they said. "Do as you have said."

⁶So Abraham ran back to the tent and said to Sarah, "Hurry! Get three large measures* of your best flour, knead it into dough, and bake some bread." ⁷Then Abraham ran out to the herd and chose a tender calf and gave it to his servant, who quickly prepared it. ⁸When the food was ready, Abraham took some yogurt and milk and the roasted meat, and he served it to the men. As they ate, Abraham waited on them in the shade of the trees.

⁹"Where is Sarah, your wife?" the visitors asked.

"She's inside the tent," Abraham replied.

¹⁰Then one of them said, "I will return to you about

---

**17:15** *Sarai* and *Sarah* both mean "princess"; the change in spelling may reflect the difference in dialect between Ur and Canaan.
**17:19** *Isaac* means "he laughs."   **18:6** Hebrew *3 seahs,* about half a bushel or 22 liters.

---

**17:10-14** Male circumcision was the sign of membership in the covenant community. However, women were equally part of the covenant. They were the daughters, wives, and mothers of circumcised men and participated under their membership. The prohibition of intermarriage with uncircumcised peoples was not motivated by prejudice but was a means of protecting covenant continuity in Abraham's family. Foreigners who lived among the Israelites were also circumcised to show that they shared in the covenant.

**17:15-16** God renamed Abram (Abraham) and Sarai (Sarah) to underscore his determination to bless their descendants, despite their unbelief and their highly dysfunctional family (see 16:1-16). Sarai and Sarah both mean "princess"; the change in spelling may reflect the difference in dialect between Ur and Canaan. The new name, fitting for one who would be the mother of kings, was a milestone in Sarah's

calling and would serve as a constant reminder to her of God's promise.

**18:5-8** Hospitality was a cardinal virtue in ancient culture. In an age before restaurants and grocery stores, travelers depended heavily upon the hospitality of people along their route. As the manager of a large household, Abraham coordinated the preparation of bread, meat, yogurt, and milk, and personally served his distinguished guests.

**18:9-15** God had already promised that Sarah would bear a son (see 17:15-19). In that account, the narrator referred to God using his divine title, the Hebrew word *Elohim* ("God" in English translations). Here, Abraham experienced a physical visitation from a speaker who identified God by his covenant name, Yahweh ("LORD" in our English translations). Sarah's response to the promise mattered. Her incredulity prompted a poignant question: "Is anything too hard for the LORD?" (18:14).

this time next year, and your wife, Sarah, will have a son!"

Sarah was listening to this conversation from the tent. ¹¹Abraham and Sarah were both very old by this time, and Sarah was long past the age of having children. ¹²So she laughed silently to herself and said, "How could a worn-out woman like me enjoy such pleasure, especially when my master—my husband—is also so old?"

¹³Then the LORD said to Abraham, "Why did Sarah laugh? Why did she say, 'Can an old woman like me have a baby?' ¹⁴Is anything too hard for the LORD? I will return about this time next year, and Sarah will have a son."

¹⁵Sarah was afraid, so she denied it, saying, "I didn't laugh."

But the LORD said, "No, you did laugh."

## Abraham Intercedes for Sodom

¹⁶Then the men got up from their meal and looked out toward Sodom. As they left, Abraham went with them to send them on their way.

¹⁷"Should I hide my plan from Abraham?" the LORD asked. ¹⁸"For Abraham will certainly become a great and mighty nation, and all the nations of the earth will be blessed through him. ¹⁹I have singled him out so that he will direct his sons and their families to keep the way of the LORD by doing what is right and just. Then I will do for Abraham all that I have promised."

²⁰So the LORD told Abraham, "I have heard a great outcry from Sodom and Gomorrah, because their sin is so flagrant. ²¹I am going down to see if their actions are as wicked as I have heard. If not, I want to know."

²²The other men turned and headed toward Sodom, but the LORD remained with Abraham. ²³Abraham approached him and said, "Will you sweep away both the righteous and the wicked? ²⁴Suppose you find fifty righteous people living there in the city—will you still sweep it away and not spare it for their sakes? ²⁵Surely you wouldn't do such a thing, destroying the righteous along with the wicked. Why, you would be treating the righteous and the wicked exactly the same! Surely you wouldn't do that! Should not the Judge of all the earth do what is right?"

²⁶And the LORD replied, "If I find fifty righteous people in Sodom, I will spare the entire city for their sake."

²⁷Then Abraham spoke again. "Since I have begun, let me speak further to my Lord, even though I am but dust and ashes. ²⁸Suppose there are only forty-five righteous people rather than fifty? Will you destroy the whole city for lack of five?"

And the LORD said, "I will not destroy it if I find forty-five righteous people there."

²⁹Then Abraham pressed his request further. "Suppose there are only forty?"

And the LORD replied, "I will not destroy it for the sake of the forty."

³⁰"Please don't be angry, my Lord," Abraham pleaded. "Let me speak—suppose only thirty righteous people are found?"

And the LORD replied, "I will not destroy it if I find thirty."

³¹Then Abraham said, "Since I have dared to speak to the Lord, let me continue—suppose there are only twenty?"

And the LORD replied, "Then I will not destroy it for the sake of the twenty."

³²Finally, Abraham said, "Lord, please don't be angry with me if I speak one more time. Suppose only ten are found there?"

And the LORD replied, "Then I will not destroy it for the sake of the ten."

³³When the LORD had finished his conversation with Abraham, he went on his way, and Abraham returned to his tent.

## Sodom and Gomorrah Destroyed

**19** That evening the two angels came to the entrance of the city of Sodom. Lot was sitting there, and when he saw them, he stood up to meet them. Then he welcomed them and bowed with his face to the ground. ²"My lords," he said, "come to my home to wash your feet, and be my guests for the night. You may then get up early in the morning and be on your way again."

"Oh no," they replied. "We'll just spend the night out here in the city square."

³But Lot insisted, so at last they went home with him. Lot prepared a feast for them, complete with fresh bread made without yeast, and they ate. ⁴But before they retired for the night, all the men of Sodom, young and old, came from all over the city and surrounded the house. ⁵They shouted to Lot, "Where are the men who came to spend the night with you? Bring them out to us so we can have sex with them!"

⁶So Lot stepped outside to talk to them, shutting the door behind him. ⁷"Please, my brothers," he begged, "don't do such a wicked thing. ⁸Look, I have two virgin daughters. Let me bring them out to you, and you can do with them as you wish. But please, leave these men alone, for they are my guests and are under my protection."

---

**19:6-8** This story of Lot is deeply troubling. He offered his daughters to be raped, prioritizing the protection of his out-of-town guests. And his future sons-in-law were among those rioting outside (19:14)! Lot's willingness for his daughters to marry men who apparently were among the violent sex offenders, his disregard for his daughters' safety, and his hesitation to leave such a corrupt city (19:16) all demonstrate how depraved he had become. He may have been morally superior to his neighbors (2 Peter 2:7-8), but not by much. God's decision to destroy the city was thoroughly justified.

⁹"Stand back!" they shouted. "This fellow came to town as an outsider, and now he's acting like our judge! We'll treat you far worse than those other men!" And they lunged toward Lot to break down the door.

¹⁰But the two angels* reached out, pulled Lot into the house, and bolted the door. ¹¹Then they blinded all the men, young and old, who were at the door of the house, so they gave up trying to get inside.

¹²Meanwhile, the angels questioned Lot. "Do you have any other relatives here in the city?" they asked. "Get them out of this place—your sons-in-law, sons, daughters, or anyone else. ¹³For we are about to destroy this city completely. The outcry against this place is so great it has reached the LORD, and he has sent us to destroy it."

¹⁴So Lot rushed out to tell his daughters' fiancés, "Quick, get out of the city! The LORD is about to destroy it." But the young men thought he was only joking.

¹⁵At dawn the next morning the angels became insistent. "Hurry," they said to Lot. "Take your wife and your two daughters who are here. Get out right now, or you will be swept away in the destruction of the city!"

¹⁶When Lot still hesitated, the angels seized his hand and the hands of his wife and two daughters and rushed them to safety outside the city, for the LORD was merciful. ¹⁷When they were safely out of the city, one of the angels ordered, "Run for your lives! And don't look back or stop anywhere in the valley! Escape to the mountains, or you will be swept away!"

¹⁸"Oh no, my lord!" Lot begged. ¹⁹"You have been so gracious to me and saved my life, and you have shown such great kindness. But I cannot go to the mountains. Disaster would catch up to me there, and I would soon die. ²⁰See, there is a small village nearby. Please let me go there instead; don't you see how small it is? Then my life will be saved."

²¹"All right," the angel said, "I will grant your request. I will not destroy the little village. ²²But hurry! Escape to it, for I can do nothing until you arrive there." (This explains why that village was known as Zoar, which means "little place.")

²³Lot reached the village just as the sun was rising over the horizon. ²⁴Then the LORD rained down fire and burning sulfur from the sky on Sodom and Gomorrah. ²⁵He utterly destroyed them, along with the other cities and villages of the plain, wiping out all the people and every bit of vegetation. ²⁶But Lot's wife looked back as she was following behind him, and she turned into a pillar of salt.

19:10 Hebrew *men;* also in 19:12, 16.

19:26 Lot's wife did not simply glance over her shoulder. The verb translated "looked" here indicates prolonged, intense gazing—toward the world she loved (compare 15:5). Lot's wife was too attached to Sodom to accept God's mercy, so she was included in the judgment as she lingered in the valley.

# Perspective

## How could Lot do that?

SCRIPTURE CONNECTION: GENESIS 19:1-8

Some of us can instantly relate to how Lot's daughters surely felt about Lot's offer to the men of Sodom: disposable. We also have been compromised by people we trusted to love and protect us.

But God reaches for us in our peril. Lot, in his cowardice, is deemed by God as worthy to save. His daughters, reduced to sexual commodities, are deemed worthy to save. This makes us curious about God's love.

Jesus knows the feeling of being forsaken. And he showed that opposing realities can simultaneously be true: We can suffer intense rejection, deprivation, abandonment, devaluing, and crushing shame, while at the same time, we can celebrate a heavenly Father who loves us so unselfishly that he gave himself rather than giving us.

Lot offered to sacrifice his own daughters, perhaps to save himself. God sacrifices himself to save us.

## VIEWPOINTS

HERS: *Based on their experiences with their earthly father, what might Lot's daughters have believed about themselves and God?*

MINE: *"As a young girl under my dad's protection, I knew I was safe. Loved. Treasured. Absent his protection, my world took a different spin. A godly father carries for us daughters a representation of God and a message of our worth."*

YOURS: *What ideas have you formed about yourself or of God based on experiences with your earthly father? In what ways might you challenge your negative beliefs as you reflect on your heavenly Father?*

MISTY ARTERBURN is an author and speaker, contributing to Bible projects, devotionals, and recovery materials for over twenty years. Wife and mom to five, Misty is the founder of Recovery Girls and the general editor of *The One Year Bible for Women.*

²⁷Abraham got up early that morning and hurried out to the place where he had stood in the Lord's presence. ²⁸He looked out across the plain toward Sodom and Gomorrah and watched as columns of smoke rose from the cities like smoke from a furnace.

²⁹But God had listened to Abraham's request and kept Lot safe, removing him from the disaster that engulfed the cities on the plain.

## Lot and His Daughters

³⁰Afterward Lot left Zoar because he was afraid of the people there, and he went to live in a cave in the mountains with his two daughters. ³¹One day the older daughter said to her sister, "There are no men left anywhere in this entire area, so we can't get married like everyone else. And our father will soon be too old to have children. ³²Come, let's get him drunk with wine, and then we will have sex with him. That way we will preserve our family line through our father."

³³So that night they got him drunk with wine, and the older daughter went in and had intercourse with her father. He was unaware of her lying down or getting up again.

³⁴The next morning the older daughter said to her younger sister, "I had sex with our father last night. Let's get him drunk with wine again tonight, and you go in and have sex with him. That way we will preserve our family line through our father." ³⁵So that night they got him drunk with wine again, and the younger daughter went in and had intercourse with him. As before, he was unaware of her lying down or getting up again.

³⁶As a result, both of Lot's daughters became pregnant by their own father. ³⁷When the older daughter gave birth to a son, she named him Moab.* He became the ancestor of the nation now known as the Moabites. ³⁸When the younger daughter gave birth to a son, she named him Ben-ammi.* He became the ancestor of the nation now known as the Ammonites.

## Abraham Deceives Abimelech

**20** Abraham moved south to the Negev and lived for a while between Kadesh and Shur, and then he moved on to Gerar. While living there as a foreigner, ²Abraham introduced his wife, Sarah, by saying, "She is my sister." So King Abimelech of Gerar sent for Sarah and had her brought to him at his palace.

³But that night God came to Abimelech in a dream and told him, "You are a dead man, for that woman you have taken is already married!"

⁴But Abimelech had not slept with her yet, so he said, "Lord, will you destroy an innocent nation? ⁵Didn't Abraham tell me, 'She is my sister'? And she herself said, 'Yes, he is my brother.' I acted in complete innocence! My hands are clean."

⁶In the dream God responded, "Yes, I know you are innocent. That's why I kept you from sinning against me, and why I did not let you touch her. ⁷Now return the woman to her husband, and he will pray for you, for he is a prophet. Then you will live. But if you don't return her to him, you can be sure that you and all your people will die."

⁸Abimelech got up early the next morning and quickly called all his servants together. When he told them what had happened, his men were terrified. ⁹Then Abimelech called for Abraham. "What have you done to us?" he demanded. "What crime have I committed that deserves treatment like this, making me and my kingdom guilty of this great sin? No one should ever do what you have done! ¹⁰Whatever possessed you to do such a thing?"

¹¹Abraham replied, "I thought, 'This is a godless place. They will want my wife and will kill me to get her.' ¹²And she really is my sister, for we both have the same father, but different mothers. And I married her. ¹³When God called me to leave my father's home and to travel from place to place, I told her, 'Do me a favor. Wherever we go, tell the people that I am your brother.'"

¹⁴Then Abimelech took some of his sheep and goats, cattle, and male and female servants, and he presented them to Abraham. He also returned his wife, Sarah, to him. ¹⁵Then Abimelech said, "Look over my land and choose any place where you would like to live." ¹⁶And he said to Sarah, "Look, I am giving your 'brother' 1,000 pieces of silver* in the presence of all these witnesses. This is to compensate you for any wrong I may have done to you. This will settle any claim against me, and your reputation is cleared."

¹⁷Then Abraham prayed to God, and God healed Abimelech, his wife, and his female servants, so they

---

**19:37** *Moab* sounds like a Hebrew term that means "from father." **19:38** *Ben-ammi* means "son of my kinsman." **20:16** Hebrew *1,000 [shekels] of silver,* about 25 pounds or 11.4 kilograms in weight.

---

**19:30-35** Lot's daughters' plan to have sex with their drunk father showed that they, too, had been corrupted by Sodom's culture. They saw incest as the only way to carry on their family line. Ironically, their father had offered them to be raped (19:6-8), but they raped him instead. Their illicit unions produced the ancestors of the Moabites and Ammonites, perennial enemies of Israel (but see Deuteronomy 2:9, 19).
**20:2** Abraham maintained his practice of introducing Sarah as his sister (see 12:13; 20:13), jeopardizing God's promise that Sarah would bear Abraham a son. His reasoning—"This is a

godless place" (20:11)—was faulty. Abimelech responded immediately when God confronted him; his household was terrified of having offended a deity (20:3-10). Abimelech was angry that Abraham's deception had made him guilty of "this great sin" (20:9). Evidently, he knew taking another man's wife was wrong.
**20:17-18** The barrenness of Abimelech's household suggests that some time had passed. The fact that infertility has been divine punishment for sin does not mean that it usually is. However, the story clearly conveys that God alone controls fertility.

# Sarah

Lies and Laughter

I can imagine Sarah being furious.

As she drew a king's attention for being beautiful, Abraham lied, "She is my sister."

"I'm your what?"

Sarah was marched off into the king's harem, even brought to the king himself.

Who we are is sometimes chosen for us. Amid the swirl of family, culture, and appearances, we can become someone we are most definitely not. And one day, as we sip our coffee, we realize that what we're doing is slowly sucking the life out of us. We wonder, "How did I get here?" Maybe someone else's fear—but most likely our own—has wrapped us in a bad-dream-of-a-life.

While Abraham got it wrong in this passage, Sarah herself got identity wrong a lot. Would she believe God was the one who could make her a mom, even though she was too old? Or would she laugh? Would she maintain faith that she would be the mother of many generations, or would she offer her servant to have a baby in her place? Would she be a "princess" (the meaning of the name Sarah) who cared for her subjects, or would she use her authority to harm her servant Hagar?

God intervened for Sarah. He spoke to the king in a dream, and the king scrambled to return her to Abraham, who fessed up. Sarah was restored to who she really was.

God knows our true identity, not just what others say about us or the ways we pigeonhole ourselves. As with Sarah, our identity, linked to his love, gives life.

> God loves the real you, not who others say you are. Your identity, trued to his love, gives life.

SARAH'S STORY IS TOLD IN GENESIS 11–23; SHE IS ALSO MENTIONED IN ISAIAH 51:2; ROMANS 4:19; 9:9; GALATIANS 4:21-31; HEBREWS 11:11; 1 PETER 3:6.

## IDENTIFY

What words have you spoken, have others spoken, or has God spoken about who you are?

*"Like Sarah, I once found myself living by others' lies. Turns out God made me for something that fits a lot better."*

**CARA DAY** is a writer and illustrator. She has served with Stonecroft Ministries helping women live "extraordinary."

could have children. ¹⁸For the LORD had caused all the women to be infertile because of what happened with Abraham's wife, Sarah.

## The Birth of Isaac

**21** The LORD kept his word and did for Sarah exactly what he had promised. ²She became pregnant, and she gave birth to a son for Abraham in his old age. This happened at just the time God had said it would. ³And Abraham named their son Isaac. ⁴Eight days after Isaac was born, Abraham

circumcised him as God had commanded. ⁵Abraham was 100 years old when Isaac was born.

⁶And Sarah declared, "God has brought me laughter.* All who hear about this will laugh with me. ⁷Who would have said to Abraham that Sarah would nurse a baby? Yet I have given Abraham a son in his old age!"

## Hagar and Ishmael Are Sent Away

⁸When Isaac grew up and was about to be weaned, Abraham prepared a huge feast to celebrate the occasion. ⁹But Sarah saw Ishmael—the son of Abraham

21:6 The name *Isaac* means "he laughs."

---

**21:1-2** Twenty-five years after God first promised Abraham a son (12:1-4), and one year after the angels visited Abraham and Sarah (18:1-15), Sarah gave birth. The intervening years had been filled with difficulty, and the wait was hard, but God kept his promise.

**21:6** The name Isaac (*yitskhaq* in Hebrew) means "he laughs." Sarah's wordplay showed that the laughter of unbelief when the promise was given (18:12) had changed to the laughter of joy at its fulfillment. Sarah knew that everyone who had heard would laugh with her, rejoicing at the news. Hebrews 11:11 commends her faith in God's promise despite her struggle with unbelief.

---

## ⑧ Come Close　　FEARFUL: GOD IS STRONGER STILL

SCRIPTURE CONNECTION: GENESIS 20:1-18

My dad has a letter from his sister, dated 1974. My favorite part is that it's in fancy, almost whimsical cursive. But she was a no-nonsense gal. She graduated college at a time when many women didn't go to college. And she was going to make sure my dad got an education too.

In many parts of the world today, women are not offered a full education. Even in Western culture, we are still gaining ground in elevating women's voices. In the ancient world, Sarah's voice would have been mostly unheard, while Abraham's voice would have rung influential and powerful.

### My strongest place is trusting in the one true God.

Sarah might have felt fearful and helpless as she was introduced to the pagan king Abimelech with the lie that she was Abraham's sister. But even as Abraham's fear held Sarah captive, God could free her still. God kept Abimelech from touching Sarah. And Sarah's faith could grow stronger as she witnessed God's deliverance.

There are a lot of strong women out there, and the ability to trust in God in the face of mistreatment is an important demonstration of strength.

**REFLECT** "That's why I kept you from sinning against me, and why I did not let you touch her." GENESIS 20:6

*God, help me trust you when I feel helpless and voiceless. Make me strong, knowing you are a strong, trustworthy God. Amen.*

**CONSIDER** "Man and woman are designed to rule together. Exclusion of women is the opposite of God's design. To exclude women is to exclude half of God's creation means of ruling the earth. This means that we must include and celebrate the influence and presence of women in all realms of life. Women should be sought after and encouraged, educated and equipped, taught, learned with and learned from, celebrated and needed as essential partners in the shared task" ELYSE FITZPATRICK AND ERIC SCHUMACHER, *Worthy: Celebrating the Value of Women.*

WHITNEY PUTNAM is the senior director of women's events and marketing at New Life Ministries. She is an overall joy-chaser and is often found dancing in her kitchen.

and her Egyptian servant Hagar—making fun of her son, Isaac.* [10]So she turned to Abraham and demanded, "Get rid of that slave woman and her son. He is not going to share the inheritance with my son, Isaac. I won't have it!"

[11]This upset Abraham very much because Ishmael was his son. [12]But God told Abraham, "Do not be upset over the boy and your servant. Do whatever Sarah tells you, for Isaac is the son through whom your descendants will be counted. [13]But I will also make a nation of the descendants of Hagar's son because he is your son, too."

[14]So Abraham got up early the next morning, prepared food and a container of water, and strapped them on Hagar's shoulders. Then he sent her away with their son, and she wandered aimlessly in the wilderness of Beersheba.

[15]When the water was gone, she put the boy in the shade of a bush. [16]Then she went and sat down by herself about a hundred yards* away. "I don't want to watch the boy die," she said, as she burst into tears.

[17]But God heard the boy crying, and the angel of God called to Hagar from heaven, "Hagar, what's wrong? Do not be afraid! God has heard the boy crying as he lies there. [18]Go to him and comfort him, for I will make a great nation from his descendants."

[19]Then God opened Hagar's eyes, and she saw a well full of water. She quickly filled her water container and gave the boy a drink.

[20]And God was with the boy as he grew up in the wilderness. He became a skillful archer, [21]and he settled in the wilderness of Paran. His mother arranged for him to marry a woman from the land of Egypt.

## Abraham's Covenant with Abimelech

[22]About this time, Abimelech came with Phicol, his army commander, to visit Abraham. "God is obviously with you, helping you in everything you do," Abimelech said. [23]"Swear to me in God's name that you will never deceive me, my children, or any of my descendants. I have been loyal to you, so now swear that you will be loyal to me and to this country where you are living as a foreigner."

[24]Abraham replied, "Yes, I swear to it!" [25]Then Abraham complained to Abimelech about a well that Abimelech's servants had taken by force from Abraham's servants.

[26]"This is the first I've heard of it," Abimelech answered. "I have no idea who is responsible. You have never complained about this before."

[27]Abraham then gave some of his sheep, goats, and cattle to Abimelech, and they made a treaty. [28]But Abraham also took seven additional female lambs and set them off by themselves. [29]Abimelech asked, "Why have you set these seven apart from the others?"

[30]Abraham replied, "Please accept these seven lambs to show your agreement that I dug this well." [31]Then he named the place Beersheba (which means "well of the oath"), because that was where they had sworn the oath.

[32]After making their covenant at Beersheba, Abimelech left with Phicol, the commander of his army, and they returned home to the land of the Philistines. [33]Then Abraham planted a tamarisk tree at Beersheba, and there he worshiped the LORD, the Eternal God.* [34]And Abraham lived as a foreigner in Philistine country for a long time.

## Abraham's Faith Tested

**22** Some time later, God tested Abraham's faith. "Abraham!" God called.

"Yes," he replied. "Here I am."

[2]"Take your son, your only son—yes, Isaac, whom you love so much—and go to the land of Moriah. Go and sacrifice him as a burnt offering on one of the mountains, which I will show you."

[3]The next morning Abraham got up early. He saddled his donkey and took two of his servants with him, along with his son, Isaac. Then he chopped wood for a fire for a burnt offering and set out for the place God had told him about. [4]On the third day of their journey, Abraham looked up and saw the place in the distance. [5]"Stay here with the donkey," Abraham told the servants. "The boy and I will travel a little farther. We will worship there, and then we will come right back."

[6]So Abraham placed the wood for the burnt offering on Isaac's shoulders, while he himself carried the fire and the knife. As the two of them walked on together, [7]Isaac turned to Abraham and said, "Father?"

"Yes, my son?" Abraham replied.

"We have the fire and the wood," the boy said, "but where is the sheep for the burnt offering?"

---

21:9 As in Greek version and Latin Vulgate; Hebrew lacks *of her son, Isaac.* 21:16 Hebrew *a bowshot.* 21:33 Hebrew *El-Olam.*

---

**21:9-10** Earlier, Sarah had mistreated Hagar to the point that Hagar had fled (16:6). When Hagar's son mistreated Isaac, Sarah demanded that "that slave woman and her son" leave. Sarah's initial lack of trust in God in giving Hagar to Abraham resulted in many years of exploitation and multigenerational rivalry.

**21:14-21** Abraham gave Hagar meager resources when he sent her away, but God kept his promise to this Egyptian woman and her son. He heard their cries and provided for their needs, reiterating his plan to "make a great nation from his descendants"

(see 16:10). Hagar later succeeded in finding Ishmael an Egyptian wife.

**22:2** God's instructions to Abraham are troubling (see Perspective on page 34), but this story does not encourage child abuse. God's unique test of Abraham's faith related directly to the covenant promise about Isaac's descendants. Abraham's immediate and unquestioning obedience showed he trusted God to provide a substitute (22:3, 5, 8) or even raise Isaac from the dead (Hebrews 11:17-19).

# Perspective

## Where are the role models?

SCRIPTURE CONNECTION: GENESIS 22:1-19

If we open the Bible in search of role models, we soon run into trouble. Most Bible stories teach us about God's righteous character, but the humans in the stories are full of flaws. Their exploits are usually not a good example.

The Bible describes, rather than prescribes, their behavior. However, we take courage from the fact that God shows mercy to people who are flawed, just like us.

Passages like Genesis 22 are even more difficult. How can I trust a God who tells a father to kill his own son? What does this tell me about God's character?

Keep in mind that Abraham's situation is unique. And, as we see by the story's end, God never intended to put Isaac to death. He certainly does not ask us to sacrifice our children. In fact, there are numerous passages in the Bible that show God abhorring such practices. His instruction to Abraham was purely a test of trust. Would Abraham cling to the boy or entrust him to God?

---

### VIEWPOINTS

HIS: *How did this experience change Abraham's view of God?*
MINE: *"Like Abraham, I am always in danger of clinging to what God has provided instead of clinging to God. Will I trust him when it looks like I may lose something dear to me?"*
YOURS: *Is there something that easily becomes more important to you than God? Does this passage help reorient your trust?*

---

CARMEN JOY IMES, PhD, is an author, speaker, blogger, YouTuber, and serves as associate professor of Old Testament at Biola University in California.

---

[8]"God will provide a sheep for the burnt offering, my son," Abraham answered. And they both walked on together.

[9]When they arrived at the place where God had told him to go, Abraham built an altar and arranged the wood on it. Then he tied his son, Isaac, and laid him on the altar on top of the wood. [10]And Abraham picked up the knife to kill his son as a sacrifice. [11]At that moment the angel of the LORD called to him from heaven, "Abraham! Abraham!"

"Yes," Abraham replied. "Here I am!"

[12]"Don't lay a hand on the boy!" the angel said. "Do not hurt him in any way, for now I know that you truly fear God. You have not withheld from me even your son, your only son."

[13]Then Abraham looked up and saw a ram caught by its horns in a thicket. So he took the ram and sacrificed it as a burnt offering in place of his son. [14]Abraham named the place Yahweh-Yireh (which means "the LORD will provide"). To this day, people still use that name as a proverb: "On the mountain of the LORD it will be provided."

[15]Then the angel of the LORD called again to Abraham from heaven. [16]"This is what the LORD says: Because you have obeyed me and have not withheld even your son, your only son, I swear by my own name that [17]I will certainly bless you. I will multiply your descendants* beyond number, like the stars in the sky and the sand on the seashore. Your descendants will conquer the cities of their enemies. [18]And through your descendants all the nations of the earth will be blessed—all because you have obeyed me."

[19]Then they returned to the servants and traveled back to Beersheba, where Abraham continued to live.

[20]Soon after this, Abraham heard that Milcah, his brother Nahor's wife, had borne Nahor eight sons. [21]The oldest was named Uz, the next oldest was Buz, followed by Kemuel (the ancestor of the Arameans), [22]Kesed, Hazo, Pildash, Jidlaph, and Bethuel. [23](Bethuel became the father of Rebekah.) In addition to these eight sons from Milcah, [24]Nahor had four other children from his concubine Reumah. Their names were Tebah, Gaham, Tahash, and Maacah.

## The Burial of Sarah

**23** When Sarah was 127 years old, [2]she died at Kiriath-arba (now called Hebron) in the land of Canaan. There Abraham mourned and wept for her.

22:17 Hebrew *seed;* also in 22:17b, 18.

---

22:24 In some ancient cultures, concubines helped landowners increase their offspring and build larger households. As a member of the household, a concubine was assured continuous provision for her needs and the needs of her children, but her social status was not equal to a full wife. She was not available to marry another man or to be sold into another family's service (see Exodus 21:7-11). The Old Testament does not explicitly condemn polygamy, but Genesis repeatedly demonstrates its perils.

³Then, leaving her body, he said to the Hittite elders, ⁴"Here I am, a stranger and a foreigner among you. Please sell me a piece of land so I can give my wife a proper burial."

⁵The Hittites replied to Abraham, ⁶"Listen, my lord, you are an honored prince among us. Choose the finest of our tombs and bury her there. No one here will refuse to help you in this way."

⁷Then Abraham bowed low before the Hittites ⁸and said, "Since you are willing to help me in this way, be so kind as to ask Ephron son of Zohar ⁹to let me buy his cave at Machpelah, down at the end of his field. I will pay the full price in the presence of witnesses, so I will have a permanent burial place for my family."

¹⁰Ephron was sitting there among the others, and he answered Abraham as the others listened, speaking publicly before all the Hittite elders of the town. ¹¹"No, my lord," he said to Abraham, "please listen to me. I will give you the field and the cave. Here in the presence of my people, I give it to you. Go and bury your dead."

¹²Abraham again bowed low before the citizens of the land, ¹³and he replied to Ephron as everyone listened. "No, listen to me. I will buy it from you. Let me pay the full price for the field so I can bury my dead there."

¹⁴Ephron answered Abraham, ¹⁵"My lord, please listen to me. The land is worth 400 pieces* of silver, but what is that between friends? Go ahead and bury your dead."

¹⁶So Abraham agreed to Ephron's price and paid the amount he had suggested—400 pieces of silver, weighed according to the market standard. The Hittite elders witnessed the transaction.

¹⁷So Abraham bought the plot of land belonging to Ephron at Machpelah, near Mamre. This included the field itself, the cave that was in it, and all the surrounding trees. ¹⁸It was transferred to Abraham as his permanent possession in the presence of the Hittite elders at the city gate. ¹⁹Then Abraham buried his wife, Sarah, there in Canaan, in the cave of Machpelah, near Mamre (also called Hebron). ²⁰So the field and the cave were transferred from the Hittites to Abraham for use as a permanent burial place.

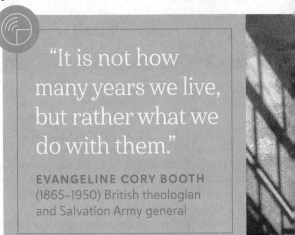

"It is not how many years we live, but rather what we do with them."

EVANGELINE CORY BOOTH
(1865–1950) British theologian and Salvation Army general

## A Wife for Isaac

24 Abraham was now a very old man, and the LORD had blessed him in every way. ²One day Abraham said to his oldest servant, the man in charge of his household, "Take an oath by putting your hand under my thigh. ³Swear by the LORD, the God of heaven and earth, that you will not allow my son to marry one of these local Canaanite women. ⁴Go instead to my homeland, to my relatives, and find a wife there for my son Isaac."

⁵The servant asked, "But what if I can't find a young woman who is willing to travel so far from home? Should I then take Isaac there to live among your relatives in the land you came from?"

⁶"No!" Abraham responded. "Be careful never to take my son there. ⁷For the LORD, the God of heaven, who took me from my father's house and my native land, solemnly promised to give this land to my descendants.* He will send his angel ahead of you, and he will see to it that you find a wife there for my son. ⁸If she is unwilling to come back with you, then you are free from this oath of mine. But under no circumstances are you to take my son there."

⁹So the servant took an oath by putting his hand under the thigh of his master, Abraham. He swore to follow Abraham's instructions. ¹⁰Then he loaded ten of Abraham's camels with all kinds of expensive gifts

---

23:15 Hebrew *400 shekels*, about 10 pounds or 4.6 kilograms in weight; also in 23:16.   24:7 Hebrew *seed*; also in 24:60.

---

**23:1-4** God had promised Abraham land, numerous descendants through Sarah, and blessing for their family (12:1-3). However, until Sarah's death they owned no land. Abraham acquired a field and a cave to use as a family tomb. This transaction was the first sign that a permanent transition had taken place, as people normally buried dead relatives in their ancestral homeland (see 49:29-32; 50:24-25).
**23:4-20** The negotiations between Abraham and the Hittites provide a fascinating window into ancient Mesopotamian culture. Although Ephron explicitly stated that he would "give" the land,

Abraham took Ephron's casual mention of the value of the land as the price he expected to receive. The witness of community elders ensured that no one would later contest Abraham's ownership.
**24:3-8** Abraham's unwillingness for Isaac to marry a Canaanite woman or to return to his father's homeland was rooted in God's covenant promises. Abraham sought to maintain faithfulness to God by avoiding intermarriage with uncircumcised Canaanites who would encourage them to worship other gods. He also insisted that Isaac remain in the land of Canaan in anticipation that it would be their land.

# Perspective

## Is the bride free to choose?

SCRIPTURE CONNECTION: GENESIS 24:1-67

The story of Isaac and Rebekah is the first explicit example of an arranged marriage in the Bible. Ironically, it's also the first mention of love between spouses. This juxtaposition of arranged marriage and love challenges those of us steeped in Western culture to ask how they coexist.

While coercion is bad, arrangements are not inherently bad. In fact, in many parts of the world today, there are flourishing arranged marriages.

Abraham was deeply invested in his son's (and his descendants') well-being. He entrusted his faithful servant with a most important mission: invite home a bride for Isaac.

When Rebekah appeared, she proved diligent in her work and generous in her spirit. She made two choices in this story—neither one by coercion. Her first choice was to eagerly serve Abraham's servant at the well. Then, when she was asked about her willingness to go with the servant, she made a second choice: "I will go."

Similarly, God entrusted Jesus with a most important mission to invite home a bride (a term used for believers, 2 Corinthians 11:2). God made the arrangements, and we freely choose. And find love.

## VIEWPOINTS

HERS: *What choices were available to Rebekah?*
MINE: *"When pressed with demands, obligations, and afflictions, I may lose sight of my options and begin feeling trapped with no path for relief or joy. I often want to make 'external choices': change my environment or change other people. But I have learned that my most powerful choices rest within my own heart—the 'internal choices.' And the condition of my heart then affects everything else that I do."*
YOURS: *When faced with life's challenges, what external and internal choices are available for you? How might the condition of your heart affect your circumstances?*

MISTY ARTERBURN is an author and speaker, contributing to Bible projects, devotionals, and recovery materials for over twenty years. Wife and mom to five, Misty is the founder of Recovery Girls and the general editor of *The One Year Bible for Women*.

from his master, and he traveled to distant Aram-naharaim. There he went to the town where Abraham's brother Nahor had settled. ¹¹He made the camels kneel beside a well just outside the town. It was evening, and the women were coming out to draw water. ¹²"O LORD, God of my master, Abraham," he prayed. "Please give me success today, and show unfailing love to my master, Abraham. ¹³See, I am standing here beside this spring, and the young women of the town are coming out to draw water. ¹⁴This is my request. I will ask one of them, 'Please give me a drink from your jug.' If she says, 'Yes, have a drink, and I will water your camels, too!'—let her be the one you have selected as Isaac's wife. This is how I will know that you have shown unfailing love to my master."

¹⁵Before he had finished praying, he saw a young woman named Rebekah coming out with her water jug on her shoulder. She was the daughter of Bethuel, who was the son of Abraham's brother Nahor and his wife, Milcah. ¹⁶Rebekah was very beautiful and old enough to be married, but she was still a virgin. She went down to the spring, filled her jug, and came up again. ¹⁷Running over to her, the servant said, "Please give me a little drink of water from your jug."

¹⁸"Yes, my lord," she answered, "have a drink." And she quickly lowered her jug from her shoulder and gave him a drink. ¹⁹When she had given him a drink, she said, "I'll draw water for your camels, too, until they have had enough to drink." ²⁰So she quickly emptied her jug into the watering trough and ran back to the well to draw water for all his camels.

²¹The servant watched her in silence, wondering whether or not the LORD had given him success in his mission. ²²Then at last, when the camels had finished drinking, he took out a gold ring for her nose and two large gold bracelets* for her wrists.

²³"Whose daughter are you?" he asked. "And please tell me, would your father have any room to put us up for the night?"

²⁴"I am the daughter of Bethuel," she replied. "My grandparents are Nahor and Milcah. ²⁵Yes, we have plenty of straw and feed for the camels, and we have room for guests."

²⁶The man bowed low and worshiped the LORD. ²⁷"Praise the LORD, the God of my master, Abraham,"

24:22 Hebrew *a gold nose-ring weighing a beka* [0.2 ounces or 6 grams] *and two gold bracelets weighing 10* [shekels] [4 ounces or 114 grams].

24:11 This is the first of many similar events in the Bible (these are known as *type scenes*). Abraham's servant found a wife for Isaac at the well outside Abraham's hometown. Later, Jacob and Moses would each find a wife in the same way (Genesis 29:1-30; Exodus 2:15-22).
24:12-20 Rebekah, Abraham's great-niece, proved herself to be kind, generous, and capable, showing stellar hospitality to Abraham's servant. Ten thirsty camels could drink two hundred to three hundred gallons of water in one sitting, so a woman who would work that hard for a stranger was remarkable!

# Rebekah

## More Than Her Circumstances

When she first entered the story, Rebekah seemed chosen. What were the chances? A man coming to town looking for a young woman who would offer him and his camels a drink, and there she was meeting that description perfectly. Then she gets whisked away to a life of comfort. It certainly looked like God's favor.

Then those problematic twins, Jacob and Esau, arrived, fighting before they were even born. Their brotherly rivalry was unmatched, and Rebekah got herself involved. She ended up deceiving her husband, Isaac, so that Jacob—her favorite—could become the family heir over his brother, Esau. They had their fair share of family issues.

At different points in her story, Rebekah might have labeled herself "blessed" or "cursed." But that dismisses how every part of her story was used for God's glory. God was present with Rebekah no matter the circumstances, the feelings, or the choices.

> God can use all of my story for his glory.

Like all of us, Rebekah is more than any single moment in her story. She could be identified at different moments as a sought-after bride, a conflicted mother, or a deceptive wife. Though each of these titles may ring true, more than anything she was known and used by God. This was true even amid her mistakes. As it turned out, Jesus was linked to Abraham's lineage through Jacob. Though God could have worked this out a million ways, he chose to make Rebekah's story part of Christ's story.

REBEKAH'S STORY IS TOLD IN GENESIS 24–27; SHE IS ALSO MENTIONED IN GENESIS 49:31 & ROMANS 9:10.

## IDENTIFY

How can God redeem every part of your story?

"As with Rebekah, God can use my mistakes in creative ways for his purposes. My identity isn't tied up in what I do 'right' or 'wrong.' God sees me and can use all of my story for his glory."

**ALEXANDRA KUYKENDALL** is a cofounder of The Open Door Sisterhood and author of several books, including *Seeking Out Goodness: Finding the True and Beautiful All around You.*

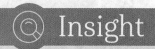

# Insight    COULD YOU LIFT THAT?

Camels have been used to transport people and goods for thousands of years. Abraham's servant took ten camels with him on his journey to Haran to find a wife for Isaac. He and his camels met Rebekah at a well, a traditional place to find a wife in the Bible. He knew Rebekah was the one when she gave him a drink and then offered to water his camels, too. Rebekah was clearly a strong woman: Ten thirsty camels can drink around two hundred to three hundred gallons of water in one sitting.

**10 CAMELS' WATER INTAKE = ~250 GALLONS OF WATER = ~2,085 POUNDS CARRIED**

he said. "The LORD has shown unfailing love and faithfulness to my master, for he has led me straight to my master's relatives."

²⁸The young woman ran home to tell her family everything that had happened. ²⁹Now Rebekah had a brother named Laban, who ran out to meet the man at the spring. ³⁰He had seen the nose-ring and the bracelets on his sister's wrists, and had heard Rebekah tell what the man had said. So he rushed out to the spring, where the man was still standing beside his camels. ³¹Laban said to him, "Come and stay with us, you who are blessed by the LORD! Why are you standing here outside the town when I have a room all ready for you and a place prepared for the camels?"

³²So the man went home with Laban, and Laban unloaded the camels, gave him straw for their bedding, fed them, and provided water for the man and the camel drivers to wash their feet. ³³Then food was served. But Abraham's servant said, "I don't want to eat until I have told you why I have come."

"All right," Laban said, "tell us."

³⁴"I am Abraham's servant," he explained. ³⁵"And the LORD has greatly blessed my master; he has become a wealthy man. The LORD has given him flocks of sheep and goats, herds of cattle, a fortune in silver and gold, and many male and female servants and camels and donkeys.

³⁶"When Sarah, my master's wife, was very old, she gave birth to my master's son, and my master has given him everything he owns. ³⁷And my master made me take an oath. He said, 'Do not allow my son to marry one of these local Canaanite women. ³⁸Go instead to my father's house, to my relatives, and find a wife there for my son.'

³⁹"But I said to my master, 'What if I can't find a young woman who is willing to go back with me?' ⁴⁰He responded, 'The LORD, in whose presence I have lived, will send his angel with you and will make your mission successful. Yes, you must find a wife for my son from among my relatives, from my father's family. ⁴¹Then you will have fulfilled your obligation. But if you go to my relatives and they refuse to let her go with you, you will be free from my oath.'

⁴²"So today when I came to the spring, I prayed this prayer: 'O LORD, God of my master, Abraham, please give me success on this mission. ⁴³See, I am standing here beside this spring. This is my request. When a young woman comes to draw water, I will say to her, "Please give me a little drink of water from your jug." ⁴⁴If she says, "Yes, have a drink, and I will draw water for your camels, too," let her be the one you have selected to be the wife of my master's son.'

⁴⁵"Before I had finished praying in my heart, I saw Rebekah coming out with her water jug on her shoulder. She went down to the spring and drew water. So I said to her, 'Please give me a drink.' ⁴⁶She quickly lowered her jug from her shoulder and said, 'Yes, have a drink, and I will water your camels, too!' So I drank, and then she watered the camels.

⁴⁷"Then I asked, 'Whose daughter are you?' She replied, 'I am the daughter of Bethuel, and my grandparents are Nahor and Milcah.' So I put the ring on her nose, and the bracelets on her wrists.

⁴⁸"Then I bowed low and worshiped the LORD. I praised the LORD, the God of my master, Abraham, because he had led me straight to my master's niece to be his son's wife. ⁴⁹So tell me—will you or won't you show unfailing love and faithfulness to my master? Please tell me yes or no, and then I'll know what to do next."

⁵⁰Then Laban and Bethuel replied, "The LORD has obviously brought you here, so there is nothing we can say. ⁵¹Here is Rebekah; take her and go. Yes, let her be the wife of your master's son, as the LORD has directed."

⁵²When Abraham's servant heard their answer, he bowed down to the ground and worshiped the LORD. ⁵³Then he brought out silver and gold jewelry and clothing and presented them to Rebekah. He also gave expensive presents to her brother and mother. ⁵⁴Then they ate their meal, and the servant and the men with him stayed there overnight.

But early the next morning, Abraham's servant said, "Send me back to my master."

⁵⁵"But we want Rebekah to stay with us at least ten days," her brother and mother said. "Then she can go."

⁵⁶But he said, "Don't delay me. The LORD has made my mission successful; now send me back so I can return to my master."

⁵⁷"Well," they said, "we'll call Rebekah and ask her what she thinks." ⁵⁸So they called Rebekah. "Are you willing to go with this man?" they asked her.

And she replied, "Yes, I will go."

⁵⁹So they said good-bye to Rebekah and sent her away with Abraham's servant and his men. The woman who had been Rebekah's childhood nurse went along with her. ⁶⁰They gave her this blessing as she parted:

"Our sister, may you become
the mother of many millions!
May your descendants be strong
and conquer the cities of their enemies."

⁶¹Then Rebekah and her servant girls mounted the camels and followed the man. So Abraham's servant took Rebekah and went on his way.

⁶²Meanwhile, Isaac, whose home was in the Negev, had returned from Beer-lahai-roi. ⁶³One evening as he was walking and meditating in the fields, he looked up and saw the camels coming. ⁶⁴When Rebekah looked up and saw Isaac, she quickly dismounted from her camel. ⁶⁵"Who is that man walking through the fields to meet us?" she asked the servant.

And he replied, "It is my master." So Rebekah covered her face with her veil. ⁶⁶Then the servant told Isaac everything he had done.

⁶⁷And Isaac brought Rebekah into his mother Sarah's tent, and she became his wife. He loved her deeply, and she was a special comfort to him after the death of his mother.

## The Death of Abraham

**25** Abraham married another wife, whose name was Keturah. ²She gave birth to Zimran, Jokshan, Medan, Midian, Ishbak, and Shuah. ³Jokshan was the father of Sheba and Dedan. Dedan's descendants were the Asshurites, Letushites, and Leummites. ⁴Midian's sons were Ephah, Epher, Hanoch, Abida, and Eldaah. These were all descendants of Abraham through Keturah.

⁵Abraham gave everything he owned to his son Isaac. ⁶But before he died, he gave gifts to the sons of his concubines and sent them off to a land in the east, away from Isaac.

⁷Abraham lived for 175 years, ⁸and he died at a ripe old age, having lived a long and satisfying life. He breathed his last and joined his ancestors in death. ⁹His sons Isaac and Ishmael buried him in the cave of Machpelah, near Mamre, in the field of Ephron son of Zohar the Hittite. ¹⁰This was the field Abraham had purchased from the Hittites and where he had buried his wife Sarah. ¹¹After Abraham's death, God blessed his son Isaac, who settled near Beer-lahai-roi in the Negev.

---

**24:51** In the ancient Near East, a woman's father normally bore responsibility for arranging her marriage. In this case, Rebekah's brother Laban also played a role, perhaps due to her father's advanced age. Given Abraham's obvious wealth and status as a close family relative, the servant quickly convinced them it was a good match. They did not consult her first, and she was not present for the negotiations the next morning (24:57), but she expressed willingness to go right away (24:58).

**24:67** Not much is known about ancient marriage ceremonies. The negotiations between male relatives were likely the most complex part. Whether Isaac and Rebekah married immediately is not clear. What is clear is that arranged marriages did not necessarily lack affection. Isaac loved Rebekah deeply.

**25:5-6** Abraham remarried after Sarah's death. The narrator has not called Keturah or Hagar concubines until this point, but clearly the status of their sons did not equal Isaac's. Abraham loved all his sons, so before he died, he gave each of them gifts. But to demonstrate and preserve Isaac's position as his heir, Abraham sent these other sons away, as he had previously sent away Ishmael (21:8-14).

## A Good Name:
## Name Changes Reveal Purpose

**MY STORY WITH GOD**

**SCRIPTURE CONNECTION: GENESIS 25:19-34; 32:22-32**

In a powerful, public ceremony in India in 2011, two hundred young girls, whose parents had named them Nakusha (meaning "unwanted"), legally chose new names reflecting their new, positive identity.

What is the meaning of your name? Five name changes occur in Genesis. Eve, Abraham, Sarah, Jacob, and Joseph all experienced a name change, and each change reflected something of God's plan to redeem people. The name changes also signaled new self-images.

Eve was initially called *ishshah*, "the woman," the companion to *ish*, "the man." Adam recognized her as "bone from my bone, and flesh from my flesh" (2:23), an equal companion. But after the Fall, Adam renamed her Eve, "mother of all who live" (3:20), which could be viewed as narrowing her function to raising children. But God's purpose for her extended to his redemption plan; he promised that her offspring would overcome evil (3:15).

God's ideal, his plan, was thus not lost when sin entered the world, and the name changes of Abram, Sarai, and Jacob also look toward God's plan to restore humanity to himself.

Abram means "exalted father," but his new name, Abraham, means "father of many," that is, many nations (17:5). This was God's vision for Abraham and his offspring. And it was a seal of God's covenant relationship with Abraham. Sarai's name change doesn't result in a change in meaning, as both Sarai and Sarah mean "princess." But it did clearly include her in God's promise and further served as an expression of God's vision for this couple (see note on 17:15-16).

Jacob's name, "heel grabber," reflects his birth as the second-born twin who held on to his brother's heel (25:26). He later grabbed Esau's birthright and tricked Isaac into blessing him as the oldest son, which led to Jacob's having to flee. On Jacob's return to Canaan, he wrestled with a mysterious stranger and demanded a blessing from him. The stranger—evidently a messenger from God— gave him the new name Israel, which means "fighting with God" or "God fights" (32:22-32).

> God gives us good names for good purposes.

Joseph (meaning "may he add") was given a name change when he was promoted by Pharaoh to second-in-command in Egypt. The new name, Zaphenath-paneah ("God speaks and lives"), is never used of Joseph again. It was his Egyptian name, and while the name positioned Joseph to later help the Israelites, it didn't change his identity as a son of Jacob, belonging to the people of Israel.

These people are a part of our spiritual heritage. And their new names reflect God's good plans for them—and for all of us who are blessed through them.

### IMAGINE

What does your name mean?

How might your name reflect how God wants to bless you and others?

*"When I learned my name's meaning ('consecrated to God'), I saw God's call on my life from birth, as a pastor and later as a professor."*

**ELIZABETH GLANVILLE, PhD,** is retired faculty from Fuller Theological Seminary, School of Mission and Theology. She is an international teacher on missions and leadership and chaplain for a local police department and her retirement community.

## Ishmael's Descendants

[12]This is the account of the family of Ishmael, the son of Abraham through Hagar, Sarah's Egyptian servant. [13]Here is a list, by their names and clans, of Ishmael's descendants: The oldest was Nebaioth, followed by Kedar, Adbeel, Mibsam, [14]Mishma, Dumah, Massa, [15]Hadad, Tema, Jetur, Naphish, and Kedemah. [16]These twelve sons of Ishmael became the founders of twelve tribes named after them, listed according to the places they settled and camped. [17]Ishmael lived for 137 years. Then he breathed his last and joined his ancestors in death. [18]Ishmael's descendants occupied the region from Havilah to Shur, which is east of Egypt in the direction of Asshur. There they lived in open hostility toward all their relatives.*

## The Births of Esau and Jacob

[19]This is the account of the family of Isaac, the son of Abraham. [20]When Isaac was forty years old, he married Rebekah, the daughter of Bethuel the Aramean from Paddan-aram and the sister of Laban the Aramean.

[21]Isaac pleaded with the LORD on behalf of his wife, because she was unable to have children. The LORD answered Isaac's prayer, and Rebekah became pregnant with twins. [22]But the two children struggled with each other in her womb. So she went to ask the LORD about it. "Why is this happening to me?" she asked.

[23]And the LORD told her, "The sons in your womb will become two nations. From the very beginning, the two nations will be rivals. One nation will be stronger than the other; and your older son will serve your younger son."

[24]And when the time came to give birth, Rebekah discovered that she did indeed have twins! [25]The first one was very red at birth and covered with thick hair like a fur coat. So they named him Esau.* [26]Then the other twin was born with his hand grasping Esau's heel. So they named him Jacob.* Isaac was sixty years old when the twins were born.

## Esau Sells His Birthright

[27]As the boys grew up, Esau became a skillful hunter. He was an outdoorsman, but Jacob had a quiet temperament, preferring to stay at home. [28]Isaac loved Esau because he enjoyed eating the wild game Esau brought home, but Rebekah loved Jacob.

[29]One day when Jacob was cooking some stew, Esau arrived home from the wilderness exhausted and hungry. [30]Esau said to Jacob, "I'm starved! Give me some of that red stew!" (This is how Esau got his other name, Edom, which means "red.")

[31]"All right," Jacob replied, "but trade me your rights as the firstborn son."

[32]"Look, I'm dying of starvation!" said Esau. "What good is my birthright to me now?"

[33]But Jacob said, "First you must swear that your birthright is mine." So Esau swore an oath, thereby selling all his rights as the firstborn to his brother, Jacob.

[34]Then Jacob gave Esau some bread and lentil stew. Esau ate the meal, then got up and left. He showed contempt for his rights as the firstborn.

## Isaac Deceives Abimelech

**26** A severe famine now struck the land, as had happened before in Abraham's time. So Isaac moved to Gerar, where Abimelech, king of the Philistines, lived.

[2]The LORD appeared to Isaac and said, "Do not go down to Egypt, but do as I tell you. [3]Live here as a foreigner in this land, and I will be with you and bless you. I hereby confirm that I will give all these lands to you and your descendants,* just as I solemnly promised Abraham, your father. [4]I will cause your descendants to become as numerous as the stars of the sky, and I will give them all these lands. And through your descendants all the nations of the earth will be blessed. [5]I will do this because Abraham listened to me and obeyed all my requirements, commands, decrees, and instructions." [6]So Isaac stayed in Gerar.

25:18 The meaning of the Hebrew is uncertain.   25:25 *Esau* sounds like a Hebrew term that means "hair."   25:26 *Jacob* sounds like the Hebrew words for "heel" and "deceiver."   26:3 Hebrew *seed;* also in 26:4, 24.

**25:21** Like Sarah before her (16:1; 18:11) and Rachel after her (29:31; 30:1, 22-23), Rebekah struggled with infertility—in her case, for twenty years. Children continued the family line, helped protect the tribe, and provided crucial labor as survival depended upon the fruitfulness of crops and herds. Children also kept property within the family, cared for aging parents, and enacted the proper funeral rites. Infertility was therefore a crushing stigma for a woman and a source of anxiety for a man. Since it was understood that God could control fertility, infertility was viewed as a spiritual issue prompting fervent prayer.
**25:22-23** Rebekah's twins frequently wrestled within her. She inquired of the Lord, seeking to understand why her children were not at peace. Although we are not told how the subsequent interaction took place, God clearly honored Rebekah's desire to know his will. God spoke to her, indicating

that her sons would be rivals, with the older serving the younger. This may have fueled her special love for her younger son, Jacob (25:28).
**25:31-33** The firstborn son had double the inheritance of his siblings, along with the responsibility to care for aging parents. Esau gave Jacob his esteemed status in exchange for a single bowl of stew, showing how shortsighted he was (see Hebrews 12:16).
**26:2-6** God assured Isaac that he would inherit the covenant promises (see 12:1-3) because Abraham had faithfully listened to God and obeyed all his requirements, commands, decrees, and instructions. Moses used these same terms in Deuteronomy to describe God's covenant with Israel, implying that Abraham would have obeyed the stipulations of the Sinai covenant if he had known them.

⁷When the men who lived there asked Isaac about his wife, Rebekah, he said, "She is my sister." He was afraid to say, "She is my wife." He thought, "They will kill me to get her, because she is so beautiful." ⁸But some time later, Abimelech, king of the Philistines, looked out his window and saw Isaac caressing Rebekah.

⁹Immediately, Abimelech called for Isaac and exclaimed, "She is obviously your wife! Why did you say, 'She is my sister'?"

"Because I was afraid someone would kill me to get her from me," Isaac replied.

¹⁰"How could you do this to us?" Abimelech exclaimed. "One of my people might easily have taken your wife and slept with her, and you would have made us guilty of great sin."

¹¹Then Abimelech issued a public proclamation: "Anyone who touches this man or his wife will be put to death!"

## Conflict over Water Rights

¹²When Isaac planted his crops that year, he harvested a hundred times more grain than he planted, for the LORD blessed him. ¹³He became a very rich man, and his wealth continued to grow. ¹⁴He acquired so many flocks of sheep and goats, herds of cattle, and servants that the Philistines became jealous of him. ¹⁵So the Philistines filled up all of Isaac's wells with dirt. These were the wells that had been dug by the servants of his father, Abraham.

¹⁶Finally, Abimelech ordered Isaac to leave the country. "Go somewhere else," he said, "for you have become too powerful for us."

¹⁷So Isaac moved away to the Gerar Valley, where he set up their tents and settled down. ¹⁸He reopened the wells his father had dug, which the Philistines had filled in after Abraham's death. Isaac also restored the names Abraham had given them.

¹⁹Isaac's servants also dug in the Gerar Valley and discovered a well of fresh water. ²⁰But then the shepherds from Gerar came and claimed the spring. "This is our water," they said, and they argued over it with Isaac's herdsmen. So Isaac named the well Esek (which means "argument"). ²¹Isaac's men then dug another well, but again there was a dispute over it. So Isaac named it Sitnah (which means "hostility"). ²²Abandoning that one, Isaac moved on and dug another well. This time there was no dispute over it, so Isaac named the place Rehoboth (which means "open space"), for he said, "At last the LORD has created enough space for us to prosper in this land."

²³From there Isaac moved to Beersheba, ²⁴where the LORD appeared to him on the night of his arrival. "I am the God of your father, Abraham," he said. "Do not be afraid, for I am with you and will bless you. I will multiply your descendants, and they will become a great nation. I will do this because of my promise to Abraham, my servant." ²⁵Then Isaac built an altar there and worshiped the LORD. He set up his camp at that place, and his servants dug another well.

## Isaac's Covenant with Abimelech

²⁶One day King Abimelech came from Gerar with his adviser, Ahuzzath, and also Phicol, his army commander. ²⁷"Why have you come here?" Isaac asked. "You obviously hate me, since you kicked me off your land."

²⁸They replied, "We can plainly see that the LORD is with you. So we want to enter into a sworn treaty with you. Let's make a covenant. ²⁹Swear that you will not harm us, just as we have never troubled you. We have always treated you well, and we sent you away from us in peace. And now look how the LORD has blessed you!"

³⁰So Isaac prepared a covenant feast to celebrate the treaty, and they ate and drank together. ³¹Early the next morning, they each took a solemn oath not to interfere with each other. Then Isaac sent them home again, and they left him in peace.

³²That very day Isaac's servants came and told him about a new well they had dug. "We've found water!" they exclaimed. ³³So Isaac named the well Shibah (which means "oath"). And to this day the town that grew up there is called Beersheba (which means "well of the oath").

³⁴At the age of forty, Esau married two Hittite wives: Judith, the daughter of Beeri, and Basemath, the daughter of Elon. ³⁵But Esau's wives made life miserable for Isaac and Rebekah.

## Jacob Steals Esau's Blessing

27 One day when Isaac was old and turning blind, he called for Esau, his older son, and said, "My son."

---

**26:7-11** Isaac not only inherited the covenant from his father, but he also learned deception from him. He deceived the residents of Gerar into believing that his wife was his sister. (This Abimelech is probably not the same man as in Genesis 20. *Abimelech* means "my father is king," so it could have been a dynastic name or title.) As with Abraham, when Isaac jeopardized the covenant, God prevented disaster and preserved the marriage.
**26:34-35** Disregarding the covenant faith of his grandfather Abraham, Esau married outside the extended family, causing tension with his parents. Intermarriage would likely lead Esau and his children to worship idols, rather than God. His marriages illustrate how unfit he was to lead the covenant people into God's blessings. His later marriage to a descendant of Ishmael further demonstrated that he did not revere the uniqueness of the covenant family (28:8-9).
**27:1-46** Jacob, whose name means "heel grabber," learned deception from his mother, Rebekah. She conspired with Jacob to deceive his father, Isaac, now blind, to gain the blessing of the firstborn before he died. In this event, the entire family acted faithlessly: Isaac disregarded the prophecy from Rebekah's pregnancy (25:23), Esau ignored his agreement with Jacob (25:33), and Rebekah acted deviously, even tricking Isaac into sending Jacob away (27:46). Favoritism produces a toxic family dynamic.

30 When Rachel saw that she wasn't having any children for Jacob, she became jealous of her sister. She pleaded with Jacob, "Give me children, or I'll die!"

²Then Jacob became furious with Rachel. "Am I God?" he asked. "He's the one who has kept you from having children!"

³Then Rachel told him, "Take my maid, Bilhah, and sleep with her. She will bear children for me,* and through her I can have a family, too." ⁴So Rachel gave her servant, Bilhah, to Jacob as a wife, and he slept with her. ⁵Bilhah became pregnant and presented him with a son. ⁶Rachel named him Dan,* for she said, "God has vindicated me! He has heard my request and given me a son." ⁷Then Bilhah became pregnant again and gave Jacob a second son. ⁸Rachel named him Naphtali,* for she said, "I have struggled hard with my sister, and I'm winning!"

⁹Meanwhile, Leah realized that she wasn't getting pregnant anymore, so she took her servant, Zilpah, and gave her to Jacob as a wife. ¹⁰Soon Zilpah presented him with a son. ¹¹Leah named him Gad,* for she said, "How fortunate I am!" ¹²Then Zilpah gave Jacob a second son. ¹³And Leah named him Asher,* for she said, "What joy is mine! Now the other women will celebrate with me."

¹⁴One day during the wheat harvest, Reuben found some mandrakes growing in a field and brought

---

30:3 Hebrew *bear children on my knees.* 30:6 *Dan* means "he judged" or "he vindicated." 30:8 *Naphtali* means "my struggle." 30:11 *Gad* means "good fortune." 30:13 *Asher* means "happy."

---

**30:1-13** In ancient Mesopotamia, it was devastating for a woman not to have children, and Rachel understandably felt wronged by her infertility. She resorted to a culturally acceptable solution for infertility in ancient times—she gave her servant to Jacob as a concubine. Rachel's decision to have children through her servant, and Jacob's compliance, recalls Sarai's use of Hagar (16:1-4). The resulting frenzy to bear children reads like an arms race, with each side stockpiling weapons (in this case, sons) to outmaneuver the other.

**30:14-16** Ancient Mesopotamian people considered mandrakes an aphrodisiac and aid to conception. Rachel thought the mandrakes would help her get pregnant, so she offered to trade sleeping with Jacob for a night in exchange for the plant. Leah ended up pregnant rather than Rachel. Rachel's desperation to get pregnant clouded her judgment and distracted her from trusting God to intervene.

---

 **Insight**   ISRAEL'S FAMILY TREE

From the time of Abraham, rivalry and competition were rife within the family, which might explain the legacy of contention among the tribes of Israel later. Hagar had contempt for Sarah (16:4-5), but Sarah felt threatened by Hagar's son, Ishmael (21:10). Rebekah and Isaac encouraged the rivalry foretold about Jacob and Esau (25:22-26, 28). The rivalry between sisters Rachel and Leah explains much of the later rivalry among their sons (see 37:1-36), and then between the tribes. But God had compassion on Leah, who was unloved, by enabling her to bear sons for Jacob. Despite Jacob's preference for Rachel and her children, Judah's kingly tribe and Levi's priestly line came through Leah.

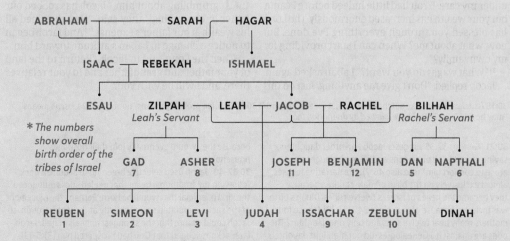

them to his mother, Leah. Rachel begged Leah, "Please give me some of your son's mandrakes."

¹⁵But Leah angrily replied, "Wasn't it enough that you stole my husband? Now will you steal my son's mandrakes, too?"

Rachel answered, "I will let Jacob sleep with you tonight if you give me some of the mandrakes."

¹⁶So that evening, as Jacob was coming home from the fields, Leah went out to meet him. "You must come and sleep with me tonight!" she said. "I have paid for you with some mandrakes that my son found." So that night he slept with Leah. ¹⁷And God answered Leah's prayers. She became pregnant again and gave birth to a fifth son for Jacob. ¹⁸She named him Issachar,* for she said, "God has rewarded me for giving my servant to my husband as a wife." ¹⁹Then Leah became pregnant again and gave birth to a sixth son for Jacob. ²⁰She named him Zebulun,* for she said, "God has given me a good reward. Now my husband will treat me with respect, for I have given him six sons." ²¹Later she gave birth to a daughter and named her Dinah.

²²Then God remembered Rachel's plight and answered her prayers by enabling her to have children. ²³She became pregnant and gave birth to a son. "God has removed my disgrace," she said. ²⁴And she named him Joseph,* for she said, "May the LORD add yet another son to my family."

## Jacob's Wealth Increases

²⁵Soon after Rachel had given birth to Joseph, Jacob said to Laban, "Please release me so I can go home to my own country. ²⁶Let me take my wives and children, for I have earned them by serving you, and let me be on my way. You certainly know how hard I have worked for you."

²⁷"Please listen to me," Laban replied. "I have become wealthy, for* the LORD has blessed me because of you. ²⁸Tell me how much I owe you. Whatever it is, I'll pay it."

²⁹Jacob replied, "You know how hard I've worked for you, and how your flocks and herds have grown under my care. ³⁰You had little indeed before I came, but your wealth has increased enormously. The LORD has blessed you through everything I've done. But now, what about me? When can I start providing for my own family?"

³¹"What wages do you want?" Laban asked again.

Jacob replied, "Don't give me anything. Just do this

one thing, and I'll continue to tend and watch over your flocks. ³²Let me inspect your flocks today and remove all the sheep and goats that are speckled or spotted, along with all the black sheep. Give these to me as my wages. ³³In the future, when you check on the animals you have given me as my wages, you'll see that I have been honest. If you find in my flock any goats without speckles or spots, or any sheep that are not black, you will know that I have stolen them from you."

³⁴"All right," Laban replied. "It will be as you say." ³⁵But that very day Laban went out and removed the male goats that were streaked and spotted, all the female goats that were speckled and spotted or had white patches, and all the black sheep. He placed them in the care of his own sons, ³⁶who took them a three-days' journey from where Jacob was. Meanwhile, Jacob stayed and cared for the rest of Laban's flock.

³⁷Then Jacob took some fresh branches from poplar, almond, and plane trees and peeled off strips of bark, making white streaks on them. ³⁸Then he placed these peeled branches in the watering troughs where the flocks came to drink, for that was where they mated. ³⁹And when they mated in front of the white-streaked branches, they gave birth to young that were streaked, speckled, and spotted. ⁴⁰Jacob separated those lambs from Laban's flock. And at mating time he turned the flock to face Laban's animals that were streaked or black. This is how he built his own flock instead of increasing Laban's.

⁴¹Whenever the stronger females were ready to mate, Jacob would place the peeled branches in the watering troughs in front of them. Then they would mate in front of the branches. ⁴²But he didn't do this with the weaker ones, so the weaker lambs belonged to Laban, and the stronger ones were Jacob's. ⁴³As a result, Jacob became very wealthy, with large flocks of sheep and goats, female and male servants, and many camels and donkeys.

## Jacob Flees from Laban

**31** But Jacob soon learned that Laban's sons were grumbling about him. "Jacob has robbed our father of everything!" they said. "He has gained all his wealth at our father's expense." ²And Jacob began to notice a change in Laban's attitude toward him.

³Then the LORD said to Jacob, "Return to the land of your father and grandfather and to your relatives there, and I will be with you."

---

30:18 *Issachar* sounds like a Hebrew term that means "reward." 30:20 *Zebulun* probably means "honor." 30:24 *Joseph* means "may he add." 30:27 Or *I have learned by divination that.*

**30:21** Genesis 37:35 suggests Jacob had other daughters, saying literally, "all of his sons and all of his daughters arose to comfort him" (see also 46:7). The narrative focuses almost exclusively on the birth of male children because they became the heads of Israel's twelve tribes. Dinah's birth was included because of her role in 34:1-31. (Did those four mothers really bear twelve sons and only one daughter? The odds are against it.) Genealogies did not highlight daughters because they would eventually join their husbands' households.

**30:37-40** Jacob used selective breeding to acquire a flock, following the traditional belief that peeled sticks influenced the kind of animal that would be born. Perhaps the placement of the sticks stimulated sexual activity at the water trough, so Jacob could ensure that the strongest animals mated. Jacob later acknowledged that God had prospered him (31:5-13).

# Leah & Rachel

## Love Triangle Tragedy

A love triangle is never where you want to find sisters, yet that is exactly where we find Rachel and Leah. Leah, with "no sparkle in [her] eyes," and Rachel, with "a beautiful figure and a lovely face," both deeply desired the favor of Jacob, a cousin hired to work their father's fields who became husband to both sisters.

"Sleep with me!" Leah would cry to Jacob.

"Give me a son!" Rachel would plead.

What a juggling act Jacob had on his hands, and what discontent Rachel and Leah lugged around!

In that culture, the badge of bearing sons was like gold. It brought deep fulfillment to a woman's life and gave her a place in society. It's no wonder that Rachel envied Leah, who kept having one son after another. Rachel raged and found a way to her own "fulfillment" by giving an enslaved woman to Jacob to conceive a son for her. Leah then did the same. They were each determined to win, focused on gaining honor in their family and chasing satisfaction in what society deemed successful.

Although God listened to these women and granted their requests, finding happiness in proving ourselves isn't the lesson here. It's clear from the hungry hearts of Leah and Rachel that true fulfillment doesn't come from what the world considers success; it comes from being loved by, and loving, God. Whenever we're experiencing brokenness in our relationships, we can remember that God's love for us is deep, whole, and perfect.

> Only God satisfies the deep hunger of my heart.

LEAH'S AND RACHEL'S STORIES ARE TOLD IN GENESIS 29–35; THEY ARE ALSO MENTIONED IN RUTH 4:11.

## IDENTIFY

What have you turned to for fulfillment?

Do you relate more to Leah or Rachel in this story? Why?

*"All too quickly I can want to appear successful by the world's standards—whether it's the social-media-ready home, the well-mannered children, the A+ job, or the corner office. I like finding worth from the outside in. But my true worth comes from God."*

WHITNEY PUTNAM is the senior director of women's events and marketing at New Life Ministries. She is an overall joy-chaser and is often found dancing in her kitchen.

[4]So Jacob called Rachel and Leah out to the field where he was watching his flock. [5]He said to them, "I have noticed that your father's attitude toward me has changed. But the God of my father has been with me. [6]You know how hard I have worked for your father, [7]but he has cheated me, changing my wages ten times. But God has not allowed him to do me any harm. [8]For if he said, 'The speckled animals will be your wages,' the whole flock began to produce speckled young. And when he changed his mind and said, 'The striped animals will be your wages,' then the whole flock produced striped young. [9]In this way, God has taken your father's animals and given them to me.

[10]"One time during the mating season, I had a dream and saw that the male goats mating with the females were streaked, speckled, and spotted. [11]Then in my dream, the angel of God said to me, 'Jacob!' And I replied, 'Yes, here I am.'

[12]"The angel said, 'Look up, and you will see that only the streaked, speckled, and spotted males are mating with the females of your flock. For I have seen how Laban has treated you. [13]I am the God who appeared to you at Bethel,* the place where you anointed the pillar of stone and made your vow to me. Now get ready and leave this country and return to the land of your birth.'"

[14]Rachel and Leah responded, "That's fine with us! We won't inherit any of our father's wealth anyway. [15]He has reduced our rights to those of foreign women. And after he sold us, he wasted the money you paid him for us. [16]All the wealth God has given you from our father legally belongs to us and our children. So go ahead and do whatever God has told you."

[17]So Jacob put his wives and children on camels, [18]and he drove all his livestock in front of him. He packed all the belongings he had acquired in Paddan-aram and set out for the land of Canaan, where his father, Isaac, lived. [19]At the time they left, Laban was some distance away, shearing his sheep. Rachel stole her father's household idols and took them with her. [20]Jacob outwitted Laban the Aramean, for they set out secretly and never told Laban they were leaving. [21]So Jacob took all his possessions with him and crossed the Euphrates River,* heading for the hill country of Gilead.

## Laban Pursues Jacob

[22]Three days later, Laban was told that Jacob had fled. [23]So he gathered a group of his relatives and set out in hot pursuit. He caught up with Jacob seven days later in the hill country of Gilead. [24]But the previous night God had appeared to Laban the Aramean in a dream and told him, "I'm warning you—leave Jacob alone!"

[25]Laban caught up with Jacob as he was camped in the hill country of Gilead, and he set up his camp not far from Jacob's. [26]"What do you mean by deceiving me like this?" Laban demanded. "How dare you drag my daughters away like prisoners of war? [27]Why did you slip away secretly? Why did you deceive me? And why didn't you say you wanted to leave? I would have given you a farewell feast, with singing and music, accompanied by tambourines and harps. [28]Why didn't you let me kiss my daughters and grandchildren and tell them good-bye? You have acted very foolishly! [29]I could destroy you, but the God of your father appeared to me last night and warned me, 'Leave Jacob alone!' [30]I can understand your feeling that you must go, and your intense longing for your father's home. But why have you stolen my gods?"

[31]"I rushed away because I was afraid," Jacob answered. "I thought you would take your daughters from me by force. [32]But as for your gods, see if you can find them, and let the person who has taken them die! And if you find anything else that belongs to you, identify it before all these relatives of ours, and I will give it back!" But Jacob did not know that Rachel had stolen the household idols.

[33]Laban went first into Jacob's tent to search there, then into Leah's, and then the tents of the two servant wives—but he found nothing. Finally, he went into Rachel's tent. [34]But Rachel had taken the household idols and hidden them in her camel saddle, and now she was sitting on them. When Laban had thoroughly searched her tent without finding them, [35]she said to her father, "Please, sir, forgive me if I don't get up for you. I'm having my monthly period." So Laban continued his search, but he could not find the household idols.

[36]Then Jacob became very angry, and he challenged Laban. "What's my crime?" he demanded. "What have I done wrong to make you chase after me as though I were a criminal? [37]You have rummaged through everything I own. Now show me what you found that belongs to you! Set it out here in front of us, before our relatives, for all to see. Let them judge between us!

[38]"For twenty years I have been with you, caring for your flocks. In all that time your sheep and goats never miscarried. In all those years I never used a

31:13 As in Greek version and an Aramaic Targum; Hebrew reads *the God of Bethel.* 31:21 Hebrew *the river.*

31:19-20 Rachel may have wanted to regain some of the assets Laban had squandered. Possessing the idols may have constituted a claim to family inheritance, as later customs indicate. It is also probable that she worshiped idols since Jacob had not yet committed to the Lord, Yahweh, alone (see 28:20-22; 35:2-4). Laban apparently felt vulnerable without the idols because he chased Jacob's company and drew attention to them in his accusations.

31:30-35 Rachel used her monthly period as an excuse not to stand when her father entered. Although we have no indication that Rachel was actually menstruating, her bleeding would have defiled the gods. Laban scarcely would have suspected she would profane the idols. Whether or not she was menstruating, she successfully deceived her deceitful father.

single ram of yours for food. ³⁹If any were attacked and killed by wild animals, I never showed you the carcass and asked you to reduce the count of your flock. No, I took the loss myself! You made me pay for every stolen animal, whether it was taken in broad daylight or in the dark of night.

⁴⁰"I worked for you through the scorching heat of the day and through cold and sleepless nights. ⁴¹Yes, for twenty years I slaved in your house! I worked for fourteen years earning your two daughters, and then six more years for your flock. And you changed my wages ten times! ⁴²In fact, if the God of my father had not been on my side—the God of Abraham and the fearsome God of Isaac*—you would have sent me away empty-handed. But God has seen your abuse and my hard work. That is why he appeared to you last night and rebuked you!"

## Jacob's Treaty with Laban

⁴³Then Laban replied to Jacob, "These women are my daughters, these children are my grandchildren, and these flocks are my flocks—in fact, everything you see is mine. But what can I do now about my daughters and their children? ⁴⁴So come, let's make a covenant, you and I, and it will be a witness to our commitment."

⁴⁵So Jacob took a stone and set it up as a monument. ⁴⁶Then he told his family members, "Gather some stones." So they gathered stones and piled them in a heap. Then Jacob and Laban sat down beside the pile of stones to eat a covenant meal. ⁴⁷To commemorate the event, Laban called the place Jegar-sahadutha (which means "witness pile" in Aramaic), and Jacob called it Galeed (which means "witness pile" in Hebrew).

⁴⁸Then Laban declared, "This pile of stones will stand as a witness to remind us of the covenant we have made today." This explains why it was called Galeed—"Witness Pile." ⁴⁹But it was also called Mizpah (which means "watchtower"), for Laban said, "May the LORD keep watch between us to make sure that we keep this covenant when we are out of each other's sight. ⁵⁰If you mistreat my daughters or if you marry other wives, God will see it even if no one else does. He is a witness to this covenant between us.

⁵¹"See this pile of stones," Laban continued, "and see this monument I have set between us. ⁵²They stand between us as witnesses of our vows. I will never pass this pile of stones to harm you, and you must never pass these stones or this monument to harm me. ⁵³I call on the God of our ancestors—the God of your grandfather Abraham and the God of my grandfather Nahor—to serve as a judge between us."

So Jacob took an oath before the fearsome God of his father, Isaac,* to respect the boundary line. ⁵⁴Then Jacob offered a sacrifice to God there on the mountain and invited everyone to a covenant feast. After they had eaten, they spent the night on the mountain.

⁵⁵*Laban got up early the next morning, and he kissed his grandchildren and his daughters and blessed them. Then he left and returned home.

32 ¹*As Jacob started on his way again, angels of God came to meet him. ²When Jacob saw them, he exclaimed, "This is God's camp!" So he named the place Mahanaim.*

## Jacob Sends Gifts to Esau

³Then Jacob sent messengers ahead to his brother, Esau, who was living in the region of Seir in the land of Edom. ⁴He told them, "Give this message to my master Esau: 'Humble greetings from your servant Jacob. Until now I have been living with Uncle Laban, ⁵and now I own cattle, donkeys, flocks of sheep and goats, and many servants, both men and women. I have sent these messengers to inform my lord of my coming, hoping that you will be friendly to me.'"

⁶After delivering the message, the messengers returned to Jacob and reported, "We met your brother, Esau, and he is already on his way to meet you—with an army of 400 men!" ⁷Jacob was terrified at the news. He divided his household, along with the flocks and herds and camels, into two groups. ⁸He thought, "If Esau meets one group and attacks it, perhaps the other group can escape."

⁹Then Jacob prayed, "O God of my grandfather Abraham, and God of my father, Isaac—O LORD, you told me, 'Return to your own land and to your relatives.' And you promised me, 'I will treat you kindly.' ¹⁰I am not worthy of all the unfailing love and faithfulness you have shown to me, your servant. When I left home and crossed the Jordan River, I owned nothing except a walking stick. Now my household fills two large camps! ¹¹O LORD, please rescue me from the hand of my brother, Esau. I am afraid that he is coming to attack me, along with my wives and children. ¹²But you promised me, 'I will surely treat you kindly, and I will multiply your descendants until they become as numerous as the sands along the seashore—too many to count.'"

¹³Jacob stayed where he was for the night. Then he selected these gifts from his possessions to present to his brother, Esau: ¹⁴200 female goats, 20 male goats, 200 ewes, 20 rams, ¹⁵30 female camels with their young, 40 cows, 10 bulls, 20 female donkeys,

31:42 Or *and the Fear of Isaac.*   31:53 Or *the Fear of his father, Isaac.*   31:55 Verse 31:55 is numbered 32:1 in Hebrew text.
32:1 Verses 32:1-32 are numbered 32:2-33 in Hebrew text.   32:2 *Mahanaim* means "two camps."

**32:1-32** God had revealed himself to Jacob as he left Canaan (28:10-22). Upon his return, Jacob saw angels and wrestled with a mysterious stranger at night. The stranger changed his name from Jacob ("heel grabber") to Israel ("fights with God" or "God fights"), indicating a divine encounter. Throughout his life, Jacob had seized God's blessing. This wrestling match symbolized his whole life. Jacob's prayer in 32:9-12 finally acknowledged his own weakness and need for God's protection.

and 10 male donkeys. [16]He divided these animals into herds and assigned each to different servants. Then he told his servants, "Go ahead of me with the animals, but keep some distance between the herds."

[17]He gave these instructions to the men leading the first group: "When my brother, Esau, meets you, he will ask, 'Whose servants are you? Where are you going? Who owns these animals?' [18]You must reply, 'They belong to your servant Jacob, but they are a gift for his master Esau. Look, he is coming right behind us.'"

[19]Jacob gave the same instructions to the second and third herdsmen and to all who followed behind the herds: "You must say the same thing to Esau when you meet him. [20]And be sure to say, 'Look, your servant Jacob is right behind us.'"

Jacob thought, "I will try to appease him by sending gifts ahead of me. When I see him in person, perhaps he will be friendly to me." [21]So the gifts were sent on ahead, while Jacob himself spent that night in the camp.

## Jacob Wrestles with God

[22]During the night Jacob got up and took his two wives, his two servant wives, and his eleven sons and crossed the Jabbok River with them. [23]After taking them to the other side, he sent over all his possessions.

[24]This left Jacob all alone in the camp, and a man came and wrestled with him until the dawn began to break. [25]When the man saw that he would not win the match, he touched Jacob's hip and wrenched it out of its socket. [26]Then the man said, "Let me go, for the dawn is breaking!"

But Jacob said, "I will not let you go unless you bless me."

[27]"What is your name?" the man asked.

He replied, "Jacob."

[28]"Your name will no longer be Jacob," the man told him. "From now on you will be called Israel,* because you have fought with God and with men and have won."

[29]"Please tell me your name," Jacob said.

"Why do you want to know my name?" the man replied. Then he blessed Jacob there.

[30]Jacob named the place Peniel (which means "face of God"), for he said, "I have seen God face to face, yet my life has been spared." [31]The sun was rising as Jacob left Peniel,* and he was limping because of the injury to his hip. [32](Even today the people of Israel don't eat the tendon near the hip socket because of what

happened that night when the man strained the tendon of Jacob's hip.)

## Jacob and Esau Make Peace

**33** Then Jacob looked up and saw Esau coming with his 400 men. So he divided the children among Leah, Rachel, and his two servant wives. [2]He put the servant wives and their children at the front, Leah and her children next, and Rachel and Joseph last. [3]Then Jacob went on ahead. As he approached his brother, he bowed to the ground seven times before him. [4]Then Esau ran to meet him and embraced him, threw his arms around his neck, and kissed him. And they both wept.

[5]Then Esau looked at the women and children and asked, "Who are these people with you?"

"These are the children God has graciously given to me, your servant," Jacob replied. [6]Then the servant wives came forward with their children and bowed before him. [7]Next came Leah with her children, and they bowed before him. Finally, Joseph and Rachel came forward and bowed before him.

[8]"And what were all the flocks and herds I met as I came?" Esau asked.

Jacob replied, "They are a gift, my lord, to ensure your friendship."

[9]"My brother, I have plenty," Esau answered. "Keep what you have for yourself."

[10]But Jacob insisted, "No, if I have found favor with you, please accept this gift from me. And what a relief to see your friendly smile. It is like seeing the face of God! [11]Please take this gift I have brought you, for God has been very gracious to me. I have more than enough." And because Jacob insisted, Esau finally accepted the gift.

[12]"Well," Esau said, "let's be going. I will lead the way."

[13]But Jacob replied, "You can see, my lord, that some of the children are very young, and the flocks and herds have their young, too. If they are driven too hard, even for one day, all the animals could die. [14]Please, my lord, go ahead of your servant. We will follow slowly, at a pace that is comfortable for the livestock and the children. I will meet you at Seir."

[15]"All right," Esau said, "but at least let me assign some of my men to guide and protect you."

Jacob responded, "That's not necessary. It's enough that you've received me warmly, my lord!"

[16]So Esau turned around and started back to Seir that same day. [17]Jacob, on the other hand, traveled on to Succoth. There he built himself a house and

---

**32:28** *Jacob* sounds like the Hebrew words for "heel" and "deceiver." *Israel* means "God fights."   **32:31** Hebrew *Penuel*, a variant spelling of Peniel.

---

**33:1-4** At first Jacob seems to be prioritizing his own safety over that of his wives and children by sending them ahead. However, as indicated in 33:3, he went ahead of all of them to meet Esau.

His encounter with the mysterious stranger and the blessing he received gave him the courage to face his fear. He had dreaded this encounter for the entire journey, but Esau forgave him.

# Insight    FAMILY TRAVELS THROUGH CANAAN

Jacob, Rachel and Leah, their servants, and their children journeyed across, around, and back through Canaan multiple times during their lifetimes. This map shows the routes they may have taken based on Genesis 32–38.

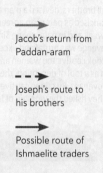

→ Jacob's return from Paddan-aram

--→ Joseph's route to his brothers

→ Possible route of Ishmaelite traders

made shelters for his livestock. That is why the place was named Succoth (which means "shelters"). ¹⁸Later, having traveled all the way from Paddan-aram, Jacob arrived safely at the town of Shechem, in the land of Canaan. There he set up camp outside the town. ¹⁹Jacob bought the plot of land where he camped from the family of Hamor, the father of Shechem, for 100 pieces of silver.* ²⁰And there he built an altar and named it El-Elohe-Israel.*

## Revenge against Shechem

**34** One day Dinah, the daughter of Jacob and Leah, went to visit some of the young women who lived in the area. ²But when the local

prince, Shechem son of Hamor the Hivite, saw Dinah, he seized her and raped her. ³But then he fell in love with her, and he tried to win her affection with tender words. ⁴He said to his father, Hamor, "Get me this young girl. I want to marry her."

⁵Soon Jacob heard that Shechem had defiled his daughter, Dinah. But since his sons were out in the fields herding his livestock, he said nothing until they returned. ⁶Hamor, Shechem's father, came to discuss the matter with Jacob. ⁷Meanwhile, Jacob's sons had come in from the field as soon as they heard what had happened. They were shocked and furious that their sister had been raped. Shechem had done a disgraceful thing against Jacob's family,* something that should never be done.

**33:19** Hebrew *100 kesitahs;* the value or weight of the kesitah is no longer known.  **33:20** *El-Elohe-Israel* means "God, the God of Israel."  **34:7** Hebrew *a disgraceful thing in Israel.*

**33:18-20** Jacob, like Abraham, built an altar to God at Shechem (see 12:6-7) and purchased land from local residents (23:1-20). Jacob's return to the land God promised to Abraham initiated the beginning of the next stage of covenant fulfillment.
**34:1-31** The narrative includes few tales of Jacob's sons in Canaan. This tragic story is important because it illustrates the depravity of the Canaanites and explains the animosity between Jacob's sons and their neighbors. It also characterizes Levi and Simeon as violent (see 49:5-7) and Jacob as passive in his old age.

**34:1-2** If Dinah's visit to the local women was unwise, the narrator does not suggest it, and she is not faulted for what she wore or what she said. The blame falls squarely on Shechem for violating Dinah. "Consent" in those days was primarily given by the men whose job it was to protect the women of their family, and Shechem had not sought Jacob's permission to wed. Instead, like Adam and Eve in the Garden of Eden, Shechem saw what he wanted and seized it—in this case, Dinah.

[8]Hamor tried to speak with Jacob and his sons. "My son Shechem is truly in love with your daughter," he said. "Please let him marry her. [9]In fact, let's arrange other marriages, too. You give us your daughters for our sons, and we will give you our daughters for your sons. [10]And you may live among us; the land is open to you! Settle here and trade with us. And feel free to buy property in the area."

[11]Then Shechem himself spoke to Dinah's father and brothers. "Please be kind to me, and let him marry her," he begged. "I will give you whatever you ask. [12]No matter what dowry or gift you demand, I will gladly pay it—just give me the girl as my wife."

[13]But since Shechem had defiled their sister, Dinah, Jacob's sons responded deceitfully to Shechem and his father, Hamor. [14]They said to them, "We couldn't possibly allow this, because you're not circumcised. It would be a disgrace for our sister to marry a man like you! [15]But here is a solution. If every man among you will be circumcised like we are, [16]then we will give you our daughters, and we'll take your daughters for ourselves. We will live among you and become one people. [17]But if you don't agree to be circumcised, we will take her and be on our way."

[18]Hamor and his son Shechem agreed to their proposal. [19]Shechem wasted no time in acting on this request, for he wanted Jacob's daughter desperately. Shechem was a highly respected member of his family, [20]and he went with his father, Hamor, to present this proposal to the leaders at the town gate.

---

**34:8-12** After sexually violating Dinah, Shechem kept her (34:26) while trying to get permission to marry her. His father, Hamor, saw intermarriage as a means to gain control of Jacob's wealth (34:10, 23), but God had promised to give Jacob the land (28:13-15). Intermarriage with the Canaanites would have jeopardized the integrity of the covenant family (24:1-8; 28:1-4). **34:13-31** Without waiting for their father to respond, Simeon and Levi, Dinah's full brothers, devised a plan to get revenge. Having been circumcised as part of an agreement, the men of Shechem were weak and in pain, giving Simeon and Levi the advantage. Their revenge was brutal and excessive. They killed every man and took captive the women and children. By using circumcision as a tool of deception, they showed disdain for the sign of the covenant. By taking captive Canaanites into their community, they risked the worship of idols.

---

## ⑧ Come Close — VIOLATED: THE REAL "FIX"

### SCRIPTURE CONNECTION: GENESIS 34:1-4

The Bible does not mention anyone talking to Dinah about what had happened or how she felt. Was she hurt, afraid, ashamed, angry, or blaming herself? How did she feel as she saw the destruction that followed? Did she feel more shame, pain, or fear?

I know these feelings, the raw emotions of a rape survivor. My father didn't know how to react and did nothing—just like Jacob. My siblings were angry and wanted to remedy the situation—just like Dinah's brothers. People wanted to fix things so they could move on but looked past me, busying themselves with action. I needed peace in my soul to calm the rage, uncertainty, shame, hurt, and fear.

The night after, feeling so completely alone in a room full of people, John 14:27 hovered around my raging thoughts—peace, *not* as the world gives; *not* fixing, but peace.

I felt a hand on my heart, a palpable blanket of peace—covering, warm, quiet, unexplainable, undefinable, life-affirming.

**REFLECT** "I am leaving you with a gift—peace of mind and heart. And the peace I give is a gift the world cannot give." JOHN 14:27

*Jesus, help me to trust you to give me what I really need—your peace. Amen.*

**CONSIDER** "Whenever his hand is laid upon you, it gives inexpressible peace and comfort, and the sense that 'underneath are the everlasting arms' (Deuteronomy 33:27), full of support, provision, comfort, and strength." OSWALD CHAMBERS, *My Utmost for His Highest.*

### Jesus gives you peace unlike anything this world has to offer.

ELISABETH SELZER ROGERS, MDiv, MA, PhD, is a passionate believer and follower of Christ, bringing his love to the secular world through mentoring, coaching, and modeling his unconditional love.

²¹"These men are our friends," they said. "Let's invite them to live here among us and trade freely. Look, the land is large enough to hold them. We can take their daughters as wives and let them marry ours. ²²But they will consider staying here and becoming one people with us only if all of our men are circumcised, just as they are. ²³But if we do this, all their livestock and possessions will eventually be ours. Come, let's agree to their terms and let them settle here among us."

²⁴So all the men in the town council agreed with Hamor and Shechem, and every male in the town was circumcised. ²⁵But three days later, when their wounds were still sore, two of Jacob's sons, Simeon and Levi, who were Dinah's full brothers, took their swords and entered the town without opposition. Then they slaughtered every male there, ²⁶including Hamor and his son Shechem. They killed them with their swords, then took Dinah from Shechem's house and returned to their camp.

²⁷Meanwhile, the rest of Jacob's sons arrived. Finding the men slaughtered, they plundered the town because their sister had been defiled there. ²⁸They seized all the flocks and herds and donkeys—everything they could lay their hands on, both inside the town and outside in the fields. ²⁹They looted all their wealth and plundered their houses. They also took all their little children and wives and led them away as captives.

³⁰Afterward Jacob said to Simeon and Levi, "You have ruined me! You've made me stink among all the people of this land—among all the Canaanites and Perizzites. We are so few that they will join forces and crush us. I will be ruined, and my entire household will be wiped out!"

³¹"But why should we let him treat our sister like a prostitute?" they retorted angrily.

## Jacob's Return to Bethel

**35** Then God said to Jacob, "Get ready and move to Bethel and settle there. Build an altar there to the God who appeared to you when you fled from your brother, Esau."

²So Jacob told everyone in his household, "Get rid of all your pagan idols, purify yourselves, and put on clean clothing. ³We are now going to Bethel, where I will build an altar to the God who answered my prayers when I was in distress. He has been with me wherever I have gone."

⁴So they gave Jacob all their pagan idols and earrings, and he buried them under the great tree near Shechem. ⁵As they set out, a terror from God spread over the people in all the towns of that area, so no one attacked Jacob's family.

⁶Eventually, Jacob and his household arrived at Luz (also called Bethel) in Canaan. ⁷Jacob built an altar there and named the place El-bethel (which means "God of Bethel"), because God had appeared to him there when he was fleeing from his brother, Esau.

⁸Soon after this, Rebekah's old nurse, Deborah, died. She was buried beneath the oak tree in the valley below Bethel. Ever since, the tree has been called Allon-bacuth (which means "oak of weeping").

⁹Now that Jacob had returned from Paddan-aram, God appeared to him again at Bethel. God blessed him, ¹⁰saying, "Your name is Jacob, but you will not be called Jacob any longer. From now on your name will be Israel."* So God renamed him Israel.

¹¹Then God said, "I am El-Shaddai—'God Almighty.' Be fruitful and multiply. You will become a great nation, even many nations. Kings will be among your descendants! ¹²And I will give you the land I once gave to Abraham and Isaac. Yes, I will give it to you and your descendants after you." ¹³Then God went up from the place where he had spoken to Jacob.

¹⁴Jacob set up a stone pillar to mark the place where God had spoken to him. Then he poured wine over it as an offering to God and anointed the pillar with olive oil. ¹⁵And Jacob named the place Bethel (which means "house of God"), because God had spoken to him there.

## The Deaths of Rachel and Isaac

¹⁶Leaving Bethel, Jacob and his clan moved on toward Ephrath. But Rachel went into labor while they were still some distance away. Her labor pains were intense. ¹⁷After a very hard delivery, the midwife finally exclaimed, "Don't be afraid—you have another son!" ¹⁸Rachel was about to die, but with her last breath she named the baby Ben-oni (which means "son of my sorrow"). The baby's father, however, called him Benjamin (which means "son of my right hand"). ¹⁹So Rachel died and was buried on the way to Ephrath (that is, Bethlehem). ²⁰Jacob set up a stone monument over Rachel's grave, and it can be seen there to this day.

²¹Then Jacob* traveled on and camped beyond

**35:10** *Jacob* sounds like the Hebrew words for "heel" and "deceiver." *Israel* means "God fights." **35:21** Hebrew *Israel;* also in 35:22a. The names "Jacob" and "Israel" are often interchanged throughout the Old Testament, referring sometimes to the individual patriarch and sometimes to the nation.

**35:1-15** Jacob had not committed himself exclusively to the God of Abraham until now. (Note his conditional worship in 28:20-22.) Here he vowed wholehearted devotion to God, requiring his family to destroy their idols. In response, God reiterated the creation blessing ("be fruitful and multiply," see 1:28) and his promise of fame and land.

**35:16-20** Benjamin's birth completed the family, but Rachel died in childbirth. Rachel found the name "son of my sorrow" appropriate, but Jacob changed it to "son of my right hand." Jacob thus turned the day of sorrow into a day of hope. The tribe of Benjamin later inherited the land where Rachel was buried (see Joshua 18:21-28).

Migdal-eder. ²²While he was living there, Reuben had intercourse with Bilhah, his father's concubine, and Jacob soon heard about it.

These are the names of the twelve sons of Jacob:

²³The sons of Leah were Reuben (Jacob's oldest son), Simeon, Levi, Judah, Issachar, and Zebulun.
²⁴The sons of Rachel were Joseph and Benjamin.
²⁵The sons of Bilhah, Rachel's servant, were Dan and Naphtali.
²⁶The sons of Zilpah, Leah's servant, were Gad and Asher.

These are the names of the sons who were born to Jacob at Paddan-aram.

²⁷So Jacob returned to his father, Isaac, in Mamre, which is near Kiriath-arba (now called Hebron), where Abraham and Isaac had both lived as foreigners. ²⁸Isaac lived for 180 years. ²⁹Then he breathed his last and died at a ripe old age, joining his ancestors in death. And his sons, Esau and Jacob, buried him.

## Descendants of Esau

**36** This is the account of the descendants of Esau (also known as Edom). ²Esau married two young women from Canaan: Adah, the daughter of Elon the Hittite; and Oholibamah, the daughter of Anah and granddaughter of Zibeon the Hivite. ³He also married his cousin Basemath, who was the daughter of Ishmael and the sister of Nebaioth. ⁴Adah gave birth to a son named Eliphaz for Esau. Basemath gave birth to a son named Reuel. ⁵Oholibamah gave birth to sons named Jeush, Jalam, and Korah. All these sons were born to Esau in the land of Canaan.

⁶Esau took his wives, his children, and his entire household, along with his livestock and cattle—all the wealth he had acquired in the land of Canaan—and moved away from his brother, Jacob. ⁷There was not enough land to support them both because of all the livestock and possessions they had acquired. ⁸So Esau (also known as Edom) settled in the hill country of Seir.

⁹This is the account of Esau's descendants, the Edomites, who lived in the hill country of Seir.

¹⁰These are the names of Esau's sons: Eliphaz, the son of Esau's wife Adah; and Reuel, the son of Esau's wife Basemath. ¹¹The descendants of Eliphaz were Teman, Omar, Zepho, Gatam, and Kenaz. ¹²Timna, the concubine of Esau's son Eliphaz, gave birth to a son named Amalek. These are the descendants of Esau's wife Adah.

¹³The descendants of Reuel were Nahath, Zerah, Shammah, and Mizzah. These are the descendants of Esau's wife Basemath.

¹⁴Esau also had sons through Oholibamah, the daughter of Anah and granddaughter of Zibeon. Their names were Jeush, Jalam, and Korah.

¹⁵These are the descendants of Esau who became the leaders of various clans:

The descendants of Esau's oldest son, Eliphaz, became the leaders of the clans of Teman, Omar, Zepho, Kenaz, ¹⁶Korah, Gatam, and Amalek. These are the clan leaders in the land of Edom who descended from Eliphaz. All these were descendants of Esau's wife Adah.

¹⁷The descendants of Esau's son Reuel became the leaders of the clans of Nahath, Zerah, Shammah, and Mizzah. These are the clan leaders in the land of Edom who descended from Reuel. All these were descendants of Esau's wife Basemath.

¹⁸The descendants of Esau and his wife Oholibamah became the leaders of the clans of Jeush, Jalam, and Korah. These are the clan leaders who descended from Esau's wife Oholibamah, the daughter of Anah.

¹⁹These are the clans descended from Esau (also known as Edom), identified by their clan leaders.

## Original Peoples of Edom

²⁰These are the names of the tribes that descended from Seir the Horite. They lived in the land of Edom: Lotan, Shobal, Zibeon, Anah, ²¹Dishon, Ezer, and Dishan. These were the Horite clan leaders, the descendants of Seir, who lived in the land of Edom.

²²The descendants of Lotan were Hori and Hemam. Lotan's sister was named Timna.
²³The descendants of Shobal were Alvan, Manahath, Ebal, Shepho, and Onam.
²⁴The descendants of Zibeon were Aiah and Anah. (This is the Anah who discovered the hot springs in the wilderness while he was grazing his father's donkeys.)
²⁵The descendants of Anah were his son, Dishon, and his daughter, Oholibamah.
²⁶The descendants of Dishon* were Hemdan, Eshban, Ithran, and Keran.

36:26 Hebrew *Dishan*, a variant spelling of Dishon; compare 36:21, 28.

**35:22** The sexual exploitation of women was frighteningly common in ancient times, as it is today. Reuben had sex with Bilhah, thus defiling his father's marriage bed. Perhaps Reuben, as the oldest son, was trying to replace his father as head of the clan (see 2 Samuel 16:15-22), but by this action he lost his birthright (see Genesis 49:3-4).
**35:23-26** The sons of Jacob appear in the order in which their mothers were intimate with Jacob. The result is a chiasm (literary sandwich), with Rachel's favored children in the center—Leah, Rachel, Bilhah, Zilpah. The last sentence is a generalization—Benjamin was born after they left Paddan-aram (35:16-18).
**36:1-43** The careful record of Esau's line shows God's continuing concern for those who were not part of the covenant family. It reminds us of God's purpose to bless all nations through Abraham and Sarah's family.

²⁷The descendants of Ezer were Bilhan, Zaavan, and Akan.

²⁸The descendants of Dishan were Uz and Aran.

²⁹So these were the leaders of the Horite clans: Lotan, Shobal, Zibeon, Anah, ³⁰Dishon, Ezer, and Dishan. The Horite clans are named after their clan leaders, who lived in the land of Seir.

## Rulers of Edom

³¹These are the kings who ruled in the land of Edom before any king ruled over the Israelites*:

³²Bela son of Beor, who ruled in Edom from his city of Dinhabah.

³³When Bela died, Jobab son of Zerah from Bozrah became king in his place.

³⁴When Jobab died, Husham from the land of the Temanites became king in his place.

³⁵When Husham died, Hadad son of Bedad became king in his place and ruled from the city of Avith. He was the one who defeated the Midianites in the land of Moab.

³⁶When Hadad died, Samlah from the city of Masrekah became king in his place.

³⁷When Samlah died, Shaul from the city of Rehoboth-on-the-River became king in his place.

³⁸When Shaul died, Baal-hanan son of Acbor became king in his place.

³⁹When Baal-hanan son of Acbor died, Hadad* became king in his place and ruled from the city of Pau. His wife was Mehetabel, the daughter of Matred and granddaughter of Me-zahab.

⁴⁰These are the names of the leaders of the clans descended from Esau, who lived in the places named for them: Timna, Alvah, Jetheth, ⁴¹Oholibamah, Elah, Pinon, ⁴²Kenaz, Teman, Mibzar, ⁴³Magdiel, and Iram. These are the leaders of the clans of Edom, listed according to their settlements in the land they occupied. They all descended from Esau, the ancestor of the Edomites.

## Joseph's Dreams

**37** So Jacob settled again in the land of Canaan, where his father had lived as a foreigner.

²This is the account of Jacob and his family. When Joseph was seventeen years old, he often tended his father's flocks. He worked for his half brothers, the sons of his father's wives Bilhah and Zilpah. But Joseph reported to his father some of the bad things his brothers were doing.

³Jacob* loved Joseph more than any of his other children because Joseph had been born to him in his old age. So one day Jacob had a special gift made for Joseph—a beautiful robe.* ⁴But his brothers hated Joseph because their father loved him more than the rest of them. They couldn't say a kind word to him.

⁵One night Joseph had a dream, and when he told his brothers about it, they hated him more than ever. ⁶"Listen to this dream," he said. ⁷"We were out in the field, tying up bundles of grain. Suddenly my bundle stood up, and your bundles all gathered around and bowed low before mine!"

⁸His brothers responded, "So you think you will be our king, do you? Do you actually think you will reign over us?" And they hated him all the more because of his dreams and the way he talked about them.

⁹Soon Joseph had another dream, and again he told his brothers about it. "Listen, I have had another dream," he said. "The sun, moon, and eleven stars bowed low before me!"

¹⁰This time he told the dream to his father as well as to his brothers, but his father scolded him. "What kind of dream is that?" he asked. "Will your mother and I and your brothers actually come and bow to the ground before you?" ¹¹But while his brothers were jealous of Joseph, his father wondered what the dreams meant.

¹²Soon after this, Joseph's brothers went to pasture their father's flocks at Shechem. ¹³When they had been gone for some time, Jacob said to Joseph, "Your brothers are pasturing the sheep at Shechem. Get ready, and I will send you to them."

"I'm ready to go," Joseph replied.

¹⁴"Go and see how your brothers and the flocks are getting along," Jacob said. "Then come back and bring me a report." So Jacob sent him on his way, and Joseph traveled to Shechem from their home in the valley of Hebron.

¹⁵When he arrived there, a man from the area noticed him wandering around the countryside. "What are you looking for?" he asked.

¹⁶"I'm looking for my brothers," Joseph replied. "Do you know where they are pasturing their sheep?"

¹⁷"Yes," the man told him. "They have moved on from here, but I heard them say, 'Let's go on to Dothan.'" So Joseph followed his brothers to Dothan and found them there.

**36:31** Or *before an Israelite king ruled over them.* **36:39** As in some Hebrew manuscripts, Samaritan Pentateuch, and Syriac version (see also 1 Chr 1:50); most Hebrew manuscripts read *Hadar.* **37:3a** Hebrew *Israel;* also in 37:13. See note on 35:21. **37:3b** Traditionally rendered *a coat of many colors.* The exact meaning of the Hebrew is uncertain.

**37:1–50:26** The Joseph saga is an important episode in the history of God's covenant people. Historians consider it one of the oldest novellas in the world, with brilliant character development and gripping dialogue. Joseph exhibited wisdom, faithfulness, and trust in God despite great suffering. God rewarded him with wealth, honor, and a family of his own. His wisdom ensured survival for both the Egyptians and his extended family during a severe famine.

**37:4** Jacob's favoritism toward Joseph inflamed his other sons' hatred. Just as Isaac's and Rebekah's favoritism separated their family, Jacob's favoritism would separate him from his son Joseph.

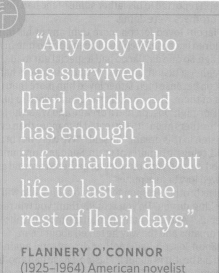

"Anybody who
has survived
[her] childhood
has enough
information about
life to last ... the
rest of [her] days."

**FLANNERY O'CONNOR**
(1925–1964) American novelist
and Christian

## Joseph Sold into Slavery

<sup>18</sup>When Joseph's brothers saw him coming, they recognized him in the distance. As he approached, they made plans to kill him. <sup>19</sup>"Here comes the dreamer!" they said. <sup>20</sup>"Come on, let's kill him and throw him into one of these cisterns. We can tell our father, 'A wild animal has eaten him.' Then we'll see what becomes of his dreams!"

<sup>21</sup>But when Reuben heard of their scheme, he came to Joseph's rescue. "Let's not kill him," he said. <sup>22</sup>"Why should we shed any blood? Let's just throw him into this empty cistern here in the wilderness. Then he'll die without our laying a hand on him." Reuben was secretly planning to rescue Joseph and return him to his father.

<sup>23</sup>So when Joseph arrived, his brothers ripped off the beautiful robe he was wearing. <sup>24</sup>Then they grabbed him and threw him into the cistern. Now the cistern was empty; there was no water in it. <sup>25</sup>Then, just as they were sitting down to eat, they looked up and saw a caravan of camels in the distance coming toward them. It was a group of Ishmaelite traders taking a load of gum, balm, and aromatic resin from Gilead down to Egypt.

<sup>26</sup>Judah said to his brothers, "What will we gain by killing our brother? We'd have to cover up the crime.* <sup>27</sup>Instead of hurting him, let's sell him to those Ishmaelite traders. After all, he is our brother—our own flesh and blood!" And his brothers agreed. <sup>28</sup>So when the Ishmaelites, who were Midianite traders, came by, Joseph's brothers pulled him out of the cistern and sold him to them for twenty pieces* of silver. And the traders took him to Egypt.

<sup>29</sup>Some time later, Reuben returned to get Joseph out of the cistern. When he discovered that Joseph was missing, he tore his clothes in grief. <sup>30</sup>Then he went back to his brothers and lamented, "The boy is gone! What will I do now?"

<sup>31</sup>Then the brothers killed a young goat and dipped Joseph's robe in its blood. <sup>32</sup>They sent the beautiful robe to their father with this message: "Look at what we found. Doesn't this robe belong to your son?"

<sup>33</sup>Their father recognized it immediately. "Yes," he said, "it is my son's robe. A wild animal must have eaten him. Joseph has clearly been torn to pieces!" <sup>34</sup>Then Jacob tore his clothes and dressed himself in burlap. He mourned deeply for his son for a long time. <sup>35</sup>His family all tried to comfort him, but he refused to be comforted. "I will go to my grave* mourning for my son," he would say, and then he would weep.

<sup>36</sup>Meanwhile, the Midianite traders* arrived in Egypt, where they sold Joseph to Potiphar, an officer of Pharaoh, the king of Egypt. Potiphar was captain of the palace guard.

## Judah and Tamar

**38** About this time, Judah left home and moved to Adullam, where he stayed with a man named Hirah. <sup>2</sup>There he saw a Canaanite woman, the daughter of Shua, and he married her. When he slept with her, <sup>3</sup>she became pregnant and gave birth to a son, and he named the boy Er. <sup>4</sup>Then she became pregnant again and gave birth to another son, and she named him Onan. <sup>5</sup>And when she gave birth to a third son, she named him Shelah. At the time of Shelah's birth, they were living at Kezib.

<sup>6</sup>In the course of time, Judah arranged for his firstborn son, Er, to marry a young woman named Tamar. <sup>7</sup>But Er was a wicked man in the LORD's sight, so the LORD took his life. <sup>8</sup>Then Judah said to Er's brother Onan, "Go and marry Tamar, as our law requires of the brother of a man who has died. You must produce an heir for your brother."

**37:26** Hebrew *cover his blood.*  **37:28** Hebrew *20 [shekels],* about 8 ounces or 228 grams in weight.  **37:35** Hebrew *go down to Sheol.*
**37:36** Hebrew *the Medanites.* The relationship between the Midianites and Medanites is unclear; compare 37:28. See also 25:2.

**37:25** The Ishmaelite traders carried spices to Egypt for embalming. From Jacob's perspective, his son had already died. Ironically, Genesis ends with Joseph embalmed in a coffin in Egypt (50:26), but his sojourn there gave life. Through it, God preserved Joseph's life and the lives of his brothers and their families.
**38:1-30** This story may seem like a random interruption to the Joseph saga, but it provides a crucial piece of the story—Judah's

character transformation. It had been Judah's idea to sell his brother Joseph into slavery, a move to profit from his disappearance (37:26-27). His claim to care about his brother in 37:27 rings hollow. However, by the end of the saga, Judah had offered himself to be enslaved in place of his brother Benjamin (44:30-34).
**38:8-10** This custom is known as levirate marriage (from the

⁹But Onan was not willing to have a child who would not be his own heir. So whenever he had intercourse with his brother's wife, he spilled the semen on the ground. This prevented her from having a child who would belong to his brother. ¹⁰But the LORD considered it evil for Onan to deny a child to his dead brother. So the LORD took Onan's life, too.

¹¹Then Judah said to Tamar, his daughter-in-law, "Go back to your parents' home and remain a widow until my son Shelah is old enough to marry you." (But Judah didn't really intend to do this because he was afraid Shelah would also die, like his two brothers.) So Tamar went back to live in her father's home.

Latin *levir*, "husband's brother"). If a man died childless, his brother or nearest relative was to marry his widow to produce a child to carry on the family name of the deceased and inherit his property (see Deuteronomy 25:5-10). The practice also provided a secure home for the childless widow. Onan demonstrated selfishness by using Tamar for sex while ensuring she would not get pregnant. God refused to tolerate this abuse.

**38:11** Judah promised to give Tamar to his third son, Shelah, when he was ready to marry, but by sending her to her family, he proved unwilling to provide for her.

## Oikos
**IMAGE** — MY STORY WITH FAMILY & FRIENDS

## No Perfect Family

SCRIPTURE CONNECTION: GENESIS 38:1-30

If you're worried your family disqualifies you from serving God's purposes, you don't have to look far in the Bible to see families just as raw and flawed as yours. Families made of real people with real issues give hope that God doesn't just use the put-together and polished to move his purposes forward. He uses all of us just as we are.

Here are three things I've learned from families in Genesis that help me live my purpose with my own family:

> There are no perfect families. Only real ones. Loved ones.

- Conflicts don't have to define families. Abram told Lot, "Let's not allow this conflict to come between us or our herdsmen. After all, we are close relatives!" (13:8). With intentional conversation we can put differences aside.
- God fills in when I can't meet my children's needs. Hagar thought she was leaving her son to die, but she discovered otherwise. "God heard the boy crying, and the angel of God called to Hagar from heaven, . . . 'Go to him and comfort him, for I will make a great nation from his descendants'" (21:17-18).
- Honoring one another gains rewards—and truth comes out. After deception on the part of both Judah and his daughter-in-law, Tamar, Judah said, "She is more righteous than I am" (38:26). Family relationships help to highlight our true character.

My family, like Bible families, is made up of imperfect people. We fail each other, but that doesn't disqualify us from God's plan. If he can use the real problems of these real families, he can use me in mine.

### IMAGINE

What do you observe about families and conflict in your experiences?

How can your family's pain points bring God glory?

*"Every family has pain that God can use to further his purposes in the world. We might not see it yet, but he can redeem any family drama."*

ALEXANDRA KUYKENDALL is a cofounder of The Open Door Sisterhood and author of several books, including *Seeking Out Goodness: Finding the True and Beautiful All around You.*

¹²Some years later Judah's wife died. After the time of mourning was over, Judah and his friend Hirah the Adullamite went up to Timnah to supervise the shearing of his sheep. ¹³Someone told Tamar, "Look, your father-in-law is going up to Timnah to shear his sheep."

¹⁴Tamar was aware that Shelah had grown up, but no arrangements had been made for her to come and marry him. So she changed out of her widow's clothing and covered herself with a veil to disguise herself. Then she sat beside the road at the entrance to the village of Enaim, which is on the road to Timnah. ¹⁵Judah noticed her and thought she was a prostitute, since she had covered her face. ¹⁶So he stopped and propositioned her. "Let me have sex with you," he said, not realizing that she was his own daughter-in-law.

"How much will you pay to have sex with me?" Tamar asked.

¹⁷"I'll send you a young goat from my flock," Judah promised.

"But what will you give me to guarantee that you will send the goat?" she asked.

¹⁸"What kind of guarantee do you want?" he replied.

She answered, "Leave me your identification seal and its cord and the walking stick you are carrying." So Judah gave them to her. Then he had intercourse with her, and she became pregnant. ¹⁹Afterward she went back home, took off her veil, and put on her widow's clothing as usual.

²⁰Later Judah asked his friend Hirah the Adullamite to take the young goat to the woman and to pick up the things he had given her as his guarantee. But Hirah couldn't find her. ²¹So he asked the men who lived there, "Where can I find the shrine prostitute who was sitting beside the road at the entrance to Enaim?"

"We've never had a shrine prostitute here," they replied.

²²So Hirah returned to Judah and told him, "I couldn't find her anywhere, and the men of the village claim they've never had a shrine prostitute there."

²³"Then let her keep the things I gave her," Judah said. "I sent the young goat as we agreed, but you couldn't find her. We'd be the laughingstock of the village if we went back again to look for her."

²⁴About three months later, Judah was told, "Tamar, your daughter-in-law, has acted like a prostitute. And now, because of this, she's pregnant."

"Bring her out, and let her be burned!" Judah demanded.

²⁵But as they were taking her out to kill her, she sent this message to her father-in-law: "The man who owns these things made me pregnant. Look closely. Whose seal and cord and walking stick are these?"

²⁶Judah recognized them immediately and said, "She is more righteous than I am, because I didn't arrange for her to marry my son Shelah." And Judah never slept with Tamar again.

²⁷When the time came for Tamar to give birth, it was discovered that she was carrying twins. ²⁸While she was in labor, one of the babies reached out his hand. The midwife grabbed it and tied a scarlet string around the child's wrist, announcing, "This one came out first." ²⁹But then he pulled back his hand, and out came his brother! "What!" the midwife exclaimed. "How did you break out first?" So he was named Perez.* ³⁰Then the baby with the scarlet string on his wrist was born, and he was named Zerah.*

## Joseph in Potiphar's House

**39** When Joseph was taken to Egypt by the Ishmaelite traders, he was purchased by Potiphar, an Egyptian officer. Potiphar was captain of the guard for Pharaoh, the king of Egypt.

²The LORD was with Joseph, so he succeeded in everything he did as he served in the home of his Egyptian master. ³Potiphar noticed this and realized that the LORD was with Joseph, giving him success in everything he did. ⁴This pleased Potiphar, so he soon made Joseph his personal attendant. He put him in charge of his entire household and everything he owned. ⁵From the day Joseph was put in charge of his master's household and property, the LORD began to bless Potiphar's household for Joseph's sake. All his household affairs ran smoothly, and his crops and livestock flourished. ⁶So Potiphar gave Joseph complete administrative responsibility over everything he owned. With Joseph there, he didn't worry about a thing—except what kind of food to eat!

Joseph was a very handsome and well-built young

---

38:29 *Perez* means "breaking out."   38:30 *Zerah* means "scarlet" or "brightness."

---

**38:12-24** When Tamar saw that Judah had not kept his promise or fulfilled his responsibility as the closest male relative to marry her himself, she took matters into her own hands. She disguised herself and propositioned him, not out of lust or revenge, but out of duty to carry on his family line (see Judah's response in 38:26). Her plan worked, and she became pregnant with twins. The purpose of the story is not to hold up Tamar's actions as a model but to highlight Judah's hypocrisy. He would pay for what he thought was a prostitute but condemn Tamar for prostitution, all the while failing to provide for her.
**38:25-26** Tamar became the great(times five)-grandmother of Boaz, who was the great-grandfather of King David (see Ruth

4:18-22). Her action led to the preservation of the tribe through which Israel's kings would come. At the story's climax, Tamar identified Judah as the father of her children. Rather than dismiss her charges, Judah acknowledged his wrongdoing. In the end, we see how this incident transformed his character. God can do remarkable things with those who acknowledge their sin and repent.
**39:6-18** Back-to-back with the story of Judah and Tamar is another tale of power and sex. However, this time the woman had suffered no legal wrong. Potiphar's wife, unfaithful to her husband and mastered by lust, used constant pressure and physical force to try to seduce Joseph. When she failed, she lied to destroy his reputation.

# Tamar

**IDENTITY** — ## Rewarded Anyway

*Tamar remembers …*

Sometimes it's hard to know what is right. But I believe God works for our good, like banks that direct a rushing river.

My first husband, Er, was an evil man. When he died, the law said that his next brother, Onan, was to give me an heir. He refused to fulfill that responsibility. But God saw him and caused Onan to die, too.

I thought I could rely on my father-in-law, Judah. He promised me his last son, though I would have to wait for him to come of age. It was all a lie.

When I saw an opportunity to make things right, I took it. I held Judah accountable to conceive an heir. I felt I had no other options. Judah had all the power, and I had none. So, I tricked him into obedience.

Judah realized what he did was even worse. He called me "more righteous" (38:26). More important than Judah's praise, God rewarded my desire to follow him. In time, my name would appear in the Messiah's family tree (Matthew 1:3).

Some say my action also changed Judah's heart. He acknowledged that he had failed to provide for a vulnerable woman in his family. He changed from the Judah who had sold one brother (Joseph) into slavery, to the Judah who risked his life to protect another brother (Benjamin). God redeemed not just one family, but all.

God created a way that brings life. Like banks of a rushing river, his Kingdom current rushes forward. Responding in faith, even imperfectly, can lead to reward.

> Responding to God in faith, even imperfectly, can lead to reward.

TAMAR'S STORY IS TOLD IN GENESIS 38.

## IDENTIFY

How does Tamar's story encourage us to respond in faith, even if we aren't sure how?

*"Watching others break rules to protect themselves is disheartening. I know, though, that God's ways are like the banks of a river. They keep back the flood of sin and push his Kingdom forward in a strong current of accountability and responsibility."*

CARA DAY is a writer and illustrator. She has served with Stonecroft Ministries helping women live "extraordinary."

man, [7]and Potiphar's wife soon began to look at him lustfully. "Come and sleep with me," she demanded.

[8]But Joseph refused. "Look," he told her, "my master trusts me with everything in his entire household. [9]No one here has more authority than I do. He has held back nothing from me except you, because you are his wife. How could I do such a wicked thing? It would be a great sin against God."

[10]She kept putting pressure on Joseph day after day, but he refused to sleep with her, and he kept out of her way as much as possible. [11]One day, however, no one else was around when he went in to do his work. [12]She came and grabbed him by his cloak, demanding, "Come on, sleep with me!" Joseph tore himself away, but he left his cloak in her hand as he ran from the house.

[13]When she saw that she was holding his cloak and he had fled, [14]she called out to her servants. Soon all the men came running. "Look!" she said. "My husband has brought this Hebrew slave here to make fools of us! He came into my room to rape me, but I screamed. [15]When he heard me scream, he ran outside and got away, but he left his cloak behind with me."

[16]She kept the cloak with her until her husband came home. [17]Then she told him her story. "That Hebrew slave you've brought into our house tried to come in and fool around with me," she said. [18]"But when I screamed, he ran outside, leaving his cloak with me!"

## Joseph Put in Prison

[19]Potiphar was furious when he heard his wife's story about how Joseph had treated her. [20]So he took Joseph and threw him into the prison where the

---

# ⑧ Come Close  LUST: NOTICE WHEN YOU NOTICE

**SCRIPTURE CONNECTION: GENESIS 39:1-20**

Our church service was beginning. I was about twelve years old. An older gentleman entered with three very handsome young men. My friend could not help herself.

"Oooh," she said loudly. We laughed about it for weeks.

I'm betting Potiphar's wife murmured something to a handmaiden when Joseph entered her home. According to 39:6, "Joseph was a very handsome and well-built young man." She noticed. We notice. But noticing is not where it stopped. She "soon began to look at him lustfully" (39:7).

It always starts with noticing. The eyes, the smile, the build, the laugh, the kindness, or the instant connection. Something is noticed. This should be our first warning.

Joseph was in Potiphar's home for quite some time. That meant Potiphar's wife had time for second looks, innocent-seeming interactions, and excuses to catch him alone. Each moment was likely replayed in her mind.

The noticing became lusting.

Lust is a hungry monster that demands more. "One more look," it whispers. "Surely you have a reason to talk to him," it suggests. It will not stop until it has you crossing the line it wants you to. And across that line is always the ruin of someone's life.

Joseph got thrown into jail. Marriages fester. Families erode.

We will notice. It is what we do next that matters.

**REFLECT** "Potiphar's wife soon began to look at him lustfully." GENESIS 39:7

*Lord, when I "notice," please help me, like Joseph, take immediate action to notice you noticing and flee from temptation. Amen.*

**CONSIDER** "When something is awakened in us by another man . . . we do have a choice in that moment. We choose to accept the awakening as an invitation to go find that with *our* man. . . . Or to pray, if we are single, that this sort of man . . . will come to us from God's hand" STASI AND JOHN ELDREDGE, *Captivating.*

Notice when you notice. It's what you do next that matters.

CARA DAY is a writer and illustrator. She has served with Stonecroft Ministries helping women live "extraordinary."

king's prisoners were held, and there he remained. [21]But the LORD was with Joseph in the prison and showed him his faithful love. And the LORD made Joseph a favorite with the prison warden. [22]Before long, the warden put Joseph in charge of all the other prisoners and over everything that happened in the prison. [23]The warden had no more worries, because Joseph took care of everything. The LORD was with him and caused everything he did to succeed.

## Joseph Interprets Two Dreams

**40** Some time later, Pharaoh's chief cup-bearer and chief baker offended their royal master. [2]Pharaoh became angry with these two officials, [3]and he put them in the prison where Joseph was, in the palace of the captain of the guard. [4]They remained in prison for quite some time, and the captain of the guard assigned them to Joseph, who looked after them.

[5]While they were in prison, Pharaoh's cup-bearer and baker each had a dream one night, and each dream had its own meaning. [6]When Joseph saw them the next morning, he noticed that they both looked upset. [7]"Why do you look so worried today?" he asked them.

[8]And they replied, "We both had dreams last night, but no one can tell us what they mean."

"Interpreting dreams is God's business," Joseph replied. "Go ahead and tell me your dreams."

[9]So the chief cup-bearer told Joseph his dream first. "In my dream," he said, "I saw a grapevine in front of me. [10]The vine had three branches that began to bud and blossom, and soon it produced clusters of ripe grapes. [11]I was holding Pharaoh's wine cup in my hand, so I took a cluster of grapes and squeezed the juice into the cup. Then I placed the cup in Pharaoh's hand."

[12]"This is what the dream means," Joseph said. "The three branches represent three days. [13]Within three days Pharaoh will lift you up and restore you to your position as his chief cup-bearer. [14]And please remember me and do me a favor when things go well for you. Mention me to Pharaoh, so he might let me out of this place. [15]For I was kidnapped from my homeland, the land of the Hebrews, and now I'm here in prison, but I did nothing to deserve it."

[16]When the chief baker saw that Joseph had given the first dream such a positive interpretation, he said to Joseph, "I had a dream, too. In my dream there were three baskets of white pastries stacked on my head. [17]The top basket contained all kinds of pastries for Pharaoh, but the birds came and ate them from the basket on my head."

[18]"This is what the dream means," Joseph told him. "The three baskets also represent three days. [19]Three days from now Pharaoh will lift you up and impale your body on a pole. Then birds will come and peck away at your flesh."

[20]Pharaoh's birthday came three days later, and he prepared a banquet for all his officials and staff. He summoned* his chief cup-bearer and chief baker to join the other officials. [21]He then restored the chief cup-bearer to his former position, so he could again hand Pharaoh his cup. [22]But Pharaoh impaled the chief baker, just as Joseph had predicted when he interpreted his dream. [23]Pharaoh's chief cup-bearer, however, forgot all about Joseph, never giving him another thought.

## Pharaoh's Dreams

**41** Two full years later, Pharaoh dreamed that he was standing on the bank of the Nile River. [2]In his dream he saw seven fat, healthy cows come up out of the river and begin grazing in the marsh grass. [3]Then he saw seven more cows come up behind them from the Nile, but these were scrawny and thin. These cows stood beside the fat cows on the riverbank. [4]Then the scrawny, thin cows ate the seven healthy, fat cows! At this point in the dream, Pharaoh woke up.

[5]But he fell asleep again and had a second dream. This time he saw seven heads of grain, plump and beautiful, growing on a single stalk. [6]Then seven more heads of grain appeared, but these were shriveled and withered by the east wind. [7]And these thin heads swallowed up the seven plump, well-formed heads! Then Pharaoh woke up again and realized it was a dream.

[8]The next morning Pharaoh was very disturbed by the dreams. So he called for all the magicians and wise men of Egypt. When Pharaoh told them his dreams, not one of them could tell him what they meant.

[9]Finally, the king's chief cup-bearer spoke up. "Today I have been reminded of my failure," he told Pharaoh. [10]"Some time ago, you were angry with the chief baker and me, and you imprisoned us in the palace of the captain of the guard. [11]One night the chief baker and I each had a dream, and each dream had its own meaning. [12]There was a young Hebrew man

40:20 Hebrew *He lifted up the head of.*

---

**39:19-23** In spite of false accusations resulting in Joseph's imprisonment, God was with Joseph and made him prosper. The warden soon noticed his administrative skills and put him in charge. As in Potiphar's household, Joseph excelled in his work because he was diligent, skilled, and trustworthy.
**40:1-22** Joseph did not lose faith in God's promises. Joseph's own dreams had not been fulfilled (37:5-11), but his readiness

to interpret others' dreams (40:8) shows that he had not abandoned hope in divine revelation.
**40:23–41:32** The cupbearer forgot Joseph (40:23), but God did not. Soon Pharaoh asked Joseph to interpret a dream. By honoring God as the one who could help Pharaoh understand his dreams, Joseph encouraged Pharaoh to trust God (41:16).

with us in the prison who was a slave of the captain of the guard. We told him our dreams, and he told us what each of our dreams meant. ¹³And everything happened just as he had predicted. I was restored to my position as cup-bearer, and the chief baker was executed and impaled on a pole."

¹⁴Pharaoh sent for Joseph at once, and he was quickly brought from the prison. After he shaved and changed his clothes, he went in and stood before Pharaoh. ¹⁵Then Pharaoh said to Joseph, "I had a dream last night, and no one here can tell me what it means. But I have heard that when you hear about a dream you can interpret it."

¹⁶"It is beyond my power to do this," Joseph replied. "But God can tell you what it means and set you at ease."

¹⁷So Pharaoh told Joseph his dream. "In my dream," he said, "I was standing on the bank of the Nile River, ¹⁸and I saw seven fat, healthy cows come up out of the river and begin grazing in the marsh grass. ¹⁹But then I saw seven sick-looking cows, scrawny and thin, come up after them. I've never seen such sorry-looking animals in all the land of Egypt. ²⁰These thin, scrawny cows ate the seven fat cows. ²¹But afterward you wouldn't have known it, for they were still as thin and scrawny as before! Then I woke up.

²²"In my dream I also saw seven heads of grain, full and beautiful, growing on a single stalk. ²³Then seven more heads of grain appeared, but these were blighted, shriveled, and withered by the east wind. ²⁴And the shriveled heads swallowed the seven healthy heads. I told these dreams to the magicians, but no one could tell me what they mean."

²⁵Joseph responded, "Both of Pharaoh's dreams mean the same thing. God is telling Pharaoh in advance what he is about to do. ²⁶The seven healthy cows and the seven healthy heads of grain both represent seven years of prosperity. ²⁷The seven thin, scrawny cows that came up later and the seven thin heads of grain, withered by the east wind, represent seven years of famine.

²⁸"This will happen just as I have described it, for God has revealed to Pharaoh in advance what he is about to do. ²⁹The next seven years will be a period of great prosperity throughout the land of Egypt. ³⁰But afterward there will be seven years of famine so great that all the prosperity will be forgotten in Egypt. Famine will destroy the land. ³¹This famine will be so severe that even the memory of the good years will be erased. ³²As for having two similar dreams, it means that these events have been decreed by God, and he will soon make them happen.

³³"Therefore, Pharaoh should find an intelligent and wise man and put him in charge of the entire land of Egypt. ³⁴Then Pharaoh should appoint supervisors over the land and let them collect one-fifth of all the crops during the seven good years. ³⁵Have them gather all the food produced in the good years that are just ahead and bring it to Pharaoh's storehouses. Store it away, and guard it so there will be food in the cities. ³⁶That way there will be enough to eat when the seven years of famine come to the land of Egypt. Otherwise this famine will destroy the land."

## Joseph Made Ruler of Egypt

³⁷Joseph's suggestions were well received by Pharaoh and his officials. ³⁸So Pharaoh asked his officials, "Can we find anyone else like this man so obviously filled with the spirit of God?" ³⁹Then Pharaoh said to Joseph, "Since God has revealed the meaning of the dreams to you, clearly no one else is as intelligent or wise as you are. ⁴⁰You will be in charge of my court, and all my people will take orders from you. Only I, sitting on my throne, will have a rank higher than yours."

⁴¹Pharaoh said to Joseph, "I hereby put you in charge of the entire land of Egypt." ⁴²Then Pharaoh removed his signet ring from his hand and placed it on Joseph's finger. He dressed him in fine linen clothing and hung a gold chain around his neck. ⁴³Then he had Joseph ride in the chariot reserved for his second-in-command. And wherever Joseph went, the command was shouted, "Kneel down!" So Pharaoh put Joseph in charge of all Egypt. ⁴⁴And Pharaoh said to him, "I am Pharaoh, but no one will lift a hand or foot in the entire land of Egypt without your approval."

⁴⁵Then Pharaoh gave Joseph a new Egyptian name, Zaphenath-paneah.* He also gave him a wife, whose name was Asenath. She was the daughter of Potiphera, the priest of On.* So Joseph took charge of the entire land of Egypt. ⁴⁶He was thirty years old when he began serving in the court of Pharaoh, the king of Egypt. And when Joseph left Pharaoh's presence, he inspected the entire land of Egypt.

⁴⁷As predicted, for seven years the land produced bumper crops. ⁴⁸During those years, Joseph gathered all the crops grown in Egypt and stored the grain from the surrounding fields in the cities. ⁴⁹He piled up huge amounts of grain like sand on the seashore. Finally, he stopped keeping records because there was too much to measure.

⁵⁰During this time, before the first of the famine years, two sons were born to Joseph and his wife, Asenath, the daughter of Potiphera, the priest of On. ⁵¹Joseph named his older son Manasseh,* for he

---

**41:45a** *Zaphenath-paneah* probably means "God speaks and lives." **41:45b** Greek version reads *of Heliopolis;* also in 41:50.
**41:51** *Manasseh* sounds like a Hebrew term that means "causing to forget."

---

**41:33-49** Joseph's wisdom in managing national resources during a famine blessed not just Egypt but also surrounding nations. During Joseph's tenure, God's promise to bless all nations through Abraham's descendants began to be fulfilled (12:1-3). The mention of grain "like sand on the seashore" (41:49) evokes God's promise to Abraham (22:17).

said, "God has made me forget all my troubles and everyone in my father's family." [52] Joseph named his second son Ephraim,* for he said, "God has made me fruitful in this land of my grief."

[53] At last the seven years of bumper crops throughout the land of Egypt came to an end. [54] Then the seven years of famine began, just as Joseph had predicted. The famine also struck all the surrounding countries, but throughout Egypt there was plenty of food. [55] Eventually, however, the famine spread throughout the land of Egypt as well. And when the people cried out to Pharaoh for food, he told them, "Go to Joseph, and do whatever he tells you." [56] So with severe famine everywhere, Joseph opened up the storehouses and distributed grain to the Egyptians, for the famine was severe throughout the land of Egypt. [57] And people from all around came to Egypt to buy grain from Joseph because the famine was severe throughout the world.

## Joseph's Brothers Go to Egypt

42 When Jacob heard that grain was available in Egypt, he said to his sons, "Why are you standing around looking at one another? [2] I have heard there is grain in Egypt. Go down there, and buy enough grain to keep us alive. Otherwise we'll die."

[3] So Joseph's ten older brothers went down to Egypt to buy grain. [4] But Jacob wouldn't let Joseph's younger brother, Benjamin, go with them, for fear some harm might come to him. [5] So Jacob's* sons arrived in Egypt along with others to buy food, for the famine was in Canaan as well.

[6] Since Joseph was governor of all Egypt and in charge of selling grain to all the people, it was to him that his brothers came. When they arrived, they bowed before him with their faces to the ground. [7] Joseph recognized his brothers instantly, but he pretended to be a stranger and spoke harshly to them. "Where are you from?" he demanded.

"From the land of Canaan," they replied. "We have come to buy food."

[8] Although Joseph recognized his brothers, they didn't recognize him. [9] And he remembered the dreams he'd had about them many years before. He said to them, "You are spies! You have come to see how vulnerable our land has become."

[10] "No, my lord!" they exclaimed. "Your servants have simply come to buy food. [11] We are all brothers—members of the same family. We are honest men, sir! We are not spies!"

[12] "Yes, you are!" Joseph insisted. "You have come to see how vulnerable our land has become."

[13] "Sir," they said, "there are actually twelve of us. We, your servants, are all brothers, sons of a man living in the land of Canaan. Our youngest brother is back there with our father right now, and one of our brothers is no longer with us."

[14] But Joseph insisted, "As I said, you are spies! [15] This is how I will test your story. I swear by the life of Pharaoh that you will never leave Egypt unless your youngest brother comes here! [16] One of you must go and get your brother. I'll keep the rest of you here in prison. Then we'll find out whether or not your story is true. By the life of Pharaoh, if it turns out that you don't have a younger brother, then I'll know you are spies."

[17] So Joseph put them all in prison for three days. [18] On the third day Joseph said to them, "I am a God-fearing man. If you do as I say, you will live. [19] If you really are honest men, choose one of your brothers to remain in prison. The rest of you may go home with grain for your starving families. [20] But you must bring your youngest brother back to me. This will prove that you are telling the truth, and you will not die." To this they agreed.

[21] Speaking among themselves, they said, "Clearly we are being punished because of what we did to Joseph long ago. We saw his anguish when he pleaded for his life, but we wouldn't listen. That's why we're in this trouble."

[22] "Didn't I tell you not to sin against the boy?" Reuben asked. "But you wouldn't listen. And now we have to answer for his blood!"

[23] Of course, they didn't know that Joseph understood them, for he had been speaking to them through an interpreter. [24] Now he turned away from them and began to weep. When he regained his composure, he spoke to them again. Then he chose Simeon from among them and had him tied up right before their eyes.

[25] Joseph then ordered his servants to fill the men's sacks with grain, but he also gave secret instructions to return each brother's payment at the top of his

---

41:52 *Ephraim* sounds like a Hebrew term that means "fruitful." 42:5 Hebrew *Israel's.* See note on 35:21.

---

**41:50-52** Joseph enjoyed immense success in Egypt, but his sons' names hint at his sorrow. When he named his son Ephraim, he called Egypt the "land of my grief" (41:52). Ironically, by naming his son Manasseh and declaring "God has made me forget all my troubles and everyone in my father's family," he indicated that he had not forgotten at all. He wanted to forget, but his deepest longing was to be reconciled. His strong emotional reaction to his brothers later in the story made this clear (42:24; 43:30; 45:1-15).
**42:6-9** Joseph's brothers bowed to him, which fulfilled the dreams he had experienced as a boy (37:5-11). He proceeded to test them to discern whether their hearts had changed

since selling him into slavery. The brothers had considered Joseph a spy for their father and had treated him roughly (37:2, 14, 18-28). Joseph put them in a similar situation to see how they would respond.
**42:21-28** Since Joseph spoke to his brothers through a translator, he could listen to them discuss their predicament. They clearly regretted how they had treated Joseph. However, Joseph wanted to see more than regret. He wanted evidence of transformation. By requiring them to return with Benjamin, their father's other favorite son, he would see if the brothers had overcome their tendency to be jealous.

# Work

## We Work and Rest Following God's Rhythms

God blessed the seventh day and declared it holy, because it was the day when he rested from all his work of creation. GENESIS 2:3

You have six days each week for your ordinary work, but the seventh day must be a Sabbath day of complete rest, a holy day dedicated to the LORD. EXODUS 35:2

For all who have entered into God's rest have rested from their labors, just as God did after creating the world. HEBREWS 4:10

## We Work for the Real Boss

Work willingly at whatever you do, as though you were working for the Lord rather than for people. Remember that the Lord will give you an inheritance as your reward, and that the Master you are serving is Christ. COLOSSIANS 3:23-24

## Work Justly

Do not make your hired workers wait until the next day to receive their pay. LEVITICUS 19:13

As workers who tend a fig tree are allowed to eat the fruit, so workers who protect their employer's interests will be rewarded. PROVERBS 27:18

# Work willingly at whatever you do ...

# She is energetic and strong

## Get Skilled

You have expert goldsmiths and silversmiths and workers of bronze and iron. Now begin the work, and may the LORD be with you!
1 CHRONICLES 22:16

Do you see any truly competent workers? They will serve kings rather than working for ordinary people.
PROVERBS 22:29

## Our First "Job Description"

God blessed them and said, "Be fruitful and multiply. Fill the earth and govern it. Reign over the fish in the sea, the birds in the sky, and all the animals that scurry along the ground."
GENESIS 1:28

The LORD God placed the man in the Garden of Eden to tend and watch over it. GENESIS 2:15

## A Prayer for Our Work

May the Lord our God show us his approval and make our efforts successful. Yes, make our efforts successful!
PSALM 90:17

## Work Hard

Lazy people are soon poor; hard workers get rich.
PROVERBS 10:4

A little extra sleep, a little more slumber, a little folding of the hands to rest—then poverty will pounce on you like a bandit; scarcity will attack you like an armed robber.
PROVERBS 24:33-34

She is energetic and strong, a hard worker. PROVERBS 31:17

## How We Work Matters More Than Where We Work

Work willingly at whatever you do, as though you were working for the Lord rather than for people. Remember that the Lord will give you an inheritance as your reward, and that the Master you are serving is Christ. COLOSSIANS 3:23-24

Make it your goal to live a quiet life, minding your own business and working with your hands, just as we instructed you before. Then people who are not believers will respect the way you live, and you will not need to depend on others.
1 THESSALONIANS 4:11-12

sack. He also gave them supplies for their journey home. ²⁶So the brothers loaded their donkeys with the grain and headed for home.

²⁷But when they stopped for the night and one of them opened his sack to get grain for his donkey, he found his money in the top of his sack. ²⁸"Look!" he exclaimed to his brothers. "My money has been returned; it's here in my sack!" Then their hearts sank. Trembling, they said to each other, "What has God done to us?"

²⁹When the brothers came to their father, Jacob, in the land of Canaan, they told him everything that had happened to them. ³⁰"The man who is governor of the land spoke very harshly to us," they told him. "He accused us of being spies scouting the land. ³¹But we said, 'We are honest men, not spies. ³²We are twelve brothers, sons of one father. One brother is no longer with us, and the youngest is at home with our father in the land of Canaan.'

³³"Then the man who is governor of the land told us, 'This is how I will find out if you are honest men. Leave one of your brothers here with me, and take grain for your starving families and go on home. ³⁴But you must bring your youngest brother back to me. Then I will know you are honest men and not spies. Then I will give you back your brother, and you may trade freely in the land.'"

³⁵As they emptied out their sacks, there in each man's sack was the bag of money he had paid for the grain! The brothers and their father were terrified when they saw the bags of money. ³⁶Jacob exclaimed, "You are robbing me of my children! Joseph is gone! Simeon is gone! And now you want to take Benjamin, too. Everything is going against me!"

³⁷Then Reuben said to his father, "You may kill my two sons if I don't bring Benjamin back to you. I'll be responsible for him, and I promise to bring him back."

³⁸But Jacob replied, "My son will not go down with you. His brother Joseph is dead, and he is all I have left. If anything should happen to him on your journey, you would send this grieving, white-haired man to his grave.*"

## The Brothers Return to Egypt

**43** But the famine continued to ravage the land of Canaan. ²When the grain they had brought from Egypt was almost gone, Jacob said to his sons, "Go back and buy us a little more food."

³But Judah said, "The man was serious when he warned us, 'You won't see my face again unless your brother is with you.' ⁴If you send Benjamin with us, we will go down and buy more food. ⁵But if you don't let Benjamin go, we won't go either. Remember, the man said, 'You won't see my face again unless your brother is with you.'"

⁶"Why were you so cruel to me?" Jacob* moaned. "Why did you tell him you had another brother?"

⁷"The man kept asking us questions about our family," they replied. "He asked, 'Is your father still alive? Do you have another brother?' So we answered his questions. How could we know he would say, 'Bring your brother down here'?"

⁸Judah said to his father, "Send the boy with me, and we will be on our way. Otherwise we will all die of starvation—and not only we, but you and our little ones. ⁹I personally guarantee his safety. You may hold me responsible if I don't bring him back to you. Then let me bear the blame forever. ¹⁰If we hadn't wasted all this time, we could have gone and returned twice by now."

¹¹So their father, Jacob, finally said to them, "If it can't be avoided, then at least do this. Pack your bags with the best products of this land. Take them down to the man as gifts—balm, honey, gum, aromatic resin, pistachio nuts, and almonds. ¹²Also take double the money that was put back in your sacks, as it was probably someone's mistake. ¹³Then take your brother, and go back to the man. ¹⁴May God Almighty* give you mercy as you go before the man, so that he will release Simeon and let Benjamin return. But if I must lose my children, so be it."

¹⁵So the men packed Jacob's gifts and double the money and headed off with Benjamin. They finally arrived in Egypt and presented themselves to Joseph. ¹⁶When Joseph saw Benjamin with them, he said to the manager of his household, "These men will eat with me this noon. Take them inside the palace. Then go slaughter an animal, and prepare a big feast." ¹⁷So the man did as Joseph told him and took them into Joseph's palace.

¹⁸The brothers were terrified when they saw that they were being taken into Joseph's house. "It's because of the money someone put in our sacks last time we were here," they said. "He plans to pretend that we stole it. Then he will seize us, make us slaves, and take our donkeys."

---

42:38 Hebrew *to Sheol.* 43:6 Hebrew *Israel;* also in 43:11. See note on 35:21. 43:14 Hebrew *El-Shaddai.*

---

**42:36-38** Jacob made it clear that losing Benjamin would be more than he could bear. Reuben was the first to take responsibility for Benjamin, though he offered his sons' lives rather than his own. His bargain exhibits a rather twisted logic that reminds us of Lot (19:8).

**43:9** Judah demonstrated his change of heart by offering to take personal responsibility for Benjamin. He already knew what it felt like to carry the guilt for a lost brother. His offer was serious.

**43:15—45:28** The brothers were terrified that they would be accused of stealing money, but Joseph and his household manager treated them kindly. Their relief turned to terror when Joseph's silver cup was found in Benjamin's sack. Joseph was testing them to see whether they would sacrifice themselves to prevent Benjamin's enslavement. Judah immediately stepped forward and offered himself instead of Benjamin, proving he had truly changed. Joseph revealed his identity, forgave his brothers, and invited them to move to Egypt to survive the famine.

## A Feast at Joseph's Palace

[19]The brothers approached the manager of Joseph's household and spoke to him at the entrance to the palace. [20]"Sir," they said, "we came to Egypt once before to buy food. [21]But as we were returning home, we stopped for the night and opened our sacks. Then we discovered that each man's money—the exact amount paid—was in the top of his sack! Here it is; we have brought it back with us. [22]We also have additional money to buy more food. We have no idea who put our money in our sacks."

[23]"Relax. Don't be afraid," the household manager told them. "Your God, the God of your father, must have put this treasure into your sacks. I know I received your payment." Then he released Simeon and brought him out to them.

[24]The manager then led the men into Joseph's palace. He gave them water to wash their feet and provided food for their donkeys. [25]They were told they would be eating there, so they prepared their gifts for Joseph's arrival at noon.

[26]When Joseph came home, they gave him the gifts they had brought him, then bowed low to the ground before him. [27]After greeting them, he asked, "How is your father, the old man you spoke about? Is he still alive?"

[28]"Yes," they replied. "Our father, your servant, is alive and well." And they bowed low again.

[29]Then Joseph looked at his brother Benjamin, the son of his own mother. "Is this your youngest brother, the one you told me about?" Joseph asked. "May God be gracious to you, my son." [30]Then Joseph hurried from the room because he was overcome with emotion for his brother. He went into his private room, where he broke down and wept. [31]After washing his face, he came back out, keeping himself under control. Then he ordered, "Bring out the food!"

[32]The waiters served Joseph at his own table, and his brothers were served at a separate table. The Egyptians who ate with Joseph sat at their own table, because Egyptians despise Hebrews and refuse to eat with them. [33]Joseph told each of his brothers where to sit, and to their amazement, he seated them according to age, from oldest to youngest. [34]And Joseph filled their plates with food from his own table, giving Benjamin five times as much as he gave the others. So they feasted and drank freely with him.

## Joseph's Silver Cup

44 When his brothers were ready to leave, Joseph gave these instructions to his palace manager: "Fill each of their sacks with as much grain as they can carry, and put each man's money back into his sack. [2]Then put my personal silver cup at the top of the youngest brother's sack, along with the money for his grain." So the manager did as Joseph instructed him.

[3]The brothers were up at dawn and were sent on their journey with their loaded donkeys. [4]But when they had gone only a short distance and were barely out of the city, Joseph said to his palace manager, "Chase after them and stop them. When you catch up with them, ask them, 'Why have you repaid my kindness with such evil? [5]Why have you stolen my master's silver cup,* which he uses to predict the future? What a wicked thing you have done!'"

[6]When the palace manager caught up with the men, he spoke to them as he had been instructed.

[7]"What are you talking about?" the brothers responded. "We are your servants and would never do such a thing! [8]Didn't we return the money we found in our sacks? We brought it back all the way from the land of Canaan. Why would we steal silver or gold from your master's house? [9]If you find his cup with any one of us, let that man die. And all the rest of us, my lord, will be your slaves."

[10]"That's fair," the man replied. "But only the one who stole the cup will be my slave. The rest of you may go free."

[11]They all quickly took their sacks from the backs of their donkeys and opened them. [12]The palace manager searched the brothers' sacks, from the oldest to the youngest. And the cup was found in Benjamin's sack! [13]When the brothers saw this, they tore their clothing in despair. Then they loaded their donkeys again and returned to the city.

[14]Joseph was still in his palace when Judah and his brothers arrived, and they fell to the ground before him. [15]"What have you done?" Joseph demanded. "Don't you know that a man like me can predict the future?"

[16]Judah answered, "Oh, my lord, what can we say to you? How can we explain this? How can we prove our innocence? God is punishing us for our sins. My lord, we have all returned to be your slaves—all of us, not just our brother who had your cup in his sack."

[17]"No," Joseph said. "I would never do such a thing! Only the man who stole the cup will be my slave. The rest of you may go back to your father in peace."

## Judah Speaks for His Brothers

[18]Then Judah stepped forward and said, "Please, my lord, let your servant say just one word to you. Please, do not be angry with me, even though you are as powerful as Pharaoh himself.

[19]"My lord, previously you asked us, your servants, 'Do you have a father or a brother?' [20]And we responded, 'Yes, my lord, we have a father who is an old man, and his youngest son is a child of his old age. His full brother is dead, and he alone is left of his mother's children, and his father loves him very much.'

[21]"And you said to us, 'Bring him here so I can see him with my own eyes.' [22]But we said to you, 'My lord, the boy cannot leave his father, for his father would

44:5 As in Greek version; Hebrew lacks this phrase.

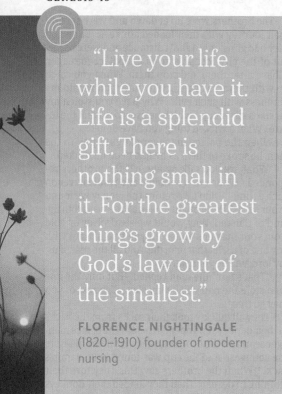

> "Live your life while you have it. Life is a splendid gift. There is nothing small in it. For the greatest things grow by God's law out of the smallest."
>
> FLORENCE NIGHTINGALE
> (1820–1910) founder of modern nursing

die.' ²³But you told us, 'Unless your youngest brother comes with you, you will never see my face again.'

²⁴"So we returned to your servant, our father, and told him what you had said. ²⁵Later, when he said, 'Go back again and buy us more food,' ²⁶we replied, 'We can't go unless you let our youngest brother go with us. We'll never get to see the man's face unless our youngest brother is with us.'

²⁷"Then my father said to us, 'As you know, my wife had two sons, ²⁸and one of them went away and never returned. Doubtless he was torn to pieces by some wild animal. I have never seen him since. ²⁹Now if you take his brother away from me, and any harm comes to him, you will send this grieving, white-haired man to his grave.*'

³⁰"And now, my lord, I cannot go back to my father without the boy. Our father's life is bound up in the boy's life. ³¹If he sees that the boy is not with us, our father will die. We, your servants, will indeed be responsible for sending that grieving, white-haired man to his grave. ³²My lord, I guaranteed to my father that I would take care of the boy. I told him, 'If I don't bring him back to you, I will bear the blame forever.'

³³"So please, my lord, let me stay here as a slave instead of the boy, and let the boy return with his brothers. ³⁴For how can I return to my father if the

boy is not with me? I couldn't bear to see the anguish this would cause my father!"

## Joseph Reveals His Identity

**45** Joseph could stand it no longer. There were many people in the room, and he said to his attendants, "Out, all of you!" So he was alone with his brothers when he told them who he was. ²Then he broke down and wept. He wept so loudly the Egyptians could hear him, and word of it quickly carried to Pharaoh's palace.

³"I am Joseph!" he said to his brothers. "Is my father still alive?" But his brothers were speechless! They were stunned to realize that Joseph was standing there in front of them. ⁴"Please, come closer," he said to them. So they came closer. And he said again, "I am Joseph, your brother, whom you sold into slavery in Egypt. ⁵But don't be upset, and don't be angry with yourselves for selling me to this place. It was God who sent me here ahead of you to preserve your lives. ⁶This famine that has ravaged the land for two years will last five more years, and there will be neither plowing nor harvesting. ⁷God has sent me ahead of you to keep you and your families alive and to preserve many survivors.* ⁸So it was God who sent me here, not you! And he is the one who made me an adviser* to Pharaoh—the manager of his entire palace and the governor of all Egypt.

⁹"Now hurry back to my father and tell him, 'This is what your son Joseph says: God has made me master over all the land of Egypt. So come down to me immediately! ¹⁰You can live in the region of Goshen, where you can be near me with all your children and grandchildren, your flocks and herds, and everything you own. ¹¹I will take care of you there, for there are still five years of famine ahead of us. Otherwise you, your household, and all your animals will starve.'"

¹²Then Joseph added, "Look! You can see for yourselves, and so can my brother Benjamin, that I really am Joseph! ¹³Go tell my father of my honored position here in Egypt. Describe for him everything you have seen, and then bring my father here quickly." ¹⁴Weeping with joy, he embraced Benjamin, and Benjamin did the same. ¹⁵Then Joseph kissed each of his brothers and wept over them, and after that they began talking freely with him.

## Pharaoh Invites Jacob to Egypt

¹⁶The news soon reached Pharaoh's palace: "Joseph's brothers have arrived!" Pharaoh and his officials were all delighted to hear this.

¹⁷Pharaoh said to Joseph, "Tell your brothers, 'This is what you must do: Load your pack animals, and hurry back to the land of Canaan. ¹⁸Then get your father and all of your families, and return here to

44:29 Hebrew *to Sheol;* also in 44:31. 45:7 Or *and to save you with an extraordinary rescue.* The meaning of the Hebrew is uncertain. 45:8 Hebrew *a father.*

me. I will give you the very best land in Egypt, and you will eat from the best that the land produces.'"

¹⁹Then Pharaoh said to Joseph, "Tell your brothers, 'Take wagons from the land of Egypt to carry your little children and your wives, and bring your father here. ²⁰Don't worry about your personal belongings, for the best of all the land of Egypt is yours.'"

²¹So the sons of Jacob* did as they were told. Joseph provided them with wagons, as Pharaoh had commanded, and he gave them supplies for the journey. ²²And he gave each of them new clothes—but to Benjamin he gave five changes of clothes and 300 pieces* of silver. ²³He also sent his father ten male donkeys loaded with the finest products of Egypt, and ten female donkeys loaded with grain and bread and other supplies he would need on his journey.

²⁴So Joseph sent his brothers off, and as they left, he called after them, "Don't quarrel about all this along the way!" ²⁵And they left Egypt and returned to their father, Jacob, in the land of Canaan.

²⁶"Joseph is still alive!" they told him. "And he is governor of all the land of Egypt!" Jacob was stunned at the news—he couldn't believe it. ²⁷But when they repeated to Jacob everything Joseph had told them, and when he saw the wagons Joseph had sent to carry him, their father's spirits revived.

²⁸Then Jacob exclaimed, "It must be true! My son Joseph is alive! I must go and see him before I die."

## Jacob's Journey to Egypt

46 So Jacob* set out for Egypt with all his possessions. And when he came to Beersheba, he offered sacrifices to the God of his father, Isaac. ²During the night God spoke to him in a vision. "Jacob! Jacob!" he called.

"Here I am," Jacob replied.

³"I am God,* the God of your father," the voice said. "Do not be afraid to go down to Egypt, for there I will make your family into a great nation. ⁴I will go with you down to Egypt, and I will bring you back again. You will die in Egypt, but Joseph will be with you to close your eyes."

⁵So Jacob left Beersheba, and his sons took him to Egypt. They carried him and their little ones and their wives in the wagons Pharaoh had provided for them. ⁶They also took all their livestock and all the personal belongings they had acquired in the land of Canaan. So Jacob and his entire family went to Egypt—⁷sons and grandsons, daughters and granddaughters—all his descendants.

⁸These are the names of the descendants of Israel—the sons of Jacob—who went to Egypt:

Reuben was Jacob's oldest son. ⁹The sons of Reuben were Hanoch, Pallu, Hezron, and Carmi. ¹⁰The sons of Simeon were Jemuel, Jamin, Ohad, Jakin, Zohar, and Shaul. (Shaul's mother was a Canaanite woman.) ¹¹The sons of Levi were Gershon, Kohath, and Merari. ¹²The sons of Judah were Er, Onan, Shelah, Perez, and Zerah (though Er and Onan had died in the land of Canaan). The sons of Perez were Hezron and Hamul. ¹³The sons of Issachar were Tola, Puah,* Jashub,* and Shimron. ¹⁴The sons of Zebulun were Sered, Elon, and Jahleel. ¹⁵These were the sons of Leah and Jacob who were born in Paddan-aram, in addition to their daughter, Dinah. The number of Jacob's descendants (male and female) through Leah was thirty-three.

¹⁶The sons of Gad were Zephon,* Haggi, Shuni, Ezbon, Eri, Arodi, and Areli. ¹⁷The sons of Asher were Imnah, Ishvah, Ishvi, and Beriah. Their sister was Serah. Beriah's sons were Heber and Malkiel. ¹⁸These were the sons of Zilpah, the servant given to Leah by her father, Laban. The number of Jacob's descendants through Zilpah was sixteen.

¹⁹The sons of Jacob's wife Rachel were Joseph and Benjamin. ²⁰Joseph's sons, born in the land of Egypt, were Manasseh and Ephraim. Their mother was Asenath, daughter of Potiphera, the priest of On.* ²¹Benjamin's sons were Bela, Beker, Ashbel, Gera, Naaman, Ehi, Rosh, Muppim, Huppim, and Ard. ²²These were the sons of Rachel and Jacob. The number of Jacob's descendants through Rachel was fourteen.

²³The son of Dan was Hushim. ²⁴The sons of Naphtali were Jahzeel, Guni, Jezer, and Shillem. ²⁵These were the sons of Bilhah, the servant given to Rachel by her father, Laban. The number of Jacob's descendants through Bilhah was seven.

²⁶The total number of Jacob's direct descendants who went with him to Egypt, not counting his sons' wives, was sixty-six. ²⁷In addition, Joseph had two sons* who were born in Egypt. So altogether, there were seventy* members of Jacob's family in the land of Egypt.

---

45:21 Hebrew *Israel;* also in 45:28. See note on 35:21.  45:22 Hebrew *300 [shekels],* about 7.5 pounds or 3.4 kilograms in weight. 46:1 Hebrew *Israel;* also in 46:29, 30. See note on 35:21.  46:3 Hebrew *I am El.*  46:13a As in Syriac version and Samaritan Pentateuch (see also 1 Chr 7:1); Hebrew reads *Puvah.*  46:13b As in some Greek manuscripts and Samaritan Pentateuch (see also Num 26:24; 1 Chr 7:1); Hebrew reads *Iob.*  46:16 As in Greek version and Samaritan Pentateuch (see also Num 26:15); Hebrew reads *Ziphion.*  46:20 Greek version reads *of Heliopolis.*  46:27a Greek version reads *nine sons,* probably including Joseph's grandsons through Ephraim and Manasseh (see 1 Chr 7:14-20).  46:27b Greek version reads *seventy-five;* see note on Exod 1:5.

---

**46:1-4** God promised to go with Jacob to Egypt, blessing his journey and bringing his descendants back to Canaan. A little over two hundred years earlier, Abraham had gone to Egypt during a famine in Canaan, and God had protected him there (12:10-20). In Scripture, Egypt was often God's source of provision for his people.

# Insight  MOTHERS AND FATHERS OF FAITH

The Bible often looks back to its beginnings—mentioning the God of Abraham, Isaac, and Jacob (see, for example, Genesis 31:42; Exodus 2:24; 6:8; Deuteronomy 6:10; 2 Kings 13:23). This same God is also the God of Sarah, Hagar, Rebekah, Leah, and Rachel. What do we see about God's way of interacting with these ancestors of faith?

| MOTHERS AND GOD'S CHARACTER | | FATHERS AND GOD'S CHARACTER | |
|---|---|---|---|
| **Eve** | Formed her in God's image 1:27<br>Brought her to her husband 2:22<br>Enabled her to have children 4:1, 25<br>Safeguarded her son's (Cain's) life 4:15 | **ADAM** | Formed him in God's image 1:27<br>Provided the "just right" companion 2:18 |
| **Sarah** | Made her beautiful 12:14<br>Blessed her with a son, made her a mother of many nations 17:15-16<br>Fulfilled covenant via her son 17:21<br>Visited her, spoke honestly to her ("you did laugh"), enabled her to have children 18:9-15<br>Kept his promises to her 21:1 | **ABRAHAM** | Called him to a new land and vocation; blessed him to be a blessing 12:1-3<br>Made a covenant with him 17:4<br>Made him father of nations and kings 17:5-6<br>Gave him land 12:7; 13:15-18; 17:8<br>Fulfilled covenant through Isaac 17:19 |
| **Hagar** | Found by God 16:7<br>Allowed to give a name to God 16:13<br>Made her a mother of nations 21:13<br>Heard her son's cries 21:17<br>Revealed how to save her son's life 21:19 | | |
| **Rebekah** | Was brought to her husband by God 24:15<br>Was made lovely 24:16<br>Loved deeply by her husband 24:67<br>Was shown God's will for her children 25:22-23 | **ISAAC** | Confirmed covenant through him 17:19<br>Showed him unfailing love by selecting Rebekah 24:14<br>Answered his prayer for Rebekah to conceive 25:21 |
| **Leah** | Not lovely or loved by her husband, but God took care of her 29:17, 31<br>Eventually praised God 29:35<br>Bore a son (Judah) whose direct line led to the Messiah Matthew 1:2-16<br>A mother of Israel Ruth 4:11 | **JACOB** | Was given land, descendants, and God's presence 28:13-15<br>Led him to his wives 29:9-12, 22-30<br>Guided him home 31:3<br>Reconciled him to his brother, Esau 33:3-4<br>Renamed him Israel 35:10 |
| **Rachel** | Lovely figure and face 29:17<br>Beloved by her husband 29:30<br>Conceived with God's help 30:22<br>Stole idols and lied, but God still made her a mother of Israel 31:34-35; Ruth 4:11<br>Birthed Joseph, who rescued Israel 35:24; 45:4-11<br>Last son honored as "son of (Jacob's) right hand" 35:18<br>Husband memorialized her grave 35:20 | | |

## Jacob's Family Arrives in Goshen

28As they neared their destination, Jacob sent Judah ahead to meet Joseph and get directions to the region of Goshen. And when they finally arrived there, 29Joseph prepared his chariot and traveled to Goshen to meet his father, Jacob. When Joseph arrived, he embraced his father and wept, holding him for a long time. 30Finally, Jacob said to Joseph, "Now I am ready to die, since I have seen your face again and know you are still alive."

31And Joseph said to his brothers and to his father's entire family, "I will go to Pharaoh and tell him, 'My brothers and my father's entire family have come to me from the land of Canaan. 32These men are shepherds, and they raise livestock. They have brought with them their flocks and herds and everything they own.'"

33Then he said, "When Pharaoh calls for you and asks you about your occupation, 34you must tell him, 'We, your servants, have raised livestock all our lives, as our ancestors have always done.' When you tell him this, he will let you live here in the region of Goshen, for the Egyptians despise shepherds."

## Jacob Blesses Pharaoh

47 Then Joseph went to see Pharaoh and told him, "My father and my brothers have arrived from the land of Canaan. They have come with all their flocks and herds and possessions, and they are now in the region of Goshen."

2Joseph took five of his brothers with him and presented them to Pharaoh. 3And Pharaoh asked the brothers, "What is your occupation?"

They replied, "We, your servants, are shepherds, just like our ancestors. 4We have come to live here in Egypt for a while, for there is no pasture for our flocks in Canaan. The famine is very severe there. So please, we request permission to live in the region of Goshen."

5Then Pharaoh said to Joseph, "Now that your father and brothers have joined you here, 6choose any place in the entire land of Egypt for them to live. Give them the best land of Egypt. Let them live in the region of Goshen. And if any of them have special skills, put them in charge of my livestock, too."

7Then Joseph brought in his father, Jacob, and presented him to Pharaoh. And Jacob blessed Pharaoh.

8"How old are you?" Pharaoh asked him.

9Jacob replied, "I have traveled this earth for 130 hard years. But my life has been short compared to the lives of my ancestors." 10Then Jacob blessed Pharaoh again before leaving his court.

11So Joseph assigned the best land of Egypt—the region of Rameses—to his father and his brothers, and he settled them there, just as Pharaoh had commanded. 12And Joseph provided food for his father and his brothers in amounts appropriate to the number of their dependents, including the smallest children.

## Joseph's Leadership in the Famine

13Meanwhile, the famine became so severe that all the food was used up, and people were starving throughout the lands of Egypt and Canaan. 14By selling grain to the people, Joseph eventually collected all the money in Egypt and Canaan, and he put the money in Pharaoh's treasury. 15When the people of Egypt and Canaan ran out of money, all the Egyptians came to Joseph. "Our money is gone!" they cried. "But please give us food, or we will die before your very eyes!"

16Joseph replied, "Since your money is gone, bring me your livestock. I will give you food in exchange for your livestock." 17So they brought their livestock to Joseph in exchange for food. In exchange for their horses, flocks of sheep and goats, herds of cattle, and donkeys, Joseph provided them with food for another year.

18But that year ended, and the next year they came again and said, "We cannot hide the truth from you, my lord. Our money is gone, and all our livestock and cattle are yours. We have nothing left to give but our bodies and our land. 19Why should we die before your very eyes? Buy us and our land in exchange for food; we offer our land and ourselves as slaves for Pharaoh. Just give us grain so we may live and not die, and so the land does not become empty and desolate."

20So Joseph bought all the land of Egypt for Pharaoh. All the Egyptians sold him their fields because the famine was so severe, and soon all the land belonged to Pharaoh. 21As for the people, he made them all slaves,* from one end of Egypt to the other. 22The only land he did not buy was the land belonging to the priests. They received an allotment of food directly from Pharaoh, so they didn't need to sell their land.

23Then Joseph said to the people, "Look, today I have bought you and your land for Pharaoh. I will provide you with seed so you can plant the fields. 24Then when you harvest it, one-fifth of your crop will belong to Pharaoh. You may keep the remaining four-fifths as seed for your fields and as food for you, your households, and your little ones."

25"You have saved our lives!" they exclaimed. "May it please you, my lord, to let us be Pharaoh's servants." 26Joseph then issued a decree still in effect in the land of Egypt, that Pharaoh should receive one-fifth of all the crops grown on his land. Only the land belonging to the priests was not given to Pharaoh.

47:21 As in Greek version and Samaritan Pentateuch; Hebrew reads *he moved them all into the towns.*

47:10 Jacob blessed Pharaoh, though Pharaoh clearly had more power and wealth. Joseph had saved Pharaoh and all of Egypt from the devastating effects of a seven-year famine. This blessing was evidence that God's promise to Abraham was already being fulfilled—Abraham's descendants were indeed blessed to be a blessing to others (12:1-3).

²⁷Meanwhile, the people of Israel settled in the region of Goshen in Egypt. There they acquired property, and they were fruitful, and their population grew rapidly. ²⁸Jacob lived for seventeen years after his arrival in Egypt, so he lived 147 years in all.

²⁹As the time of his death drew near, Jacob* called for his son Joseph and said to him, "Please do me this favor. Put your hand under my thigh and swear that you will treat me with unfailing love by honoring this last request: Do not bury me in Egypt. ³⁰When I die, please take my body out of Egypt and bury me with my ancestors."

So Joseph promised, "I will do as you ask."

³¹"Swear that you will do it," Jacob insisted. So Joseph gave his oath, and Jacob bowed humbly at the head of his bed.*

## Jacob Blesses Manasseh and Ephraim

**48** One day not long after this, word came to Joseph, "Your father is failing rapidly." So Joseph went to visit his father, and he took with him his two sons, Manasseh and Ephraim.

²When Joseph arrived, Jacob was told, "Your son Joseph has come to see you." So Jacob* gathered his strength and sat up in his bed.

³Jacob said to Joseph, "God Almighty* appeared to me at Luz in the land of Canaan and blessed me. ⁴He said to me, 'I will make you fruitful, and I will multiply your descendants. I will make you a multitude of nations. And I will give this land of Canaan to your descendants* after you as an everlasting possession.'

⁵"Now I am claiming as my own sons these two boys of yours, Ephraim and Manasseh, who were born here in the land of Egypt before I arrived. They will be my sons, just as Reuben and Simeon are. ⁶But any children born to you in the future will be your own, and they will inherit land within the territories of their brothers Ephraim and Manasseh.

⁷"Long ago, as I was returning from Paddan-aram,* Rachel died in the land of Canaan. We were still on the way, some distance from Ephrath (that is, Bethlehem). So with great sorrow I buried her there beside the road to Ephrath."

⁸Then Jacob looked over at the two boys. "Are these your sons?" he asked.

⁹"Yes," Joseph told him, "these are the sons God has given me here in Egypt."

And Jacob said, "Bring them closer to me, so I can bless them."

¹⁰Jacob was half blind because of his age and could hardly see. So Joseph brought the boys close to him, and Jacob kissed and embraced them. ¹¹Then Jacob said to Joseph, "I never thought I would see your face again, but now God has let me see your children, too!"

¹²Joseph moved the boys, who were at their grandfather's knees, and he bowed with his face to the ground. ¹³Then he positioned the boys in front of Jacob. With his right hand he directed Ephraim toward Jacob's left hand, and with his left hand he put Manasseh at Jacob's right hand. ¹⁴But Jacob crossed his arms as he reached out to lay his hands on the boys' heads. He put his right hand on the head of Ephraim, though he was the younger boy, and his left hand on the head of Manasseh, though he was the firstborn. ¹⁵Then he blessed Joseph and said,

"May the God before whom my grandfather Abraham
　and my father, Isaac, walked—
the God who has been my shepherd
　all my life, to this very day,
¹⁶ the Angel who has redeemed me from all harm—
　may he bless these boys.
May they preserve my name
　and the names of Abraham and Isaac.
And may their descendants multiply greatly
　throughout the earth."

¹⁷But Joseph was upset when he saw that his father placed his right hand on Ephraim's head. So Joseph lifted it to move it from Ephraim's head to Manasseh's head. ¹⁸"No, my father," he said. "This one is the firstborn. Put your right hand on his head."

¹⁹But his father refused. "I know, my son; I know," he replied. "Manasseh will also become a great people, but his younger brother will become even greater. And his descendants will become a multitude of nations."

²⁰So Jacob blessed the boys that day with this blessing: "The people of Israel will use your names when they give a blessing. They will say, 'May God make you as prosperous as Ephraim and Manasseh.'" In this way, Jacob put Ephraim ahead of Manasseh.

²¹Then Jacob said to Joseph, "Look, I am about to die, but God will be with you and will take you back to Canaan, the land of your ancestors. ²²And beyond

---

**47:29** Hebrew *Israel;* also in 47:31b. See note on 35:21. **47:31** Greek version reads *and Israel bowed in worship as he leaned on his staff.* Compare Heb 11:21. **48:2** Hebrew *Israel;* also in 48:8, 10, 11, 13, 14, 21. See note on 35:21. **48:3** Hebrew *El-Shaddai.* **48:4** Hebrew *seed;* also in 48:19. **48:7** Hebrew *Paddan,* referring to Paddan-aram; compare Gen 35:9.

---

**47:27-31** The Israelites increased in number in Egypt in fulfillment of the creation blessing (1:26-28). However, Jacob insisted that Joseph not bury him in Egypt. Jacob chose God's promises over Egypt's provision, knowing he belonged with his ancestors in Canaan, the land God promised him.
**48:1-6** Jacob blessed Joseph by elevating his two sons as coheirs with their uncles—the tribes of Manasseh and Ephraim would receive land along with the other tribes. This

doubled the size of Joseph's share of the inheritance, effectively treating Joseph as the firstborn. Ephraim and Manasseh became large and powerful tribes.
**48:8-22** The right hand was for the head of the firstborn, but Jacob deliberately gave that position to the younger son, Ephraim. Four consecutive generations followed that pattern: Isaac over Ishmael, Jacob over Esau, Joseph over Reuben, and Ephraim over Manasseh. God refused to be limited by cultural convention.

what I have given your brothers, I am giving you an extra portion of the land* that I took from the Amorites with my sword and bow."

## Jacob's Last Words to His Sons

49 Then Jacob called together all his sons and said, "Gather around me, and I will tell you what will happen to each of you in the days to come.

2 "Come and listen, you sons of Jacob;
    listen to Israel, your father.

3 "Reuben, you are my firstborn, my strength,
    the child of my vigorous youth.
    You are first in rank and first in power.
4 But you are as unruly as a flood,
    and you will be first no longer.
For you went to bed with my wife;
    you defiled my marriage couch.

5 "Simeon and Levi are two of a kind;
    their weapons are instruments of violence.
6 May I never join in their meetings;
    may I never be a party to their plans.
For in their anger they murdered men,
    and they crippled oxen just for sport.
7 A curse on their anger, for it is fierce;
    a curse on their wrath, for it is cruel.
I will scatter them among the descendants of Jacob;
    I will disperse them throughout Israel.

8 "Judah, your brothers will praise you.
    You will grasp your enemies by the neck.
    All your relatives will bow before you.
9 Judah, my son, is a young lion
    that has finished eating its prey.
Like a lion he crouches and lies down;
    like a lioness—who dares to rouse him?
10 The scepter will not depart from Judah,
    nor the ruler's staff from his descendants,*
until the coming of the one to whom it belongs,*
    the one whom all nations will honor.
11 He ties his foal to a grapevine,
    the colt of his donkey to a choice vine.
He washes his clothes in wine,
    his robes in the blood of grapes.
12 His eyes are darker than wine,
    and his teeth are whiter than milk.

13 "Zebulun will settle by the seashore
    and will be a harbor for ships;
    his borders will extend to Sidon.

14 "Issachar is a sturdy donkey,
    resting between two saddlepacks.*
15 When he sees how good the countryside is
    and how pleasant the land,
he will bend his shoulder to the load
    and submit himself to hard labor.

16 "Dan will govern his people,
    like any other tribe in Israel.
17 Dan will be a snake beside the road,
    a poisonous viper along the path
that bites the horse's hooves
    so its rider is thrown off.
18 I trust in you for salvation, O LORD!

19 "Gad will be attacked by marauding bands,
    but he will attack them when they retreat.

20 "Asher will dine on rich foods
    and produce food fit for kings.

21 "Naphtali is a doe set free
    that bears beautiful fawns.

22 "Joseph is the foal of a wild donkey,
    the foal of a wild donkey at a spring—
    one of the wild donkeys on the ridge.*
23 Archers attacked him savagely;
    they shot at him and harassed him.
24 But his bow remained taut,
    and his arms were strengthened
by the hands of the Mighty One of Jacob,
    by the Shepherd, the Rock of Israel.
25 May the God of your father help you;
    may the Almighty bless you
with the blessings of the heavens above,
    and blessings of the watery depths below,
    and blessings of the breasts and womb.
26 May my fatherly blessings on you
    surpass the blessings of my ancestors,*
    reaching to the heights of the eternal hills.
May these blessings rest on the head of
        Joseph,
    who is a prince among his brothers.

27 "Benjamin is a ravenous wolf,
    devouring his enemies in the morning
    and dividing his plunder in the evening."

28 These are the twelve tribes of Israel, and this is what their father said as he told his sons good-bye. He blessed each one with an appropriate message.

---

**48:22** Or *an extra ridge of land.* The meaning of the Hebrew is uncertain.   **49:10a** Hebrew *from between his feet.*   **49:10b** Or *until tribute is brought to him and the peoples obey;* traditionally rendered *until Shiloh comes.*   **49:14** Or *sheepfolds,* or *hearths.* **49:22** Or *Joseph is a fruitful tree, / a fruitful tree beside a spring. / His branches reach over the wall.* The meaning of the Hebrew is uncertain.   **49:26** Or *of the ancient mountains.*

---

**49:1-28** God's blessings in Genesis contrasted sharply with those of pagan religions, which sought fortune and fertility through magic. Pagan cultic observances at shrines were performed to induce deities to act on behalf of the worshipers. By contrast, in Genesis, all life, fertility, and blessing came by God's decree. Jacob deliberately crafted prophetic oracles regarding the future settlement of Canaan. All the tribes would enter the land, but they would not participate equally. Their inheritance would partly reflect their degree of exemplary behavior.

## Jacob's Death and Burial

²⁹Then Jacob instructed them, "Soon I will die and join my ancestors. Bury me with my father and grandfather in the cave in the field of Ephron the Hittite. ³⁰This is the cave in the field of Machpelah, near Mamre in Canaan, that Abraham bought from Ephron the Hittite as a permanent burial site. ³¹There Abraham and his wife Sarah are buried. There Isaac and his wife, Rebekah, are buried. And there I buried Leah. ³²It is the plot of land and the cave that my grandfather Abraham bought from the Hittites."

³³When Jacob had finished this charge to his sons, he drew his feet into the bed, breathed his last, and joined his ancestors in death.

50 Joseph threw himself on his father and wept over him and kissed him. ²Then Joseph told the physicians who served him to embalm his father's body; so Jacob* was embalmed. ³The embalming process took the usual forty days. And the Egyptians mourned his death for seventy days.

⁴When the period of mourning was over, Joseph approached Pharaoh's advisers and said, "Please do me this favor and speak to Pharaoh on my behalf. ⁵Tell him that my father made me swear an oath. He said to me, 'Listen, I am about to die. Take my body back to the land of Canaan, and bury me in the tomb I prepared for myself.' So please allow me to go and bury my father. After his burial, I will return without delay."

⁶Pharaoh agreed to Joseph's request. "Go and bury your father, as he made you promise," he said. ⁷So Joseph went up to bury his father. He was accompanied by all of Pharaoh's officials, all the senior members of Pharaoh's household, and all the senior officers of Egypt. ⁸Joseph also took his entire household and his brothers and their households. But they left their little children and flocks and herds in the land of Goshen. ⁹A great number of chariots and charioteers accompanied Joseph.

¹⁰When they arrived at the threshing floor of Atad, near the Jordan River, they held a very great and solemn memorial service, with a seven-day period of mourning for Joseph's father. ¹¹The local residents, the Canaanites, watched them mourning at the threshing floor of Atad. Then they renamed that place (which is near the Jordan) Abel-mizraim,* for they said, "This is a place of deep mourning for these Egyptians."

¹²So Jacob's sons did as he had commanded them. ¹³They carried his body to the land of Canaan and buried him in the cave in the field of Machpelah, near Mamre. This is the cave that Abraham had bought as a permanent burial site from Ephron the Hittite.

## Joseph Reassures His Brothers

¹⁴After burying Jacob, Joseph returned to Egypt with his brothers and all who had accompanied him to his father's burial. ¹⁵But now that their father was dead, Joseph's brothers became fearful. "Now Joseph will show his anger and pay us back for all the wrong we did to him," they said.

¹⁶So they sent this message to Joseph: "Before your father died, he instructed us ¹⁷to say to you: 'Please forgive your brothers for the great wrong they did to you—for their sin in treating you so cruelly.' So we, the servants of the God of your father, beg you to forgive our sin." When Joseph received the message, he broke down and wept. ¹⁸Then his brothers came and threw themselves down before Joseph. "Look, we are your slaves!" they said.

¹⁹But Joseph replied, "Don't be afraid of me. Am I God, that I can punish you? ²⁰You intended to harm me, but God intended it all for good. He brought me to this position so I could save the lives of many people. ²¹No, don't be afraid. I will continue to take care of you and your children." So he reassured them by speaking kindly to them.

## The Death of Joseph

²²So Joseph and his brothers and their families continued to live in Egypt. Joseph lived to the age of 110. ²³He lived to see three generations of descendants of his son Ephraim, and he lived to see the birth of the children of Manasseh's son Makir, whom he claimed as his own.*

²⁴"Soon I will die," Joseph told his brothers, "but God will surely come to help you and lead you out of this land of Egypt. He will bring you back to the land he solemnly promised to give to Abraham, to Isaac, and to Jacob."

²⁵Then Joseph made the sons of Israel swear an oath, and he said, "When God comes to help you and lead you back, you must take my bones with you." ²⁶So Joseph died at the age of 110. The Egyptians embalmed him, and his body was placed in a coffin in Egypt

50:2 Hebrew *Israel.* See note on 35:21. **50:11** *Abel-mizraim* means "mourning of the Egyptians." **50:23** Hebrew *who were born on Joseph's knees.*

**50:1-13** Jacob's burial in Machpelah signified that Joseph and his brothers still believed God's promise to give them their true home, Canaan, though they lived in Egypt. Sarah was buried there (23:19), marking Abraham's first possession of land in Canaan. Others buried at the cave of Machpelah near Hebron were Abraham, Isaac, Rebekah, and Leah (49:30-31). **50:22-26** Joseph had succeeded in Egypt and lived a long life, but he insisted on being buried in Canaan. The book ends with Joseph's coffin in Egypt but points ahead to the day when Abraham's descendants would return to Canaan, the land God promised them. Joseph was eventually buried in Shechem (Joshua 24:32). We tend to think of death as the tragic end of life, but ancient people were satisfied knowing their families would carry on.

# Koinonia

**IMAGE** — MY STORY WITH COMMUNITY, WORKPLACE & CHURCH

## Work Is More Than a Four-Letter Word

**SCRIPTURE CONNECTION: GENESIS 50:14-21**

A mentor once encouraged me that, from God's perspective, work is a four-letter word: *GIFT.* Work is God's gift to us, and when we bring our gifts to the work he assigns, we enter a divinely directed realm of service.

Joseph's life was marked by his devotion to God and the faithful stewardship of assignments he was given. He brought his gifts to his work, and God used Joseph in his plan to save the children of Israel. Joseph's example inspires my view of work, as I labor alongside leaders of more than twelve hundred faith-based nonprofits. Here is what I see in Joseph that I want more of in me:

> The gift of work and our gifts at work have the power to transform!

- Confidence—Joseph knew God was with him (39:2).
- Conviction—Joseph quickly discerned situations and resisted temptation (39:12).
- Consistency—Joseph focused on the task at hand, ready to put his gifts to work (40:8).
- Compassion—Joseph resisted bitterness and chose forgiveness and mercy (50:20-21).

The gift of our work and our gifts at work have the power to transform us and advance God's greater purpose.

## IMAGINE

If Joseph were your mentor, what lessons from his life might help you?

How would you put his story to work for you today?

*"While Joseph was given big dreams, he trusted God and focused on the task at hand. I give thanks that God still gives us big dreams and the gift of pursuing them through everyday faithfulness."*

**TAMI HEIM** is president and CEO of Christian Leadership Alliance and serves on many nonprofit boards. She and her husband lead mission teams to Haiti to love and disciple orphans.

# Exodus

**WHAT DO WE LEARN ABOUT GOD'S MISSION AND OURS?**
God's presence and laws enable the people of Israel to fulfill God's mission.

**WHO WROTE IT?** Exodus is anonymous, but Jewish and Christian traditions attribute it to Moses (see 24:4).

**WHEN DID IT HAPPEN?** Either in the 1400s or 1200s BC, hundreds of years after the final events of Genesis.

## HOW IS IT ORGANIZED?

- 1–2: God begins his rescue through Shiphrah and Puah, Moses' Mother and Miriam, and Pharaoh's daughter
- 3–15: God rescues his people from slavery in Egypt
- 16–18: God provides for his people's needs in the wilderness
- 19–24: God gives his people instructions for living
- 32: The people rebel against God
- 33–34: God speaks to Moses again
- 35–40: Building the Tabernacle

## FEATURE HIGHLIGHTS

+ *Five Women Who Made a Difference: Delivering and Raising Moses (81)*
+ *Why So Long? (82)*
+ *Failure Not Enough or Not Willing (85)*
+ *The Lord Himself Leads Us (99)*

*Words to Remember are highlighted throughout this book*

## HOW LONG DOES IT TAKE TO READ?

| | | | 2:30 | | | |
|---|---|---|---|---|---|---|
| :30 | 1:00 | 1:30 | 2:00 | 2:30 | 3:00 | 3:30 |

## Timeline

**BC**

- 1805 ● JOSEPH DIES
- c. 1800 –1446 ● ISRAELITES ENSLAVED IN EGYPT
- 1533 ● MIRIAM BORN TO AMRAM AND JOCHEBED
- 1529 ● AARON, BROTHER TO MIRIAM AND MOSES, BORN
- 1526 ● JOCHEBED GIVES BIRTH TO MOSES
  — *Five women save Moses' life (Shiphrah, Puah, Jochebed, Miriam, and Pharaoh's daughter)*
- 1486 ● MOSES FLEES TO MIDIAN, MARRIES ZIPPORAH
  — *Zipporah saves Moses' life by circumcising their son*
- 1446 ● EXODUS FROM EGYPT
  — *Miriam leads the women in dancing, worship, celebration of God's victory*
- 1445 ● TEN COMMANDMENTS GIVEN
  — *Miriam and Aaron oppose Moses*
  — *Moses pleads for God to heal Miriam*
- 1406 ● ISRAEL ENTERS CANAAN
- 1375 ● JUDGES (INCLUDING DEBORAH, GIDEON, AND SAMSON) BEGIN TO RULE
- 1050 ● KINGDOM UNITED UNDER SAUL

## The Israelites in Egypt

1 These are the names of the sons of Israel (that is, Jacob) who moved to Egypt with their father, each with his family: ²Reuben, Simeon, Levi, Judah, ³Issachar, Zebulun, Benjamin, ⁴Dan, Naphtali, Gad, and Asher. ⁵In all, Jacob had seventy* descendants in Egypt, including Joseph, who was already there.

⁶In time, Joseph and all of his brothers died, ending that entire generation. ⁷But their descendants, the Israelites, had many children and grandchildren. In fact, they multiplied so greatly that they became extremely powerful and filled the land.

⁸Eventually, a new king came to power in Egypt who knew nothing about Joseph or what he had done. ⁹He said to his people, "Look, the people of Israel now outnumber us and are stronger than we are. ¹⁰We must make a plan to keep them from growing even more. If we don't, and if war breaks out, they will join our enemies and fight against us. Then they will escape from the country.*"

¹¹So the Egyptians made the Israelites their slaves. They appointed brutal slave drivers over them, hoping to wear them down with crushing labor. They forced them to build the cities of Pithom and Rameses as supply centers for the king. ¹²But the more the Egyptians oppressed them, the more the Israelites multiplied and spread, and the more alarmed the Egyptians became. ¹³So the Egyptians worked the people of Israel without mercy. ¹⁴They made their lives bitter, forcing them to mix mortar and make bricks and do all the work in the fields. They were ruthless in all their demands.

¹⁵Then Pharaoh, the king of Egypt, gave this order to the Hebrew midwives, Shiphrah and Puah: ¹⁶"When you help the Hebrew women as they give birth, watch as they deliver.* If the baby is a boy, kill him; if it is a girl, let her live." ¹⁷But because the midwives feared God, they refused to obey the king's orders. They allowed the boys to live, too.

¹⁸So the king of Egypt called for the midwives. "Why have you done this?" he demanded. "Why have you allowed the boys to live?"

¹⁹"The Hebrew women are not like the Egyptian women," the midwives replied. "They are more vigorous and have their babies so quickly that we cannot get there in time."

²⁰So God was good to the midwives, and the Israelites continued to multiply, growing more and more powerful. ²¹And because the midwives feared God, he gave them families of their own.

²²Then Pharaoh gave this order to all his people: "Throw every newborn Hebrew boy into the Nile River. But you may let the girls live."

## The Birth of Moses

2 About this time, a man and woman from the tribe of Levi got married. ²The woman became pregnant and gave birth to a son. She saw that he was a special baby and kept him hidden for three months. ³But when she could no longer hide him, she got a basket made of papyrus reeds and waterproofed it with tar and pitch. She put the baby in the basket and laid it among the reeds along the bank of the Nile River. ⁴The baby's sister then stood at a distance, watching to see what would happen to him.

⁵Soon Pharaoh's daughter came down to bathe in the river, and her attendants walked along the riverbank. When the princess saw the basket among the reeds, she sent her maid to get it for her. ⁶When the princess opened it, she saw the baby. The little boy was crying, and she felt sorry for him. "This must be one of the Hebrew children," she said.

⁷Then the baby's sister approached the princess. "Should I go and find one of the Hebrew women to nurse the baby for you?" she asked.

⁸"Yes, do!" the princess replied. So the girl went and called the baby's mother.

⁹"Take this baby and nurse him for me," the princess told the baby's mother. "I will pay you for your help." So the woman took her baby home and nursed him.

¹⁰Later, when the boy was older, his mother brought him back to Pharaoh's daughter, who adopted him as her own son. The princess named him Moses,* for she explained, "I lifted him out of the water."

## Moses Escapes to Midian

¹¹Many years later, when Moses had grown up, he went out to visit his own people, the Hebrews, and saw how hard they were forced to work. During his visit, he saw an Egyptian beating one of his fellow Hebrews. ¹²After looking in all directions to make

---

1:5 Dead Sea Scrolls and Greek version read *seventy-five;* see notes on Gen 46:27. 1:10 Or *will take the country.* 1:16 Hebrew *look upon the two stones;* perhaps the reference is to a birthstool. 2:10 *Moses* sounds like a Hebrew term that means "to lift out."

---

**1:15-22** Pharaoh was unaware of the history regarding Jacob's descendants and viewed them as a threat rather than a blessing. His method of controlling them toem ensure a robust labor force for his building projects was counterproductive. Killing the boys would mean fewer enslaved men. He let the girls live, underestimating their strength. Women undermined Pharaoh at every turn in this story, mostly because they feared God rather than him. The midwives, Moses' mom and sister, and even Pharaoh's daughter defied his edict. **2:1-9** The baby's mom saw that he was "special" (literally, "good"), echoing God's assessment of his creative work in Genesis (1:4, 10, 12, 18, 25, 31). All babies are good because each one is made in God's image (Genesis 1:26-28). Pharaoh's murderous policy contradicted God's creation blessing to produce offspring and fill the earth. These women conspired together at great danger to themselves to rescue a baby boy under a death sentence. The key players in this narrative remain nameless as if to protect their identity. **2:10** The princess named the baby Moses, which in Egyptian means "son of" and in Hebrew means "one who draws out." She memorialized his questionable origin (son of who?) as well as her audacity—rather than throwing him into the Nile as her father had commanded, she drew him out of it. Moses himself would draw the Hebrews out through the sea and into freedom.

# *Five Women* WHO MADE A DIFFERENCE

## Delivering and Raising Moses

Can we make a difference in difficult situations? Yes! When we creatively invest our faith, abilities, and resources, God can do great things through us. Take these examples:

- *Two Midwives: Shiphrah and Puah.* Pharaoh felt threatened by the escalating population of Hebrews in Egypt. Unable to contain them through slavery, he directed these two midwives to kill all newborn Hebrew boys. But they let the boys live and told Pharaoh that the mothers were giving birth and hiding the babies before they arrived (Exodus 1:15-21).
- *Moses' Mother: Jochebed.* Three months after giving birth to her third child, a boy, Jochebed couldn't hide him any longer and developed a plan. She reinforced a papyrus basket and set her baby afloat in the Nile (Exodus 2:1-3).
- *Pharaoh's Daughter.* While heading to bathe in the Nile, she discovered the crying baby in a basket and felt sorry for him. She rescued the baby and later adopted him (Exodus 2:5-10).
- *Moses' Sister: Miriam.* Jochebed stationed her firstborn along the bank to watch the basket. When Pharaoh's daughter discovered the baby, Miriam offered to find a nurse. Pharaoh's daughter agreed and even paid Jochebed to do it. Mother, sister, and baby were reunited until Moses joined Pharaoh's household, positioning him to become the rescuer of the Hebrew people (Exodus 2:4, 7-10).

> When we invest ourselves in creative obedience, God can do great things through us.

These five women creatively invested themselves in difficult situations and great good resulted.

THESE FIVE WOMEN'S STORIES ARE TOLD IN EXODUS 1–2.

## IDENTIFY

How many lives might those midwives have saved?

How does Jochebed's instinct to save her son reflect God's heart to save his people?

While Pharaoh's daughter likely didn't know Israel's God, how might God have been working behind the scenes?

Could Miriam have possibly imagined serving at her brother's side, helping to lead Israel out of slavery?

*"It's easy to hang back, thinking our actions won't matter. But they do! Even what may seem small, unnoticed, frivolous, or frowned upon by others, when done in love for God, can change a life forever."*

ELISA MORGAN, MDiv, speaks, writes, and cohosts podcasts for Our Daily Bread Ministries. For twenty years, she served as president of MOPS International, now as president emerita. Her motto is "Living really … Really living."

# Perspective

## Why so long?

SCRIPTURE CONNECTION: EXODUS 2:23-25

If God cared about the Israelites, why did he let them be enslaved? And why did he wait so long to intervene?

God doesn't always reveal the reasons for his timing. But this passage shows that even though the wait was long, God had not forgotten his promise to bless the descendants of Abraham (see Genesis 12:1-3).

Egypt had provided refuge for the Israelites during a major famine, and Joseph had helped Egypt create a system to ensure survival. However, a later pharaoh exploited the Israelites to help himself. God's delay during their slavery in Egypt gave ample time for the oppressors to change their ways. It also allowed a broader demonstration of his power when he did free the Israelites.

The brokenness we experience drives us to cry out to God, too. Our earnest prayers cultivate trust that God will someday make all things new. And when he does, our only response will be to give him glory.

### VIEWPOINTS

THEIRS: *Did the Israelites wonder if God has forgotten his promises?*
MINE: *"Reconciliation and healing can seem so far away. When it feels like the world around me falls apart, will I trust God's promise to restore all things?"*
YOURS: *Does it seem like God is absent? Let this passage remind you: God has not forgotten you.*

CARMEN JOY IMES, PhD, is an author, speaker, blogger, YouTuber, and serves as associate professor of Old Testament at Biola University in California.

sure no one was watching, Moses killed the Egyptian and hid the body in the sand.

13The next day, when Moses went out to visit his people again, he saw two Hebrew men fighting. "Why are you beating up your friend?" Moses said to the one who had started the fight.

14The man replied, "Who appointed you to be our prince and judge? Are you going to kill me as you killed that Egyptian yesterday?"

Then Moses was afraid, thinking, "Everyone knows what I did." 15And sure enough, Pharaoh heard what had happened, and he tried to kill Moses. But Moses fled from Pharaoh and went to live in the land of Midian.

When Moses arrived in Midian, he sat down beside a well. 16Now the priest of Midian had seven daughters who came as usual to draw water and fill the water troughs for their father's flocks. 17But some other shepherds came and chased them away. So Moses jumped up and rescued the girls from the shepherds. Then he drew water for their flocks.

18When the girls returned to Reuel, their father, he asked, "Why are you back so soon today?"

19"An Egyptian rescued us from the shepherds," they answered. "And then he drew water for us and watered our flocks."

20"Then where is he?" their father asked. "Why did you leave him there? Invite him to come and eat with us."

21Moses accepted the invitation, and he settled there with him. In time, Reuel gave Moses his daughter Zipporah to be his wife. 22Later she gave birth to a son, and Moses named him Gershom,* for he explained, "I have been a foreigner in a foreign land."

23Years passed, and the king of Egypt died. But the Israelites continued to groan under their burden of slavery. They cried out for help, and their cry rose up to God. 24God heard their groaning, and he remembered his covenant promise to Abraham, Isaac, and Jacob. 25He looked down on the people of Israel and knew it was time to act.*

## Moses and the Burning Bush

3 One day Moses was tending the flock of his father-in-law, Jethro,* the priest of Midian. He led the flock far into the wilderness and came to Sinai,* the mountain of God. 2There the angel of the LORD appeared to him in a blazing fire from the middle of a bush. Moses stared in amazement. Though the bush was engulfed in flames, it didn't burn up. 3"This is amazing," Moses said to himself. "Why isn't that bush burning up? I must go see it."

4When the LORD saw Moses coming to take a closer look, God called to him from the middle of the bush, "Moses! Moses!"

"Here I am!" Moses replied.

5"Do not come any closer," the LORD warned. "Take off your sandals, for you are standing on holy ground. 6I am

---

2:22 *Gershom* sounds like a Hebrew term that means "a foreigner there."  2:25 Or *and acknowledged his obligation to help them.*
3:1a Moses' father-in-law went by two names, Jethro and Reuel.  3:1b Hebrew *Horeb,* another name for Sinai.

---

2:11-22 Moses seemed to share both his birth mother's and his adoptive mother's concern for justice. He acted to avenge the beating of a Hebrew man (2:11-12) and the bullying of Midianite women (2:17). However, his passionate burst in Egypt was no match for systemic injustice. He needed the Lord's calling and empowerment to rescue the Israelites from slavery.

# Insight · THE RELUCTANT LEADER

When God appeared to Moses in a burning bush and told him to lead the Israelites out of slavery in Egypt, Moses tried everything he could to avoid God's calling (3:1–4:17). Moses' excuses might sound familiar to you if you've ever wanted to avoid your calling. God responds to Moses point by point, answering his excuses with reassurance and provision.

| MOSES | | GOD |
|---|---|---|
| I'm not enough. (3:11) | 1 | I will be with you. (3:12) |
| People will ask: What makes you think you're the person for this job? (3:13) | 2 | It's not about you—it's about me. Tell them my name: I AM WHO I AM. Remind them that I know where they came from. (3:14-18) |
| What if they won't believe or listen to me? (4:1) | 3 | Here are two miracles I will do to get their attention. (4:2-9) |
| I'm terrified of public speaking. (4:10) | 4 | Who made you to speak and who gives you the words to say? I did and I will! (4:11-12) |
| Please! Send someone else. (4:13) | 5 | All right, I'll give you a partner to work with, your brother. Now, go! (4:14-17) |

the God of your father*—the God of Abraham, the God of Isaac, and the God of Jacob." When Moses heard this, he covered his face because he was afraid to look at God.

⁷Then the LORD told him, "I have certainly seen the oppression of my people in Egypt. I have heard their cries of distress because of their harsh slave drivers. Yes, I am aware of their suffering. ⁸So I have come down to rescue them from the power of the Egyptians and lead them out of Egypt into their own fertile and spacious land. It is a land flowing with milk and honey—the land where the Canaanites, Hittites, Amorites, Perizzites, Hivites, and Jebusites now live. ⁹Look! The cry of the people of Israel has reached me, and I have seen how harshly the Egyptians abuse them. ¹⁰Now go, for I am sending you to Pharaoh. You must lead my people Israel out of Egypt."

¹¹But Moses protested to God, "Who am I to appear before Pharaoh? Who am I to lead the people of Israel out of Egypt?"

¹²God answered, "I will be with you. And this is your sign that I am the one who has sent you: When you have brought the people out of Egypt, you will worship God at this very mountain."

¹³But Moses protested, "If I go to the people of Israel and tell them, 'The God of your ancestors has sent me to you,' they will ask me, 'What is his name?' Then what should I tell them?"

¹⁴God replied to Moses, "I AM WHO I AM.* Say this to the people of Israel: I AM has sent me to you." ¹⁵God also said to Moses, "Say this to the people of Israel: Yahweh,* the God of your ancestors—the God of Abraham, the God of Isaac, and the God of Jacob—has sent me to you.

**3:6** Greek version reads *your fathers.* **3:14** Or *I WILL BE WHAT I WILL BE.* **3:15** *Yahweh* (also in 3:16) is a transliteration of the proper name *YHWH* that is sometimes rendered "Jehovah"; in this translation it is usually rendered "the LORD" (note the use of small capitals).

**3:6** Who was Moses? Born of a Hebrew woman, raised by an Egyptian, he fled to the east and married a Midianite. So where did he belong? The name of his firstborn, Gershom, means "a foreigner there." Moses didn't feel at home anywhere. Here at the mountain, the Lord simultaneously revealed his own identity as well as Moses': "I am the God of your father." Which father? Hebrew? Egyptian? Midianite? "The God of Abraham." Moses found his true place with God's covenant people.

**3:14-16** God graciously revealed his intimate name, Yahweh, to Moses, inviting him to be on a first-name basis. Yahweh is usually rendered "the LORD" (in all capital letters) in English. In Hebrew, Yahweh's name sounds like the statement "He is" or "He will be." God's name identifies him but does not limit him. He is The One Who Is, and the Israelites would discover the fullness of his character as he demonstrated it on their behalf.

This is my eternal name,
my name to remember for all generations.

16"Now go and call together all the elders of Israel. Tell them, 'Yahweh, the God of your ancestors—the God of Abraham, Isaac, and Jacob—has appeared to me. He told me, "I have been watching closely, and I see how the Egyptians are treating you. 17I have promised to rescue you from your oppression in Egypt. I will lead you to a land flowing with milk and honey—the land where the Canaanites, Hittites, Amorites, Perizzites, Hivites, and Jebusites now live."'

18"The elders of Israel will accept your message. Then you and the elders must go to the king of Egypt and tell him, 'The LORD, the God of the Hebrews, has met with us. So please let us take a three-day journey into the wilderness to offer sacrifices to the LORD, our God.'

19"But I know that the king of Egypt will not let you go unless a mighty hand forces him.* 20So I will raise my hand and strike the Egyptians, performing all kinds of miracles among them. Then at last he will let you go. 21And I will cause the Egyptians to look favorably on you. They will give you gifts when you go so you will not leave empty-handed. 22Every Israelite woman will ask for articles of silver and gold and fine clothing from her Egyptian neighbors and from the foreign women in their houses. You will dress your sons and daughters with these, stripping the Egyptians of their wealth."

## Signs of the LORD's Power

4 But Moses protested again, "What if they won't believe me or listen to me? What if they say, 'The LORD never appeared to you'?"

2Then the LORD asked him, "What is that in your hand?"

"A shepherd's staff," Moses replied.

3"Throw it down on the ground," the LORD told him. So Moses threw down the staff, and it turned into a snake! Moses jumped back.

4Then the LORD told him, "Reach out and grab its tail." So Moses reached out and grabbed it, and it turned back into a shepherd's staff in his hand.

5"Perform this sign," the LORD told him. "Then they will believe that the LORD, the God of their ancestors—the God of Abraham, the God of Isaac, and the God of Jacob—really has appeared to you."

6Then the LORD said to Moses, "Now put your hand inside your cloak." So Moses put his hand inside his cloak, and when he took it out again, his hand was white as snow with a severe skin disease.* 7"Now put your hand back into your cloak," the LORD said. So

Moses put his hand back in, and when he took it out again, it was as healthy as the rest of his body.

8The LORD said to Moses, "If they do not believe you and are not convinced by the first miraculous sign, they will be convinced by the second sign. 9And if they don't believe you or listen to you even after these two signs, then take some water from the Nile River and pour it out on the dry ground. When you do, the water from the Nile will turn to blood on the ground."

10But Moses pleaded with the LORD, "O Lord, I'm not very good with words. I never have been, and I'm not now, even though you have spoken to me. I get tongue-tied, and my words get tangled."

11Then the LORD asked Moses, "Who makes a person's mouth? Who decides whether people speak or do not speak, hear or do not hear, see or do not see? Is it not I, the LORD? 12Now go! I will be with you as you speak, and I will instruct you in what to say."

13But Moses again pleaded, "Lord, please! Send anyone else."

14Then the LORD became angry with Moses. "All right," he said. "What about your brother, Aaron the Levite? I know he speaks well. And look! He is on his way to meet you now. He will be delighted to see you. 15Talk to him, and put the words in his mouth. I will be with both of you as you speak, and I will instruct you both in what to do. 16Aaron will be your spokesman to the people. He will be your mouthpiece, and you will stand in the place of God for him, telling him what to say. 17And take your shepherd's staff with you, and use it to perform the miraculous signs I have shown you."

## Moses Returns to Egypt

18So Moses went back home to Jethro, his father-in-law. "Please let me return to my relatives in Egypt," Moses said. "I don't even know if they are still alive."

"Go in peace," Jethro replied.

19Before Moses left Midian, the LORD said to him, "Return to Egypt, for all those who wanted to kill you have died."

20So Moses took his wife and sons, put them on a donkey, and headed back to the land of Egypt. In his hand he carried the staff of God.

21And the LORD told Moses, "When you arrive back in Egypt, go to Pharaoh and perform all the miracles I have empowered you to do. But I will harden his heart so he will refuse to let the people go. 22Then you will tell him, 'This is what the LORD says: Israel is my firstborn son. 23I commanded you, "Let my son go, so he can worship me." But since you have refused, I will now kill your firstborn son!'"

---

3:19 As in Greek and Latin versions; Hebrew reads *will not let you go, not by a mighty hand.* 4:6 Or *with leprosy.* The Hebrew word used here can describe various skin diseases.

---

3:22 Pharaoh had not worried about the Hebrew women, but a Hebrew woman gave birth to and raised the deliverer of God's people. Women would freely carry away the wealth of Egypt, and no one would object. Just as Pharaoh's daughter paid Moses' mother to nurse him, the Egyptians would give generously toward the Hebrews as they left Egypt. Perhaps the Egyptians desired to make reparations for years of exploitation at Pharaoh's hands (see 11:2-3).

²⁴On the way to Egypt, at a place where Moses and his family had stopped for the night, the LORD confronted him and was about to kill him. ²⁵But Moses' wife, Zipporah, took a flint knife and circumcised her son. She touched his feet* with the foreskin and said, "Now you are a bridegroom of blood to me." ²⁶(When she said "a bridegroom of blood," she was referring to the circumcision.) After that, the LORD left him alone.

²⁷Now the LORD had said to Aaron, "Go out into the wilderness to meet Moses." So Aaron went and met Moses at the mountain of God, and he embraced him. ²⁸Moses then told Aaron everything the LORD had commanded him to say. And he told him about the miraculous signs the LORD had commanded him to perform.

²⁹Then Moses and Aaron returned to Egypt and called all the elders of Israel together. ³⁰Aaron told them everything the LORD had told Moses, and Moses performed the miraculous signs as they watched. ³¹Then the people of Israel were convinced that the LORD had sent Moses and Aaron. When they heard that the LORD was concerned about them and had seen their misery, they bowed down and worshiped.

**4:25** The Hebrew word for "feet" may refer here to the male sex organ.

**4:24-26** This story may seem strange, but it underscores how essential it was for Moses to obey God. Male circumcision was the only command given to Abraham (Genesis 17:10) and was the sign of God's covenant with him. Moses could not lead the covenant people without complying himself. As in Exodus 1–2, a woman saved Moses from death. In Hebrew, Zipporah sounds like Shiphrah, the midwife's name in 1:15. These rescue stories frame Moses' call narrative in Exodus 3–4.

---

## ⑧ Come Close        FAILURE: NOT ENOUGH OR NOT WILLING?

SCRIPTURE CONNECTION: EXODUS 3:1–4:17

I know failure. I know trying hard, throwing myself in, and coming up short. As a result of such experiences, I longed for a simple, quiet life with low-key plans. That was before I knew how far God would go for me.

Moses knew failure too. Raised in a royal household, expectations were heaped upon his head, but a murder changed everything. Self-banishment seemed appropriate. In the wilderness, he would spend his days quietly. He'd watch after sheep. That would give him a lot of alone time to think about failure.

Then God appeared inside a burning bush and offered Moses a new job. I do not blame Moses one bit for trying five times to change God's mind. Sheep might be smelly and stupid, but they don't judge.

"Who am I?" Moses asked.

God's answer to that question isn't about Moses: It's about God. God gave his name, a miracle staff, multiple signs, the promise of riches, and someone to speak on Moses' behalf if he should get tongue-tied. And even when Moses' reluctance angered God, God didn't retaliate. Instead, he provided.

And that is what I am learning about God. His provision clears the path. God's call is bigger than our deficits. His call flows from his love, and he does the amazing when we finally say yes.

**REFLECT** "For everything comes from him and exists by his power and is intended for his glory." ROMANS 11:36

*Lord, may I remember that what you invite me to do is by you and through you and for you. Amen.*

**CONSIDER** "No one can hurt us if we don't do anything. We can't be rejected if we never attempt to blossom. *We won't have regrets*, we tell ourselves. But ... every woman longs to dream ... to move beyond coping and surviving." BONNIE GRAY, *Whispers of Rest*

## When God calls, he provides, clearing the path for my "yes."

CARA DAY is a writer and illustrator. She has served with Stonecroft Ministries helping women live "extraordinary."

## Moses and Aaron Speak to Pharaoh

5 After this presentation to Israel's leaders, Moses and Aaron went and spoke to Pharaoh. They told him, "This is what the LORD, the God of Israel, says: Let my people go so they may hold a festival in my honor in the wilderness."

2"Is that so?" retorted Pharaoh. "And who is the LORD? Why should I listen to him and let Israel go? I don't know the LORD, and I will not let Israel go."

3But Aaron and Moses persisted. "The God of the Hebrews has met with us," they declared. "So let us take a three-day journey into the wilderness so we can offer sacrifices to the LORD our God. If we don't, he will kill us with a plague or with the sword."

4Pharaoh replied, "Moses and Aaron, why are you distracting the people from their tasks? Get back to work! 5Look, there are many of your people in the land, and you are stopping them from their work."

## Making Bricks without Straw

6That same day Pharaoh sent this order to the Egyptian slave drivers and the Israelite foremen: 7"Do not supply any more straw for making bricks. Make the people get it themselves! 8But still require them to make the same number of bricks as before. Don't reduce the quota. They are lazy. That's why they are crying out, 'Let us go and offer sacrifices to our God.' 9Load them down with more work. Make them sweat! That will teach them to listen to lies!"

10So the slave drivers and foremen went out and told the people: "This is what Pharaoh says: I will not provide any more straw for you. 11Go and get it yourselves. Find it wherever you can. But you must produce just as many bricks as before!" 12So the people scattered throughout the land of Egypt in search of stubble to use as straw.

13Meanwhile, the Egyptian slave drivers continued to push hard. "Meet your daily quota of bricks, just as you did when we provided you with straw!" they demanded. 14Then they whipped the Israelite foremen they had put in charge of the work crews. "Why haven't you met your quotas either yesterday or today?" they demanded.

15So the Israelite foremen went to Pharaoh and pleaded with him. "Please don't treat your servants like this," they begged. 16"We are given no straw, but the slave drivers still demand, 'Make bricks!' We are being beaten, but it isn't our fault! Your own people are to blame!"

17But Pharaoh shouted, "You're just lazy! Lazy! That's why you're saying, 'Let us go and offer sacrifices to the LORD.' 18Now get back to work! No straw will be given to you, but you must still produce the full quota of bricks."

19The Israelite foremen could see that they were in serious trouble when they were told, "You must not reduce the number of bricks you make each day." 20As they left Pharaoh's court, they confronted Moses and Aaron, who were waiting outside for them. 21The foremen said to them, "May the LORD judge and punish you for making us stink before Pharaoh and his officials. You have put a sword into their hands, an excuse to kill us!"

22Then Moses went back to the LORD and protested, "Why have you brought all this trouble on your own people, Lord? Why did you send me? 23Ever since I came to Pharaoh as your spokesman, he has been even more brutal to your people. And you have done nothing to rescue them!"

## Promises of Deliverance

6 Then the LORD told Moses, "Now you will see what I will do to Pharaoh. When he feels the force of my strong hand, he will let the people go. In fact, he will force them to leave his land!"

2And God said to Moses, "I am Yahweh—'the LORD.'* 3I appeared to Abraham, to Isaac, and to Jacob as El-Shaddai—'God Almighty'*—but I did not reveal my name, Yahweh, to them. 4And I reaffirmed my covenant with them. Under its terms, I promised to give them the land of Canaan, where they were living as foreigners. 5You can be sure that I have heard the groans of the people of Israel, who are now slaves to the Egyptians. And I am well aware of my covenant with them.

6"Therefore, say to the people of Israel: 'I am the LORD. I will free you from your oppression and will rescue you from your slavery in Egypt. I will redeem you with a powerful arm and great acts of judgment. 7I will claim you as my own people, and I will be your God. Then you will know that I am the LORD your God who has freed you from your oppression in Egypt. 8I will bring you into the land I swore to give to Abraham, Isaac, and Jacob. I will give it to you as your very own possession. I am the LORD!'"

9So Moses told the people of Israel what the LORD had said, but they refused to listen anymore. They had become too discouraged by the brutality of their slavery.

---

6:2 *Yahweh* is a transliteration of the proper name *YHWH* that is sometimes rendered "Jehovah"; in this translation it is usually rendered "the LORD" (note the use of small capitals).  6:3 *El-Shaddai,* which means "God Almighty," is the name for God used in Gen 17:1; 28:3; 35:11; 43:14; 48:3.

**5:1-2** The stated purpose for Israel's release was worship. The symmetry is clear: The people who served Pharaoh asked for time off to serve Yahweh. Pharaoh refused even this reasonable request, revealing his extreme greed. He claimed not to know who Yahweh was, but through the plagues, God would reveal himself.

**6:1-13** God renewed his promises to his people. The declaration of rescue brought the real question to the surface, the question Pharaoh articulated earlier: Who is the Lord (5:2)? As much as the Israelites needed rescue from bondage, their greater need was to know the Lord. The climax of God's renewed promises was "you will know that I am the LORD your God" (6:7).

¹⁰Then the LORD said to Moses, ¹¹"Go back to Pharaoh, the king of Egypt, and tell him to let the people of Israel leave his country."

¹²"But LORD!" Moses objected. "My own people won't listen to me anymore. How can I expect Pharaoh to listen? I'm such a clumsy speaker!*"

¹³But the LORD spoke to Moses and Aaron and gave them orders for the Israelites and for Pharaoh, the king of Egypt. The LORD commanded Moses and Aaron to lead the people of Israel out of Egypt.

## The Ancestors of Moses and Aaron

¹⁴These are the ancestors of some of the clans of Israel:

The sons of Reuben, Israel's oldest son, were Hanoch, Pallu, Hezron, and Carmi. Their descendants became the clans of Reuben.

¹⁵The sons of Simeon were Jemuel, Jamin, Ohad, Jakin, Zohar, and Shaul. (Shaul's mother was a Canaanite woman.) Their descendants became the clans of Simeon.

¹⁶These are the descendants of Levi, as listed in their family records: The sons of Levi were Gershon, Kohath, and Merari. (Levi lived to be 137 years old.)

¹⁷The descendants of Gershon included Libni and Shimei, each of whom became the ancestor of a clan.

¹⁸The descendants of Kohath included Amram, Izhar, Hebron, and Uzziel. (Kohath lived to be 133 years old.)

¹⁹The descendants of Merari included Mahli and Mushi.

These are the clans of the Levites, as listed in their family records.

²⁰Amram married his father's sister Jochebed, and she gave birth to his sons, Aaron and Moses. (Amram lived to be 137 years old.)

²¹The sons of Izhar were Korah, Nepheg, and Zicri.

²²The sons of Uzziel were Mishael, Elzaphan, and Sithri.

²³Aaron married Elisheba, the daughter of Amminadab and sister of Nahshon, and she gave birth to his sons, Nadab, Abihu, Eleazar, and Ithamar.

²⁴The sons of Korah were Assir, Elkanah, and Abiasaph. Their descendants became the clans of Korah.

²⁵Eleazar son of Aaron married one of the daughters of Putiel, and she gave birth to his son, Phinehas.

These are the ancestors of the Levite families, listed according to their clans.

²⁶The Aaron and Moses named in this list are the same ones to whom the LORD said, "Lead the people of Israel out of the land of Egypt like an army." ²⁷It was Moses and Aaron who spoke to Pharaoh, the king of Egypt, about leading the people of Israel out of Egypt.

²⁸When the LORD spoke to Moses in the land of Egypt, ²⁹he said to him, "I am the LORD! Tell Pharaoh, the king of Egypt, everything I am telling you." ³⁰But Moses argued with the LORD, saying, "I can't do it! I'm such a clumsy speaker! Why should Pharaoh listen to me?"

## Aaron's Staff Becomes a Serpent

**7** Then the LORD said to Moses, "Pay close attention to this. I will make you seem like God to Pharaoh, and your brother, Aaron, will be your prophet. ²Tell Aaron everything I command you, and Aaron must command Pharaoh to let the people of Israel leave his country. ³But I will make Pharaoh's heart stubborn so I can multiply my miraculous signs and wonders in the land of Egypt. ⁴Even then Pharaoh will refuse to listen to you. So I will bring down my fist on Egypt. Then I will rescue my forces—my people, the Israelites—from the land of Egypt with great acts of judgment. ⁵When I raise my powerful hand and bring out the Israelites, the Egyptians will know that I am the LORD."

⁶So Moses and Aaron did just as the LORD had commanded them. ⁷Moses was eighty years old, and Aaron was eighty-three when they made their demands to Pharaoh.

6:12 Hebrew *I have uncircumcised lips;* also in 6:30.

---

**6:14-30** This genealogical interruption identifies how Moses and Aaron fit among Israel's families. It shows that God was continuing what he had done for their ancestors. The book of Exodus's recurring emphasis on Yahweh as the God of their ancestors comes explicitly (3:6 onward) and implicitly (1:1 onward). What God was about to do was not an unrelated action by some new god who devalued powerless older gods (a typical theme in ancient pagan literature). Unlike pagan gods, who aimed at personal power and fought among themselves, the true God has always had a single, overarching purpose for his creation to find fulfillment in proper relationship to him. Although God carries out that purpose in ever-expanding displays of creativity, the new activities always align with what he has already revealed of himself. Moses and Aaron did not suddenly appear out of the unknown. Rather, they belonged to those same people who God first revealed himself to. They belonged to the same people who God would soon show himself to even more grandly. The genealogies of Jesus have a similar purpose (Matthew 1:1-16; Luke 3:23-38).

**7:3** God announced several times that he would harden Pharaoh's heart (4:21; 9:12; 10:1). Here he gave an exact reason: Pharaoh's stubbornness would demonstrate God's miraculous power. God's hardening of Pharaoh's heart did not override Pharaoh's own will. Pharaoh hardened his own heart many times (7:13, 22; 8:15, 32; 9:35). God gave him ample opportunity to respond in repentance, but Pharaoh persistently refused, so God confirmed Pharaoh's rebellious decision.

**7:14–11:10** Each plague was an act of *uncreation.* The

⁸Then the LORD said to Moses and Aaron, ⁹"Pharaoh will demand, 'Show me a miracle.' When he does this, say to Aaron, 'Take your staff and throw it down in front of Pharaoh, and it will become a serpent.*'"

¹⁰So Moses and Aaron went to Pharaoh and did what the LORD had commanded them. Aaron threw down his staff before Pharaoh and his officials, and it became a serpent! ¹¹Then Pharaoh called in his own wise men and sorcerers, and these Egyptian magicians did the same thing with their magic. ¹²They threw down their staffs, which also became serpents! But then Aaron's staff swallowed up their staffs. ¹³Pharaoh's heart, however, remained hard. He still refused to listen, just as the LORD had predicted.

## A Plague of Blood

¹⁴Then the LORD said to Moses, "Pharaoh's heart is stubborn,* and he still refuses to let the people go. ¹⁵So go to Pharaoh in the morning as he goes down to the river. Stand on the bank of the Nile and meet him there. Be sure to take along the staff that turned into a snake. ¹⁶Then announce to him, 'The LORD, the God of the Hebrews, has sent me to tell you, "Let my people go, so they can worship me in the wilderness." Until now, you have refused to listen to him. ¹⁷So this is what the LORD says: "I will show you that I am the LORD." Look! I will strike the water of the Nile with this staff in my hand, and the river will turn to blood. ¹⁸The fish in it will die, and the river will stink. The Egyptians will not be able to drink any water from the Nile.'"

¹⁹Then the LORD said to Moses: "Tell Aaron, 'Take your staff and raise your hand over the waters of Egypt—all its rivers, canals, ponds, and all the reservoirs. Turn all the water to blood. Everywhere in Egypt the water will turn to blood, even the water stored in wooden bowls and stone pots.'"

²⁰So Moses and Aaron did just as the LORD commanded them. As Pharaoh and all of his officials watched, Aaron raised his staff and struck the water of the Nile. Suddenly, the whole river turned to blood! ²¹The fish in the river died, and the water became so foul that the Egyptians couldn't drink it. There was blood everywhere throughout the land of Egypt. ²²But again the magicians of Egypt used their magic, and they, too, turned water into blood. So Pharaoh's heart remained hard. He refused to listen to Moses and Aaron, just as the LORD had predicted. ²³Pharaoh returned to his palace and put the whole thing out of his mind. ²⁴Then all the Egyptians dug along the riverbank to find drinking water, for they couldn't drink the water from the Nile.

²⁵Seven days passed from the time the LORD struck the Nile.

## A Plague of Frogs

8 ¹*Then the LORD said to Moses, "Go back to Pharaoh and announce to him, 'This is what the LORD says: Let my people go, so they can worship me. ²If you refuse to let them go, I will send a plague of frogs across your entire land. ³The Nile River will swarm with frogs. They will come up out of the river and into your palace, even into your bedroom and onto your bed! They will enter the houses of your officials and your people. They will even jump into your ovens and your kneading bowls. ⁴Frogs will jump on you, your people, and all your officials.'"

⁵*Then the LORD said to Moses, "Tell Aaron, 'Raise the staff in your hand over all the rivers, canals, and ponds of Egypt, and bring up frogs over all the land.'" ⁶So Aaron raised his hand over the waters of Egypt, and frogs came up and covered the whole land! ⁷But the magicians were able to do the same thing with their magic. They, too, caused frogs to come up on the land of Egypt.

⁸Then Pharaoh summoned Moses and Aaron and begged, "Plead with the LORD to take the frogs away from me and my people. I will let your people go, so they can offer sacrifices to the LORD."

⁹"You set the time!" Moses replied. "Tell me when you want me to pray for you, your officials, and your people. Then you and your houses will be rid of the frogs. They will remain only in the Nile River."

¹⁰"Do it tomorrow," Pharaoh said.

"All right," Moses replied, "it will be as you have said. Then you will know that there is no one like the LORD our God. ¹¹The frogs will leave you and your houses, your officials, and your people. They will remain only in the Nile River."

¹²So Moses and Aaron left Pharaoh's palace, and Moses cried out to the LORD about the frogs he had inflicted on Pharaoh. ¹³And the LORD did just what Moses had predicted. The frogs in the houses, the courtyards, and the fields all died. ¹⁴The Egyptians piled them into great heaps, and a terrible stench filled the land. ¹⁵But when Pharaoh saw that relief had come, he became stubborn.* He refused to listen to Moses and Aaron, just as the LORD had predicted.

---

**7:9** Hebrew *tannin*, which elsewhere refers to a sea monster. Greek version translates it "dragon."  **7:14** Hebrew *heavy*.  **8:1** Verses 8:1-4 are numbered 7:26-29 in Hebrew text.  **8:5** Verses 8:5-32 are numbered 8:1-28 in Hebrew text.  **8:15** Hebrew *made his heart heavy;* also in 8:32.

---

destructive policies of the pharaohs (killing infants and working enslaved people ruthlessly) opposed God's creation design by bringing death and bondage, rather than human flourishing. God responded by bringing disorder to Egypt: Water became undrinkable, frogs ran amok, gnats and flies filled the air, livestock died, people broke out in boils, hail destroyed crops, locusts ate what

remained, and daytime turned into darkness. Eventually, the firstborn children of Egypt died.

**8:25** Pharaoh attempted to bargain with God. He wanted to obey partially while still retaining control. James says people who divide loyalty between God and the world "[are] as unsettled as a wave of the sea that is blown and tossed by the wind" (James 1:6). Similarly,

# Insight  TEN PLAGUES AGAINST TEN FALSE GODS

When God rescued his people from Egypt after many years of slavery there, he displayed his power over Egypt's gods through a series of plagues (7:14–11:10). Each plague can be understood as a direct challenge to a specific Egyptian deity.

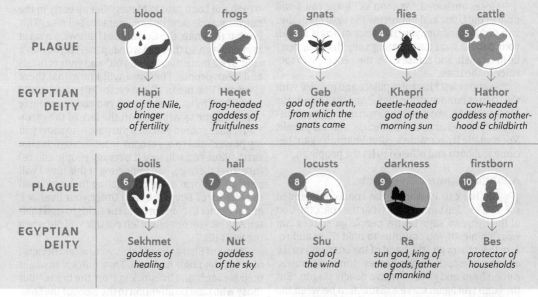

| | blood | frogs | gnats | flies | cattle |
|---|---|---|---|---|---|
| PLAGUE | 1 | 2 | 3 | 4 | 5 |
| EGYPTIAN DEITY | Hapi *god of the Nile, bringer of fertility* | Heqet *frog-headed goddess of fruitfulness* | Geb *god of the earth, from which the gnats came* | Khepri *beetle-headed god of the morning sun* | Hathor *cow-headed goddess of mother-hood & childbirth* |

| | boils | hail | locusts | darkness | firstborn |
|---|---|---|---|---|---|
| PLAGUE | 6 | 7 | 8 | 9 | 10 |
| EGYPTIAN DEITY | Sekhmet *goddess of healing* | Nut *goddess of the sky* | Shu *god of the wind* | Ra *sun god, king of the gods, father of mankind* | Bes *protector of households* |

## A Plague of Gnats

¹⁶So the LORD said to Moses, "Tell Aaron, 'Raise your staff and strike the ground. The dust will turn into swarms of gnats throughout the land of Egypt.'" ¹⁷So Moses and Aaron did just as the LORD had commanded them. When Aaron raised his hand and struck the ground with his staff, gnats infested the entire land, covering the Egyptians and their animals. All the dust in the land of Egypt turned into gnats. ¹⁸Pharaoh's magicians tried to do the same thing with their secret arts, but this time they failed. And the gnats covered everyone, people and animals alike.

¹⁹"This is the finger of God!" the magicians exclaimed to Pharaoh. But Pharaoh's heart remained hard. He wouldn't listen to them, just as the LORD had predicted.

## A Plague of Flies

²⁰Then the LORD told Moses, "Get up early in the morning and stand in Pharaoh's way as he goes down to the river. Say to him, 'This is what the LORD says: Let my people go, so they can worship me. ²¹If you refuse, then I will send swarms of flies on you, your officials, your people, and all the houses. The Egyptian homes will be filled with flies, and the ground will be covered with them. ²²But this time I will spare the region of Goshen, where my people live. No flies will be found there. Then you will know that I am the LORD and that I am present even in the heart of your land. ²³I will make a clear distinction between* my people and your people. This miraculous sign will happen tomorrow.'"

²⁴And the LORD did just as he had said. A thick swarm of flies filled Pharaoh's palace and the houses of his officials. The whole land of Egypt was thrown into chaos by the flies.

²⁵Pharaoh called for Moses and Aaron. "All right! Go ahead and offer sacrifices to your God," he said. "But do it here in this land."

²⁶But Moses replied, "That wouldn't be right. The Egyptians detest the sacrifices that we offer to the LORD our God. Look, if we offer our sacrifices here

8:23 As in Greek and Latin versions; Hebrew reads *I will set redemption between*.

Jesus explains that anyone who divides their commitment works against God (Matthew 12:22-30).
**8:26-27** Moses pointed out the impossibility of Pharaoh's request by noting the Egyptians' own prejudice. The Egyptians thought the Hebrew people were beneath them (see Genesis 43:32). The Hebrews asked to leave Egypt to worship God (see Exodus 5:1; 7:16; 8:1, 20). God's purpose for the Exodus was to lead his people into a proper relationship with him. The first step was to free them from Pharaoh's oppressive rule and the Egyptians' prejudice.

where the Egyptians can see us, they will stone us. ²⁷We must take a three-day trip into the wilderness to offer sacrifices to the LORD our God, just as he has commanded us."

²⁸"All right, go ahead," Pharaoh replied. "I will let you go into the wilderness to offer sacrifices to the LORD your God. But don't go too far away. Now hurry and pray for me."

²⁹Moses answered, "As soon as I leave you, I will pray to the LORD, and tomorrow the swarms of flies will disappear from you and your officials and all your people. But I am warning you, Pharaoh, don't lie to us again and refuse to let the people go to sacrifice to the LORD."

³⁰So Moses left Pharaoh's palace and pleaded with the LORD to remove all the flies. ³¹And the LORD did as Moses asked and caused the swarms of flies to disappear from Pharaoh, his officials, and his people. Not a single fly remained. ³²But Pharaoh again became stubborn and refused to let the people go.

## A Plague against Livestock

9 "Go back to Pharaoh," the LORD commanded Moses. "Tell him, 'This is what the LORD, the God of the Hebrews, says: Let my people go, so they can worship me. ²If you continue to hold them and refuse to let them go, ³the hand of the LORD will strike all your livestock—your horses, donkeys, camels, cattle, sheep, and goats—with a deadly plague. ⁴But the LORD will again make a distinction between the livestock of the Israelites and that of the Egyptians. Not a single one of Israel's animals will die! ⁵The LORD has already set the time for the plague to begin. He has declared that he will strike the land tomorrow.'"

⁶And the LORD did just as he had said. The next morning all the livestock of the Egyptians died, but the Israelites didn't lose a single animal. ⁷Pharaoh sent his officials to investigate, and they discovered that the Israelites had not lost a single animal! But even so, Pharaoh's heart remained stubborn,* and he still refused to let the people go.

## A Plague of Festering Boils

⁸Then the LORD said to Moses and Aaron, "Take handfuls of soot from a brick kiln, and have Moses toss it into the air while Pharaoh watches. ⁹The ashes will spread like fine dust over the whole land of Egypt, causing festering boils to break out on people and animals throughout the land."

¹⁰So they took soot from a brick kiln and went and stood before Pharaoh. As Pharaoh watched, Moses threw the soot into the air, and boils broke out on people and animals alike. ¹¹Even the magicians were unable to stand before Moses, because the boils had broken out on them and all the Egyptians. ¹²But the LORD hardened Pharaoh's heart, and just as the LORD had predicted to Moses, Pharaoh refused to listen.

## A Plague of Hail

¹³Then the LORD said to Moses, "Get up early in the morning and stand before Pharaoh. Tell him, 'This is what the LORD, the God of the Hebrews, says: Let my people go, so they can worship me. ¹⁴If you don't, I will send more plagues on you* and your officials and your people. Then you will know that there is no one like me in all the earth. ¹⁵By now I could have lifted my hand and struck you and your people with a plague to wipe you off the face of the earth. ¹⁶But I have spared you for a purpose—to show you my power* and to spread my fame throughout the earth. ¹⁷But you still lord it over my people and refuse to let them go. ¹⁸So tomorrow at this time I will send a hailstorm more devastating than any in all the history of Egypt. ¹⁹Quick! Order your livestock and servants to come in from the fields to find shelter. Any person or animal left outside will die when the hail falls.'"

²⁰Some of Pharaoh's officials were afraid because of what the LORD had said. They quickly brought their servants and livestock in from the fields. ²¹But those who paid no attention to the word of the LORD left theirs out in the open.

²²Then the LORD said to Moses, "Lift your hand toward the sky so hail may fall on the people, the livestock, and all the plants throughout the land of Egypt."

²³So Moses lifted his staff toward the sky, and the LORD sent thunder and hail, and lightning flashed toward the earth. The LORD sent a tremendous hailstorm against all the land of Egypt. ²⁴Never in all the history of Egypt had there been a storm like that, with such devastating hail and continuous lightning. ²⁵It left all of Egypt in ruins. The hail struck down everything in the open field—people, animals, and plants alike. Even the trees were destroyed. ²⁶The only place without hail was the region of Goshen, where the people of Israel lived.

²⁷Then Pharaoh quickly summoned Moses and Aaron. "This time I have sinned," he confessed. "The LORD is the righteous one, and my people and I are wrong. ²⁸Please beg the LORD to end this terrifying thunder and hail. We've had enough. I will let you go; you don't need to stay any longer."

9:7 Hebrew *heavy.* 9:14 Hebrew *on your heart.* 9:16 Greek version reads *to display my power in you;* compare Rom 9:17.

**9:14-17** God explained the plagues' purpose: to reveal (especially to Pharaoh) that "there is no one like me in all the earth" (9:14; see also Isaiah 46:9; Jeremiah 10:6-7). Thus, God did not destroy Pharaoh and Egypt in a single blow, as he could have done. Instead, God spared them (Exodus 9:16), allowing them to submit to his power, repent of their sins, and let the Israelites leave Egypt. But Pharaoh refused to humble himself and stop playing lord over the Lord's people (9:17).

²⁹"All right," Moses replied. "As soon as I leave the city, I will lift my hands and pray to the LORD. Then the thunder and hail will stop, and you will know that the earth belongs to the LORD. ³⁰But I know that you and your officials still do not fear the LORD God."

³¹(All the flax and barley were ruined by the hail, because the barley had formed heads and the flax was budding. ³²But the wheat and the emmer wheat were spared, because they had not yet sprouted from the ground.)

³³So Moses left Pharaoh's court and went out of the city. When he lifted his hands to the LORD, the thunder and hail stopped, and the downpour ceased. ³⁴But when Pharaoh saw that the rain, hail, and thunder had stopped, he and his officials sinned again, and Pharaoh again became stubborn.* ³⁵Because his heart was hard, Pharaoh refused to let the people leave, just as the LORD had predicted through Moses.

## A Plague of Locusts

10 Then the LORD said to Moses, "Return to Pharaoh and make your demands again. I have made him and his officials stubborn* so I can display my miraculous signs among them. ²I've also done it so you can tell your children and grandchildren about how I made a mockery of the Egyptians and about the signs I displayed among them—and so you will know that I am the LORD."

³So Moses and Aaron went to Pharaoh and said, "This is what the LORD, the God of the Hebrews, says: How long will you refuse to submit to me? Let my people go, so they can worship me. ⁴If you refuse, watch out! For tomorrow I will bring a swarm of locusts on your country. ⁵They will cover the land so that you won't be able to see the ground. They will devour what little is left of your crops after the hailstorm, including all the trees growing in the fields. ⁶They will overrun your palaces and the homes of your officials and all the houses in Egypt. Never in the history of Egypt have your ancestors seen a plague like this one!" And with that, Moses turned and left Pharaoh.

⁷Pharaoh's officials now came to Pharaoh and appealed to him. "How long will you let this man hold us hostage? Let the men go to worship the LORD their God! Don't you realize that Egypt lies in ruins?"

⁸So Moses and Aaron were brought back to Pharaoh. "All right," he told them, "go and worship the LORD your God. But who exactly will be going with you?"

⁹Moses replied, "We will all go—young and old, our sons and daughters, and our flocks and herds. We must all join together in celebrating a festival to the LORD."

¹⁰Pharaoh retorted, "The LORD will certainly need to be with you if I let you take your little ones! I can see through your evil plan. ¹¹Never! Only the men may go and worship the LORD, since that is what you requested." And Pharaoh threw them out of the palace.

¹²Then the LORD said to Moses, "Raise your hand over the land of Egypt to bring on the locusts. Let them cover the land and devour every plant that survived the hailstorm."

¹³So Moses raised his staff over Egypt, and the LORD caused an east wind to blow over the land all that day and through the night. When morning arrived, the east wind had brought the locusts. ¹⁴And the locusts swarmed over the whole land of Egypt, settling in dense swarms from one end of the country to the other. It was the worst locust plague in Egyptian history, and there has never been another one like it. ¹⁵For the locusts covered the whole country and darkened the land. They devoured every plant in the fields and all the fruit on the trees that had survived the hailstorm. Not a single leaf was left on the trees and plants throughout the land of Egypt.

¹⁶Pharaoh quickly summoned Moses and Aaron. "I have sinned against the LORD your God and against you," he confessed. ¹⁷"Forgive my sin, just this once, and plead with the LORD your God to take away this death from me."

¹⁸So Moses left Pharaoh's court and pleaded with the LORD. ¹⁹The LORD responded by shifting the wind, and the strong west wind blew the locusts into the Red Sea.* Not a single locust remained in all the land of Egypt. ²⁰But the LORD hardened Pharaoh's heart again, so he refused to let the people go.

## A Plague of Darkness

²¹Then the LORD said to Moses, "Lift your hand toward heaven, and the land of Egypt will be covered with a darkness so thick you can feel it." ²²So Moses lifted his hand to the sky, and a deep darkness covered the entire land of Egypt for three days. ²³During all that time the people could not see each other, and no one moved. But there was light as usual where the people of Israel lived.

²⁴Finally, Pharaoh called for Moses. "Go and worship the LORD," he said. "But leave your flocks and herds here. You may even take your little ones with you."

²⁵"No," Moses said, "you must provide us with animals for sacrifices and burnt offerings to the LORD our God. ²⁶All our livestock must go with us, too; not a hoof can be left behind. We must choose our

9:34 Hebrew *made his heart heavy.* 10:1 Hebrew *have made his heart and his officials' hearts heavy.* 10:19 Hebrew *sea of reeds.*

9:29 There is no one like the Lord in all the earth (9:14), and all "the earth belongs to the LORD." This was the plagues' inescapable message, though the Egyptians had difficulty accepting it.

10:16-17 Pharaoh's recognition of his sin grew deeper the more he experienced God's judgment. He admitted that his pride and refusal to keep his word were sins. He recognized that sin cannot be ignored but requires God's forgiveness. But unfortunately, his correct theological understanding did not change his heart.

sacrifices for the LORD our God from among these animals. And we won't know how we are to worship the LORD until we get there."

27But the LORD hardened Pharaoh's heart once more, and he would not let them go. 28"Get out of here!" Pharaoh shouted at Moses. "I'm warning you. Never come back to see me again! The day you see my face, you will die!"

29"Very well," Moses replied. "I will never see your face again."

## Death for Egypt's Firstborn

11 Then the LORD said to Moses, "I will strike Pharaoh and the land of Egypt with one more blow. After that, Pharaoh will let you leave this country. In fact, he will be so eager to get rid of you that he will force you all to leave. 2Tell all the Israelite men and women to ask their Egyptian neighbors for articles of silver and gold." 3(Now the LORD had caused the Egyptians to look favorably on the people of Israel. And Moses was considered a very great man in the land of Egypt, respected by Pharaoh's officials and the Egyptian people alike.)

4Moses had announced to Pharaoh, "This is what the LORD says: At midnight tonight I will pass through the heart of Egypt. 5All the firstborn sons will die in every family in Egypt, from the oldest son of Pharaoh, who sits on his throne, to the oldest son of his lowliest servant girl who grinds the flour. Even the firstborn of all the livestock will die. 6Then a loud wail will rise throughout the land of Egypt, a wail like no one has heard before or will ever hear again. 7But among the Israelites it will be so peaceful that not even a dog will bark. Then you will know that the LORD makes a distinction between the Egyptians and the Israelites. 8All the officials of Egypt will run to me and fall to the ground before me. 'Please leave!' they will beg. 'Hurry! And take all your followers with you.' Only then will I go!" Then, burning with anger, Moses left Pharaoh.

9Now the LORD had told Moses earlier, "Pharaoh will not listen to you, but then I will do even more mighty miracles in the land of Egypt." 10Moses and Aaron performed these miracles in Pharaoh's presence, but the LORD hardened Pharaoh's heart, and he wouldn't let the Israelites leave the country.

12:11 Hebrew *Bind up your loins.*

## The First Passover

12 While the Israelites were still in the land of Egypt, the LORD gave the following instructions to Moses and Aaron: 2"From now on, this month will be the first month of the year for you. 3Announce to the whole community of Israel that on the tenth day of this month each family must choose a lamb or a young goat for a sacrifice, one animal for each household. 4If a family is too small to eat a whole animal, let them share with another family in the neighborhood. Divide the animal according to the size of each family and how much they can eat. 5The animal you select must be a one-year-old male, either a sheep or a goat, with no defects.

6"Take special care of this chosen animal until the evening of the fourteenth day of this first month. Then the whole assembly of the community of Israel must slaughter their lamb or young goat at twilight. 7They are to take some of the blood and smear it on the sides and top of the doorframes of the houses where they eat the animal. 8That same night they must roast the meat over a fire and eat it along with bitter salad greens and bread made without yeast. 9Do not eat any of the meat raw or boiled in water. The whole animal—including the head, legs, and internal organs—must be roasted over a fire. 10Do not leave any of it until the next morning. Burn whatever is not eaten before morning.

11"These are your instructions for eating this meal: Be fully dressed,* wear your sandals, and carry your walking stick in your hand. Eat the meal with urgency, for this is the LORD's Passover. 12On that night I will pass through the land of Egypt and strike down every firstborn son and firstborn male animal in the land of Egypt. I will execute judgment against all the gods of Egypt, for I am the LORD! 13But the blood on your doorposts will serve as a sign, marking the houses where you are staying. When I see the blood, I will pass over you. This plague of death will not touch you when I strike the land of Egypt.

14"This is a day to remember. Each year, from generation to generation, you must celebrate it as a special festival to the LORD. This is a law for all time. 15For seven days the bread you eat must be made without yeast. On the first day of the festival,

---

**10:27-29** Pharaoh seemed to realize that he had reached a point of no return. If he would not submit—the only appropriate response to what he had learned from the plagues—then he must kill the messenger. This reasoning resembles what the Gospels say about the religious leaders' plot to kill Jesus. They refused to learn from Jesus' life and ministry appropriately, so they arranged to kill him (see John 11:45-53).

**11:4-8** After months of stubborn resistance to the Lord's demands, Pharaoh brought a terrible consequence on his people. A previous pharaoh had demanded the death of Hebrew boys; now, Egyptian sons would die. In 4:22-23, God

called Israel his firstborn son and stated that because Pharaoh refused to let Israel worship Yahweh, he would kill Pharaoh's firstborn son. Meanwhile, the Hebrew firstborn sons would be under God's protection as long as they showed allegiance to him through the Passover ritual.

**12:1** This chapter of ritual instructions may feel like an odd interruption to an otherwise gripping story, but it serves an important function. The yearly Passover celebration would ensure that every generation would own the Exodus from Egypt as their story. The sounds, smells, and tastes of Passover made the Exodus come alive again every year.

remove every trace of yeast from your homes. Anyone who eats bread made with yeast during the seven days of the festival will be cut off from the community of Israel. ¹⁶On the first day of the festival and again on the seventh day, all the people must observe an official day for holy assembly. No work of any kind may be done on these days except in the preparation of food.

¹⁷"Celebrate this Festival of Unleavened Bread, for it will remind you that I brought your forces out of the land of Egypt on this very day. This festival will be a permanent law for you; celebrate this day from generation to generation. ¹⁸The bread you eat must be made without yeast from the evening of the fourteenth day of the first month until the evening of the twenty-first day of that month. ¹⁹During those seven days, there

# Insight    ISRAEL'S CALENDAR OF FESTIVALS

Ancient Israel marked the beginning of each month at the new moon, which occurs on average every 29.5 days. Twelve lunar cycles results in a 354-day calendar, which is 11 days shorter than the solar year. The Israelites also celebrated several annual festivals. This regular cycle of celebrations helped the people of Israel remember what God had done for them in the past and how he would provide for them as they journeyed to a new land.

## ANNUAL FESTIVALS

**Passover**
Leviticus 23:5

**Unleavened Bread**
Leviticus 23:6-8

**First Harvest**
Leviticus 23:9-14

**Later Passover**
Numbers 9:4-12

**Harvest**
Leviticus 23:15-22

**Trumpets**
Leviticus 23:23-25

**Day of Atonement**
Leviticus 23:26-32

**Shelters**
Leviticus 23:33-43

**Dedication**
John 10:22

**Purim**
Esther 9:1-32

Modern months, for comparison

Months were most often referred to by numbers

> "When I left the house of bondage, … I went to the Lord and asked Him to give me a new name. And the Lord gave me Sojourner, because I was to travel up and down the land, showing the people their sins, and being a sign unto them. Afterwards I told the Lord I wanted another name, … and the Lord gave me Truth, because I was to declare the truth to the people."
>
> **SOJOURNER TRUTH**
> (1797–1883) evangelist, abolitionist, and women's rights activist

your houses. And no one may go out through the door until morning. ²³For the LORD will pass through the land to strike down the Egyptians. But when he sees the blood on the top and sides of the doorframe, the LORD will pass over your home. He will not permit his death angel to enter your house and strike you down.

²⁴"Remember, these instructions are a permanent law that you and your descendants must observe forever. ²⁵When you enter the land the LORD has promised to give you, you will continue to observe this ceremony. ²⁶Then your children will ask, 'What does this ceremony mean?' ²⁷And you will reply, 'It is the Passover sacrifice to the LORD, for he passed over the houses of the Israelites in Egypt. And though he struck the Egyptians, he spared our families.'" When Moses had finished speaking, all the people bowed down to the ground and worshiped.

²⁸So the people of Israel did just as the LORD had commanded through Moses and Aaron. ²⁹And that night at midnight, the LORD struck down all the firstborn sons in the land of Egypt, from the firstborn son of Pharaoh, who sat on his throne, to the firstborn son of the prisoner in the dungeon. Even the firstborn of their livestock were killed. ³⁰Pharaoh and all his officials and all the people of Egypt woke up during the night, and loud wailing was heard throughout the land of Egypt. There was not a single house where someone had not died.

### Israel's Exodus from Egypt

³¹Pharaoh sent for Moses and Aaron during the night. "Get out!" he ordered. "Leave my people—and take the rest of the Israelites with you! Go and worship the LORD as you have requested. ³²Take your flocks and herds, as you said, and be gone. Go, but bless me as you leave." ³³All the Egyptians urged the people of Israel to get out of the land as quickly as possible, for they thought, "We will all die!"

³⁴The Israelites took their bread dough before yeast was added. They wrapped their kneading boards in their cloaks and carried them on their shoulders. ³⁵And the people of Israel did as Moses had instructed; they asked the Egyptians for clothing and articles of silver and gold. ³⁶The LORD caused the Egyptians to look favorably on the Israelites, and they gave the Israelites whatever they asked for. So they stripped the Egyptians of their wealth!

³⁷That night the people of Israel left Rameses and started for Succoth. There were about 600,000 men,* plus all the women and children. ³⁸A rabble

must be no trace of yeast in your homes. Anyone who eats anything made with yeast during this week will be cut off from the community of Israel. These regulations apply both to the foreigners living among you and to the native-born Israelites. ²⁰During those days you must not eat anything made with yeast. Wherever you live, eat only bread made without yeast."

²¹Then Moses called all the elders of Israel together and said to them, "Go, pick out a lamb or young goat for each of your families, and slaughter the Passover animal. ²²Drain the blood into a basin. Then take a bundle of hyssop branches and dip it into the blood. Brush the hyssop across the top and sides of the doorframes of

---

**12:37** Or *fighting men;* Hebrew reads *men on foot.*

---

**12:37** This large number implies a total of about 2.5 million Hebrews who left Egypt, which raises logistical problems: First, their camp would cover about 400 square miles; second, a line of people 1,000 across would be nearly a mile wide and would take 20 hours to pass a single point; and third, no other armies were so large at that time. As a result, two viable alternatives have been proposed: The number is symbolic, perhaps reflecting the number of Israelites during a later period; or the Hebrew word for "thousand" (*eleph*) can also mean "military unit." So this could be read as "600 military units of fighting men." With an average military unit of approximately 10 to 15 men, standard for that time, the total population would be closer to 22,000.

of non-Israelites went with them, along with great flocks and herds of livestock. ³⁹For bread they baked flat cakes from the dough without yeast they had brought from Egypt. It was made without yeast because the people were driven out of Egypt in such a hurry that they had no time to prepare the bread or other food.

⁴⁰The people of Israel had lived in Egypt* for 430 years. ⁴¹In fact, it was on the last day of the 430th year that all the LORD's forces left the land. ⁴²On this night the LORD kept his promise to bring his people out of the land of Egypt. So this night belongs to him, and it must be commemorated every year by all the Israelites, from generation to generation.

## Instructions for the Passover

⁴³Then the LORD said to Moses and Aaron, "These are the instructions for the festival of Passover. No outsiders are allowed to eat the Passover meal. ⁴⁴But any slave who has been purchased may eat it if he has been circumcised. ⁴⁵Temporary residents and hired servants may not eat it. ⁴⁶Each Passover lamb must be eaten in one house. Do not carry any of its meat outside, and do not break any of its bones. ⁴⁷The whole community of Israel must celebrate this Passover festival.

⁴⁸"If there are foreigners living among you who want to celebrate the LORD's Passover, let all their males be circumcised. Only then may they celebrate the Passover with you like any native-born Israelite. But no uncircumcised male may ever eat the Passover meal. ⁴⁹This instruction applies to everyone, whether a native-born Israelite or a foreigner living among you."

⁵⁰So all the people of Israel followed all the LORD's commands to Moses and Aaron. ⁵¹On that very day the LORD brought the people of Israel out of the land of Egypt like an army.

## Dedication of the Firstborn

**13** Then the LORD said to Moses, ²"Dedicate to me every firstborn among the Israelites. The first offspring to be born, of both humans and animals, belongs to me."

³So Moses said to the people, "This is a day to remember forever—the day you left Egypt, the place of your slavery. Today the LORD has brought you out by the power of his mighty hand. (Remember, eat no food containing yeast.) ⁴On this day in early spring,

in the month of Abib,* you have been set free. ⁵You must celebrate this event in this month each year after the LORD brings you into the land of the Canaanites, Hittites, Amorites, Hivites, and Jebusites. (He swore to your ancestors that he would give you this land—a land flowing with milk and honey.) ⁶For seven days the bread you eat must be made without yeast. Then on the seventh day, celebrate a feast to the LORD. ⁷Eat bread without yeast during those seven days. In fact, there must be no yeast bread or any yeast at all found within the borders of your land during this time.

⁸"On the seventh day you must explain to your children, 'I am celebrating what the LORD did for me when I left Egypt.' ⁹This annual festival will be a visible sign to you, like a mark branded on your hand or your forehead. Let it remind you always to recite this teaching of the LORD: 'With a strong hand, the LORD rescued you from Egypt.'* ¹⁰So observe the decree of this festival at the appointed time each year.

¹¹"This is what you must do when the LORD fulfills the promise he swore to you and to your ancestors. When he gives you the land where the Canaanites now live, ¹²you must present all firstborn sons and firstborn male animals to the LORD, for they belong to him. ¹³A firstborn donkey may be bought back from the LORD by presenting a lamb or young goat in its place. But if you do not buy it back, you must break its neck. However, you must buy back every firstborn son.

¹⁴"And in the future, your children will ask you, 'What does all this mean?' Then you will tell them, 'With the power of his mighty hand, the LORD brought us out of Egypt, the place of our slavery. ¹⁵Pharaoh stubbornly refused to let us go, so the LORD killed all the firstborn males throughout the land of Egypt, both people and animals. That is why I now sacrifice all the firstborn males to the LORD—except that the firstborn sons are always bought back.' ¹⁶This ceremony will be like a mark branded on your hand or your forehead. It is a reminder that the power of the LORD's mighty hand brought us out of Egypt."

## Israel's Wilderness Detour

¹⁷When Pharaoh finally let the people go, God did not lead them along the main road that runs through Philistine territory, even though that was the shortest route to the Promised Land. God said, "If the people are faced with a battle, they might change

---

**12:40** Samaritan Pentateuch reads *in Canaan and Egypt;* Greek version reads *in Egypt and Canaan.* **13:4** Hebrew *On this day in the month of Abib.* This first month of the ancient Hebrew lunar calendar usually occurs within the months of March and April. **13:9** Or *Let it remind you always to keep the instructions of the LORD on the tip of your tongue, because with a strong hand, the LORD rescued you from Egypt.*

---

**12:48** For the Israelites, male circumcision was a sign of covenant membership. While only men were circumcised, women were included in the covenant through their connection to circumcised men—their fathers, husbands, and sons. Foreigners were welcome to join the Israelite community by adopting this practice.

**13:12** Selecting firstborn sons to belong to the Lord probably reflects Pharaoh's attempts to target Hebrew boys (1:16, 22). God set up a perpetual reminder that the Israelites were *his* people, rather than Pharaoh's.

their minds and return to Egypt." ¹⁸So God led them in a roundabout way through the wilderness toward the Red Sea.* Thus the Israelites left Egypt like an army ready for battle.*

¹⁹Moses took the bones of Joseph with him, for Joseph had made the sons of Israel swear to do this. He said, "God will certainly come to help you. When he does, you must take my bones with you from this place."

²⁰The Israelites left Succoth and camped at Etham on the edge of the wilderness. ²¹The LORD went ahead of them. He guided them during the day with a pillar of cloud, and he provided light at night with a pillar of fire. This allowed them to travel by day or by night. ²²And the LORD did not remove the pillar of cloud or pillar of fire from its place in front of the people.

**14** Then the LORD gave these instructions to Moses: ²"Order the Israelites to turn back and camp by Pi-hahiroth between Migdol and the sea. Camp there along the shore, across from Baal-zephon. ³Then Pharaoh will think, 'The Israelites are confused. They are trapped in the wilderness!' ⁴And once again I will harden Pharaoh's heart, and he will chase after you.* I have planned this in order to display my glory through Pharaoh and his whole army. After this the Egyptians will know that I am the LORD!" So the Israelites camped there as they were told.

## The Egyptians Pursue Israel

⁵When word reached the king of Egypt that the Israelites had fled, Pharaoh and his officials changed their minds. "What have we done, letting all those Israelite slaves get away?" they asked. ⁶So Pharaoh harnessed his chariot and called up his troops. ⁷He took with him 600 of Egypt's best chariots, along with the rest of the chariots of Egypt, each with its commander. ⁸The LORD hardened the heart of Pharaoh, the king of Egypt, so he chased after the people of Israel, who had left with fists raised in defiance. ⁹The Egyptians chased after them with all the forces in Pharaoh's army—all his horses and chariots, his charioteers, and his troops. The Egyptians caught up with the people of Israel as they were camped beside the shore near Pi-hahiroth, across from Baal-zephon.

¹⁰As Pharaoh approached, the people of Israel looked up and panicked when they saw the Egyptians overtaking them. They cried out to the LORD, ¹¹and they said to Moses, "Why did you bring us out here to die in the wilderness? Weren't there enough graves for us in Egypt? What have you done to us? Why did you make us leave Egypt? ¹²Didn't we tell you this would happen while we were still in Egypt? We said, 'Leave us alone! Let us be slaves to the Egyptians. It's better to be a slave in Egypt than a corpse in the wilderness!'"

¹³But Moses told the people, "Don't be afraid. Just stand still and watch the LORD rescue you today. The Egyptians you see today will never be seen again. ¹⁴The LORD himself will fight for you. Just stay calm."

## Escape through the Red Sea

¹⁵Then the LORD said to Moses, "Why are you crying out to me? Tell the people to get moving! ¹⁶Pick up your staff and raise your hand over the sea. Divide the water so the Israelites can walk through the middle of the sea on dry ground. ¹⁷And I will harden the hearts of the Egyptians, and they will charge in after the Israelites. My great glory will be displayed through Pharaoh and his troops, his chariots, and his charioteers. ¹⁸When my glory is displayed through them, all Egypt will see my glory and know that I am the LORD!"

¹⁹Then the angel of God, who had been leading the people of Israel, moved to the rear of the camp. The pillar of cloud also moved from the front and stood behind them. ²⁰The cloud settled between the Egyptian and Israelite camps. As darkness fell, the cloud turned to fire, lighting up the night. But the Egyptians and Israelites did not approach each other all night.

²¹Then Moses raised his hand over the sea, and the LORD opened up a path through the water with a strong east wind. The wind blew all that night, turning the seabed into dry land. ²²So the people of Israel walked through the middle of the sea on dry ground, with walls of water on each side!

²³Then the Egyptians—all of Pharaoh's horses, chariots, and charioteers—chased them into the middle of the sea. ²⁴But just before dawn the LORD looked down on the Egyptian army from the pillar

---

**13:18a** Hebrew *sea of reeds.* **13:18b** Greek version reads *left Egypt in the fifth generation.* **14:4** Hebrew *after them.*

**13:21-22** God graciously led his people with a cloud they could see day and night. This had a practical benefit since travel by night would be advantageous in a hot desert. The cloud also visibly demonstrated Yahweh's presence with them—a striking testimony to surrounding nations (see Joshua 2:8-11). God's people usually experience his guidance less dramatically—for example, through the Spirit convicting us of sin or giving us peace.

**14:10-12** This complaint is the first time we see the sad refrain that the Israelites will repeat for the next forty years, as they

wander in the wilderness. Instead of believing that God, who demonstrated his power so overwhelmingly, could now save them, the Israelites turned on their rescuer. The cry of the unsurrendered heart is always "Give me the security of slavery rather than the risk of faith!"

**14:22** As with the plagues, naturalistic explanations for this event fall short. A strong, steady wind blowing across a shallow, contained body of water can change its depth dramatically. But it does not produce "dry ground, with walls of water on each side." The Lord can intervene and do with nature as he wishes.

of fire and cloud, and he threw their forces into total confusion. [25]He twisted* their chariot wheels, making their chariots difficult to drive. "Let's get out of here—away from these Israelites!" the Egyptians shouted. "The LORD is fighting for them against Egypt!"

[26]When all the Israelites had reached the other side, the LORD said to Moses, "Raise your hand over the sea again. Then the waters will rush back and cover the Egyptians and their chariots and charioteers." [27]So as the sun began to rise, Moses raised his hand over the sea, and the water rushed back into its usual place. The Egyptians tried to escape, but the LORD swept them into the sea. [28]Then the waters returned and covered all the chariots and charioteers—the entire army of Pharaoh. Of all the Egyptians who had chased the Israelites into the sea, not a single one survived.

[29]But the people of Israel had walked through the middle of the sea on dry ground, as the water stood up like a wall on both sides. [30]That is how the LORD rescued Israel from the hand of the Egyptians that day. And the Israelites saw the bodies of the Egyptians washed up on the seashore. [31]When the people of Israel saw the mighty power that the LORD had unleashed against the Egyptians, they were filled with awe before him. They put their faith in the LORD and in his servant Moses.

## A Song of Deliverance

**15** Then Moses and the people of Israel sang this song to the LORD:

"I will sing to the LORD,
    for he has triumphed gloriously;

14:25 As in Greek version, Samaritan Pentateuch, and Syriac version; Hebrew reads *He removed.*

---

## ⑧ Come Close   OPPRESSED: CONFRONTING FEAR

**SCRIPTURE CONNECTION: EXODUS 14:5-31**

The overarching theme in all of God's signs is very clear to those of us who have been delivered from oppression: Do not be afraid. See, fear is the currency of oppression. To confront oppression is to confront fear.

I always understood that fear was a driving force in how power oppresses. Fear is what keeps people quiet when wrong things happen. Fear is what allows people to keep bowing under pressure. Fear is instilled in oppressed people to get them to submit to the oppression. It's how so many oppressors can govern and oppress people who outnumber them. The Israelites were afraid of Pharaoh, and that fear kept them under his control. I knew that. What I didn't know—and this information would change the way I think of oppression forever—is that Pharaoh was afraid of the Israelites.

Make no mistake. Both the oppressed and the oppressor are participating in the same fear. If you participate in fear, you will either oppress or you will be oppressed. Give it some thought and study. Every despot, every oppressive leader in the world, was terrified. ... Terrified leaders oppress terrified people.

Is it any wonder that whenever God encounters his people, he leads with, "Do not be afraid"? He says this 365 times in the Bible—like we need to be reminded every day.

**REFLECT** "When the people of Israel saw the mighty power that the LORD had unleashed ... [t]hey put their faith in the LORD and in his servant Moses." EXODUS 14:31

*Lord, when I feel oppressed, help me look and point to you for courage. Amen.*

**CONSIDER** "God's signs are not for themselves; they serve a purpose—have you listened to them lately?" DANIELLE STRICKLAND, *The Ultimate Exodus*

### Courageous people uplift those who feel oppressed by looking and pointing to God.

DANIELLE STRICKLAND • Content taken from *The Ultimate Exodus* by Danielle Strickland. Copyright © 2017 by The Salvation Army. Used by permission of NavPress, represented by Tyndale House Publishers. All rights reserved.

he has hurled both horse and rider
  into the sea.
2 The LORD is my strength and my song;
  he has given me victory.
This is my God, and I will praise him—
  my father's God, and I will exalt him!
3 The LORD is a warrior;
  Yahweh* is his name!
4 Pharaoh's chariots and army
  he has hurled into the sea.
The finest of Pharaoh's officers
  are drowned in the Red Sea.*
5 The deep waters gushed over them;
  they sank to the bottom like a stone.

6 "Your right hand, O LORD,
  is glorious in power.
Your right hand, O LORD,
  smashes the enemy.
7 In the greatness of your majesty,
  you overthrow those who rise against you.
You unleash your blazing fury;
  it consumes them like straw.
8 At the blast of your breath,
  the waters piled up!
The surging waters stood straight like a wall;
  in the heart of the sea the deep waters became
  hard.

9 "The enemy boasted, 'I will chase them
  and catch up with them.
I will plunder them
  and consume them.
I will flash my sword;
  my powerful hand will destroy them.'
10 But you blew with your breath,
  and the sea covered them.
They sank like lead
  in the mighty waters.

11 "Who is like you among the gods, O LORD—
  glorious in holiness,
awesome in splendor,
  performing great wonders?
12 You raised your right hand,
  and the earth swallowed our enemies.

13 "With your unfailing love you lead
  the people you have redeemed.
In your might, you guide them
  to your sacred home.
14 The peoples hear and tremble;

anguish grips those who live in Philistia.
15 The leaders of Edom are terrified;
  the nobles of Moab tremble.
All who live in Canaan melt away;
16   terror and dread fall upon them.
The power of your arm
  makes them lifeless as stone
until your people pass by, O LORD,
  until the people you purchased pass by.
17 You will bring them in and plant them on your
    own mountain—
  the place, O LORD, reserved for your own
    dwelling,
  the sanctuary, O Lord, that your hands have
    established.
18 The LORD will reign forever and ever!"

19When Pharaoh's horses, chariots, and chari-oteers rushed into the sea, the LORD brought the water crashing down on them. But the people of Israel had walked through the middle of the sea on dry ground! 20Then Miriam the prophet, Aaron's sister, took a tambourine and led all the women as they played their tambourines and danced. 21And Miriam sang this song:

"Sing to the LORD,
  for he has triumphed gloriously;
he has hurled both horse and rider
  into the sea."

## Bitter Water at Marah

22Then Moses led the people of Israel away from the Red Sea, and they moved out into the desert of Shur. They traveled in this desert for three days without finding any water. 23When they came to the oasis of Marah, the water was too bitter to drink. So they called the place Marah (which means "bitter"). 24Then the people complained and turned against Moses. "What are we going to drink?" they demanded. 25So Moses cried out to the LORD for help, and the LORD showed him a piece of wood. Moses threw it into the water, and this made the water good to drink.

It was there at Marah that the LORD set before them the following decree as a standard to test their faithfulness to him. 26He said, "If you will listen care-fully to the voice of the LORD your God and do what is right in his sight, obeying his commands and keep-ing all his decrees, then I will not make you suffer any of the diseases I sent on the Egyptians; for I am the LORD who heals you."

15:3 Yahweh is a transliteration of the proper name YHWH that is sometimes rendered "Jehovah"; in this translation it is usually rendered "the LORD" (note the use of small capitals). 15:4 Hebrew sea of reeds; also in 15:22.

15:20-21 Miriam led the women in celebration of the Lord's victory over the Egyptian army. She is referred to as a prophet, making her the first in a long line of female prophets and teachers in the Bible, including Deborah (Judges 4:4), Hannah (1 Samuel 2:1-10), Huldah (2 Kings 22:14), Elizabeth (Luke 1:39-45), Mary (Luke 1:46-55), Anna (Luke 2:36), Priscilla (Acts 18:26), Philip's daughters (Acts 21:8-9), and Phoebe (Romans 16:1). Paul's restrictions on women's public ministry (see, for example, 1 Corinthians 14:34-35) seem to relate to problems particular to that context; Paul elsewhere permitted women to pray and prophesy in public (1 Corinthi-ans 11:4-5).

²⁷After leaving Marah, the Israelites traveled on to the oasis of Elim, where they found twelve springs and seventy palm trees. They camped there beside the water.

## Manna and Quail from Heaven

**16** Then the whole community of Israel set out from Elim and journeyed into the wilderness of Sin,* between Elim and Mount Sinai. They arrived there on the fifteenth day of the second month, one month after leaving the land of Egypt.* ²There, too, the whole community of Israel complained about Moses and Aaron.

³"If only the LORD had killed us back in Egypt," they moaned. "There we sat around pots filled with meat and ate all the bread we wanted. But now you have brought us into this wilderness to starve us all to death."

16:1a The geographical name *Sin* is related to *Sinai* and should not be confused with the English word *sin.* 16:1b The Exodus had occurred on the fifteenth day of the first month (see Num 33:3).

---

## Koinonia

**IMAGE**    MY STORY WITH COMMUNITY, WORKPLACE & CHURCH

### The Lord Himself Leads Us

SCRIPTURE CONNECTION:
EXODUS 14:1-31; 15:13; 16:12; 23:20-23; 29:42-46

I often think that if I'd witnessed God parting the Red Sea, it would be easier to trust him. And yet those who did witness it (and many other miracles) seem to have had short memories and a nearly immediate distrust of the Lord's leading. Amazingly, God didn't give up on them! Instead, he promised to lead them into a land of milk and honey. And all along the way, he longed for them to know him—the Lord their God.

When God has led me to try to turn around difficult situations, I've complained. I've wondered if God led me "out of Egypt" only to leave me "stranded in the wilderness." In those moments of wondering, I've forgotten who God is and why he leads us. Thankfully, God hasn't forgotten me. He also hasn't given up on his purpose to release the whole world from bondage to sin. He may even be leading me to play some small part in that grand plan.

> The Lord leads us out of bondage and into his promises.

The people's journey from Egypt to Israel reminds us how God faithfully loves us: He leads us from bondage to freedom. He hears our cries. And he keeps leading us to the Promised Land.

### IMAGINE

How can you remember those times when God has led you and delivered you?

Where is he leading you now?

*"Every time God leads me out of Egypt to wander in the wilderness, I may forget his bigger plan for the world. Thankfully, he has not. I can rest in knowing that all his plans unfold just as he intends, with the people he means to include, even me."*

KATHERINE LEARY ALSDORF founded and directed Redeemer Church's Center for Faith & Work. She co-authored *Every Good Endeavor: Connecting Your Work to God's Work* with Timothy Keller.

# Insight

## IF YOU COULD BRING JUST ONE FOOD ON A TRIP...

God provided for the people's nutritional needs miraculously while they were traveling from Egypt to Canaan with manna, quail, and water (Exodus 16–17). Why was manna the perfect food for the Israelites' journey to the Promised Land? How does it compare to what we eat today?

Food for
the Journey
to the
Promised Land

### Manna Compared to Recent Snacking Trends*

✔ **LESS SUGAR**
Manna tasted like honey but was healthy. 16:31

✔ **HIGH PROTEIN**
Custom made by the Creator for his creation's needs 16:15

✔ **FUNCTIONAL NUTRITION**
Manna provided energy, focus, and calm. Knowing God would feed them daily must have felt pretty peaceful! 16:35

✔ **FRESH**
Manna, made daily! 16:4

✔ **BITE-SIZED**
Manna was a similar color to a coriander seed and was "a flaky substance as fine as frost," so it potentially appeared as small wafers just perfect for packing and eating on the go. 16:14, 31

*Source: Glanbia Nutritionals

⁴Then the LORD said to Moses, "Look, I'm going to rain down food from heaven for you. Each day the people can go out and pick up as much food as they need for that day. I will test them in this to see whether or not they will follow my instructions. ⁵On the sixth day they will gather food, and when they prepare it, there will be twice as much as usual."

⁶So Moses and Aaron said to all the people of Israel, "By evening you will realize it was the LORD who brought you out of the land of Egypt. ⁷In the morning you will see the glory of the LORD, because he has heard your complaints, which are against him, not against us. What have we done that you should complain about us?" ⁸Then Moses added, "The LORD will give you meat to eat in the evening and bread to satisfy you in the morning, for he has heard all your complaints against him. What have we done? Yes, your complaints are against the LORD, not against us."

⁹Then Moses said to Aaron, "Announce this to the entire community of Israel: 'Present yourselves before the LORD, for he has heard your complaining.'" ¹⁰And as Aaron spoke to the whole community of Israel, they looked out toward the wilderness. There they could see the awesome glory of the LORD in the cloud.

¹¹Then the LORD said to Moses, ¹²"I have heard the Israelites' complaints. Now tell them, 'In the evening you will have meat to eat, and in the morning you will have all the bread you want. Then you will know that I am the LORD your God.'"

¹³That evening vast numbers of quail flew in and covered the camp. And the next morning the area around the camp was wet with dew. ¹⁴When the dew evaporated, a flaky substance as fine as frost blanketed the ground. ¹⁵The Israelites were puzzled when they saw it. "What is it?" they asked each other. They had no idea what it was.

**16:4-5** These are the Lord's instructions for gathering the food he would provide in the wilderness. He gave enough for each day, with a double amount on the sixth day so that the people would not have to gather any on the Sabbath (see 16:21-30). The Israelites thus observed the Sabbath even before it was commanded (see 20:8-11). We instinctively resist a lifestyle in which we need to depend on God each day to supply our needs. We wish to have supplies in advance so that we can feel independent. God was training the people for a life of faith (see Matthew 6:11).

**16:15** The Hebrew phrase *man hu* (which means "What is it?") became the name of the miraculous food "manna" (see 16:31). For forty years, the people ate *what is it?* Jesus referred to himself as the "true bread from heaven" that gives life. In this way, Jesus embodied this manna-miracle (John 6:32-35, 48, 51, 58).

And Moses told them, "It is the food the LORD has given you to eat. <sup>16</sup>These are the LORD's instructions: Each household should gather as much as it needs. Pick up two quarts* for each person in your tent."

<sup>17</sup>So the people of Israel did as they were told. Some gathered a lot, some only a little. <sup>18</sup>But when they measured it out,* everyone had just enough. Those who gathered a lot had nothing left over, and those who gathered only a little had enough. Each family had just what it needed.

<sup>19</sup>Then Moses told them, "Do not keep any of it until morning." <sup>20</sup>But some of them didn't listen and kept some of it until morning. But by then it was full of maggots and had a terrible smell. Moses was very angry with them.

<sup>21</sup>After this the people gathered the food morning by morning, each family according to its need. And as the sun became hot, the flakes they had not picked up melted and disappeared. <sup>22</sup>On the sixth day, they gathered twice as much as usual—four quarts* for each person instead of two. Then all the leaders of the community came and asked Moses for an explanation. <sup>23</sup>He told them, "This is what the LORD commanded: Tomorrow will be a day of complete rest, a holy Sabbath day set apart for the LORD. So bake or boil as much as you want today, and set aside what is left for tomorrow."

<sup>24</sup>So they put some aside until morning, just as Moses had commanded. And in the morning the leftover food was wholesome and good, without maggots or odor. <sup>25</sup>Moses said, "Eat this food today, for today is a Sabbath day dedicated to the LORD. There will be no food on the ground today. <sup>26</sup>You may gather the food for six days, but the seventh day is the Sabbath. There will be no food on the ground that day."

<sup>27</sup>Some of the people went out anyway on the seventh day, but they found no food. <sup>28</sup>The LORD asked Moses, "How long will these people refuse to obey my commands and instructions? <sup>29</sup>They must realize that the Sabbath is the LORD's gift to you. That is why he gives you a two-day supply on the sixth day, so there will be enough for two days. On the Sabbath day you must each stay in your place. Do not go out to pick up food on the seventh day." <sup>30</sup>So the people did not gather any food on the seventh day.

<sup>31</sup>The Israelites called the food manna.* It was white like coriander seed, and it tasted like honey wafers.

<sup>32</sup>Then Moses said, "This is what the LORD has commanded: Fill a two-quart container with manna to preserve it for your descendants. Then later generations will be able to see the food I gave you in the wilderness when I set you free from Egypt."

<sup>33</sup>Moses said to Aaron, "Get a jar and fill it with two quarts of manna. Then put it in a sacred place before the LORD to preserve it for all future generations." <sup>34</sup>Aaron did just as the LORD had commanded Moses. He eventually placed it in the Ark of the Covenant—in front of the stone tablets inscribed with the terms of the covenant.* <sup>35</sup>So the people of Israel ate manna for forty years until they arrived at the land where they would settle. They ate manna until they came to the border of the land of Canaan.

<sup>36</sup>The container used to measure the manna was an omer, which was one-tenth of an ephah; it held about two quarts.*

## Water from the Rock

**17** At the LORD's command, the whole community of Israel left the wilderness of Sin* and moved from place to place. Eventually they camped at Rephidim, but there was no water there for the people to drink. <sup>2</sup>So once more the people complained against Moses. "Give us water to drink!" they demanded.

"Quiet!" Moses replied. "Why are you complaining against me? And why are you testing the LORD?"

<sup>3</sup>But tormented by thirst, they continued to argue with Moses. "Why did you bring us out of Egypt? Are you trying to kill us, our children, and our livestock with thirst?"

<sup>4</sup>Then Moses cried out to the LORD, "What should I do with these people? They are ready to stone me!"

<sup>5</sup>The LORD said to Moses, "Walk out in front of the people. Take your staff, the one you used when you struck the water of the Nile, and call some of the elders of Israel to join you. <sup>6</sup>I will stand before you on the rock at Mount Sinai.* Strike the rock, and water will come gushing out. Then the people will be able to drink." So Moses struck the rock as he was told, and water gushed out as the elders looked on.

<sup>7</sup>Moses named the place Massah (which means "test") and Meribah (which means "arguing") because the people of Israel argued with Moses and tested the LORD by saying, "Is the LORD here with us or not?"

## Israel Defeats the Amalekites

<sup>8</sup>While the people of Israel were still at Rephidim, the warriors of Amalek attacked them. <sup>9</sup>Moses commanded Joshua, "Choose some men to go out and fight the army of Amalek for us. Tomorrow, I will stand at the top of the hill, holding the staff of God in my hand."

<sup>10</sup>So Joshua did what Moses had commanded and fought the army of Amalek. Meanwhile, Moses,

---

**16:16** Hebrew *1 omer* [2.2 liters]; also in 16:32, 33. **16:18** Hebrew *measured it with an omer.* **16:22** Hebrew *2 omers* [4.4 liters]. **16:31** *Manna* means "What is it?" See 16:15. **16:34** Hebrew *He placed it in front of the Testimony;* see note on 25:16. **16:36** Hebrew *An omer is one-tenth of an ephah.* **17:1** The geographical name *Sin* is related to *Sinai* and should not be confused with the English word *sin.* **17:6** Hebrew *Horeb,* another name for Sinai.

---

**17:2** The people doubted that God stayed with or cared for them, and they demanded proof of his presence and care with a test (see 17:7). God invites a test based on faith ("I do believe, but help me overcome my unbelief," Mark 9:24). Still, he detests a test based on doubt (for example, *I don't believe, and I think God should prove himself to me,* as in John 6:30). A test based on doubt makes us the judge and God the defendant, which is the opposite of our rightful position.

Aaron, and Hur climbed to the top of a nearby hill. ¹¹As long as Moses held up the staff in his hand, the Israelites had the advantage. But whenever he dropped his hand, the Amalekites gained the advantage. ¹²Moses' arms soon became so tired he could no longer hold them up. So Aaron and Hur found a stone for him to sit on. Then they stood on each side of Moses, holding up his hands. So his hands held steady until sunset. ¹³As a result, Joshua overwhelmed the army of Amalek in battle.

¹⁴After the victory, the LORD instructed Moses, "Write this down on a scroll as a permanent reminder, and read it aloud to Joshua: I will erase the memory of Amalek from under heaven." ¹⁵Moses built an altar there and named it Yahweh-Nissi (which means "the LORD is my banner"). ¹⁶He said, "They have raised their fist against the LORD's throne, so now* the LORD will be at war with Amalek generation after generation."

## Jethro's Visit to Moses

18 Moses' father-in-law, Jethro, the priest of Midian, heard about everything God had done for Moses and his people, the Israelites. He heard especially about how the LORD had rescued them from Egypt.

²Earlier, Moses had sent his wife, Zipporah, and his two sons back to Jethro, who had taken them in. ³(Moses' first son was named Gershom,* for Moses had said when the boy was born, "I have been a foreigner in a foreign land." ⁴His second son was named Eliezer,* for Moses had said, "The God of my ancestors was my helper; he rescued me from the sword of Pharaoh.") ⁵Jethro, Moses' father-in-law, now came to visit Moses in the wilderness. He brought Moses' wife and two sons with him, and they arrived while Moses and the people were camped near the mountain of God. ⁶Jethro had sent a message to Moses, saying, "I, Jethro, your father-in-law, am coming to see you with your wife and your two sons."

⁷So Moses went out to meet his father-in-law. He bowed low and kissed him. They asked about each other's welfare and then went into Moses' tent. ⁸Moses told his father-in-law everything the LORD had done to Pharaoh and Egypt on behalf of Israel. He also told about all the hardships they had experienced along the way and how the LORD had rescued his people from all their troubles. ⁹Jethro was delighted when he heard about all the good things the LORD had done for Israel as he rescued them from the hand of the Egyptians.

¹⁰"Praise the LORD," Jethro said, "for he has rescued you from the Egyptians and from Pharaoh. Yes, he has rescued Israel from the powerful hand of Egypt! ¹¹I know now that the LORD is greater than all other gods, because he rescued his people from the oppression of the proud Egyptians."

¹²Then Jethro, Moses' father-in-law, brought a burnt offering and sacrifices to God. Aaron and all the elders of Israel came out and joined him in a sacrificial meal in God's presence.

## Jethro's Wise Advice

¹³The next day, Moses took his seat to hear the people's disputes against each other. They waited before him from morning till evening.

¹⁴When Moses' father-in-law saw all that Moses was doing for the people, he asked, "What are you really accomplishing here? Why are you trying to do all this alone while everyone stands around you from morning till evening?"

¹⁵Moses replied, "Because the people come to me to get a ruling from God. ¹⁶When a dispute arises, they come to me, and I am the one who settles the case between the quarreling parties. I inform the people of God's decrees and give them his instructions."

¹⁷"This is not good!" Moses' father-in-law exclaimed. ¹⁸"You're going to wear yourself out—and the people, too. This job is too heavy a burden for you to handle all by yourself. ¹⁹Now listen to me, and let me give you a word of advice, and may God be with you. You should continue to be the people's representative before God, bringing their disputes to him. ²⁰Teach them God's decrees, and give them his instructions. Show them how to conduct their lives. ²¹But select from all the people some capable, honest men who fear God and hate bribes. Appoint them as leaders over groups of one thousand, one hundred, fifty, and ten. ²²They should always be available to solve the people's common disputes, but have them bring the major cases to you. Let the leaders decide the smaller matters themselves. They will help you carry the load, making the task easier for you. ²³If you follow this advice, and if God commands you to do so, then you will be able to endure the pressures, and all these people will go home in peace."

²⁴Moses listened to his father-in-law's advice and followed his suggestions. ²⁵He chose capable men from all over Israel and appointed them as leaders over the people. He put them in charge of groups of one thousand, one hundred, fifty, and ten. ²⁶These

---

17:16 Or *Hands have been lifted up to the LORD's throne, and now.* 18:3 *Gershom* sounds like a Hebrew term that means "a foreigner there." 18:4 *Eliezer* means "God is my helper."

17:9-13 This victory was God's gift, as the description here makes clear. The determining factor was God's blessing, as indicated by Moses' upraised hands. This principle appears again and again in the conquest of the land of Canaan. Without God's blessing, Israel could do nothing (see Numbers 14:42-45; Joshua 7:10-12). 18:2 Moses and Zipporah may have had irreconcilable differences resulting in divorce ("sent . . . back" could imply this). Or they may have lived separately for a time for the sake of the task God had given Moses to do. Numbers 12:1 refers to Moses' "Cushite" wife, which may have been intended as a sort of racial slur about Zipporah, or it could imply that Zipporah was no longer in the picture (had either died or was divorced).

# Zipporah

**IDENTITY** ## A Surprising Marriage

*Zipporah remembers...*

I met the man of my dreams—strong and handsome. He rescued me and my sisters from the shepherds who kept us from using a well. Then Father invited him to stay with us and arranged for me to be his wife. Life was looking good.

But then Moses' God appeared in a burning bush, and Moses said he had to go back to Egypt to save his people. What was that all about? Heading to Egypt wasn't part of my dream.

On the journey, I had to save Moses from God's anger. My husband hadn't circumcised our son, even though God had commanded Abraham and his descendants to do so. I took immediate action, and when God accepted the offering, we continued to Egypt.

Later, we went into the wilderness with all of Moses' people. After a while, Moses sent me and our two sons back to my father. Maybe Moses was too busy. Maybe he wanted to protect me. Maybe he was trying to leave me. I don't know.

But my father later brought me back to Moses. He helped Moses lighten his huge workload, and I stayed, but, wow, it was a hard life. It certainly wasn't my dream.

ZIPPORAH'S STORY IS TOLD IN EXODUS 2:15-22; 4:20-26; 18:1-8.

> Life is a journey of unexpected turns, but God's faithfulness helps us navigate it.

## IDENTIFY

Have you ever found yourself in a place you never expected?

How did God meet you there?

*"When I married my husband, our dream was to work with college students at a Christian student organization. That never happened. God made sense of my wandering path in my fifties, calling me to start a career teaching at a seminary, working with students in a totally different capacity. While not what I planned, I am amazed and fulfilled."*

ELIZABETH GLANVILLE, PhD, is retired faculty from Fuller Theological Seminary, School of Mission and Theology. She is an international teacher on missions and leadership and chaplain for a local police department and her retirement community.

men were always available to solve the people's common disputes. They brought the major cases to Moses, but they took care of the smaller matters themselves.

²⁷Soon after this, Moses said good-bye to his father-in-law, who returned to his own land.

## The LORD Reveals Himself at Sinai

**19** Exactly two months after the Israelites left Egypt,* they arrived in the wilderness of Sinai. ²After breaking camp at Rephidim, they came to the wilderness of Sinai and set up camp there at the base of Mount Sinai.

³Then Moses climbed the mountain to appear before God. The LORD called to him from the mountain and said, "Give these instructions to the family of Jacob; announce it to the descendants of Israel: ⁴'You have seen what I did to the Egyptians. You know how I carried you on eagles' wings and brought you to myself. ⁵Now if you will obey me and keep my covenant, you will be my own special treasure from among all the peoples on earth; for all the earth belongs to me. ⁶And you will be my kingdom of priests, my holy nation.' This is the message you must give to the people of Israel."

⁷So Moses returned from the mountain and called together the elders of the people and told them everything the LORD had commanded him. ⁸And all the people responded together, "We will do everything the LORD has commanded." So Moses brought the people's answer back to the LORD.

⁹Then the LORD said to Moses, "I will come to you in a thick cloud, Moses, so the people themselves can hear me when I speak with you. Then they will always trust you."

Moses told the LORD what the people had said. ¹⁰Then the LORD told Moses, "Go down and prepare the people for my arrival. Consecrate them today and tomorrow, and have them wash their clothing. ¹¹Be sure they are ready on the third day, for on that day the LORD will come down on Mount Sinai as all the people watch. ¹²Mark off a boundary all around the mountain. Warn the people, 'Be careful! Do not go up on the mountain or even touch its boundaries. Anyone who touches the mountain will certainly be put to death. ¹³No hand may touch the person or animal

that crosses the boundary; instead, stone them or shoot them with arrows. They must be put to death.' However, when the ram's horn sounds a long blast, then the people may go up on the mountain.*"

¹⁴So Moses went down to the people. He consecrated them for worship, and they washed their clothes. ¹⁵He told them, "Get ready for the third day, and until then abstain from having sexual intercourse."

¹⁶On the morning of the third day, thunder roared and lightning flashed, and a dense cloud came down on the mountain. There was a long, loud blast from a ram's horn, and all the people trembled. ¹⁷Moses led them out from the camp to meet with God, and they stood at the foot of the mountain. ¹⁸All of Mount Sinai was covered with smoke because the LORD had descended on it in the form of fire. The smoke billowed into the sky like smoke from a brick kiln, and the whole mountain shook violently. ¹⁹As the blast of the ram's horn grew louder and louder, Moses spoke, and God thundered his reply. ²⁰The LORD came down on the top of Mount Sinai and called Moses to the top of the mountain. So Moses climbed the mountain.

²¹Then the LORD told Moses, "Go back down and warn the people not to break through the boundaries to see the LORD, or they will die. ²²Even the priests who regularly come near to the LORD must purify themselves so that the LORD does not break out and destroy them."

²³"But LORD," Moses protested, "the people cannot come up to Mount Sinai. You already warned us. You told me, 'Mark off a boundary all around the mountain to set it apart as holy.'"

²⁴But the LORD said, "Go down and bring Aaron back up with you. In the meantime, do not let the priests or the people break through to approach the LORD, or he will break out and destroy them."

²⁵So Moses went down to the people and told them what the LORD had said.

## Ten Commandments for the Covenant Community

**20** Then God gave the people all these instructions*:

²"I am the LORD your God, who rescued you from the land of Egypt, the place of your slavery.

---

**19:1** Hebrew *In the third month after the Israelites left Egypt, on the very day,* i.e., two lunar months to the day after leaving Egypt. Compare Num 33:3. **19:13** Or *up to the mountain.* **20:1** Hebrew *all these words.*

---

**19:4-6** God had rescued the Israelites from serving Pharaoh, and now they were to serve him. At this crucial juncture in the Lord's relationship with Israel, he defined their new role. To be God's "own special treasure" indicated their appointment as Yahweh's preferred treaty partner. As a "kingdom of priests" and "holy nation," the Israelites' obedience to the terms of the covenant would set them apart for Yahweh's service.

**19:7-8** The Israelites willingly signed on to their new role as the Lord's representatives. God did not impose the laws in Exodus 20–24 against their will. They agreed to God's reasonable

instructions for a well-ordered society (see also 24:3). While the laws do not represent the ultimate ideal for society, they help regulate life in a fallen world.

**19:10-15** The people received commands that would prepare them to receive God's covenant. They were to wash their clothing because God is pure. They were to prepare a boundary all around the mountain and be careful not to cross it because God is holy. They were to abstain from sex because that would ensure ritual purity. Things that are natural and right under ordinary circumstances were to be set aside for the extraordinary purpose of meeting God.

³"You must not have any other god but me.
⁴"You must not make for yourself an idol of any
kind or an image of anything in the heavens or
on the earth or in the sea. ⁵You must not bow
down to them or worship them, for I, the LORD
your God, am a jealous God who will not tolerate
your affection for any other gods. I lay the sins of
the parents upon their children; the entire family
is affected—even children in the third and
fourth generations of those who reject me. ⁶But I
lavish unfailing love for a thousand generations
on those* who love me and obey my commands.
⁷"You must not misuse the name of the LORD your
God. The LORD will not let you go unpunished if
you misuse his name.
⁸"Remember to observe the Sabbath day by
keeping it holy. ⁹You have six days each week
for your ordinary work, ¹⁰but the seventh
day is a Sabbath day of rest dedicated to the
LORD your God. On that day no one in your
household may do any work. This includes
you, your sons and daughters, your male
and female servants, your livestock, and any
foreigners living among you. ¹¹For in six days
the LORD made the heavens, the earth, the sea,
and everything in them; but on the seventh
day he rested. That is why the LORD blessed the
Sabbath day and set it apart as holy.
¹²"Honor your father and mother. Then you will
live a long, full life in the land the LORD your God
is giving you.
¹³"You must not murder.
¹⁴"You must not commit adultery.
¹⁵"You must not steal.
¹⁶"You must not testify falsely against your neighbor.
¹⁷"You must not covet your neighbor's house. You
must not covet your neighbor's wife, male or
female servant, ox or donkey, or anything else
that belongs to your neighbor."

**20:6** Hebrew *for thousands of those.*

**20:1-17** The Ten Commandments outlined God's expectations
for the covenant community. The Lord underscored his role as
the one who rescued them from slavery (20:2). In response,
they were to be a people who looked out for their neighbors and
protected each other's right to rest, honor, life, property, reputation, and exclusive marriage. They were also to be a people
who worshiped Yahweh exclusively and recognized that they
belonged to him. The commands were addressed to male heads
of households who were to use their power to protect, rather
than exploit, the vulnerable.

**20:5-6** "In the third and fourth generations . . . for a thousand
generations": It is vital to keep both sides of this equation
together. God does not punish children for their parents'
sins. Rather, he says that our sins affect future generations.
He graciously restricts sins' effects to three or four generations while extending obedience's effects to a thousand
generations (literally "for thousands"; see also Exodus 34:6-7;
Deuteronomy 7:9).

# Perspective

## Are women property or partners?

SCRIPTURE CONNECTION: EXODUS 20:17

Some aspects of biblical law sound jarring to
our modern ears. It seems reasonable to prevent
men from desiring someone else's wife, but
why do wives appear in a list of what "belongs
to your neighbor"? Were women considered
property?

Not exactly. In ancient Israel, women lived
under the protection and authority of their
fathers and husbands. A wedding did include a
wealth exchange (a bride price and a dowry).
However, the money did not indicate a "sale."
Instead, it ensured the marriage's stability
and extended the family's support for the new
union.

Perhaps Moses anticipated how this command could be misconstrued. In Deuteronomy
5:21, where he repeats God's instructions for the
next generation, Moses rearranges the list. This
time, he mentions the wife first, separate from
the list of possessions.

## VIEWPOINTS

**HERS:** *The Israelite wife found security in a
marriage where she and her husband partnered
in fulfilling God's commands with their families'
support.*
**MINE:** *"When my husband and I married, my
parents paid for the ceremony, while my mother-
in-law provided the rehearsal dinner. Both
families invested in our future."*
**YOURS:** *What is your attitude toward
marriage? Do you see it as the partnering
of two families?*

CARMEN JOY IMES, PhD, is an author, speaker,
blogger, YouTuber, and serves as associate
professor of Old Testament at Biola University
in California.

¹⁸When the people heard the thunder and the loud blast of the ram's horn, and when they saw the flashes of lightning and the smoke billowing from the mountain, they stood at a distance, trembling with fear.

¹⁹And they said to Moses, "You speak to us, and we will listen. But don't let God speak directly to us, or we will die!"

²⁰"Don't be afraid," Moses answered them, "for God has come in this way to test you, and so that your fear of him will keep you from sinning!"

²¹As the people stood in the distance, Moses approached the dark cloud where God was.

## Proper Use of Altars

²²And the LORD said to Moses, "Say this to the people of Israel: You saw for yourselves that I spoke to you from heaven. ²³Remember, you must not make any idols of silver or gold to rival me.

²⁴"Build for me an altar made of earth, and offer your sacrifices to me—your burnt offerings and peace offerings, your sheep and goats, and your cattle. Build my altar wherever I cause my name to be remembered, and I will come to you and bless you. ²⁵If you use stones to build my altar, use only natural, uncut stones. Do not shape the stones with a tool, for that would make the altar unfit for holy use. ²⁶And do not approach my altar by going up steps. If you do, someone might look up under your clothing and see your nakedness.

## Fair Treatment of Slaves

21 "These are the regulations you must present to Israel.

²"If you buy a Hebrew slave, he may serve for no more than six years. Set him free in the seventh year, and he will owe you nothing for his freedom. ³If he was single when he became your slave, he shall leave single. But if he was married before he became a slave, then his wife must be freed with him. ⁴"If his master gave him a wife while he was a slave and they had sons or daughters, then only the man will be free in the seventh year, but his wife

and children will still belong to his master. ⁵But the slave may declare, 'I love my master, my wife, and my children. I don't want to go free.' ⁶If he does this, his master must present him before God.* Then his master must take him to the door or doorpost and publicly pierce his ear with an awl. After that, the slave will serve his master for life.

⁷"When a man sells his daughter as a slave, she will not be freed at the end of six years as the men are. ⁸If she does not satisfy her owner, he must allow her to be bought back again. But he is not allowed to sell her to foreigners, since he is the one who broke the contract with her. ⁹But if the slave's owner arranges for her to marry his son, he may no longer treat her as a slave but as a daughter.

¹⁰"If a man who has married a slave wife takes another wife for himself, he must not neglect the rights of the first wife to food, clothing, and sexual intimacy. ¹¹If he fails in any of these three obligations, she may leave as a free woman without making any payment.

## Cases of Personal Injury

¹²"Anyone who assaults and kills another person must be put to death. ¹³But if it was simply an accident permitted by God, I will appoint a place of refuge where the slayer can run for safety. ¹⁴However, if someone deliberately kills another person, then the slayer must be dragged even from my altar and be put to death.

¹⁵"Anyone who strikes father or mother must be put to death.

¹⁶"Kidnappers must be put to death, whether they are caught in possession of their victims or have already sold them as slaves.

¹⁷"Anyone who dishonors* father or mother must be put to death.

¹⁸"Now suppose two men quarrel, and one hits the other with a stone or fist, and the injured person does not die but is confined to bed. ¹⁹If he is later able to walk outside again, even with a crutch, the assailant will not be punished but must compensate his victim for lost wages and provide for his full recovery.

---

21:6 Or *before the judges.*  21:17 Greek version reads *Anyone who speaks disrespectfully of.* Compare Matt 15:4; Mark 7:10.

---

**20:26** God carefully protected against indecent exposure in worship to set the Israelites apart from other nations. Sex was an integral part of many Canaanite rituals because they associated fertility with the favor of certain gods. By prohibiting nakedness in the Tabernacle, Yahweh blessed the people with children and crops without compromising the exclusive sexual commitment between husband and wife. The fact that all of Israel's priests were fully clothed men distinguished them from other nations, who employed female cult prostitutes and priestesses to promote fertility (see also 28:42-43).

**21:2-6** To prevent exploitation in Israel, God strictly regulated slavery. Obedience to the entire law would protect Israel's indentured servants from mistreatment, such as they had experienced

in Egypt. Men could hire themselves out as indentured servants for a limited time. They might do so to avoid starvation or pay a debt incurred by theft. They retained the rights to marry and go free after they paid their debt. If they preferred serving the man who had purchased them, they could volunteer to serve for life.

**21:7-11** The roles of an enslaved woman often included marriage. As with nearly all ancient marriages, the father made the arrangements. Her new home was to be permanent to prevent exploitation. If the man married her, he could not sell her if she displeased him or if he took another wife. If he arranged for her to marry his son instead, she was not available to the father as a sexual partner. These regulations were intended to preserve her dignity and rights.

²⁰"If a man beats his male or female slave with a club and the slave dies as a result, the owner must be punished. ²¹But if the slave recovers within a day or two, then the owner shall not be punished, since the slave is his property.

²²"Now suppose two men are fighting, and in the process they accidentally strike a pregnant woman so she gives birth prematurely.* If no further injury results, the man who struck the woman must pay the amount of compensation the woman's husband demands and the judges approve. ²³But if there is further injury, the punishment must match the injury: a life for a life, ²⁴an eye for an eye, a tooth for a tooth, a hand for a hand, a foot for a foot, ²⁵a burn for a burn, a wound for a wound, a bruise for a bruise.

²⁶"If a man hits his male or female slave in the eye and the eye is blinded, he must let the slave go free to compensate for the eye. ²⁷And if a man knocks out the tooth of his male or female slave, he must let the slave go free to compensate for the tooth.

²⁸"If an ox* gores a man or woman to death, the ox must be stoned, and its flesh may not be eaten. In such a case, however, the owner will not be held liable. ²⁹But suppose the ox had a reputation for goring, and the owner had been informed but failed to keep it under control. If the ox then kills someone, it must be stoned, and the owner must also be put to death. ³⁰However, the dead person's relatives may accept payment to compensate for the loss of life. The owner of the ox may redeem his life by paying whatever is demanded.

21:22 Or *so she has a miscarriage;* Hebrew reads *so her children come out.*  21:28 Or *bull,* or *cow;* also in 21:29-36.

**21:20-21** In ancient Israelite culture, corporal punishment was considered acceptable. The Hebrew phrase translated here as "the slave is his property" reads literally, "he is his silver." Unlike 21:19, where an assailant had to compensate the victim for lost wages during the recovery period, in this case, it was the enslaver's loss if the enslaved person had to take time off work to recover from injuries the enslaver had inflicted. It was in his best interest to treat enslaved people well. Both enslaved women and men were considered fully human. Therefore, someone who killed an enslaved person was subject to the death penalty.
**21:22-25** It appears that if a fight caused a child's premature birth and the child died (that is, there was further injury), the penalty for murder was to be enacted (a life for a life). The law of retaliation called for a penalty that matched the victim's injury. This law also served to limit the punishment, so that it did not exceed the original damage.
**21:26-32** An enslaver did not have the right to injure an enslaved person's body. Permanent injury resulted in freedom, effectively canceling the enslaved person's debt. The life of an enslaved person—male or female—was valued just as highly as a free person's life. An animal who killed an enslaved person must die, and payment was made to the enslaver for the lost labor. This payment was equivalent to the unpaid debt as the slavery in view here was an indentured servitude.

# Perspective

## Does God condone slavery?

SCRIPTURE CONNECTION: EXODUS 21:1-11

God clearly opposed the Israelites' enslavement in Egypt. After all, he freed them. Why, then, would he allow the Israelites to keep enslaved people?

Israel's laws did not represent an ideal, just as our laws often fall short. They often aimed to minimize the effects of living in a broken world.

Slavery among the Israelites was generally the result of extreme poverty. Rather than starving to death, a person could willingly serve a benefactor to pay a debt. As we see in this passage, enslaved men and women had different parameters because when the women married, they entered the household of their enslaver. Even so, there were certain protections for the women as well (21:7-11). Many of the Israelite laws guarded against the exploitation of enslaved people and other vulnerable people (see, for example, 20:10; 21:16; 22:21-27).

Despite how this played out in Israel's legal system, slavery is not God's design. Every person —regardless of gender, ethnicity, or financial status—is an image-bearer of God, and he does not condone slavery in the past or the present.

### VIEWPOINTS

HERS: *Marriage, even if it meant slavery, was one way to escape extreme poverty.*
MINE: *"I cannot imagine someone choosing a husband for me, but in many cultures, arranged marriages are the norm. A father was to look after his daughter's best interests."*
YOURS: *How has God provided for you when you had no good options?*

CARMEN JOY IMES, PhD, is an author, speaker, blogger, YouTuber, and serves as associate professor of Old Testament at Biola University in California.

³¹"The same regulation applies if the ox gores a boy or a girl. ³²But if the ox gores a slave, either male or female, the animal's owner must pay the slave's owner thirty silver coins,* and the ox must be stoned.

³³"Suppose someone digs or uncovers a pit and fails to cover it, and then an ox or a donkey falls into it. ³⁴The owner of the pit must pay full compensation to the owner of the animal, but then he gets to keep the dead animal.

³⁵"If someone's ox injures a neighbor's ox and the injured ox dies, then the two owners must sell the live ox and divide the price equally between them. They must also divide the dead animal. ³⁶But if the ox had a reputation for goring, yet its owner failed to keep it under control, he must pay full compensation—a live ox for the dead one—but he may keep the dead ox.

## Protection of Property

**22** ¹*"If someone steals an ox* or sheep and then kills or sells it, the thief must pay back five oxen for each ox stolen, and four sheep for each sheep stolen.

²*"If a thief is caught in the act of breaking into a house and is struck and killed in the process, the person who killed the thief is not guilty of murder. ³But if it happens in daylight, the one who killed the thief is guilty of murder.

"A thief who is caught must pay in full for everything he stole. If he cannot pay, he must be sold as a slave to pay for his theft. ⁴If someone steals an ox or a donkey or a sheep and it is found in the thief's possession, then the thief must pay double the value of the stolen animal.

⁵"If an animal is grazing in a field or vineyard and the owner lets it stray into someone else's field to graze, then the animal's owner must pay compensation from the best of his own grain or grapes.

⁶"If you are burning thornbushes and the fire gets out of control and spreads into another person's field, destroying the sheaves or the uncut grain or the whole crop, the one who started the fire must pay for the lost crop.

⁷"Suppose someone leaves money or goods with a neighbor for safekeeping, and they are stolen from the neighbor's house. If the thief is caught, the compensation is double the value of what was stolen.

⁸But if the thief is not caught, the neighbor must appear before God,* who will determine if he stole the property.

⁹"Suppose there is a dispute between two people who both claim to own a particular ox, donkey, sheep, article of clothing, or any lost property. Both parties must come before God, and the person whom God declares* guilty must pay double compensation to the other.

¹⁰"Now suppose someone leaves a donkey, ox, sheep, or any other animal with a neighbor for safekeeping, but it dies or is injured or is taken away, and no one sees what happened. ¹¹The neighbor must then take an oath in the presence of the Lord. If the Lord confirms that the neighbor did not steal the property, the owner must accept the verdict, and no payment will be required. ¹²But if the animal was indeed stolen, the guilty person must pay compensation to the owner. ¹³If it was torn to pieces by a wild animal, the remains of the carcass must be shown as evidence, and no compensation will be required.

¹⁴"If someone borrows an animal from a neighbor and it is injured or dies when the owner is absent, the person who borrowed it must pay full compensation. ¹⁵But if the owner was present, no compensation is required. And no compensation is required if the animal was rented, for this loss is covered by the rental fee.

## Social Responsibility

¹⁶"If a man seduces a virgin who is not engaged to anyone and has sex with her, he must pay the customary bride price and marry her. ¹⁷But if her father refuses to let him marry her, the man must still pay him an amount equal to the bride price of a virgin.

¹⁸"You must not allow a sorceress to live.

¹⁹"Anyone who has sexual relations with an animal must certainly be put to death.

²⁰"Anyone who sacrifices to any god other than the Lord must be destroyed.*

²¹"You must not mistreat or oppress foreigners in any way. Remember, you yourselves were once foreigners in the land of Egypt.

²²"You must not exploit a widow or an orphan. ²³If you exploit them in any way and they cry out to me, then I will certainly hear their cry. ²⁴My anger will blaze against you, and I will kill you with the sword.

**21:32** Hebrew *30 shekels of silver*, about 12 ounces or 342 grams in weight. **22:1a** Verse 22:1 is numbered 21:37 in Hebrew text. **22:1b** Or *bull, or cow;* also in 22:4, 9, 10. **22:2** Verses 22:2-31 are numbered 22:1-30 in Hebrew text. **22:8** Or *before the judges.* **22:9** Or *before the judges, and the person whom the judges declare.* **22:20** The Hebrew term used here refers to the complete consecration of things or people to the Lord, either by destroying them or by giving them as an offering.

**22:16-17** This passage seems shocking—require a woman to marry the first man she slept with? However, the law was designed to underscore the seriousness of sex: Any man who seduced a woman had to be prepared to marry her. God did not tolerate sex outside of marriage. A woman's father could refuse the marriage if it were not in his daughter's best interests, but since the woman would likely never marry, the man had to pay the bride price to support her. **22:22-24** God takes seriously the care of vulnerable members of society. Exploitation incurs God's anger, and the penalty for taking advantage of the vulnerable was death.

## Plans for the Altar of Burnt Offering

**27** "Using acacia wood, construct a square altar 7½ feet wide, 7½ feet long, and 4½ feet high.* ²Make horns for each of its four corners so that the horns and altar are all one piece. Overlay the altar with bronze. ³Make ash buckets, shovels, basins, meat forks, and firepans, all of bronze. ⁴Make a bronze grating for it, and attach four bronze rings at its four corners. ⁵Install the grating halfway down the side of the altar, under the ledge. ⁶For carrying the altar, make poles from acacia wood, and overlay them with bronze. ⁷Insert the poles through the rings on the two sides of the altar. ⁸The altar must be hollow, made from planks. Build it just as you were shown on the mountain.

## Plans for the Courtyard

⁹"Then make the courtyard for the Tabernacle, enclosed with curtains made of finely woven linen. On the south side, make the curtains 150 feet long.* ¹⁰They will be held up by twenty posts set securely in twenty bronze bases. Hang the curtains with silver hooks and rings. ¹¹Make the curtains the same on the north side—150 feet of curtains held up by twenty posts set securely in bronze bases. Hang the curtains with silver hooks and rings. ¹²The curtains

27:1 Hebrew *5 cubits* [2.3 meters] *wide, 5 cubits long, a square, and 3 cubits* [1.4 meters] *high.*   27:9 Hebrew *100 cubits* [46 meters]; also in 27:11.

**27:1-19** These plans move outward from the center of the Tabernacle, from the altar of burnt offering to the courtyard. As with the sanctuary, the plans for the courtyard furnishings appear (27:1-8) before the plans for the courtyard itself (27:9-19).

---

## ⊙ Insight   THE TABERNACLE

Exodus 36–40 describes the construction of the Tabernacle and its accessories. The Tabernacle was the mobile sanctuary of God's presence with his people and the place where Israel made sacrifices and offerings in worship of the Lord.

**ALTAR OF BURNT OFFERING**
Exodus 27:1-8

**WASHBASIN**
Exodus 30:18; 38:8
Leviticus 8:11

**INCENSE ALTAR**
Exodus 30:1-10

**GOLD LAMPSTAND**
Exodus 25:31-39

**TABLE FOR THE BREAD OF THE PRESENCE**
Exodus 25:23-30
Leviticus 24:5-9

**ARK OF THE COVENANT**
Exodus 25:10-22; 40:20
Numbers 7:89; 10:33
Joshua 3:14-17
1 Samuel 4–6
2 Samuel 6:1-15

**HOLY PLACE**
Exodus 28:29

**MOST HOLY PLACE**
Exodus 26:34
Leviticus 16

**MODEL OF THE TABERNACLE**
This full-scale model of the Tabernacle is located in Timna Park in southern Israel. It is a near replica of the Tabernacle Moses and the Israelites constructed in the wilderness.

on the west end of the courtyard will be 75 feet long,* supported by ten posts set into ten bases. ¹³The east end of the courtyard, the front, will also be 75 feet long. ¹⁴The courtyard entrance will be on the east end, flanked by two curtains. The curtain on the right side will be 22½ feet long,* supported by three posts set into three bases. ¹⁵The curtain on the left side will also be 22½ feet long, supported by three posts set into three bases.

¹⁶"For the entrance to the courtyard, make a curtain that is 30 feet long.* Make it from finely woven linen, and decorate it with beautiful embroidery in blue, purple, and scarlet thread. Support it with four posts, each securely set in its own base. ¹⁷All the posts around the courtyard must have silver rings and hooks and bronze bases. ¹⁸So the entire courtyard will be 150 feet long and 75 feet wide, with curtain walls 7½ feet high,* made from finely woven linen. The bases for the posts will be made of bronze.

¹⁹"All the articles used in the rituals of the Tabernacle, including all the tent pegs used to support the Tabernacle and the courtyard curtains, must be made of bronze.

## Light for the Tabernacle

²⁰"Command the people of Israel to bring you pure oil of pressed olives for the light, to keep the lamps burning continually. ²¹The lampstand will stand in the Tabernacle, in front of the inner curtain that shields the Ark of the Covenant.* Aaron and his sons must keep the lamps burning in the LORD's presence all night. This is a permanent law for the people of Israel, and it must be observed from generation to generation.

## Clothing for the Priests

28 "Call for your brother, Aaron, and his sons, Nadab, Abihu, Eleazar, and Ithamar. Set them apart from the rest of the people of Israel so they may minister to me and be my priests. ²Make sacred garments for Aaron that are glorious and beautiful. ³Instruct all the skilled craftsmen whom I have filled with the spirit of wisdom. Have them make garments for Aaron that will distinguish him as a priest set apart for my service. ⁴These are the garments they are to make: a chestpiece, an ephod, a robe, a patterned tunic, a turban, and a sash. They

are to make these sacred garments for your brother, Aaron, and his sons to wear when they serve me as priests. ⁵So give them fine linen cloth, gold thread, and blue, purple, and scarlet thread.

## Design of the Ephod

⁶"The craftsmen must make the ephod of finely woven linen and skillfully embroider it with gold and with blue, purple, and scarlet thread. ⁷It will consist of two pieces, front and back, joined at the shoulders with two shoulder-pieces. ⁸The decorative sash will be made of the same materials: finely woven linen embroidered with gold and with blue, purple, and scarlet thread.

⁹"Take two onyx stones, and engrave on them the names of the tribes of Israel. ¹⁰Six names will be on each stone, arranged in the order of the births of the original sons of Israel. ¹¹Engrave these names on the two stones in the same way a jeweler engraves a seal. Then mount the stones in settings of gold filigree. ¹²Fasten the two stones on the shoulder-pieces of the ephod as a reminder that Aaron represents the people of Israel. Aaron will carry these names on his shoulders as a constant reminder whenever he goes before the LORD. ¹³Make the settings of gold filigree, ¹⁴then braid two cords of pure gold and attach them to the filigree settings on the shoulders of the ephod.

## Design of the Chestpiece

¹⁵"Then, with great skill and care, make a chestpiece to be worn for seeking a decision from God.* Make it to match the ephod, using finely woven linen embroidered with gold and with blue, purple, and scarlet thread. ¹⁶Make the chestpiece of a single piece of cloth folded to form a pouch nine inches* square. ¹⁷Mount four rows of gemstones* on it. The first row will contain a red carnelian, a pale-green peridot, and an emerald. ¹⁸The second row will contain a turquoise, a blue lapis lazuli, and a white moonstone. ¹⁹The third row will contain an orange jacinth, an agate, and a purple amethyst. ²⁰The fourth row will contain a blue-green beryl, an onyx, and a green jasper. All these stones will be set in gold filigree. ²¹Each stone will represent one of the twelve sons of Israel, and the name of that tribe will be engraved on it like a seal.

27:12 Hebrew *50 cubits* [23 meters]; also in 27:13. 27:14 Hebrew *15 cubits* [6.9 meters]; also in 27:15. 27:16 Hebrew *20 cubits* [9.2 meters]. 27:18 Hebrew *100 cubits* [46 meters] *long and 50 by 50* [23 meters] *wide and 5 cubits* [2.3 meters] *high.* 27:21 Hebrew *in the Tent of Meeting, outside the inner curtain that is in front of the Testimony.* See note on 25:16. 28:15 Hebrew *a chestpiece for decision.* 28:16 Hebrew *1 span* [23 centimeters]. 28:17 The identification of some of these gemstones is uncertain.

**27:20–30:38** Following the structural designs for the Tabernacle comes instructions for the people and elements involved in service. Included are priestly functions (27:20-21; 29:38-46), clothing (28:1-43), dedication ceremonies (29:1-37), furnishings (30:1-10, 17-21), and supplies (30:11-16, 22-38).

**28:1–29:46** The high priest was the best-dressed Israelite. The twelve gemstones on his chest symbolized his representative role, indicating that all twelve tribes would have a

permanent share in his ministry. The gold medallion on his forehead bearing Yahweh's name showed the priest's status as Yahweh's representative. Later, the entire nation was called "a holy people, who belong to the LORD your God" (Deuteronomy 7:6). This phrase echoed the high priest's medallion to reinforce the people's priestly status (Exodus 19:6). The high priest was a visual model of the vocation of the entire nation.

²²"To attach the chestpiece to the ephod, make braided cords of pure gold thread. ²³Then make two gold rings and attach them to the top corners of the chestpiece. ²⁴Tie the two gold cords to the two rings on the chestpiece. ²⁵Tie the other ends of the cords to the gold settings on the shoulder-pieces of the ephod. ²⁶Then make two more gold rings and attach them to the inside edges of the chestpiece next to the ephod. ²⁷And make two more gold rings and attach them to the front of the ephod, below the shoulder-pieces, just above the knot where the decorative sash is fastened to the ephod. ²⁸Then attach the bottom rings of the chestpiece to the rings on the ephod with blue cords. This will hold the chestpiece securely to the ephod above the decorative sash.

²⁹"In this way, Aaron will carry the names of the tribes of Israel on the sacred chestpiece* over his heart when he goes into the Holy Place. This will be a continual reminder that he represents the people when he comes before the LORD. ³⁰Insert the Urim and Thummim into the sacred chestpiece so they will be carried over Aaron's heart when he goes into the LORD's presence. In this way, Aaron will always carry over his heart the objects used to determine the LORD's will for his people whenever he goes in before the LORD.

## Additional Clothing for the Priests

³¹"Make the robe that is worn with the ephod from a single piece of blue cloth, ³²with an opening for Aaron's head in the middle of it. Reinforce the opening with a woven collar* so it will not tear. ³³Make pomegranates out of blue, purple, and scarlet yarn, and attach them to the hem of the robe, with gold bells between them. ³⁴The gold bells and pomegranates are to alternate all around the hem. ³⁵Aaron will wear this robe whenever he ministers before the LORD, and the bells will tinkle as he goes in and out of the LORD's presence in the Holy Place. If he wears it, he will not die.

³⁶"Next make a medallion of pure gold, and engrave it like a seal with these words: HOLY TO THE LORD. ³⁷Attach the medallion with a blue cord to the front of Aaron's turban, where it must remain. ³⁸Aaron must wear it on his forehead so he may take on himself any guilt of the people of Israel when they consecrate their sacred offerings. He must always wear it on his forehead so the LORD will accept the people.

³⁹"Weave Aaron's patterned tunic from fine linen cloth. Fashion the turban from this linen as well. Also make a sash, and decorate it with colorful embroidery.

⁴⁰"For Aaron's sons, make tunics, sashes, and special head coverings that are glorious and beautiful. ⁴¹Clothe your brother, Aaron, and his sons with these garments, and then anoint and ordain them. Consecrate them so they can serve as my priests. ⁴²Also make linen undergarments for them, to be worn next to their bodies, reaching from their hips to their thighs. ⁴³These must be worn whenever Aaron and his sons enter the Tabernacle* or approach the altar in the Holy Place to perform their priestly duties. Then they will not incur guilt and die. This is a permanent law for Aaron and all his descendants after him.

## Dedication of the Priests

29 "This is the ceremony you must follow when you consecrate Aaron and his sons to serve me as priests: Take a young bull and two rams with no defects. ²Then, using choice wheat flour and no yeast, make loaves of bread, thin cakes mixed with olive oil, and wafers spread with oil. ³Place them all in a single basket, and present them at the entrance of the Tabernacle, along with the young bull and the two rams.

⁴"Present Aaron and his sons at the entrance of the Tabernacle,* and wash them with water. ⁵Dress Aaron in his priestly garments—the tunic, the robe worn with the ephod, the ephod itself, and the chestpiece. Then wrap the decorative sash of the ephod around him. ⁶Place the turban on his head, and fasten the sacred medallion to the turban. ⁷Then anoint him by pouring the anointing oil over his head. ⁸Next present his sons, and dress them in their tunics. ⁹Wrap the sashes around the waists of Aaron and his sons, and put their special head coverings on them. Then the right to the priesthood will be theirs by law forever. In this way, you will ordain Aaron and his sons.

¹⁰"Bring the young bull to the entrance of the Tabernacle, where Aaron and his sons will lay their hands on its head. ¹¹Then slaughter the bull in the LORD's presence at the entrance of the Tabernacle. ¹²Put some of its blood on the horns of the altar with your finger, and pour out the rest at the base of the altar. ¹³Take all the fat around the internal organs,

---

28:29 Hebrew *the chestpiece for decision;* also in 28:30. See 28:15.   28:32 The meaning of the Hebrew is uncertain.
28:43 Hebrew *Tent of Meeting.*   29:4 Hebrew *Tent of Meeting;* also in 29:10, 11, 30, 32, 42, 44.

---

**29:1-37** Moses consecrated (or sanctified, set apart as sacred) Aaron and his sons to serve the Lord. This emphasis on making the priests holy appears throughout the ceremonies (29:4-9, 21, 28, 29, 34, 36, 37). The priests were set apart not merely to serve but to serve a God whose nature is utterly different from that of fallen, sinful humans. Leviticus 8–9 reports how the people carried out these instructions.
**29:10-34** Consecrating Aaron into priesthood involved a sin

offering (29:10-14), a burnt offering (29:15-18), and an ordination offering (29:19-28). The same patterns are expanded to the regular offerings of the people (see 29:38-46; Leviticus 1–7). In all three offerings, "Aaron and his sons will lay their hands on [the] head" of the sacrificial animals (Exodus 29:10, 15, 19). All three indicate that sin is a matter of life and death and that only death can remove it. Because blood represents life, it is prominent in these ceremonies (29:12, 16, 20, 21).

the long lobe of the liver, and the two kidneys and the fat around them, and burn it all on the altar. ¹⁴Then take the rest of the bull, including its hide, meat, and dung, and burn it outside the camp as a sin offering.

¹⁵"Next Aaron and his sons must lay their hands on the head of one of the rams. ¹⁶Then slaughter the ram, and splatter its blood against all sides of the altar. ¹⁷Cut the ram into pieces, and wash off the internal organs and the legs. Set them alongside the head and the other pieces of the body, ¹⁸then burn the entire animal on the altar. This is a burnt offering to the LORD; it is a pleasing aroma, a special gift presented to the LORD.

¹⁹"Now take the other ram, and have Aaron and his sons lay their hands on its head. ²⁰Then slaughter it, and apply some of its blood to the right earlobes of Aaron and his sons. Also put it on the thumbs of their right hands and the big toes of their right feet. Splatter the rest of the blood against all sides of the altar. ²¹Then take some of the blood from the altar and some of the anointing oil, and sprinkle it on Aaron and his sons and on their garments. In this way, they and their garments will be set apart as holy.

²²"Since this is the ram for the ordination of Aaron and his sons, take the fat of the ram, including the fat of the broad tail, the fat around the internal organs, the long lobe of the liver, and the two kidneys and the fat around them, along with the right thigh. ²³Then take one round loaf of bread, one thin cake mixed with olive oil, and one wafer from the basket of bread without yeast that was placed in the LORD's presence. ²⁴Put all these in the hands of Aaron and his sons to be lifted up as a special offering to the LORD. ²⁵Afterward take the various breads from their hands, and burn them on the altar along with the burnt offering. It is a pleasing aroma to the LORD, a special gift for him. ²⁶Then take the breast of Aaron's ordination ram, and lift it up in the LORD's presence as a special offering to him. Then keep it as your own portion.

²⁷"Set aside the portions of the ordination ram that belong to Aaron and his sons. This includes the breast and the thigh that were lifted up before the LORD as a special offering. ²⁸In the future, whenever the people of Israel lift up a peace offering, a portion of it must be set aside for Aaron and his descendants. This is their permanent right, and it is a sacred offering from the Israelites to the LORD.

²⁹"Aaron's sacred garments must be preserved for his descendants who succeed him, and they will wear them when they are anointed and ordained. ³⁰The descendant who succeeds him as high priest will wear these clothes for seven days as he ministers in the Tabernacle and the Holy Place.

³¹"Take the ram used in the ordination ceremony, and boil its meat in a sacred place. ³²Then Aaron and his sons will eat this meat, along with the bread in the basket, at the Tabernacle entrance. ³³They alone may eat the meat and bread used for their purification* in the ordination ceremony. No one else may eat them, for these things are set apart and holy. ³⁴If any of the ordination meat or bread remains until the morning, it must be burned. It may not be eaten, for it is holy.

³⁵"This is how you will ordain Aaron and his sons to their offices, just as I have commanded you. The ordination ceremony will go on for seven days. ³⁶Each day you must sacrifice a young bull as a sin offering to purify them, making them right with the LORD.* Afterward, cleanse the altar by purifying it*; make it holy by anointing it with oil. ³⁷Purify the altar, and consecrate it every day for seven days. After that, the altar will be absolutely holy, and whatever touches it will become holy.

³⁸"These are the sacrifices you are to offer regularly on the altar. Each day, offer two lambs that are a year old, ³⁹one in the morning and the other in the evening. ⁴⁰With one of them, offer two quarts of choice flour mixed with one quart of pure oil of pressed olives; also, offer one quart of wine* as a liquid offering. ⁴¹Offer the other lamb in the evening, along with the same offerings of flour and wine as in the morning. It will be a pleasing aroma, a special gift presented to the LORD.

⁴²"These burnt offerings are to be made each day from generation to generation. Offer them in the LORD's presence at the Tabernacle entrance; there I will meet with you and speak with you. ⁴³I will meet the people of Israel there, in the place made holy by my glorious presence. ⁴⁴Yes, I will consecrate the Tabernacle and the altar, and I will consecrate Aaron and his sons to serve me as priests. ⁴⁵Then I will live among the people of Israel and be their God, ⁴⁶and they will know that I am the LORD their God. I am the one who brought them out of the land of Egypt so that I could live among them. I am the LORD their God.

## Plans for the Incense Altar

**30** "Then make another altar of acacia wood for burning incense. ²Make it 18 inches square and 36 inches high,* with horns at the corners carved from the same piece of wood as the altar itself. ³Overlay the top, sides, and horns of the altar with pure gold, and run a gold molding around the entire altar. ⁴Make two gold rings, and attach them on opposite sides of the altar below the gold molding to hold the carrying poles. ⁵Make the poles of acacia wood and overlay them with gold. ⁶Place the incense altar just outside the inner curtain that shields the Ark of the Covenant,* in front of the Ark's cover—the place of atonement—that covers the tablets

The LORD himself will fight for you. Just stay calm.

inscribed with the terms of the covenant.* I will meet with you there.

7"Every morning when Aaron maintains the lamps, he must burn fragrant incense on the altar. 8And each evening when he lights the lamps, he must again burn incense in the LORD's presence. This must be done from generation to generation. 9Do not offer any unholy incense on this altar, or any burnt offerings, grain offerings, or liquid offerings.

10"Once a year Aaron must purify* the altar by smearing its horns with blood from the offering made to purify the people from their sin. This will be a regular, annual event from generation to generation, for this is the LORD's most holy altar."

## Money for the Tabernacle

11Then the LORD said to Moses, 12"Whenever you take a census of the people of Israel, each man who is counted must pay a ransom for himself to the LORD. Then no plague will strike the people as you count them. 13Each person who is counted must give a small piece of silver as a sacred offering to the LORD. (This payment is half a shekel,* based on the sanctuary shekel, which equals twenty gerahs.) 14All who have reached their twentieth birthday must give this sacred offering to the LORD. 15When this offering is given to the LORD to purify your lives, making you right with him,* the rich must not give more than the specified amount, and the poor must not give less. 16Receive this ransom money from the Israelites, and use it for the care of the Tabernacle.* It will bring the Israelites to the LORD's attention, and it will purify your lives."

## Plans for the Washbasin

17Then the LORD said to Moses, 18"Make a bronze washbasin with a bronze stand. Place it between the Tabernacle and the altar, and fill it with water. 19Aaron and his sons will wash their hands and feet there. 20They must wash with water whenever they go into the Tabernacle to appear before the LORD and when they approach the altar to burn up their special gifts to the LORD—or they will die! 21They must always wash their hands and feet, or they will die. This is a permanent law for Aaron and his descendants, to be observed from generation to generation."

## The Anointing Oil

22Then the LORD said to Moses, 23"Collect choice spices—12½ pounds of pure myrrh, 6¼ pounds of fragrant cinnamon, 6¼ pounds of fragrant calamus,* 24and 12½ pounds of cassia*—as measured by the weight of the sanctuary shekel. Also get one gallon of olive oil.* 25Like a skilled incense maker, blend these ingredients to make a holy anointing oil. 26Use this sacred oil to anoint the Tabernacle, the Ark of the Covenant, 27the table and all its utensils, the lampstand and all its accessories, the incense altar, 28the altar of burnt offering and all its utensils, and the washbasin with its stand. 29Consecrate them to make them absolutely holy. After this, whatever touches them will also become holy.

30"Anoint Aaron and his sons also, consecrating them to serve me as priests. 31And say to the people of Israel, 'This holy anointing oil is reserved for me from generation to generation. 32It must never be used to anoint anyone else, and you must never make any blend like it for yourselves. It is holy, and you must treat it as holy. 33Anyone who makes a blend like it or anoints someone other than a priest will be cut off from the community.'"

## The Incense

34Then the LORD said to Moses, "Gather fragrant spices—resin droplets, mollusk shell, and galbanum—and mix these fragrant spices with pure frankincense, weighed out in equal amounts. 35Using the usual techniques of the incense maker, blend the spices together and sprinkle them with salt to produce a pure and holy incense. 36Grind some of the mixture into a very fine powder and put it in front of the Ark of the Covenant,* where I will meet with you in the Tabernacle. You must treat this incense as most holy. 37Never use this formula to make this incense for yourselves. It is reserved for the LORD, and you must treat it as holy. 38Anyone who makes incense like this for personal use will be cut off from the community."

## Craftsmen: Bezalel and Oholiab

31 Then the LORD said to Moses, 2"Look, I have specifically chosen Bezalel son of Uri, grandson of Hur, of the tribe of Judah. 3I have filled him with the Spirit of God, giving him great wisdom, ability, and

---

30:6b Hebrew *that covers the Testimony;* see note on 25:16.  **30:10** Or *make atonement for;* also in 30:10b.  **30:13** Or *0.2 ounces* [6 grams].  **30:15** Or *to make atonement for your lives;* similarly in 30:16.  **30:16** Hebrew *Tent of Meeting;* also in 30:18, 20, 26, 36.  **30:23** Hebrew *500 [shekels]* [5.7 kilograms] *of pure myrrh, 250 [shekels]* [2.9 kilograms] *of fragrant cinnamon, 250 [shekels] of fragrant calamus.*  **30:24a** Hebrew *500 [shekels]* [5.7 kilograms] *of cassia.*  **30:24b** Hebrew *1 hin* [3.8 liters] *of olive oil.*  **30:36** Hebrew *in front of the Testimony;* see note on 25:16.

---

**30:22-38** These recipes were designed for the Tabernacle's anointing oil and incense, and the people could not use them for other purposes. The worship of God was to be set apart from daily life. Even its aroma was distinct! Anyone who treated worship lightly was a danger to the community, so they had to be cut off from the community. (For a sobering example of this, see Leviticus 10:1-3, where Aaron's sons try a different recipe in the Tabernacle.)

**31:1-11** The construction of the Tabernacle required trained craftspeople. Bezalel and Oholiab led the project, and the Spirit of God gave them special inspiration (31:3), but generous and skilled men and women assisted them in their work (see also 35:10-24). God is honored by people who use their creative gifts for his service.

expertise in all kinds of crafts. ⁴He is a master crafts-man, expert in working with gold, silver, and bronze. ⁵He is skilled in engraving and mounting gemstones and in carving wood. He is a master at every craft!

⁶"And I have personally appointed Oholiab son of Ahisamach, of the tribe of Dan, to be his assistant. Moreover, I have given special skill to all the gifted craftsmen so they can make all the things I have commanded you to make:

⁷ the Tabernacle;*
  the Ark of the Covenant;*
  the Ark's cover—the place of atonement;
  all the furnishings of the Tabernacle;
⁸ the table and its utensils;
  the pure gold lampstand with all its accessories;
  the incense altar;
⁹ the altar of burnt offering with all its utensils;
  the washbasin with its stand;
¹⁰ the beautifully stitched garments—the
    sacred garments for Aaron the priest, and
    the garments for his sons to wear as they
    minister as priests;
¹¹ the anointing oil;
  the fragrant incense for the Holy Place.

The craftsmen must make everything as I have com-manded you."

## Instructions for the Sabbath

¹²The LORD then gave these instructions to Moses: ¹³"Tell the people of Israel: 'Be careful to keep my Sabbath day, for the Sabbath is a sign of the covenant between me and you from generation to generation. It is given so you may know that I am the LORD, who makes you holy. ¹⁴You must keep the Sabbath day, for it is a holy day for you. Anyone who desecrates it must be put to death; anyone who works on that day will be cut off from the community. ¹⁵You have six days each week for your ordinary work, but the seventh day must be a Sabbath day of complete rest, a holy day dedicated to the LORD. Anyone who works on the Sabbath must be put to death. ¹⁶The people of Israel must keep the Sabbath day by observing it from generation to generation. This is a covenant obligation for all time. ¹⁷It is a permanent sign of my covenant with the people of Israel. For in six days the LORD made heaven and earth, but on the seventh day he stopped working and was refreshed.'"

¹⁸When the LORD finished speaking with Moses on Mount Sinai, he gave him the two stone tablets inscribed with the terms of the covenant,* written by the finger of God.

## The Gold Calf

**32** When the people saw how long it was tak-ing Moses to come back down the mountain, they gathered around Aaron. "Come on," they said, "make us some gods who can lead us. We don't know what happened to this fellow Moses, who brought us here from the land of Egypt."

²So Aaron said, "Take the gold rings from the ears of your wives and sons and daughters, and bring them to me."

³All the people took the gold rings from their ears and brought them to Aaron. ⁴Then Aaron took the gold, melted it down, and molded it into the shape of a calf. When the people saw it, they exclaimed, "O Israel, these are the gods who brought you out of the land of Egypt!"

⁵Aaron saw how excited the people were, so he built an altar in front of the calf. Then he announced, "Tomorrow will be a festival to the LORD!"

⁶The people got up early the next morning to sac-rifice burnt offerings and peace offerings. After this, they celebrated with feasting and drinking, and they indulged in pagan revelry.

⁷The LORD told Moses, "Quick! Go down the moun-tain! Your people whom you brought from the land of Egypt have corrupted themselves. ⁸How quickly they have turned away from the way I commanded them to live! They have melted down gold and made a calf, and they have bowed down and sacrificed to it. They are saying, 'These are your gods, O Israel, who brought you out of the land of Egypt.'"

⁹Then the LORD said, "I have seen how stubborn and rebellious these people are. ¹⁰Now leave me alone so my fierce anger can blaze against them, and I will destroy them. Then I will make you, Moses, into a great nation."

¹¹But Moses tried to pacify the LORD his God. "O LORD!" he said. "Why are you so angry with your own people whom you brought from the land of Egypt with such great power and such a strong hand? ¹²Why let the Egyptians say, 'Their God res-cued them with the evil intention of slaughtering them in the mountains and wiping them from the face of the earth'? Turn away from your fierce anger. Change your mind about this terrible disaster you have threatened against your people! ¹³Remem-ber your servants Abraham, Isaac, and Jacob.* You bound yourself with an oath to them, saying, 'I will make your descendants as numerous as the stars of heaven. And I will give them all of this land that I have promised to your descendants, and they will possess it forever.'"

---

31:7a Hebrew *the Tent of Meeting.* 31:7b Hebrew *the Ark of the Testimony.* 31:18 Hebrew *the two tablets of the Testimony;* see note on 25:16. 32:13 Hebrew *Israel.* The names "Jacob" and "Israel" are often interchanged throughout the Old Testament, referring sometimes to the individual patriarch and sometimes to the nation.

---

**32:11-14** Moses interceded on Israel's behalf, persuading God that his promise to Abraham should result in protection rather than judgment. God was within his rights to punish the people for their rebellion. However, as this story illustrates, prayer is powerful. God invited Moses into his deliberations, entrusting him with his plans and responding to his request.

¹⁴So the LORD changed his mind about the terrible disaster he had threatened to bring on his people.

¹⁵Then Moses turned and went down the mountain. He held in his hands the two stone tablets inscribed with the terms of the covenant.* They were inscribed on both sides, front and back. ¹⁶These tablets were God's work; the words on them were written by God himself.

¹⁷When Joshua heard the boisterous noise of the people shouting below them, he exclaimed to Moses, "It sounds like war in the camp!"

¹⁸But Moses replied, "No, it's not a shout of victory nor the wailing of defeat. I hear the sound of a celebration."

¹⁹When they came near the camp, Moses saw the calf and the dancing, and he burned with anger. He threw the stone tablets to the ground, smashing them at the foot of the mountain. ²⁰He took the calf they had made and burned it. Then he ground it into powder, threw it into the water, and forced the people to drink it.

²¹Finally, he turned to Aaron and demanded, "What did these people do to you to make you bring such terrible sin upon them?"

²²"Don't get so upset, my lord," Aaron replied. "You yourself know how evil these people are. ²³They said to me, 'Make us gods who will lead us. We don't know what happened to this fellow Moses, who brought us here from the land of Egypt.' ²⁴So I told them, 'Whoever has gold jewelry, take it off.' When they brought it to me, I simply threw it into the fire—and out came this calf!"

²⁵Moses saw that Aaron had let the people get completely out of control, much to the amusement of their enemies.* ²⁶So he stood at the entrance to the camp and shouted, "All of you who are on the LORD's side, come here and join me." And all the Levites gathered around him.

²⁷Moses told them, "This is what the LORD, the God of Israel, says: Each of you, take your swords and go back and forth from one end of the camp to the other. Kill everyone—even your brothers, friends, and neighbors." ²⁸The Levites obeyed Moses' command, and about 3,000 people died that day.

²⁹Then Moses told the Levites, "Today you have ordained yourselves* for the service of the LORD, for you obeyed him even though it meant killing your own sons and brothers. Today you have earned a blessing."

## Moses Intercedes for Israel

³⁰The next day Moses said to the people, "You have committed a terrible sin, but I will go back up to the LORD on the mountain. Perhaps I will be able to obtain forgiveness* for your sin."

³¹So Moses returned to the LORD and said, "Oh, what a terrible sin these people have committed. They have made gods of gold for themselves. ³²But now, if you will only forgive their sin—but if not, erase my name from the record you have written!"

³³But the LORD replied to Moses, "No, I will erase the name of everyone who has sinned against me. ³⁴Now go, lead the people to the place I told you about. Look! My angel will lead the way before you. And when I come to call the people to account, I will certainly hold them responsible for their sins."

³⁵Then the LORD sent a great plague upon the people because they had worshiped the calf Aaron had made.

**33** The LORD said to Moses, "Get going, you and the people you brought up from the land of Egypt. Go up to the land I swore to give to Abraham, Isaac, and Jacob. I told them, 'I will give this land to your descendants.' ²And I will send an angel before you to drive out the Canaanites, Amorites, Hittites, Perizzites, Hivites, and Jebusites. ³Go up to this land that flows with milk and honey. But I will not travel among you, for you are a stubborn and rebellious people. If I did, I would surely destroy you along the way."

⁴When the people heard these stern words, they went into mourning and stopped wearing their jewelry and fine clothes. ⁵For the LORD had told Moses to tell them, "You are a stubborn and rebellious people. If I were to travel with you for even a moment, I would destroy you. Remove your jewelry and fine clothes while I decide what to do with you." ⁶So from the time they left Mount Sinai,* the Israelites wore no more jewelry or fine clothes.

⁷It was Moses' practice to take the Tent of Meeting* and set it up some distance from the camp. Everyone who wanted to make a request of the LORD would go to the Tent of Meeting outside the camp.

---

**32:15** Hebrew *the two tablets of the Testimony;* see note on 25:16. **32:25** Or *out of control, and they mocked anyone who opposed them.* The meaning of the Hebrew is uncertain. **32:29** As in Greek and Latin versions; Hebrew reads *Today ordain yourselves.* **32:30** Or *to make atonement.* **33:6** Hebrew *Horeb,* another name for Sinai. **33:7** This "Tent of Meeting" is different from the Tabernacle described in chapters 26 and 36.

---

**32:19-29** Moses' anger over the Israelites' rebellion mirrored God's (32:9-10). Although God had determined not to wipe out the entire nation, those responsible for this offense still suffered the death penalty. The Levites showed their commitment to worshiping Yahweh alone by carrying out God's judgment. Their loyalty to God was higher than their loyalty to family members.
**33:1-23** Given the people's rebellious tendencies, God determined that he would not travel with them (33:3). This provoked great mourning (33:4), and Moses pled for God's presence to go with them, marking them as his people (33:15-16).
**33:7** Before the Tabernacle existed, Moses would go outside the camp to meet with God. The Tabernacle would symbolize God's presence in the center of the Israelite community, where they would have reliable access to God. Previously, God showed up unpredictably at his initiative (for example, in Eden, in dreams, and on Mount Sinai). Now, in the Tabernacle, the Lord would make himself perpetually available to his people.

⁸Whenever Moses went out to the Tent of Meeting, all the people would get up and stand in the entrances of their own tents. They would all watch Moses until he disappeared inside. ⁹As he went into the tent, the pillar of cloud would come down and hover at its entrance while the LORD spoke with Moses. ¹⁰When the people saw the cloud standing at the entrance of the tent, they would stand and bow down in front of their own tents. ¹¹Inside the Tent of Meeting, the LORD would speak to Moses face to face, as one speaks to a friend. Afterward Moses would return to the camp, but the young man who assisted him, Joshua son of Nun, would remain behind in the Tent of Meeting.

## Moses Sees the LORD's Glory

¹²One day Moses said to the LORD, "You have been telling me, 'Take these people up to the Promised Land.' But you haven't told me whom you will send with me. You have told me, 'I know you by name, and I look favorably on you.' ¹³If it is true that you look favorably on me, let me know your ways so I may understand you more fully and continue to enjoy your favor. And remember that this nation is your very own people."

¹⁴The LORD replied, "I will personally go with you, Moses, and I will give you rest—everything will be fine for you."

¹⁵Then Moses said, "If you don't personally go with us, don't make us leave this place. ¹⁶How will anyone know that you look favorably on me—on me and on your people—if you don't go with us? For your presence among us sets your people and me apart from all other people on the earth."

¹⁷The LORD replied to Moses, "I will indeed do what you have asked, for I look favorably on you, and I know you by name."

¹⁸Moses responded, "Then show me your glorious presence."

¹⁹The LORD replied, "I will make all my goodness pass before you, and I will call out my name, Yahweh,* before you. For I will show mercy to anyone I choose, and I will show compassion to anyone I choose. ²⁰But you may not look directly at my face, for no one may see me and live." ²¹The LORD continued, "Look, stand near me on this rock. ²²As my glorious presence passes by, I will hide you in the crevice of the rock and cover you with my hand until I have passed by. ²³Then I will remove my hand and let you see me from behind. But my face will not be seen."

## A New Copy of the Covenant

**34** Then the LORD told Moses, "Chisel out two stone tablets like the first ones. I will write on them the same words that were on the tablets you smashed. ²Be ready in the morning to climb up Mount Sinai and present yourself to me on the top of the mountain. ³No one else may come with you. In fact, no one is to appear anywhere on the mountain. Do not even let the flocks or herds graze near the mountain."

⁴So Moses chiseled out two tablets of stone like the first ones. Early in the morning he climbed Mount Sinai as the LORD had commanded him, and he carried the two stone tablets in his hands.

⁵Then the LORD came down in a cloud and stood there with him; and he called out his own name, Yahweh.* ⁶The LORD passed in front of Moses, calling out,

"Yahweh!* The LORD!
　The God of compassion and mercy!
I am slow to anger
　and filled with unfailing love and faithfulness.
⁷ I lavish unfailing love to a thousand
　　generations.*
　I forgive iniquity, rebellion, and sin.
But I do not excuse the guilty.
　I lay the sins of the parents upon their
　　children and grandchildren;
the entire family is affected—
　even children in the third and fourth
　　generations."

⁸Moses immediately threw himself to the ground and worshiped. ⁹And he said, "O Lord, if it is true that I have found favor with you, then please travel with us. Yes, this is a stubborn and rebellious people, but please forgive our iniquity and our sins. Claim us as your own special possession."

¹⁰The LORD replied, "Listen, I am making a covenant with you in the presence of all your people. I will perform miracles that have never been performed anywhere in all the earth or in any nation. And all the people around you will see the power of the LORD—the awesome power I will display for you. ¹¹But listen carefully to everything I command you today. Then I will go ahead of you and drive out the Amorites, Canaanites, Hittites, Perizzites, Hivites, and Jebusites.

---

**33:19** *Yahweh* is a transliteration of the proper name *YHWH* that is sometimes rendered "Jehovah"; in this translation it is usually rendered "the LORD" (note the use of small capitals). **34:5** *Yahweh* is a transliteration of the proper name *YHWH* that is sometimes rendered "Jehovah"; in this translation it is usually rendered "the LORD" (note the use of small capitals). **34:6** See note on 34:5. **34:7** Hebrew *for thousands.*

---

**34:7** This passage describes God's actions in response to sin rather than his ideal for humanity. Our sins affect our descendants, but God restricts those natural effects to three or four generations (see also 20:5-6).
**34:10-16** This covenant is not a different covenant than that described in Exodus 19–24. Here, God reiterated it to Moses to explain why he prohibited treaties with other nations. The prohibition of intermarriage with other ethnic groups in 34:16 served one purpose: to guard against worshiping other gods. Presumably, anyone who joined the Israelites (signified by male circumcision) and obeyed and worshiped Yahweh was exempt from this prohibition.

# Extended Family

## Speak Kindly

Never speak harshly to an older man, but appeal to him respectfully as you would to your own father. Talk to younger men as you would to your own brothers. Treat older women as you would your mother, and treat younger women with all purity as you would your own sisters. **1 TIMOTHY 5:1-2**

## Honor Them

"I ... know about everything you have done for your mother-in-law since the death of your husband. I have heard how you left your father and mother and your own land to live here among complete strangers. May the LORD, the God of Israel, under whose wings you have come to take refuge, reward you fully for what you have done." **RUTH 2:11-12**

Esther continued to keep her family background and nationality a secret. She was still following Mordecai's directions, just as she did when she lived in his home. **ESTHER 2:20**

## Honor God First

"I have come to set a man
against his father,
     a daughter against her
     mother,
and a daughter-in-law against
her mother-in-law.
     Your enemies will be right in
     your own household!"
**MATTHEW 10:35-36**

"Father will be divided against son
     and son against father;
mother against daughter
     and daughter against
     mother;
and mother-in-law against
daughter-in-law
     and daughter-in-law against
     mother-in-law." **LUKE 12:53**

# Never speak harshly...

## Listen to Them

"I will do everything you say," Ruth replied. So she went down to the threshing floor that night and followed the instructions of her mother-in-law. **RUTH 3:5-6**

"If you follow this advice, and if God commands you to do so, then you will be able to endure the pressures, and all these people will go home in peace." Moses listened to his father-in-law's advice and followed his suggestions. **EXODUS 18:23-24**

¹²"Be very careful never to make a treaty with the people who live in the land where you are going. If you do, you will follow their evil ways and be trapped. ¹³Instead, you must break down their pagan altars, smash their sacred pillars, and cut down their Asherah poles. ¹⁴You must worship no other gods, for the LORD, whose very name is Jealous, is a God who is jealous about his relationship with you.

¹⁵"You must not make a treaty of any kind with the people living in the land. They lust after their gods, offering sacrifices to them. They will invite you to join them in their sacrificial meals, and you will go with them. ¹⁶Then you will accept their daughters, who sacrifice to other gods, as wives for your sons. And they will seduce your sons to commit adultery against me by worshiping other gods. ¹⁷You must not make any gods of molten metal for yourselves.

¹⁸"You must celebrate the Festival of Unleavened Bread. For seven days the bread you eat must be made without yeast, just as I commanded you. Celebrate this festival annually at the appointed time in early spring, in the month of Abib,* for that is the anniversary of your departure from Egypt.

¹⁹"The firstborn of every animal belongs to me, including the firstborn males* from your herds of cattle and your flocks of sheep and goats. ²⁰A firstborn donkey may be bought back from the LORD by presenting a lamb or young goat in its place. But if you do not buy it back, you must break its neck. However, you must buy back every firstborn son.

"No one may appear before me without an offering.

²¹"You have six days each week for your ordinary work, but on the seventh day you must stop working, even during the seasons of plowing and harvest.

²²"You must celebrate the Festival of Harvest* with the first crop of the wheat harvest, and celebrate the Festival of the Final Harvest* at the end of the harvest season. ²³Three times each year every man in Israel must appear before the Sovereign, the LORD, the God of Israel. ²⁴I will drive out the other nations ahead of you and expand your territory, so no one will covet and conquer your land while you appear before the LORD your God three times each year.

²⁵"You must not offer the blood of my sacrificial offerings together with any baked goods containing yeast. And none of the meat of the Passover sacrifice may be kept over until the next morning.

²⁶"As you harvest your crops, bring the very best of the first harvest to the house of the LORD your God.

"You must not cook a young goat in its mother's milk."

²⁷Then the LORD said to Moses, "Write down all these instructions, for they represent the terms of the covenant I am making with you and with Israel."

²⁸Moses remained there on the mountain with the LORD forty days and forty nights. In all that time he ate no bread and drank no water. And the LORD* wrote the terms of the covenant—the Ten Commandments*—on the stone tablets.

²⁹When Moses came down Mount Sinai carrying the two stone tablets inscribed with the terms of the covenant,* he wasn't aware that his face had become radiant because he had spoken to the LORD. ³⁰So when Aaron and the people of Israel saw the radiance of Moses' face, they were afraid to come near him. ³¹But Moses called out to them and asked Aaron and all the leaders of the community to come over, and he talked with them. ³²Then all the people of Israel approached him, and Moses gave them all the instructions the LORD had given him on Mount Sinai. ³³When Moses finished speaking with them, he covered his face with a veil. ³⁴But whenever he went into the Tent of Meeting to speak with the LORD, he would remove the veil until he came out again. Then he would give the people whatever instructions the LORD had given him, ³⁵and the people of Israel would see the radiant glow of his face. So he would put the veil over his face until he returned to speak with the LORD.

## Instructions for the Sabbath

**35** Then Moses called together the whole community of Israel and told them, "These are the instructions the LORD has commanded you to follow. ²You have six days each week for your ordinary work, but the seventh day must be a Sabbath day of complete rest, a holy day dedicated to the LORD. Anyone who works on that day must be put to death. ³You must not even light a fire in any of your homes on the Sabbath."

## Offerings for the Tabernacle

⁴Then Moses said to the whole community of Israel, "This is what the LORD has commanded: ⁵Take a sacred offering for the LORD. Let those with generous hearts present the following gifts to the LORD:

---

34:18 Hebrew *appointed time in the month of Abib*. This first month of the ancient Hebrew lunar calendar usually occurs within the months of March and April. **34:19** As in Greek version; the meaning of the Hebrew word is uncertain. **34:22a** Hebrew *Festival of Weeks;* compare 23:16. This was later called the Festival of Pentecost. It is celebrated today as Shavuot (or Shabuoth). **34:22b** Or *Festival of Ingathering*. This was later called the Festival of Shelters or Festival of Tabernacles (see Lev 23:33-36). It is celebrated today as Sukkot (or Succoth). **34:28a** Hebrew *he*. **34:28b** Hebrew *the ten words*. **34:29** Hebrew *the two tablets of the Testimony;* see note on 25:16.

---

**35:4–36:7** Unlike when Aaron created the gold calf and demanded one type of material (earrings), this passage invites people to bring various gifts (35:4-9). People gave as their "hearts were stirred" and "spirits were moved" (35:21).

Perhaps because the variety of gifts meant that everyone could bring something, and the giving was voluntary, the people gave too much. Moses had to command them to stop (36:4-7).

gold, silver, and bronze;
6 blue, purple, and scarlet thread;
fine linen and goat hair for cloth;
7 tanned ram skins and fine goatskin leather;
acacia wood;
8 olive oil for the lamps;
spices for the anointing oil and the fragrant incense;
9 onyx stones, and other gemstones to be set in the ephod and the priest's chestpiece.

10"Come, all of you who are gifted craftsmen. Construct everything that the LORD has commanded:

11 the Tabernacle and its sacred tent, its covering, clasps, frames, crossbars, posts, and bases;
12 the Ark and its carrying poles;
the Ark's cover—the place of atonement;
the inner curtain to shield the Ark;
13 the table, its carrying poles, and all its utensils;
the Bread of the Presence;
14 for light, the lampstand, its accessories, the lamp cups, and the olive oil for lighting;
15 the incense altar and its carrying poles;
the anointing oil and fragrant incense;
the curtain for the entrance of the Tabernacle;
16 the altar of burnt offering;
the bronze grating of the altar and its carrying poles and utensils;
the washbasin with its stand;
17 the curtains for the walls of the courtyard;
the posts and their bases;
the curtain for the entrance to the courtyard;
18 the tent pegs of the Tabernacle and courtyard and their ropes;
19 the beautifully stitched garments for the priests to wear while ministering in the Holy Place—the sacred garments for Aaron the priest, and the garments for his sons to wear as they minister as priests."

20So the whole community of Israel left Moses and returned to their tents. 21All whose hearts were stirred and whose spirits were moved came and brought their sacred offerings to the LORD. They brought all the materials needed for the Tabernacle,* for the performance of its rituals, and for the sacred garments. 22Both men and women came, all whose hearts were willing. They brought to the LORD their offerings of gold—brooches, earrings, rings from their fingers, and necklaces. They presented gold objects of every kind as a special offering to the LORD. 23All those who owned the following items willingly brought them: blue, purple, and scarlet thread; fine

linen and goat hair for cloth; and tanned ram skins and fine goatskin leather. 24And all who had silver and bronze objects gave them as a sacred offering to the LORD. And those who had acacia wood brought it for use in the project.

25All the women who were skilled in sewing and spinning prepared blue, purple, and scarlet thread, and fine linen cloth. 26All the women who were willing used their skills to spin the goat hair into yarn. 27The leaders brought onyx stones and the special gemstones to be set in the ephod and the priest's chestpiece. 28They also brought spices and olive oil for the light, the anointing oil, and the fragrant incense. 29So the people of Israel—every man and woman who was eager to help in the work the LORD had given them through Moses—brought their gifts and gave them freely to the LORD.

30Then Moses told the people of Israel, "The LORD has specifically chosen Bezalel son of Uri, grandson of Hur, of the tribe of Judah. 31The LORD has filled Bezalel with the Spirit of God, giving him great wisdom, ability, and expertise in all kinds of crafts. 32He is a master craftsman, expert in working with gold, silver, and bronze. 33He is skilled in engraving and mounting gemstones and in carving wood. He is a master at every craft. 34And the LORD has given both him and Oholiab son of Ahisamach, of the tribe of Dan, the ability to teach their skills to others. 35The LORD has given them special skills as engravers, designers, embroiderers in blue, purple, and scarlet thread on fine linen cloth, and weavers. They excel as craftsmen and as designers.

**36** "The LORD has gifted Bezalel, Oholiab, and the other skilled craftsmen with wisdom and ability to perform any task involved in building the sanctuary. Let them construct and furnish the Tabernacle, just as the LORD has commanded."

2So Moses summoned Bezalel and Oholiab and all the others who were specially gifted by the LORD and were eager to get to work. 3Moses gave them the materials donated by the people of Israel as sacred offerings for the completion of the sanctuary. But the people continued to bring additional gifts each morning. 4Finally the craftsmen who were working on the sanctuary left their work. 5They went to Moses and reported, "The people have given more than enough materials to complete the job the LORD has commanded us to do!"

6So Moses gave the command, and this message was sent throughout the camp: "Men and women, don't prepare any more gifts for the sanctuary. We

35:21 Hebrew *Tent of Meeting.*

**35:25-29** Both women and men participated in preparing the Tabernacle by using their skills and donating their finest possessions. These luxury items were likely those given to them by their neighbors as they left Egypt (12:35-36).

**37:1-29** While the passage says Bezalel made the Ark, all the rest of the furnishings (37:1, 10, 17, 25) and the courtyard and its furnishings (38:1, 8, 9, 18), this likely means he was responsible. He probably directed other craftsmen and seamstresses.

have enough!" So the people stopped bringing their sacred offerings. ⁷Their contributions were more than enough to complete the whole project.

## Building the Tabernacle

⁸The skilled craftsmen made ten curtains of finely woven linen for the Tabernacle. Then Bezalel* decorated the curtains with blue, purple, and scarlet thread and with skillfully embroidered cherubim. ⁹All ten curtains were exactly the same size—42 feet long and 6 feet wide.* ¹⁰Five of these curtains were joined together to make one long curtain, and the other five were joined to make a second long curtain. ¹¹He made fifty loops of blue yarn and put them along the edge of the last curtain in each set. ¹²The fifty loops along the edge of one curtain matched the fifty loops along the edge of the other curtain. ¹³Then he made fifty gold clasps and fastened the long curtains together with the clasps. In this way, the Tabernacle was made of one continuous piece.

¹⁴He made eleven curtains of goat-hair cloth to serve as a tent covering for the Tabernacle. ¹⁵These eleven curtains were all exactly the same size—45 feet long and 6 feet wide.* ¹⁶Bezalel joined five of these curtains together to make one long curtain, and the other six were joined to make a second long curtain. ¹⁷He made fifty loops for the edge of each large curtain. ¹⁸He also made fifty bronze clasps to fasten the long curtains together. In this way, the tent covering was made of one continuous piece. ¹⁹He completed the tent covering with a layer of tanned ram skins and a layer of fine goatskin leather.

²⁰For the framework of the Tabernacle, Bezalel constructed frames of acacia wood. ²¹Each frame was 15 feet high and 27 inches wide,* ²²with two pegs under each frame. All the frames were identical. ²³He made twenty of these frames to support the curtains on the south side of the Tabernacle. ²⁴He also made forty silver bases—two bases under each frame, with the pegs fitting securely into the bases. ²⁵For the north side of the Tabernacle, he made another twenty frames, ²⁶with their forty silver bases, two bases under each frame. ²⁷He made six frames for the rear—the west side of the Tabernacle—²⁸along with two additional frames to reinforce the rear corners of the Tabernacle. ²⁹These corner frames were matched at the bottom and firmly attached at the top with a single ring, forming a single corner unit. Both of these corner units were made the same way. ³⁰So there were eight frames at the rear of the Tabernacle, set in sixteen silver bases—two bases under each frame.

³¹Then he made crossbars of acacia wood to link the frames, five crossbars for the north side of the Tabernacle ³²and five for the south side. He also made five crossbars for the rear of the Tabernacle, which faced west. ³³He made the middle crossbar to attach halfway up the frames; it ran all the way from one end of the Tabernacle to the other. ³⁴He overlaid the frames with gold and made gold rings to hold the crossbars. Then he overlaid the crossbars with gold as well.

³⁵For the inside of the Tabernacle, Bezalel made a special curtain of finely woven linen. He decorated it with blue, purple, and scarlet thread and with skillfully embroidered cherubim. ³⁶For the curtain, he made four posts of acacia wood and four gold hooks. He overlaid the posts with gold and set them in four silver bases.

³⁷Then he made another curtain for the entrance to the sacred tent. He made it of finely woven linen and embroidered it with exquisite designs using blue, purple, and scarlet thread. ³⁸This curtain was hung on gold hooks attached to five posts. The posts with their decorated tops and hooks were overlaid with gold, and the five bases were cast from bronze.

## Building the Ark of the Covenant

**37** Next Bezalel made the Ark of acacia wood—a sacred chest 45 inches long, 27 inches wide, and 27 inches high.* ²He overlaid it inside and outside with pure gold, and he ran a molding of gold all around it. ³He cast four gold rings and attached them to its four feet, two rings on each side. ⁴Then he made poles from acacia wood and overlaid them with gold. ⁵He inserted the poles into the rings at the sides of the Ark to carry it.

⁶Then he made the Ark's cover—the place of atonement—from pure gold. It was 45 inches long and 27 inches wide.* ⁷He made two cherubim from hammered gold and placed them on the two ends of the atonement cover. ⁸He molded the cherubim on each end of the atonement cover, making it all of one piece of gold. ⁹The cherubim faced each other and looked down on the atonement cover. With their wings spread above it, they protected it.

## Building the Table

¹⁰Then Bezalel* made the table of acacia wood, 36 inches long, 18 inches wide, and 27 inches high.* ¹¹He overlaid it with pure gold and ran a gold molding around the edge. ¹²He decorated it with a 3-inch border* all around, and he ran a gold molding along the border. ¹³Then he cast four gold rings for the table

---

36:8 Hebrew *he;* also in 36:16, 20, 35. See 37:1.  36:9 Hebrew *28 cubits* [12.9 meters] *long and 4 cubits* [1.8 meters] *wide.*
36:15 Hebrew *30 cubits* [13.8 meters] *long and 4 cubits* [1.8 meters] *wide.*  36:21 Hebrew *10 cubits* [4.6 meters] *high and 1.5 cubits* [69 centimeters] *wide.*  37:1 Hebrew *2.5 cubits* [115 centimeters] *long, 1.5 cubits* [69 centimeters] *wide, and 1.5 cubits high.*  37:6 Hebrew *2.5 cubits* [115 centimeters] *long and 1.5 cubits* [69 centimeters] *wide.*  37:10a Hebrew *he;* also in 37:17, 25.  37:10b Hebrew *2 cubits* [92 centimeters] *long, 1 cubit* [46 centimeters] *wide, and 1.5 cubits* [69 centimeters] *high.*
37:12 Hebrew *a border of a handbreadth* [8 centimeters].

and attached them at the four corners next to the four legs. ¹⁴The rings were attached near the border to hold the poles that were used to carry the table. ¹⁵He made these poles from acacia wood and overlaid them with gold. ¹⁶Then he made special containers of pure gold for the table—bowls, ladles, jars, and pitchers—to be used in pouring out liquid offerings.

## Building the Lampstand

¹⁷Then Bezalel made the lampstand of pure, hammered gold. He made the entire lampstand and its decorations of one piece—the base, center stem, lamp cups, buds, and petals. ¹⁸The lampstand had six branches going out from the center stem, three on each side. ¹⁹Each of the six branches had three lamp cups shaped like almond blossoms, complete with buds and petals. ²⁰The center stem of the lampstand was crafted with four lamp cups shaped like almond blossoms, complete with buds and petals. ²¹There was an almond bud beneath each pair of branches where the six branches extended from the center stem, all made of one piece. ²²The almond buds and branches were all of one piece with the center stem, and they were hammered from pure gold.

²³He also made seven lamps for the lampstand, lamp snuffers, and trays, all of pure gold. ²⁴The entire lampstand, along with its accessories, was made from 75 pounds* of pure gold.

## Building the Incense Altar

²⁵Then Bezalel made the incense altar of acacia wood. It was 18 inches square and 36 inches high,* with horns at the corners carved from the same piece of wood as the altar itself. ²⁶He overlaid the top, sides, and horns of the altar with pure gold, and he ran a gold molding around the entire altar. ²⁷He made two gold rings and attached them on opposite sides of the altar below the gold molding to hold the carrying poles. ²⁸He made the poles of acacia wood and overlaid them with gold.

²⁹Then he made the sacred anointing oil and the fragrant incense, using the techniques of a skilled incense maker.

## Building the Altar of Burnt Offering

**38** Next Bezalel* used acacia wood to construct the square altar of burnt offering. It was 7½ feet wide, 7½ feet long, and 4½ feet high.* ²He made horns for each of its four corners so that the

horns and altar were all one piece. He overlaid the altar with bronze. ³Then he made all the altar utensils of bronze—the ash buckets, shovels, basins, meat forks, and firepans. ⁴Next he made a bronze grating and installed it halfway down the side of the altar, under the ledge. ⁵He cast four rings and attached them to the corners of the bronze grating to hold the carrying poles. ⁶He made the poles from acacia wood and overlaid them with bronze. ⁷He inserted the poles through the rings on the sides of the altar. The altar was hollow and was made from planks.

## Building the Washbasin

⁸Bezalel made the bronze washbasin and its bronze stand from bronze mirrors donated by the women who served at the entrance of the Tabernacle.*

## Building the Courtyard

⁹Then Bezalel made the courtyard, which was enclosed with curtains made of finely woven linen. On the south side the curtains were 150 feet long.* ¹⁰They were held up by twenty posts set securely in twenty bronze bases. He hung the curtains with silver hooks and rings. ¹¹He made a similar set of curtains for the north side—150 feet of curtains held up by twenty posts set securely in bronze bases. He hung the curtains with silver hooks and rings. ¹²The curtains on the west end of the courtyard were 75 feet long,* hung with silver hooks and rings and supported by ten posts set into ten bases. ¹³The east end, the front, was also 75 feet long.

¹⁴The courtyard entrance was on the east end, flanked by two curtains. The curtain on the right side was 22½ feet long* and was supported by three posts set into three bases. ¹⁵The curtain on the left side was also 22½ feet long and was supported by three posts set into three bases. ¹⁶All the curtains used in the courtyard were made of finely woven linen. ¹⁷Each post had a bronze base, and all the hooks and rings were silver. The tops of the posts of the courtyard were overlaid with silver, and the rings to hold up the curtains were made of silver.

¹⁸He made the curtain for the entrance to the courtyard of finely woven linen, and he decorated it with beautiful embroidery in blue, purple, and scarlet thread. It was 30 feet long, and its height was 7½ feet,* just like the curtains of the courtyard walls. ¹⁹It was supported by four posts, each set securely in its own bronze base. The tops of the posts were

37:24 Hebrew *1 talent* [34 kilograms]. **37:25** Hebrew *1 cubit* [46 centimeters] *long and 1 cubit wide, a square, and 2 cubits* [92 centimeters] *high.* **38:1a** Hebrew *he;* also in 38:8, 9. **38:1b** Hebrew *5 cubits* [2.3 meters] *wide, 5 cubits long, a square, and 3 cubits* [1.4 meters] *high.* **38:8** Hebrew *Tent of Meeting;* also in 38:30. **38:9** Hebrew *100 cubits* [46 meters]; also in 38:11. **38:12** Hebrew *50 cubits* [23 meters]; also in 38:13. **38:14** Hebrew *15 cubits* [6.9 meters]; also in 38:15. **38:18** Hebrew *20 cubits* [9.2 meters] *long and 5 cubits* [2.3 meters] *high.*

**38:1-20** This section reports on building the courtyard (38:9-20) and its equipment, including the altar of burnt offering (38:1-7) and the washbasin (38:8).
**38:21-29** The immense amount of metal in this inventory (more

than a ton of gold, almost four tons of silver, and two-and-a-half tons of bronze) reflects the Egyptians' eagerness to send the Israelites away. They gave the Israelites anything they asked for their departure (see 12:35-36).

# Leviticus

**WHAT DO WE LEARN ABOUT GOD'S MISSION AND OURS?** God gives instructions about how to pursue our holiness so that we can be close to him.

**WHO WROTE IT?** Leviticus is anonymous, but Jewish and Christian traditions attribute it to Moses.

**WHEN DID IT HAPPEN?** In the 1400s or 1200s BC, while the Israelites were at Sinai.

**HOW IS IT ORGANIZED?**

1–7: Instructions for offering the five main sacrifices

8–10: The beginning of Israel's priesthood: Aaron and his sons

11–15: Laws about purity

16: Marking the Day of Atonement

17–26: Holy practices for God's people

27: Dedicating people or things to God

**FEATURE HIGHLIGHTS**

+ *Distant: Called Close (133)*
+ *What's Up with All These Sacrifices? (134)*
+ *Israel's Sacrifices (136)*
+ *God's Glory (141)*
+ *Nourishing Our Bodies and Spirits (152)*

*Words to Remember are highlighted throughout this book*

**HOW LONG DOES IT TAKE TO READ?**

| | 2:00 | | | | | |
|---|---|---|---|---|---|---|
| :30 | 1:00 | 1:30 | 2:00 | 2:30 | 3:00 | 3:30 |

## Timeline

| BC | |
|---|---|
| 1446 | EXODUS FROM EGYPT |
| 1445 | TEN COMMANDMENTS GIVEN |
| 1444 | ISRAEL CAMPS AT MOUNT SINAI |
| 1406 | MOSES DIES; ISRAELITES ENTER CANAAN |
| 1375 | JUDGES (INCLUDING DEBORAH, GIDEON, AND SAMSON) BEGIN TO RULE |
| 1050 | KINGDOM UNITED UNDER SAUL |

## Procedures for the Burnt Offering

**1** The LORD called to Moses from the Tabernacle* and said to him, [2]"Give the following instructions to the people of Israel. When you present an animal as an offering to the LORD, you may take it from your herd of cattle or your flock of sheep and goats.

[3]"If the animal you present as a burnt offering is from the herd, it must be a male with no defects. Bring it to the entrance of the Tabernacle so you* may be accepted by the LORD. [4]Lay your hand on the animal's head, and the LORD will accept its death in your place to purify you, making you right with him.* [5]Then slaughter the young bull in the LORD's presence, and Aaron's sons, the priests, will present the animal's blood by splattering it against all sides of the altar that stands at the entrance to the Tabernacle. [6]Then skin the animal and cut it into pieces. [7]The sons of Aaron the priest will build a wood fire on the altar. [8]They will arrange the pieces of the offering, including the head and fat, on the wood burning on the altar. [9]But the internal organs and the legs must first be washed with water. Then the priest will burn the entire sacrifice on the altar as a burnt offering. It is a special gift, a pleasing aroma to the LORD.

[10]"If the animal you present as a burnt offering is from the flock, it may be either a sheep or a goat, but it must be a male with no defects. [11]Slaughter the animal on the north side of the altar in the LORD's presence, and Aaron's sons, the priests, will splatter its blood against all sides of the altar. [12]Then cut the animal in pieces, and the priests will arrange the pieces of the offering, including the head and fat, on the wood burning on the altar. [13]But the internal organs and the legs must first be washed with water. Then the priest will burn the entire sacrifice on the altar as a burnt offering. It is a special gift, a pleasing aroma to the LORD.

[14]"If you present a bird as a burnt offering to the LORD, choose either a turtledove or a young pigeon. [15]The priest will take the bird to the altar, wring off its head, and burn it on the altar. But first he must drain its blood against the side of the altar. [16]The priest must also remove the crop and the feathers* and throw them in the ashes on the east side of the altar. [17]Then, grasping the bird by its wings, the priest will tear the bird open, but without tearing it apart. Then he will burn it as a burnt offering on the wood burning on the altar. It is a special gift, a pleasing aroma to the LORD.

## Procedures for the Grain Offering

**2** "When you present grain as an offering to the LORD, the offering must consist of choice flour. You are to pour olive oil on it, sprinkle it with frankincense, [2]and bring it to Aaron's sons, the priests. The priest will scoop out a handful of the flour moistened with oil, together with all the frankincense, and burn this representative portion on the altar. It is a special gift, a pleasing aroma to the LORD. [3]The rest of the grain offering will then be given to Aaron and his sons. This offering will be considered a most holy part of the special gifts presented to the LORD.

[4]"If your offering is a grain offering baked in an oven, it must be made of choice flour, but without any yeast. It may be presented in the form of thin cakes mixed with olive oil or wafers spread with olive oil. [5]If your grain offering is cooked on a griddle, it must be made of choice flour mixed with olive oil but without any yeast. [6]Break it in pieces and pour olive oil on it; it is a grain offering. [7]If your grain offering is prepared in a pan, it must be made of choice flour and olive oil.

[8]"No matter how a grain offering for the LORD has been prepared, bring it to the priest, who will

---

**1:1** Hebrew *Tent of Meeting;* also in 1:3, 5.　**1:3** Or *it.*　**1:4** Or *to make atonement for you.*　**1:16** Or *the crop and its contents.* The meaning of the Hebrew is uncertain.

---

**1:1** At the end of Exodus, the Lord's visible presence filled the Tabernacle (Exodus 40:34-38), raising the question of how the people could approach. In Leviticus 1:1, though, God calls out to Moses and gives instructions for living near the Lord's presence. While to modern eyes Leviticus can at first seem difficult to comprehend, Jewish people actually begin their instruction of children in the Torah (the first five books of the Bible) with Leviticus. Admittedly, many of the book's practices do not apply directly to Christians. But underlying those practices are principles about holiness and ethics that continue to reveal God and his ways.

**1:3-17** By laying a hand on the animal's head, the individual created a symbolic identification with the animal: The animal was dying in the person's place. And as we see elsewhere in Leviticus, even unintentional sin was costly. In these sacrifices, the *person had to provide* the animal and then personally slaughter it (unless they were offering a bird). The priests then performed the rest of the sacrificial ritual. While this section does not mention repentance, Micah 6:6-8 reveals that the person's intentions mattered. The ritual alone was not enough.

**1:3-17** The Lord accepted different animals, allowing the

sacrifice of a bull, a sheep, a goat, a turtledove, or a pigeon, depending on the person's economic status. The animal had to be "with no defects" since a defect would have decreased the offering's value. In addition to the offerings mentioned in Leviticus 1–7, the priests were to offer two daily burnt offerings, one in the morning and one in the evening. The animals offered in these daily sacrifices were lambs (Numbers 28:3-8).

**2:1-16** In secular contexts, the Hebrew word *minkhah* ("grain offering") refers to a gift or the tribute of a subordinate vassal to their sovereign ruler. Here, then, we can view the offering as the gift of God's vassal people to their sovereign King. A handful of the grain from the *minkhah* would burn on the altar for the Lord; the remainder would make unleavened bread for the priest.

**3:1-17** There were three types of peace offerings: the thanksgiving offering, the vow offering, and the voluntary offering (7:11-21). The worshiper made these offerings when in right standing with God, and they were often associated with a burnt offering. Only part of the peace offering was burned on the altar. The rest created a celebratory meal that included the worshiper, their family and friends, and the priest.

present it at the altar. [9]The priest will take a representative portion of the grain offering and burn it on the altar. It is a special gift, a pleasing aroma to the LORD. [10]The rest of the grain offering will then be given to Aaron and his sons as their food. This offering will be considered a most holy part of the special gifts presented to the LORD.

[11]"Do not use yeast in preparing any of the grain offerings you present to the LORD, because no yeast or honey may be burned as a special gift presented to the LORD. [12]You may add yeast and honey to an offering of the first crops of your harvest, but these must never be offered on the altar as a pleasing aroma to the LORD. [13]Season all your grain offerings with salt to remind you of God's eternal covenant. Never forget to add salt to your grain offerings.

**3:2** Hebrew *Tent of Meeting;* also in 3:8, 13.

[14]"If you present a grain offering to the LORD from the first portion of your harvest, bring fresh grain that is coarsely ground and roasted on a fire. [15]Put olive oil on this grain offering, and sprinkle it with frankincense. [16]The priest will take a representative portion of the grain moistened with oil, together with all the frankincense, and burn it as a special gift presented to the LORD.

## Procedures for the Peace Offering

**3** "If you present an animal from the herd as a peace offering to the LORD, it may be a male or a female, but it must have no defects. [2]Lay your hand on the animal's head, and slaughter it at the entrance of the Tabernacle.* Then Aaron's sons, the priests, will splatter its blood against all sides of the altar.

---

## ⑧ Come Close    DISTANT: CALLED CLOSE

**SCRIPTURE CONNECTION: LEVITICUS 1:4**

Nothing brings comfort like being in God's presence. But during one season, I felt disconnected from God's closeness. It was a dull sensation. I knew God was still beside me, but it felt like I was constantly missing something. A tiredness of the soul seeped into my whole life.

At first, Leviticus may seem to be a book filled with confusing laws and intricate details about a time and culture that have nothing to do with our lives. How could ancient purification rituals help us draw closer to God? So I was shocked when the Holy Spirit used Leviticus 1:4 to open my eyes to see God's law and my season of distance in a fresh way.

This verse is about so much more than one detail of the ancient rituals; it is about a loving God calling his people into relationship. (In fact, the first words of this book, "The LORD called" [Leviticus 1:1], show how God reaches out to us *first*.) God was asking the Israelites to offer to him what was causing separation so he could remove the burden and guilt of sin and build a relationship. I asked, *Am I ready to do what the altar represents—give everything to God?*

I wanted to skip the surrender part and do it myself. I was trying to make myself right, but I was leaving out the key part: letting God do it! I needed to ask, *Lord, what am I unwilling to sacrifice?* by saying, "Help me to freely surrender *all* to you."

Jesus made the ultimate sacrifice for our sins when he died on the cross, but so often we continue to try to purify ourselves. The Lord is saying, "Come close to me. Give me the offering of your burdens, timelines, to-do lists, anxieties, sins. Let's do this together."

**REFLECT** "Lay your hand on the animal's head, and the LORD will accept its death in your place to purify you, making you right with him." LEVITICUS 1:4

*Lord, what am I unwilling to sacrifice? Help me to freely surrender all to you. Amen.*

**CONSIDER** "You must be willing to [eliminate] . . . every desire and affection not grounded in or directed toward God. But *you* don't eliminate it, God does." OSWALD CHAMBERS, *My Utmost for His Highest*

### I wanted to skip surrender, but I was leaving out the key part: letting God do it!

EVIE POLSLEY, MS, loves stories of how God uses everyday people. A manager at Tyndale, her favorite roles are wife and mom.

# Perspective

## What's up with all these sacrifices?

SCRIPTURE CONNECTION: LEVITICUS 1:1–7:38

At the end of Exodus, the visible presence of the Lord filled the Tabernacle. God's presence made it sacred, which meant it needed to be pure.

We can compare impurity and sacrifices to our modern understanding of bacteria and washing. We know that surgical areas need to be sterile, protecting the patient from harmful bacteria. Just as bacteria can't be allowed near a surgical patient, impurity can't come into God's presence.

Sacrifices were a means of cleansing those who wanted to be in the Lord's presence. Sometimes they needed cleansing because of sin. Other times they needed cleansing for different types of impurity, such as bodily emissions or skin diseases. These things weren't wrong or bad; they just weren't pure.

But some sacrifices weren't for cleansing sin or impurity. Instead, they were a way of saying thank you to God in worship. These offerings frequently included a meal shared with others.

Throughout the Bible, we see God making provision for his people to be pure so that we can be in his presence. In the Old Testament, God provided animal sacrifices. In the New Testament, God provided Jesus' death to purify us. In both eras, God invites his people to celebrate the sacrifice with one another and to delight in his presence.

## VIEWPOINTS

THEIRS: *How can I enter the presence of a holy God?*
MINE: *"Jesus is the perfect sacrifice, making my relationship with God possible. Do I take that gift as seriously as I should? God is good, but he deserves reverence. I need to enter his presence with respect, awe, and gratitude."*
YOURS: *How might I demonstrate a recognition of God's holiness in my prayer, service, and worship?*

JENNIFER BROWN JONES, PhD, is an author, speaker, and instructor of Old Testament for Liberty University's PhD of Bible Exposition program. She loves helping others see how God speaks to them through the Bible today.

³The priest must present part of this peace offering as a special gift to the LORD. This includes all the fat around the internal organs, ⁴the two kidneys and the fat around them near the loins, and the long lobe of the liver. These must be removed with the kidneys, ⁵and Aaron's sons will burn them on top of the burnt offering on the wood burning on the altar. It is a special gift, a pleasing aroma to the LORD.

⁶"If you present an animal from the flock as a peace offering to the LORD, it may be a male or a female, but it must have no defects. ⁷If you present a sheep as your offering, bring it to the LORD, ⁸lay your hand on its head, and slaughter it in front of the Tabernacle. Aaron's sons will then splatter the sheep's blood against all sides of the altar. ⁹The priest must present the fat of this peace offering as a special gift to the LORD. This includes the fat of the broad tail cut off near the backbone, all the fat around the internal organs, ¹⁰the two kidneys and the fat around them near the loins, and the long lobe of the liver. These must be removed with the kidneys, ¹¹and the priest will burn them on the altar. It is a special gift of food presented to the LORD.

¹²"If you present a goat as your offering, bring it to the LORD, ¹³lay your hand on its head, and slaughter it in front of the Tabernacle. Aaron's sons will then splatter the goat's blood against all sides of the altar. ¹⁴The priest must present part of this offering as a special gift to the LORD. This includes all the fat around the internal organs, ¹⁵the two kidneys and the fat around them near the loins, and the long lobe of the liver. These must be removed with the kidneys, ¹⁶and the priest will burn them on the altar. It is a special gift of food, a pleasing aroma to the LORD. All the fat belongs to the LORD.

¹⁷"You must never eat any fat or blood. This is a permanent law for you, and it must be observed from generation to generation, wherever you live."

## Procedures for the Sin Offering

4 Then the LORD said to Moses, ²"Give the following instructions to the people of Israel. This is how you are to deal with those who sin unintentionally by doing anything that violates one of the LORD's commands.

³"If the high priest* sins, bringing guilt upon the entire community, he must give a sin offering for the sin he has committed. He must present to the LORD a young bull with no defects. ⁴He must bring the bull to the LORD at the entrance of the Tabernacle,* lay

4:3 Hebrew *the anointed priest;* also in 4:5, 16. 4:4 Hebrew *Tent of Meeting;* also in 4:5, 7, 14, 16, 18.

4:1–5:13 The sin offering may be better understood as a purification offering since it appears in contexts that involve both sin and ritual impurity. Merely offering a sacrifice did not suffice, though. The offeror also needed to repent or acknowledge impurity (5:5). The purification offering addressed unintentional violations rather than deliberate disobedience (Numbers 15:30-31).

his hand on the bull's head, and slaughter it before the LORD. ⁵The high priest will then take some of the bull's blood into the Tabernacle, ⁶dip his finger in the blood, and sprinkle it seven times before the LORD in front of the inner curtain of the sanctuary. ⁷The priest will then put some of the blood on the horns of the altar for fragrant incense that stands in the LORD's presence inside the Tabernacle. He will pour out the rest of the bull's blood at the base of the altar for burnt offerings at the entrance of the Tabernacle. ⁸Then the priest must remove all the fat of the bull to be offered as a sin offering. This includes all the fat around the internal organs, ⁹the two kidneys and the fat around them near the loins, and the long lobe of the liver. He must remove these along with the kidneys, ¹⁰just as he does with cattle offered as a peace offering, and burn them on the altar of burnt offerings. ¹¹But he must take whatever is left of the bull—its hide, meat, head, legs, internal organs, and dung—¹²and carry it away to a place outside the camp that is ceremonially clean, the place where the ashes are dumped. There, on the ash heap, he will burn it on a wood fire.

¹³"If the entire Israelite community sins by violating one of the LORD's commands, but the people don't realize it, they are still guilty. ¹⁴When they become aware of their sin, the people must bring a young bull as an offering for their sin and present it before the Tabernacle. ¹⁵The elders of the community must then lay their hands on the bull's head and slaughter it before the LORD. ¹⁶The high priest will then take some of the bull's blood into the Tabernacle, ¹⁷dip his finger in the blood, and sprinkle it seven times before the LORD in front of the inner curtain. ¹⁸He will then put some of the blood on the horns of the altar for fragrant incense that stands in the LORD's presence inside the Tabernacle. He will pour out the rest of the blood at the base of the altar for burnt offerings at the entrance of the Tabernacle. ¹⁹Then the priest must remove all the animal's fat and burn it on the altar, ²⁰just as he does with the bull offered as a sin offering for the high priest. Through this process, the priest will purify the people, making them right with the LORD,* and they will be forgiven. ²¹Then the priest must take what is left of the bull and carry it outside the camp and burn it there, just as is done with the sin offering for the high priest. This offering is for the sin of the entire congregation of Israel.

²²"If one of Israel's leaders sins by violating one of the commands of the LORD his God but doesn't realize it, he is still guilty. ²³When he becomes aware of his sin, he must bring as his offering a male goat with no defects. ²⁴He must lay his hand on the goat's head and slaughter it at the place where burnt offerings are slaughtered before the LORD. This is an offering for his sin. ²⁵Then the priest will dip his finger in the blood of the sin offering and put it on the horns of the altar for burnt offerings. He will pour out the rest of the blood at the base of the altar. ²⁶Then he must burn all the goat's fat on the altar, just as he does with the peace offering. Through this process, the priest will purify the leader from his sin, making him right with the LORD, and he will be forgiven.

²⁷"If any of the common people sin by violating one of the LORD's commands, but they don't realize it, they are still guilty. ²⁸When they become aware of their sin, they must bring as an offering for their sin a female goat with no defects. ²⁹They will lay a hand on the head of the sin offering and slaughter it at the place where burnt offerings are slaughtered. ³⁰Then the priest will dip his finger in the blood and put it on the horns of the altar for burnt offerings. He will pour out the rest of the blood at the base of the altar. ³¹Then he must remove all the goat's fat, just as he does with the fat of the peace offering. He will burn the fat on the altar, and it will be a pleasing aroma to the LORD. Through this process, the priest will purify the people, making them right with the LORD, and they will be forgiven.

³²"If the people bring a sheep as their sin offering, it must be a female with no defects. ³³They must lay a hand on the head of the sin offering and slaughter it at the place where burnt offerings are slaughtered. ³⁴Then the priest will dip his finger in the blood of the sin offering and put it on the horns of the altar for burnt offerings. He will pour out the rest of the blood at the base of the altar. ³⁵Then he must remove all the sheep's fat, just as he does with the fat of a sheep presented as a peace offering. He will burn the fat on the altar on top of the special gifts presented to the LORD. Through this process, the priest will purify the people from their sin, making them right with the LORD, and they will be forgiven.

## Sins Requiring a Sin Offering

5 "If you are called to testify about something you have seen or that you know about, it is sinful to refuse to testify, and you will be punished for your sin.

²"Or suppose you unknowingly touch something that is ceremonially unclean, such as the carcass of an unclean animal. When you realize what you have done, you must admit your defilement and your guilt. This is true whether it is a wild animal, a domestic animal, or an animal that scurries along the ground.

³"Or suppose you unknowingly touch something that makes a person unclean. When you realize what you have done, you must admit your guilt.

⁴"Or suppose you make a foolish vow of any kind, whether its purpose is for good or for bad. When you realize its foolishness, you must admit your guilt.

⁵"When you become aware of your guilt in any of

4:20 Or *will make atonement for the people;* similarly in 4:26, 31, 35.

# Insight
## ISRAEL'S SACRIFICES

The book of Leviticus details instructions for sacrifices the people were to give to God. Some offered so God could forgive wrongdoing, or sin, while others simply honored and thanked God. All the sacrifices helped the Israelites live in God's presence. This chart describes each sacrifice in Leviticus 1–7.

| OFFERING | DESCRIPTION | PURPOSE | EXAMPLES |
|---|---|---|---|
| **BURNT OFFERING** Leviticus 1:2-17; 6:8-13 | *Atoning sacrifice* of a bull, ram, or male bird with no physical defect | To restore a person to closeness with God by forgiving wrongdoing, or sin. | Exodus 18:12; 29:38-42; 1 Chronicles 21:18–22:1; Job 42:8; Isaiah 1:11-20; Hebrews 10:1-18 |
| **GRAIN OFFERING** Leviticus 2; 6:14-23; 7:9-10 | *Non-atoning sacrifice* of grain, choice flour, or baked breads with olive oil, frankincense, and salt | To honor God with a worshipful gift | Nehemiah 10:33-39; 2 Corinthians 9:6-15 |
| **PEACE OFFERING** Leviticus 3; 7:11-36; 22:21 | *Non-atoning sacrifice* of any animal from the flock or herd, along with baked breads | To thank God through worship and sharing a meal with family and friends | Exodus 24:9-11; 1 Samuel 9:15-25; Acts 2:42; 1 Corinthians 11:17-34 |
| **SIN OFFERING** Leviticus 4:1–5:13; 6:24-30; 16:3-22 | *Atoning sacrifice* of animals with no physical defects. The required offering varied with the situation and station of the person receiving its benefits. | To seek forgiveness from God for unintentional sins of ritual impurity, neglect, or thoughtlessness | Numbers 15:22-31; Hebrews 10:26-31; 1 John 1:8-9 |
| **GUILT OFFERING** Leviticus 5:14–6:7; 7:1-7 | *Atoning sacrifice* of a ram or lamb with no physical defects | To pay for sins against God and the community | Matthew 5:23-24; Romans 6:12-23; 7:21–8:4 |

these ways, you must confess your sin. ⁶Then you must bring to the LORD as the penalty for your sin a female from the flock, either a sheep or a goat. This is a sin offering with which the priest will purify you from your sin, making you right with the LORD.*

⁷"But if you cannot afford to bring a sheep, you may bring to the LORD two turtledoves or two young pigeons as the penalty for your sin. One of the birds will be for a sin offering, and the other for a burnt offering. ⁸You must bring them to the priest, who will present the first bird as the sin offering. He will wring its neck but without severing its head from the body. ⁹Then he will sprinkle some of the blood of the sin offering against the sides of the altar, and the rest of the blood will be drained out at the base of the altar. This is an offering for sin. ¹⁰The priest will then prepare the second bird as a burnt offering,

following all the procedures that have been prescribed. Through this process the priest will purify you from your sin, making you right with the LORD, and you will be forgiven.

¹¹"If you cannot afford to bring two turtledoves or two young pigeons, you may bring two quarts* of choice flour for your sin offering. Since it is an offering for sin, you must not moisten it with olive oil or put any frankincense on it. ¹²Take the flour to the priest, who will scoop out a handful as a representative portion. He will burn it on the altar on top of the special gifts presented to the LORD. It is an offering for sin. ¹³Through this process, the priest will purify those who are guilty of any of these sins, making them right with the LORD, and they will be forgiven. The rest of the flour will belong to the priest, just as with the grain offering."

5:6 Or *will make atonement for you for your sin;* similarly in 5:10, 13, 16, 18.  5:11 Hebrew *¹⁄₁₀ of an ephah* [2.2 liters].

## Procedures for the Guilt Offering

[14]Then the LORD said to Moses, [15]"If one of you commits a sin by unintentionally defiling the LORD's sacred property, you must bring a guilt offering to the LORD. The offering must be your own ram with no defects, or you may buy one of equal value with silver, as measured by the weight of the sanctuary shekel.* [16]You must make restitution for the sacred property you have harmed by paying for the loss, plus an additional 20 percent. When you give the payment to the priest, he will purify you with the ram sacrificed as a guilt offering, making you right with the LORD, and you will be forgiven.

[17]"Suppose you sin by violating one of the LORD's commands. Even if you are unaware of what you have done, you are guilty and will be punished for your sin. [18]For a guilt offering, you must bring to the priest your own ram with no defects, or you may buy one of equal value. Through this process the priest will purify you from your unintentional sin, making you right with the LORD, and you will be forgiven. [19]This is a guilt offering, for you have been guilty of an offense against the LORD."

## Sins Requiring a Guilt Offering

6 [1]*Then the LORD said to Moses, [2]"Suppose one of you sins against your associate and is unfaithful to the LORD. Suppose you cheat in a deal involving a security deposit, or you steal or commit fraud, [3]or you find lost property and lie about it, or you lie while swearing to tell the truth, or you commit any other such sin. [4]If you have sinned in any of these ways, you are guilty. You must give back whatever you stole, or the money you took by extortion, or the security deposit, or the lost property you found, [5]or anything obtained by swearing falsely. You must make restitution by paying the full price plus an additional 20 percent to the person you have harmed. On the same day you must present a guilt offering. [6]As a guilt offering to the LORD, you must bring to the priest your own ram with no defects, or you may buy one of equal value. [7]Through this process, the priest will purify you before the LORD, making you right with him,* and you will be forgiven for any of these sins you have committed."

## Further Instructions for the Burnt Offering

[8]*Then the LORD said to Moses, [9]"Give Aaron and his sons the following instructions regarding the burnt offering. The burnt offering must be left on top of the altar until the next morning, and the fire on the altar must be kept burning all night. [10]In the morning, after the priest on duty has put on his official linen clothing and linen undergarments, he must clean out the ashes of the burnt offering and put them beside the altar. [11]Then he must take off these garments, change back into his regular clothes, and carry the ashes outside the camp to a place that is ceremonially clean. [12]Meanwhile, the fire on the altar must be kept burning; it must never go out. Each morning the priest will add fresh wood to the fire and arrange the burnt offering on it. He will then burn the fat of the peace offerings on it. [13]Remember, the fire must be kept burning on the altar at all times. It must never go out.

## Further Instructions for the Grain Offering

[14]"These are the instructions regarding the grain offering. Aaron's sons must present this offering to the LORD in front of the altar. [15]The priest on duty will take from the grain offering a handful of the choice flour moistened with olive oil, together with all the frankincense. He will burn this representative portion on the altar as a pleasing aroma to the LORD. [16]Aaron and his sons may eat the rest of the flour, but it must be baked without yeast and eaten in a sacred place within the courtyard of the Tabernacle.* [17]Remember, it must never be prepared with yeast. I have given it to the priests as their share of the special gifts presented to me. Like the sin offering and the guilt offering, it is most holy. [18]Any of Aaron's male descendants may eat from the special gifts presented to the LORD. This is their permanent right from generation to generation. Anyone or anything that touches these offerings will become holy."

## Procedures for the Ordination Offering

[19]Then the LORD said to Moses, [20]"On the day Aaron and his sons are anointed, they must present to the

---

**5:15** Each shekel was about 0.4 ounces or 11 grams in weight.  **6:1** Verses 6:1-7 are numbered 5:20-26 in Hebrew text.  **6:7** Or *will make atonement for you before the LORD.*  **6:8** Verses 6:8-30 are numbered 6:1-23 in Hebrew text.  **6:16** Hebrew *Tent of Meeting;* also in 6:26, 30.

---

**5:14–6:7** The guilt offering covered wrongful actions involving sacred things. It also provided for sins against other people when the offender was unaware of the wrong. Finally, the guilt offering was used in situations where someone acted fraudulently or deceitfully toward another. In such cases, the offender needed to make restitution to the person they had harmed.
**6:2-3** For those who follow God, there really is no such thing as a "secular" sin. All sin involves God, even sin directed against another person or group. In the sins requiring a guilt offering, God's forgiveness was needed and would be granted, but restitution to the injured individual had to be made first (6:4-7; see

also Matthew 5:23-24). A guilt offering could free a person from punishment for unintentional offenses against *sacred* property (Leviticus 5:14-16), as well as accidental and intentional offenses against *secular* property could be forgiven.
**6:5** The instructions for the guilt offering assumed that a person's conscience would induce voluntary repayment for damages. When restitution was voluntary, the surcharge for loss of use to the owner was always 20 percent. Penalties were more severe in other cases (see Exodus 22:1-15). There is a clear difference between voluntary confession and simply admitting sin after being caught.

Lord the standard grain offering of two quarts* of choice flour, half to be offered in the morning and half to be offered in the evening. ²¹It must be carefully mixed with olive oil and cooked on a griddle. Then slice* this grain offering and present it as a pleasing aroma to the Lord. ²²In each generation, the high priest* who succeeds Aaron must prepare this same offering. It belongs to the Lord and must be burned up completely. This is a permanent law. ²³All such grain offerings of a priest must be burned up entirely. None of it may be eaten."

## Further Instructions for the Sin Offering

²⁴Then the Lord said to Moses, ²⁵"Give Aaron and his sons the following instructions regarding the sin offering. The animal given as an offering for sin is a most holy offering, and it must be slaughtered in the Lord's presence at the place where the burnt offerings are slaughtered. ²⁶The priest who offers the sacrifice as a sin offering must eat his portion in a sacred place within the courtyard of the Tabernacle. ²⁷Anyone or anything that touches the sacrificial meat will become holy. If any of the sacrificial blood spatters on a person's clothing, the soiled garment must be washed in a sacred place. ²⁸If a clay pot is used to boil the sacrificial meat, it must then be broken. If a bronze pot is used, it must be scoured and thoroughly rinsed with water. ²⁹Any male from a priest's family may eat from this offering; it is most holy. ³⁰But the offering for sin may not be eaten if its blood was brought into the Tabernacle as an offering for purification* in the Holy Place. It must be completely burned with fire.

## Further Instructions for the Guilt Offering

7 "These are the instructions for the guilt offering. It is most holy. ²The animal sacrificed as a guilt offering must be slaughtered at the place where the burnt offerings are slaughtered, and its blood must be splattered against all sides of the altar. ³The priest will then offer all its fat on the altar, including the fat of the broad tail, the fat around the internal organs, ⁴the two kidneys and the fat around them near the loins, and the long lobe of the liver. These are to be removed with the kidneys, ⁵and the priests will burn them on the altar as a special gift presented to the Lord. This is the guilt offering. ⁶Any male from a priest's family may eat the meat. It must be eaten in a sacred place, for it is most holy.

⁷"The same instructions apply to both the guilt offering and the sin offering. Both belong to the priest who uses them to purify someone, making that person right with the Lord.* ⁸In the case of the burnt offering, the priest may keep the hide of the sacrificed

animal. ⁹Any grain offering that has been baked in an oven, prepared in a pan, or cooked on a griddle belongs to the priest who presents it. ¹⁰All other grain offerings, whether made of dry flour or flour moistened with olive oil, are to be shared equally among all the priests, the descendants of Aaron.

## Further Instructions for the Peace Offering

¹¹"These are the instructions regarding the different kinds of peace offerings that may be presented to the Lord. ¹²If you present your peace offering as an expression of thanksgiving, the usual animal sacrifice must be accompanied by various kinds of bread made without yeast—thin cakes mixed with olive oil, wafers spread with oil, and cakes made of choice flour mixed with olive oil. ¹³This peace offering of thanksgiving must also be accompanied by loaves of bread made with yeast. ¹⁴One of each kind of bread must be presented as a gift to the Lord. It will then belong to the priest who splatters the blood of the peace offering against the altar. ¹⁵The meat of the peace offering of thanksgiving must be eaten on the same day it is offered. None of it may be saved for the next morning.

¹⁶"If you bring an offering to fulfill a vow or as a voluntary offering, the meat must be eaten on the same day the sacrifice is offered, but whatever is left over may be eaten on the second day. ¹⁷Any meat left over until the third day must be completely burned up. ¹⁸If any of the meat from the peace offering is eaten on the third day, the person who presented it will not be accepted by the Lord. You will receive no credit for offering it. By then the meat will be contaminated; if you eat it, you will be punished for your sin.

¹⁹"Meat that touches anything ceremonially unclean may not be eaten; it must be completely burned up. The rest of the meat may be eaten, but only by people who are ceremonially clean. ²⁰If you are ceremonially unclean and you eat meat from a peace offering that was presented to the Lord, you will be cut off from the community. ²¹If you touch anything that is unclean (whether it is human defilement or an unclean animal or any other unclean, detestable thing) and then eat meat from a peace offering presented to the Lord, you will be cut off from the community."

## The Forbidden Blood and Fat

²²Then the Lord said to Moses, ²³"Give the following instructions to the people of Israel. You must never eat fat, whether from cattle, sheep, or goats. ²⁴The fat of an animal found dead or torn to pieces by wild animals must never be eaten, though it may be used for any other purpose. ²⁵Anyone who eats fat from

---

**6:20** Hebrew ¹⁄₁₀ of an ephah [2.2 liters]. **6:21** The meaning of this Hebrew term is uncertain. **6:22** Hebrew the anointed priest.
**6:30** Or an offering to make atonement. **7:7** Or to make atonement.

an animal presented as a special gift to the LORD will be cut off from the community. <sup>26</sup>No matter where you live, you must never consume the blood of any bird or animal. <sup>27</sup>Anyone who consumes blood will be cut off from the community."

## A Portion for the Priests

<sup>28</sup>Then the LORD said to Moses, <sup>29</sup>"Give the following instructions to the people of Israel. When you presented a peace offering to the LORD, bring part of it as a gift to the LORD. <sup>30</sup>Present it to the LORD with your own hands as a special gift to the LORD. Bring the fat of the animal, together with the breast, and lift up the breast as a special offering to the LORD. <sup>31</sup>Then the priest will burn the fat on the altar, but the breast will belong to Aaron and his descendants. <sup>32</sup>Give the right thigh of your peace offering to the priest as a gift. <sup>33</sup>The right thigh must always be given to the priest who offers the blood and the fat of the peace offering. <sup>34</sup>For I have reserved the breast of the special offering and the right thigh of the sacred offering for the priests. It is the permanent right of Aaron and his descendants to share in the peace offerings brought by the people of Israel. <sup>35</sup>This is their rightful share. The special gifts presented to the LORD have been reserved for Aaron and his descendants from the time they were set apart to serve the LORD as priests. <sup>36</sup>On the day they were anointed, the LORD commanded the Israelites to give these portions to the priests as their permanent share from generation to generation."

<sup>37</sup>These are the instructions for the burnt offering, the grain offering, the sin offering, and the guilt offering, as well as the ordination offering and the peace offering. <sup>38</sup>The LORD gave these instructions to Moses on Mount Sinai when he commanded the Israelites to present their offerings to the LORD in the wilderness of Sinai.

## Ordination of the Priests

8 Then the LORD said to Moses, <sup>2</sup>"Bring Aaron and his sons, along with their sacred garments, the anointing oil, the bull for the sin offering, the two rams, and the basket of bread made without yeast, <sup>3</sup>and call the entire community of Israel together at the entrance of the Tabernacle.*"

<sup>4</sup>So Moses followed the LORD's instructions, and the whole community assembled at the Tabernacle entrance. <sup>5</sup>Moses announced to them, "This is what the LORD has commanded us to do!" <sup>6</sup>Then he presented Aaron and his sons and washed them with water. <sup>7</sup>He put the official tunic on Aaron and tied the sash around his waist. He dressed him in the robe, placed the ephod on him, and attached the ephod securely with its decorative sash. <sup>8</sup>Then Moses placed the chestpiece on Aaron and put the Urim and the Thummim inside it. <sup>9</sup>He placed the turban on Aaron's head and attached the gold medallion—the badge of holiness—to the front of the turban, just as the LORD had commanded him.

<sup>10</sup>Then Moses took the anointing oil and anointed the Tabernacle and everything in it, making them holy. <sup>11</sup>He sprinkled the oil on the altar seven times, anointing it and all its utensils, as well as the washbasin and its stand, making them holy. <sup>12</sup>Then he poured some of the anointing oil on Aaron's head, anointing him and making him holy for his work. <sup>13</sup>Next Moses presented Aaron's sons. He clothed them in their tunics, tied their sashes around them, and put their special head coverings on them, just as the LORD had commanded him.

<sup>14</sup>Then Moses presented the bull for the sin offering. Aaron and his sons laid their hands on the bull's head, <sup>15</sup>and Moses slaughtered it. Moses took some of the blood, and with his finger he put it on the four horns of the altar to purify it. He poured out the rest of the blood at the base of the altar. Through this process, he made the altar holy by purifying it.* <sup>16</sup>Then Moses took all the fat around the internal organs, the long lobe of the liver, and the two kidneys and the fat around them, and he burned it all on the altar. <sup>17</sup>He took the rest of the bull, including its hide, meat, and dung, and burned it on a fire outside the camp, just as the LORD had commanded him.

<sup>18</sup>Then Moses presented the ram for the burnt offering. Aaron and his sons laid their hands on the ram's head, <sup>19</sup>and Moses slaughtered it. Then Moses took the ram's blood and splattered it against all sides of the altar. <sup>20</sup>Then he cut the ram into pieces, and he burned the head, some of its pieces, and the fat on the altar. <sup>21</sup>After washing the internal organs and the legs with water, Moses burned the entire ram on the altar as a burnt offering. It was a pleasing aroma, a special gift presented to the LORD, just as the LORD had commanded him.

<sup>22</sup>Then Moses presented the other ram, which was the ram of ordination. Aaron and his sons laid their hands on the ram's head, <sup>23</sup>and Moses slaughtered

---

8:3 Hebrew *Tent of Meeting;* also in 8:4, 31, 33, 35.  8:15 Or *by making atonement for it;* or *that offerings for purification might be made on it.*

---

7:28-36 While only men of a specific family lineage could be priests, all adult Israelites were invited and instructed to participate in worship. Women brought sacrifices, made vows, participated in sacred festivals, and shared in the food from the offerings.
8:1-36 In Exodus 28–29, the Lord gave Moses specific instructions for clothing and for ordaining Aaron and his sons

as priests. In Exodus 39:1-31; 40:12-16; and Leviticus 8, the commands were carried out. Moses didn't just pass along the instructions verbally; he enacted the rituals to provide an example for the priests down to the last detail, "just as the LORD had commanded him" (8:9, 13, 17, 21, 29). Because the penalty for disobedience was death, God made sure the priests knew exactly what to do.

it. Then Moses took some of its blood and applied it to the lobe of Aaron's right ear, the thumb of his right hand, and the big toe of his right foot. ²⁴Next Moses presented Aaron's sons and applied some of the blood to the lobes of their right ears, the thumbs of their right hands, and the big toes of their right feet. He then splattered the rest of the blood against all sides of the altar.

²⁵Next Moses took the fat, including the fat of the broad tail, the fat around the internal organs, the long lobe of the liver, and the two kidneys and the fat around them, along with the right thigh. ²⁶On top of these he placed a thin cake of bread made without yeast, a cake of bread mixed with olive oil, and a wafer spread with olive oil. All these were taken from the basket of bread made without yeast that was placed in the LORD's presence. ²⁷He put all these in the hands of Aaron and his sons, and he lifted these gifts as a special offering to the LORD. ²⁸Moses then took all the offerings back from them and burned them on the altar on top of the burnt offering. This was the ordination offering. It was a pleasing aroma, a special gift presented to the LORD. ²⁹Then Moses took the breast and lifted it up as a special offering to the LORD. This was Moses' portion of the ram of ordination, just as the LORD had commanded him.

³⁰Next Moses took some of the anointing oil and some of the blood that was on the altar, and he sprinkled them on Aaron and his garments and on his sons and their garments. In this way, he made Aaron and his sons and their garments holy.

³¹Then Moses said to Aaron and his sons, "Boil the remaining meat of the offerings at the Tabernacle entrance, and eat it there, along with the bread that is in the basket of offerings for the ordination, just as I commanded when I said, 'Aaron and his sons will eat it.' ³²Any meat or bread that is left over must then be burned up. ³³You must not leave the Tabernacle entrance for seven days, for that is when the ordination ceremony will be completed. ³⁴Everything we have done today was commanded by the LORD in order to purify you, making you right with him.* ³⁵Now stay at the entrance of the Tabernacle day and night for seven days, and do everything the LORD requires. If you fail to do this, you will die, for this is what the LORD has commanded." ³⁶So Aaron and his sons did everything the LORD had commanded through Moses.

## The Priests Begin Their Work

9 After the ordination ceremony, on the eighth day, Moses called together Aaron and his sons and the elders of Israel. ²He said to Aaron, "Take a young bull for a sin offering and a ram for a burnt offering, both without defects, and present them to the LORD. ³Then tell the Israelites, 'Take a male goat for a sin offering, and take a calf and a lamb, both a year old and without defects, for a burnt offering. ⁴Also take a bull* and a ram for a peace offering and flour moistened with olive oil for a grain offering. Present all these offerings to the LORD because the LORD will appear to you today.'"

⁵So the people presented all these things at the entrance of the Tabernacle,* just as Moses had commanded. Then the whole community came forward and stood before the LORD. ⁶And Moses said, "This is what the LORD has commanded you to do so that the glory of the LORD may appear to you."

⁷Then Moses said to Aaron, "Come to the altar and sacrifice your sin offering and your burnt offering to purify yourself and the people. Then present the offerings of the people to purify them, making them right with the LORD,* just as he has commanded."

⁸So Aaron went to the altar and slaughtered the calf as a sin offering for himself. ⁹His sons brought him the blood, and he dipped his finger in it and put it on the horns of the altar. He poured out the rest of the blood at the base of the altar. ¹⁰Then he burned on the altar the fat, the kidneys, and the long lobe of the liver from the sin offering, just as the LORD had commanded Moses. ¹¹The meat and the hide, however, he burned outside the camp.

¹²Next Aaron slaughtered the animal for the burnt offering. His sons brought him the blood, and he splattered it against all sides of the altar. ¹³Then they handed him each piece of the burnt offering, including the head, and he burned them on the altar. ¹⁴Then he washed the internal organs and the legs and burned them on the altar along with the rest of the burnt offering.

¹⁵Next Aaron presented the offerings of the people. He slaughtered the people's goat and presented it as

---

8:34 Or *to make atonement for you.* 9:4 Or *cow;* also in 9:18, 19. 9:5 Hebrew *Tent of Meeting;* also in 9:23. 9:7 Or *to make atonement for them.*

---

**8:34** The details of the sacrifice rituals were symbolic and important in their own right. But most important, the priests were to obey God's commands. Complete obedience to God is a major theme in both the Old Testament and the New Testament: "Obedience is better than sacrifice" (1 Samuel 15:22).

**9:2-4** These sacrifices—the sin and burnt offerings for the priests and the sin, burnt, peace, and grain offerings for the people—were offered at the beginning of the priests' ministry to make certain that all sin was atoned for and the covenant with God affirmed. Only the guilt offering was omitted.

**9:6** Just as holiness describes God's person and nature, the "glory of the LORD" tangibly expresses his power and majesty (see Ezekiel 1:28; 10:4). God's glory was revealed on Mount Sinai (Exodus 24:16), at the dedication of the Tabernacle (Exodus 40:34-35), and in Solomon's Temple (1 Kings 8:11; 2 Chronicles 7:1). Yet it remained as vast as the heavens (Psalm 19:1). The New Testament speaks of God's glory being manifested by the Son and of Christ's glory as the image of God (2 Corinthians 4:4). Jesus was glorified in his death and resurrection (John 17:1-5).

an offering for their sin, just as he had first done with the offering for his own sin. ¹⁶Then he presented the burnt offering and sacrificed it in the prescribed way. ¹⁷He also presented the grain offering, burning a handful of the flour mixture on the altar, in addition to the regular burnt offering for the morning.

¹⁸Then Aaron slaughtered the bull and the ram for the people's peace offering. His sons brought him the blood, and he splattered it against all sides of the altar. ¹⁹Then he took the fat of the bull and

the ram—the fat of the broad tail and from around the internal organs—along with the kidneys and the long lobes of the livers. ²⁰He placed these fat portions on top of the breasts of these animals and burned them on the altar. ²¹Aaron then lifted up the breasts and right thighs as a special offering to the LORD, just as Moses had commanded.

²²After that, Aaron raised his hands toward the people and blessed them. Then, after presenting the sin offering, the burnt offering, and the peace

## Theos
### IMAGE — MY STORY WITH GOD

## God's Glory: An Invitation to Awe

**SCRIPTURE CONNECTION: LEVITICUS 9:22-24**

Have you ever seen something that took your breath away? Maybe it was a newborn baby. Or a double rainbow on the horizon. Such things arrest our attention, leading us to pause in awe.

These sights give us a faint glimpse of what the Bible calls the glory of the Lord. They are visible reminders that show the goodness, greatness, and grandeur of our invisible God. Seeing God's glory shows us what God is like. God is marked by absolute perfection. Pure goodness. True gentleness. Undistracted, undiluted, unconditional love.

We can also glimpse God's glory in simple things—the unprovoked kindness of a stranger, the effervescent joy of a child, the undeserved forgiveness of someone we wronged.

All of these glimpses remind me that God is real, powerful, active, creative, and purposeful. My perspective elevates, and my hope swells that God will also bring power, creativity, and purpose to my life. As I notice God's glory, my expectations and my courage lift. I, too, can choose goodness, gentleness, and unconditional love.

> God is marked by absolute perfection. Pure goodness. True gentleness. Undistracted, undiluted, unconditional love.

### IMAGINE

What makes you pause in awe?

Whose life has shown you God?

*"As we bring goodness, gentleness, and unconditional love into our relationships and world, we extend God's glory into the homes and workplaces where we live and lead. God worked through Moses to help his community experience God's glory; our lives can do the same."*

**MINDY CALIGUIRE** is founder and president of Soul Care, dedicated to increasing soul health in the Body of Christ. Her books include *Discovering Soul Care* and *Spiritual Friendships*.

offering, he stepped down from the altar. ²³Then Moses and Aaron went into the Tabernacle, and when they came back out, they blessed the people again, and the glory of the LORD appeared to the whole community. ²⁴Fire blazed forth from the LORD's presence and consumed the burnt offering and the fat on the altar. When the people saw this, they shouted with joy and fell face down on the ground.

## The Sin of Nadab and Abihu

10 Aaron's sons Nadab and Abihu put coals of fire in their incense burners and sprinkled incense over them. In this way, they disobeyed the LORD by burning before him the wrong kind of fire, different than he had commanded. ²So fire blazed forth from the LORD's presence and burned them up, and they died there before the LORD.

³Then Moses said to Aaron, "This is what the LORD meant when he said,

'I will display my holiness
    through those who come near me.
I will display my glory
    before all the people.'"

And Aaron was silent.

⁴Then Moses called for Mishael and Elzaphan, Aaron's cousins, the sons of Aaron's uncle Uzziel. He said to them, "Come forward and carry away the bodies of your relatives from in front of the sanctuary to a place outside the camp." ⁵So they came forward and picked them up by their garments and carried them out of the camp, just as Moses had commanded.

⁶Then Moses said to Aaron and his sons Eleazar and Ithamar, "Do not show grief by leaving your hair uncombed* or by tearing your clothes. If you do, you will die, and the LORD's anger will strike the whole community of Israel. However, the rest of the Israelites, your relatives, may mourn because of the LORD's fiery destruction of Nadab and Abihu. ⁷But you must not leave the entrance of the Tabernacle* or you will die, for you have been anointed with the LORD's anointing oil." So they did as Moses commanded.

## Instructions for Priestly Conduct

⁸Then the LORD said to Aaron, ⁹"You and your descendants must never drink wine or any other alcoholic drink before going into the Tabernacle. If you do, you

will die. This is a permanent law for you, and it must be observed from generation to generation. ¹⁰You must distinguish between what is sacred and what is common, between what is ceremonially unclean and what is clean. ¹¹And you must teach the Israelites all the decrees that the LORD has given them through Moses."

¹²Then Moses said to Aaron and his remaining sons, Eleazar and Ithamar, "Take what is left of the grain offering after a portion has been presented as a special gift to the LORD, and eat it beside the altar. Make sure it contains no yeast, for it is most holy. ¹³You must eat it in a sacred place, for it has been given to you and your descendants as your portion of the special gifts presented to the LORD. These are the commands I have been given. ¹⁴But the breast and thigh that were lifted up as a special offering may be eaten in any place that is ceremonially clean. These parts have been given to you and your descendants as your portion of the peace offerings presented by the people of Israel. ¹⁵You must lift up the thigh and breast as a special offering to the LORD, along with the fat of the special gifts. These parts will belong to you and your descendants as your permanent right, just as the LORD has commanded."

¹⁶Moses then asked them what had happened to the goat of the sin offering. When he discovered it had been burned up, he became very angry with Eleazar and Ithamar, Aaron's remaining sons. ¹⁷"Why didn't you eat the sin offering in the sacred area?" he demanded. "It is a holy offering! The LORD has given it to you to remove the guilt of the community and to purify the people, making them right with the LORD.* ¹⁸Since the animal's blood was not brought into the Holy Place, you should have eaten the meat in the sacred area as I ordered you."

¹⁹Then Aaron answered Moses, "Today my sons presented both their sin offering and their burnt offering to the LORD. And yet this tragedy has happened to me. If I had eaten the people's sin offering on such a tragic day as this, would the LORD have been pleased?" ²⁰And when Moses heard this, he was satisfied.

## Ceremonially Clean and Unclean Animals

11 Then the LORD said to Moses and Aaron, ²"Give the following instructions to the people of Israel.

"Of all the land animals, these are the ones you may use for food. ³You may eat any animal that has completely split hooves and chews the cud. ⁴You may not,

---

10:6 Or *by uncovering your heads.* 10:7 Hebrew *Tent of Meeting;* also in 10:9. 10:17 Or *to make atonement for the people before the LORD.*

---

**10:1-7** God is good, but being in his holy presence can be a dangerous thing. In fact, as the ancient Israelites discovered, it was a matter of life and death, and thus something to be taken very seriously. *For failing to demonstrate reverence and obedience,* Nadab and Abihu paid with their lives. Moses commanded the priests not to mourn, as mourning could have conveyed sympathy for or solidarity with family members who had blatantly disobeyed God's instructions.

**11:1–15:33** These chapters detail the regulations pertaining to

purity. The mixing of types of things was forbidden (see Deuteronomy 22:9-11) because it represented a violation of the normal created order. "Abnormal" creatures—such as fish without fins and scales, carnivores, crawling insects, and animals without split hooves—were not to cross boundaries with "normal" types and were unfit for food or offerings (see also Deuteronomy 14:1-21). The dietary, health, and sanitary laws were meant to distinguish Israel as a holy people from those of the surrounding nations (Leviticus 11:44-45).

# Insight   HOLY, CLEAN, AND UNCLEAN

The practices establishing cleanness and uncleanness set Israel apart as God's chosen people and enabled them to live in the presence of a holy God. What is unclean is not necessarily sinful but represents a kind of unworthiness that cannot come into contact with what is holy. If it is cleansed, it acquires the potential for holiness and may be dedicated to God. Clean and unclean were not moral designations, and people and most objects would go through normal cycles of holy, clean, and unclean.

Make Holy, Devote, Set Apart      Purify

**HOLY**        **CLEAN**        **UNCLEAN**

Dishonor, Violate      Corrupt, Taint, Spoil

however, eat the following animals* that have split hooves or that chew the cud, but not both. The camel chews the cud but does not have split hooves, so it is ceremonially unclean for you. ⁵The hyrax* chews the cud but does not have split hooves, so it is unclean. ⁶The hare chews the cud but does not have split hooves, so it is unclean. ⁷The pig has evenly split hooves but does not chew the cud, so it is unclean. ⁸You may not eat the meat of these animals or even touch their carcasses. They are ceremonially unclean for you.

⁹"Of all the marine animals, these are ones you may use for food. You may eat anything from the water if it has both fins and scales, whether taken from salt water or from streams. ¹⁰But you must never eat animals from the sea or from rivers that do not have both fins and scales. They are detestable to you. This applies both to little creatures that live in shallow water and to all creatures that live in deep water. ¹¹They will always be detestable to you. You

must never eat their meat or even touch their dead bodies. ¹²Any marine animal that does not have both fins and scales is detestable to you.

¹³"These are the birds that are detestable to you. You must never eat them: the griffon vulture, the bearded vulture, the black vulture, ¹⁴the kite, falcons of all kinds, ¹⁵ravens of all kinds, ¹⁶the eagle owl, the short-eared owl, the seagull, hawks of all kinds, ¹⁷the little owl, the cormorant, the great owl, ¹⁸the barn owl, the desert owl, the Egyptian vulture, ¹⁹the stork, herons of all kinds, the hoopoe, and the bat.

²⁰"You must not eat winged insects that walk along the ground; they are detestable to you. ²¹You may, however, eat winged insects that walk along the ground and have jointed legs so they can jump. ²²The insects you are permitted to eat include all kinds of locusts, bald locusts, crickets, and grasshoppers. ²³All other winged insects that walk along the ground are detestable to you.

**11:4** The identification of some of the animals, birds, and insects in this chapter is uncertain.   **11:5** Or *coney,* or *rock badger.*

**11:2-8** Some scholars have suggested that unclean animals were to be avoided for reasons of public health, but the evidence does not support this. Horse meat, for example, is no less healthy than beef, yet it was considered unclean because the horse does

not have a split hoof (see 11:2-3). The regulations existed because an unclean animal was unacceptable as an offering to God and, therefore, it was also unacceptable as food for God's people. Jesus proclaimed all foods clean (Mark 7:14-19; Acts 10:9-16).

# Perspective

## Why did having a baby make her unclean?

SCRIPTURE CONNECTION: LEVITICUS 12:1-8

Levitical laws addressed safety, protection, and quality of life. After a woman gave birth to a child, she was considered unclean (for a period of seven days for a son and fourteen days for a daughter) because of the bodily discharges of giving birth. She could not take part in religious activities until she completed her purification (a process that took forty days for a son and eighty days for a daughter).

From today's vantage point, this may seem excessive. But if we consider this purification period as a means of rest and protection for the mother and baby, we find God's wisdom and kindness for women woven into this ritual.

## VIEWPOINTS

HERS: *Would an Israelite woman have viewed her season of purification as a blessing or setback? Why?*

MINE: *"When I read about purification here, I think of the 'forgotten ones'—postpartum mamas who must try to return to the tasks of life and do 'everything' during a vulnerable season. I advocate for women so they will not fall prey to postpartum depression and so their babies can thrive in their first year."*

YOURS: *How have you seen God's wisdom and kindness in a season of pause? Could he use that time to purify you? To protect you and give you rest?*

QUANTRILLA ARD, PhD, is a faith-based personal and spiritual development author, speaker, Bible teacher, and literary agent who believes in the power of collective strength, community, and fellowship.

²⁴"The following creatures will make you ceremonially unclean. If any of you touch their carcasses, you will be defiled until evening. ²⁵If you pick up their carcasses, you must wash your clothes, and you will remain defiled until evening.

²⁶"Any animal that has split hooves that are not evenly divided or that does not chew the cud is unclean for you. If you touch the carcass of such an animal, you will be defiled. ²⁷Of the animals that walk on all fours, those that have paws are unclean. If you touch the carcass of such an animal, you will be defiled until evening. ²⁸If you pick up its carcass, you must wash your clothes, and you will remain defiled until evening. These animals are unclean for you.

²⁹"Of the small animals that scurry along the ground, these are unclean for you: the mole rat, the rat, large lizards of all kinds, ³⁰the gecko, the monitor lizard, the common lizard, the sand lizard, and the chameleon. ³¹All these small animals are unclean for you. If any of you touch the dead body of such an animal, you will be defiled until evening. ³²If such an animal dies and falls on something, that object will be unclean. This is true whether the object is made of wood, cloth, leather, or burlap. Whatever its use, you must dip it in water, and it will remain defiled until evening. After that, it will be ceremonially clean and may be used again.

³³"If such an animal falls into a clay pot, everything in the pot will be defiled, and the pot must be smashed. ³⁴If the water from such a container spills on any food, the food will be defiled. And any beverage in such a container will be defiled. ³⁵Any object on which the carcass of such an animal falls will be defiled. If it is an oven or hearth, it must be destroyed, for it is defiled, and you must treat it accordingly.

³⁶"However, if the carcass of such an animal falls into a spring or a cistern, the water will still be clean. But anyone who touches the carcass will be defiled. ³⁷If the carcass falls on seed grain to be planted in the field, the seed will still be considered clean. ³⁸But if the seed is wet when the carcass falls on it, the seed will be defiled.

³⁹"If an animal you are permitted to eat dies and you touch its carcass, you will be defiled until evening. ⁴⁰If you eat any of its meat or carry away its carcass, you must wash your clothes, and you will remain defiled until evening.

⁴¹"All small animals that scurry along the ground are detestable, and you must never eat them. ⁴²This includes all animals that slither along on their bellies, as well as those with four legs and those with many feet. All such animals that scurry along the ground are detestable, and you must never eat them. ⁴³Do not defile yourselves by touching them. You must not make yourselves ceremonially unclean because of them. ⁴⁴For I am the LORD your God. You must consecrate yourselves and be holy, because I am holy. So do not defile yourselves with any of these small animals that scurry along the ground. ⁴⁵For I, the LORD, am the one who brought you up from the land of Egypt, that I might be your God. Therefore, you must be holy because I am holy.

⁴⁶"These are the instructions regarding land animals, birds, marine creatures, and animals that scurry along the ground. ⁴⁷By these instructions you will know what is unclean and clean, and which animals may be eaten and which may not be eaten."

## Purification after Childbirth

**12** The LORD said to Moses, [2]"Give the following instructions to the people of Israel. If a woman becomes pregnant and gives birth to a son, she will be ceremonially unclean for seven days, just as she is unclean during her menstrual period. [3]On the eighth day the boy's foreskin must be circumcised. [4]After waiting thirty-three days, she will be purified from the bleeding of childbirth. During this time of purification, she must not touch anything that is set apart as holy. And she must not enter the sanctuary until her time of purification is over. [5]If a woman gives birth to a daughter, she will be ceremonially unclean for two weeks, just as she is unclean during her menstrual period. After waiting sixty-six days, she will be purified from the bleeding of childbirth.

[6]"When the time of purification is completed for either a son or a daughter, the woman must bring a one-year-old lamb for a burnt offering and a young pigeon or turtledove for a purification offering. She must bring her offerings to the priest at the entrance of the Tabernacle.* [7]The priest will then present them to the LORD to purify her.* Then she will be ceremonially clean again after her bleeding at childbirth. These are the instructions for a woman after the birth of a son or a daughter.

[8]"If a woman cannot afford to bring a lamb, she must bring two turtledoves or two young pigeons. One will be for the burnt offering and the other for the purification offering. The priest will sacrifice them to purify her, and she will be ceremonially clean."

## Serious Skin Diseases

**13** The LORD said to Moses and Aaron, [2]"If anyone has a swelling or a rash or discolored skin that might develop into a serious skin disease,* that person must be brought to Aaron the priest or to one of his sons.* [3]The priest will examine the affected area of the skin. If the hair in the affected area has turned white and the problem appears to be more than skin-deep, it is a serious skin disease, and the priest who examines it must pronounce the person ceremonially unclean.

[4]"But if the affected area of the skin is only a white discoloration and does not appear to be more than skin-deep, and if the hair on the spot has not turned white, the priest will quarantine the person for seven days. [5]On the seventh day the priest will make another examination. If he finds the affected area has not changed and the problem has not spread on the skin, the priest will quarantine the person for seven more days. [6]On the seventh day the priest will make another examination. If he finds the affected area has faded and has not spread, the priest will pronounce the person ceremonially clean. It was only a rash. The person's clothing must be washed, and the person will be ceremonially clean. [7]But if the rash continues to spread after the person has been examined by the priest and has been pronounced clean, the infected person must return to be examined again. [8]If the priest finds that the rash has spread, he must pronounce the person ceremonially unclean, for it is indeed a skin disease.

[9]"Anyone who develops a serious skin disease must go to the priest for an examination. [10]If the priest finds a white swelling on the skin, and some hair on the spot has turned white, and there is an open sore in the affected area, [11]it is a chronic skin disease, and the priest must pronounce the person ceremonially unclean. In such cases the person need not be quarantined, for it is obvious that the skin is defiled by the disease.

[12]"Now suppose the disease has spread all over the person's skin, covering the body from head to foot. [13]When the priest examines the infected person and finds that the disease covers the entire body, he will pronounce the person ceremonially clean. Since the skin has turned completely white, the person is clean. [14]But if any open sores appear, the infected person will be pronounced ceremonially unclean. [15]The priest must make this pronouncement as soon as he sees an open sore, since open sores indicate the presence of a skin disease. [16]However, if the open sores heal and turn white like the rest of the skin, the person must return to the priest [17]for another examination. If the affected areas have indeed turned white, the priest will then pronounce the person ceremonially clean by declaring, 'You are clean!'

[18]"If anyone has a boil on the skin that has started to heal, [19]but a white swelling or a reddish white

---

**12:6** Hebrew *Tent of Meeting.* **12:7** Or *to make atonement for her;* also in 12:8. **13:2a** Traditionally rendered *leprosy.* The Hebrew word used throughout this passage is used to describe various skin diseases. **13:2b** Or *one of his descendants.*

---

**12:2-5** Various reasons have been proposed for the longer impurity period following a daughter's birth. One possibility is that, since the female infant carried the prospect of future menstrual bleeding, the mother was also thought to bear the daughter's potential for ritual uncleanness—thus necessitating the longer timeframe (see also Leviticus 15:25). Regardless, these special provisions are not meant to construe a value judgment. Women were a source of life and the continuation of God's holy people; all people bear the image of God (Genesis 1:26-27).
**13:1–14:57** Concerning the regulations pertaining to infections, the principle of normal and abnormal comes into play again (see "Holy, Clean, and Unclean" on page 143). Whether

in a person, clothing, or a building, infections are not normal: They indicate disease and death, the opposite of wholeness, and were therefore declared unclean.
**13:2** Skin disorders that were potentially contagious, such as "swelling or a rash or discolored skin," required precautions to stop their spread. Until a disorder was healed, the person was considered unclean. The diseases described in this section (Leviticus 13:1-46) may range from something as simple as an allergic rash, ringworm, or eczema to something as serious as gangrene. In Old Testament times, skin conditions were diagnosed by observation. The priests not only had a religious function but they also served as physicians.

spot develops in its place, that person must go to the priest to be examined. [20]If the priest examines it and finds it to be more than skin-deep, and if the hair in the affected area has turned white, the priest must pronounce the person ceremonially unclean. The boil has become a serious skin disease. [21]But if the priest finds no white hair on the affected area and the problem appears to be no more than skin-deep and has faded, the priest must quarantine the person for seven days. [22]If during that time the affected area spreads on the skin, the priest must pronounce the person ceremonially unclean, because it is a serious disease. [23]But if the area grows no larger and does not spread, it is merely the scar from the boil, and the priest will pronounce the person ceremonially clean.

[24]"If anyone has suffered a burn on the skin and the burned area changes color, becoming either reddish white or shiny white, [25]the priest must examine it. If he finds that the hair in the affected area has turned white and the problem appears to be more than skin-deep, a skin disease has broken out in the burn. The priest must then pronounce the person ceremonially unclean, for it is clearly a serious skin disease. [26]But if the priest finds no white hair on the affected area and the problem appears to be no more than skin-deep and has faded, the priest must quarantine the infected person for seven days. [27]On the seventh day the priest must examine the person again. If the affected area has spread on the skin, the priest must pronounce that person ceremonially unclean, for it is clearly a serious skin disease. [28]But if the affected area has not changed or spread on the skin and has faded, it is simply a swelling from the burn. The priest will then pronounce the person ceremonially clean, for it is only the scar from the burn.

[29]"If anyone, either a man or woman, has a sore on the head or chin, [30]the priest must examine it. If he finds it is more than skin-deep and has fine yellow hair on it, the priest must pronounce the person ceremonially unclean. It is a scabby sore of the head or chin. [31]If the priest examines the scabby sore and finds that it is only skin-deep but there is no black hair on it, he must quarantine the person for seven days. [32]On the seventh day the priest must examine the sore again. If he finds that the scabby sore has not spread, and there is no yellow hair on it, and it appears to be only skin-deep, [33]the person must shave off all hair except the hair on the affected area. Then the priest must quarantine the person for another seven days. [34]On the seventh day he will examine the sore again. If it has not spread and appears to be no more than skin-deep, the priest will pronounce the person ceremonially clean. The person's clothing must be washed, and the person will be ceremonially clean. [35]But if the scabby sore begins to spread after the person is pronounced clean, [36]the

priest must do another examination. If he finds that the sore has spread, the priest does not need to look for yellow hair. The infected person is ceremonially unclean. [37]But if the color of the scabby sore does not change and black hair has grown on it, it has healed. The priest will then pronounce the person ceremonially clean.

[38]"If anyone, either a man or woman, has shiny white patches on the skin, [39]the priest must examine the affected area. If he finds that the shiny patches are only pale white, this is a harmless skin rash, and the person is ceremonially clean.

[40]"If a man loses his hair and his head becomes bald, he is still ceremonially clean. [41]And if he loses hair on his forehead, he simply has a bald forehead; he is still clean. [42]However, if a reddish white sore appears on the bald area on top of his head or on his forehead, this is a skin disease. [43]The priest must examine him, and if he finds swelling around the reddish white sore anywhere on the man's head and it looks like a skin disease, [44]the man is indeed infected with a skin disease and is unclean. The priest must pronounce him ceremonially unclean because of the sore on his head.

[45]"Those who suffer from a serious skin disease must tear their clothing and leave their hair uncombed.* They must cover their mouth and call out, 'Unclean! Unclean!' [46]As long as the serious disease lasts, they will be ceremonially unclean. They must live in isolation in their place outside the camp.

## Treatment of Contaminated Clothing

[47]"Now suppose mildew* contaminates some woolen or linen clothing, [48]woolen or linen fabric, the hide of an animal, or anything made of leather. [49]If the contaminated area in the clothing, the animal hide, the fabric, or the leather article has turned greenish or reddish, it is contaminated with mildew and must be shown to the priest. [50]After examining the affected spot, the priest will put the article in quarantine for seven days. [51]On the seventh day the priest must inspect it again. If the contaminated area has spread, the clothing or fabric or leather is clearly contaminated by a serious mildew and is ceremonially unclean. [52]The priest must burn the item— the clothing, the woolen or linen fabric, or piece of leather—for it has been contaminated by a serious mildew. It must be completely destroyed by fire.

[53]"But if the priest examines it and finds that the contaminated area has not spread in the clothing, the fabric, or the leather, [54]the priest will order the object to be washed and then quarantined for seven more days. [55]Then the priest must examine the object again. If he finds that the contaminated area has not changed color after being washed, even if it did not spread, the object is defiled. It must be completely burned up, whether the contaminated spot* is on the inside or outside. [56]But if the priest

13:45 Or *and uncover their heads.*　13:47 Traditionally rendered *leprosy.* The Hebrew term used throughout this passage is the same term used for the various skin diseases described in 13:1-46.　13:55 The meaning of the Hebrew is uncertain.

examines it and finds that the contaminated area has faded after being washed, he must cut the spot from the clothing, the fabric, or the leather. ⁵⁷If the spot later reappears on the clothing, the fabric, or the leather article, the mildew is clearly spreading, and the contaminated object must be burned up. ⁵⁸But if the spot disappears from the clothing, the fabric, or the leather article after it has been washed, it must be washed again; then it will be ceremonially clean.

⁵⁹"These are the instructions for dealing with mildew that contaminates woolen or linen clothing or fabric or anything made of leather. This is how the priest will determine whether these items are ceremonially clean or unclean."

## Cleansing from Skin Diseases

14 And the LORD said to Moses, ²"The following instructions are for those seeking ceremonial purification from a skin disease.* Those who have been healed must be brought to the priest, ³who will examine them at a place outside the camp. If the priest finds that someone has been healed of a serious skin disease, ⁴he will perform a purification ceremony, using two live birds that are ceremonially clean, a stick of cedar,* some scarlet yarn, and a hyssop branch. ⁵The priest will order that one bird be slaughtered over a clay pot filled with fresh water. ⁶He will take the live bird, the cedar stick, the scarlet yarn, and the hyssop branch, and dip them into the blood of the bird that was slaughtered over the fresh water. ⁷The priest will then sprinkle the blood of the dead bird seven times on the person being purified of the skin disease. When the priest has purified the person, he will release the live bird in the open field to fly away.

⁸"The persons being purified must then wash their clothes, shave off all their hair, and bathe themselves in water. Then they will be ceremonially clean and may return to the camp. However, they must remain outside their tents for seven days. ⁹On the seventh day they must again shave all the hair from their heads, including the hair of the beard and eyebrows. They must also wash their clothes and bathe themselves in water. Then they will be ceremonially clean.

¹⁰"On the eighth day each person being purified must bring two male lambs and a one-year-old female lamb, all with no defects, along with a grain offering of six quarts* of choice flour moistened with

olive oil, and a cup* of olive oil. ¹¹Then the officiating priest will present that person for purification, along with the offerings, before the LORD at the entrance of the Tabernacle.* ¹²The priest will take one of the male lambs and the olive oil and present them as a guilt offering, lifting them up as a special offering before the LORD. ¹³He will then slaughter the male lamb in the sacred area where sin offerings and burnt offerings are slaughtered. As with the sin offering, the guilt offering belongs to the priest. It is a most holy offering. ¹⁴The priest will then take some of the blood of the guilt offering and apply it to the lobe of the right ear, the thumb of the right hand, and the big toe of the right foot of the person being purified.

¹⁵"Then the priest will pour some of the olive oil into the palm of his own left hand. ¹⁶He will dip his right finger into the oil in his palm and sprinkle some of it with his finger seven times before the LORD. ¹⁷The priest will then apply some of the oil in his palm over the blood from the guilt offering that is on the lobe of the right ear, the thumb of the right hand, and the big toe of the right foot of the person being purified. ¹⁸The priest will apply the oil remaining in his hand to the head of the person being purified. Through this process, the priest will purify* the person before the LORD.

¹⁹"Then the priest must present the sin offering to purify the person who was cured of the skin disease. After that, the priest will slaughter the burnt offering ²⁰and offer it on the altar along with the grain offering. Through this process, the priest will purify the person who was healed, and the person will be ceremonially clean.

²¹"But anyone who is too poor and cannot afford these offerings may bring one male lamb for a guilt offering, to be lifted up as a special offering for purification. The person must also bring two quarts* of choice flour moistened with olive oil for the grain offering and a cup of olive oil. ²²The offering must also include two turtledoves or two young pigeons, whichever the person can afford. One of the pair must be used for the sin offering and the other for a burnt offering. ²³On the eighth day of the purification ceremony, the person being purified must bring the offerings to the priest in the LORD's presence at the entrance of the Tabernacle. ²⁴The priest will take the lamb for the guilt offering, along with the olive oil, and lift them up as a special offering to the LORD. ²⁵Then the priest will slaughter the lamb for the guilt offering. He will take

14:2 Traditionally rendered *leprosy;* see note on 13:2a.   14:4 Or *juniper;* also in 14:6, 49, 51.   14:10a Hebrew ³⁄₁₀ *of an ephah* [6.6 liters].   14:10b Hebrew *1 log* [0.3 liters]; also in 14:21.   14:11 Hebrew *Tent of Meeting;* also in 14:23.   14:18 Or *will make atonement for;* similarly in 14:19, 20, 21, 29, 31, 53.   14:21 Hebrew ¹⁄₁₀ *of an ephah* [2.2 liters].

14:1-32 These verses, dealing with the purification of infected individuals, are best understood when read in conjunction with 13:1-46.
14:15-18 In the ancient world, olive oil was commonly used to aid healing (see Isaiah 1:6 where "soothing ointments" could

alternately be translated "olive oil"; Luke 10:34). Its use here might symbolize the healing and cleansing of the infection, which allowed the person to return to the community. Perhaps it also represented restored union between God, the priest, and the worshiper.

some of its blood and apply it to the lobe of the right ear, the thumb of the right hand, and the big toe of the right foot of the person being purified. ²⁶"The priest will also pour some of the olive oil into the palm of his own left hand. ²⁷He will dip his right finger into the oil in his palm and sprinkle some of it seven times before the LORD. ²⁸The priest will then apply some of the oil in his palm over the blood from the guilt offering that is on the lobe of the right ear, the thumb of the right hand, and the big toe of the right foot of the person being purified. ²⁹The priest will apply the oil remaining in his hand to the head of the person being purified. Through this process, the priest will purify the person before the LORD.

³⁰"Then the priest will offer the two turtledoves or the two young pigeons, whichever the person can afford. ³¹One of them is for a sin offering and the other for a burnt offering, to be presented along with the grain offering. Through this process, the priest will purify the person before the LORD. ³²These are the instructions for purification for those who have recovered from a serious skin disease but who cannot afford to bring the offerings normally required for the ceremony of purification."

## Treatment of Contaminated Houses

³³Then the LORD said to Moses and Aaron, ³⁴"When you arrive in Canaan, the land I am giving you as your own possession, I may contaminate some of the houses in your land with mildew.* ³⁵The owner of such a house must then go to the priest and say, 'It appears that my house has some kind of mildew.' ³⁶Before the priest goes in to inspect the house, he must have the house emptied so nothing inside will be pronounced ceremonially unclean. ³⁷Then the priest will go in and examine the mildew on the walls. If he finds greenish or reddish streaks and the contamination appears to go deeper than the wall's surface, ³⁸the priest will step outside the door and put the house in quarantine for seven days. ³⁹On the seventh day the priest must return for another inspection. If he finds that the mildew on the walls of the house has spread, ⁴⁰the priest must order that the stones from those areas be removed. The contaminated material will then be taken outside the town to an area designated as ceremonially unclean. ⁴¹Next the inside walls of the entire house must be scraped thoroughly and the scrapings dumped in the unclean place outside the town. ⁴²Other stones will be brought in to replace the ones that were removed, and the walls will be replastered.

⁴³"But if the mildew reappears after all the stones have been replaced and the house has been scraped and replastered, ⁴⁴the priest must return and inspect the house again. If he finds that the mildew has spread, the walls are clearly contaminated with a serious mildew, and the house is defiled. ⁴⁵It must be torn down, and all its stones, timbers, and plaster must be carried out of town to the place designated as ceremonially unclean. ⁴⁶Those who enter the house during the period of quarantine will be ceremonially unclean until evening, ⁴⁷and all who sleep or eat in the house must wash their clothing.

⁴⁸"But if the priest returns for his inspection and finds that the mildew has not reappeared in the house after the fresh plastering, he will pronounce it clean because the mildew is clearly gone. ⁴⁹To purify the house the priest must take two birds, a stick of cedar, some scarlet yarn, and a hyssop branch. ⁵⁰He will slaughter one of the birds over a clay pot filled with fresh water. ⁵¹He will take the cedar stick, the hyssop branch, the scarlet yarn, and the live bird, and dip them into the blood of the slaughtered bird and into the fresh water. Then he will sprinkle the house seven times. ⁵²When the priest has purified the house in exactly this way, ⁵³he will release the live bird in the open fields outside the town. Through this process, the priest will purify the house, and it will be ceremonially clean.

⁵⁴"These are the instructions for dealing with serious skin diseases,* including scabby sores; ⁵⁵and mildew,* whether on clothing or in a house; ⁵⁶and a swelling on the skin, a rash, or discolored skin. ⁵⁷This procedure will determine whether a person or object is ceremonially clean or unclean.

"These are the instructions regarding skin diseases and mildew."

## Bodily Discharges

**15** The LORD said to Moses and Aaron, ²"Give the following instructions to the people of Israel.

"Any man who has a bodily discharge is ceremonially unclean. ³This defilement is caused by his discharge, whether the discharge continues or stops. In either case the man is unclean. ⁴Any bed on which the man with the discharge lies and anything on which he sits will be ceremonially unclean. ⁵So if you touch the man's bed, you must wash your clothes and bathe yourself in water, and you will remain unclean until evening. ⁶If you sit where the man with the discharge has sat, you must wash your clothes and bathe yourself in water, and you will remain unclean until evening. ⁷If you touch the man with the discharge, you must wash your clothes and bathe yourself in water, and you will remain unclean until evening. ⁸If the man spits on you, you must wash your clothes and bathe yourself in water, and you will remain unclean until evening. ⁹Any saddle blanket on

---

14:34 Traditionally rendered *leprosy;* see note on 13:47.   14:54 Traditionally rendered *leprosy;* see note on 13:2a.
14:55 Traditionally rendered *leprosy;* see note on 13:47.

---

**14:33-53** The contamination of buildings by rot or mildew made them unhealthy or even unsafe. These buildings were considered diseased and therefore not whole or clean (see "Holy, Clean, and Unclean" on page 143). The inspection and treatment process was similar to the one for mildew in clothing (13:47-59).

which the man rides will be ceremonially unclean. [10]If you touch anything that was under the man, you will be unclean until evening. You must wash your clothes and bathe yourself in water, and you will remain unclean until evening. [11]If the man touches you without first rinsing his hands, you must wash your clothes and bathe yourself in water, and you will remain unclean until evening. [12]Any clay pot the man touches must be broken, and any wooden utensil he touches must be rinsed with water.

[13]"When the man with the discharge is healed, he must count off seven days for the period of purification. Then he must wash his clothes and bathe himself in fresh water, and he will be ceremonially clean. [14]On the eighth day he must get two turtledoves or two young pigeons and come before the LORD at the entrance of the Tabernacle* and give his offerings to the priest. [15]The priest will offer one bird for a sin offering and the other for a burnt offering. Through this process, the priest will purify* the man before the LORD for his discharge.

[16]"Whenever a man has an emission of semen, he must bathe his entire body in water, and he will remain ceremonially unclean until the next evening.* [17]Any clothing or leather with semen on it must be washed in water, and it will remain unclean until evening. [18]After a man and a woman have sexual intercourse, they must each bathe in water, and they will remain unclean until the next evening.

[19]"Whenever a woman has her menstrual period, she will be ceremonially unclean for seven days. Anyone who touches her during that time will be unclean until evening. [20]Anything on which the woman lies or sits during the time of her period will be unclean. [21]If any of you touch her bed, you must wash your clothes and bathe yourself in water, and you will remain unclean until evening. [22]If you touch any object she has sat on, you must wash your clothes and bathe yourself in water, and you will remain unclean until evening. [23]This includes her bed or any other object she has sat on; you will be unclean until evening if you touch it. [24]If a man has sexual intercourse with her and her blood touches him, her menstrual impurity will be transmitted to him. He will remain unclean for seven days, and any bed on which he lies will be unclean.

[25]"If a woman has a flow of blood for many days that is unrelated to her menstrual period, or if the blood continues beyond the normal period, she is ceremonially unclean. As during her menstrual period, the woman will be unclean as long as the discharge continues. [26]Any bed she lies on and any object she sits on during that time will be unclean, just as during her normal menstrual period. [27]If any of you touch these things, you will be ceremonially unclean. You must wash your clothes and bathe yourself in water, and you will remain unclean until evening.

[28]"When the woman's bleeding stops, she must count off seven days. Then she will be ceremonially clean. [29]On the eighth day she must bring two turtledoves or two young pigeons and present them to the priest at the entrance of the Tabernacle. [30]The priest will offer one for a sin offering and the other for a burnt offering. Through this process, the priest will purify her before the LORD for the ceremonial impurity caused by her bleeding.

[31]"This is how you will guard the people of Israel from ceremonial uncleanness. Otherwise they would die, for their impurity would defile my Tabernacle that stands among them. [32]These are the instructions for dealing with anyone who has a bodily discharge—a man who is unclean because of an emission of semen, [33]or a woman during her menstrual period. It applies to any man or woman who has a bodily discharge, and to a man who has sexual intercourse with a woman who is ceremonially unclean."

## The Day of Atonement

**16** The LORD spoke to Moses after the death of Aaron's two sons, who died after they entered the LORD's presence and burned the wrong kind of fire before him. [2]The LORD said to Moses, "Warn your brother, Aaron, not to enter the Most Holy Place behind the inner curtain whenever he chooses; if he does, he will die. For the Ark's cover—the place of atonement—is there, and I myself am present in the cloud above the atonement cover.

[3]"When Aaron enters the sanctuary area, he must follow these instructions fully. He must bring a young bull for a sin offering and a ram for a burnt offering. [4]He must put on his linen tunic and the linen undergarments worn next to his body. He must tie the linen sash around his waist and put the linen turban on his head. These are sacred garments, so he must bathe himself in water before he puts them on.

**15:14** Hebrew *Tent of Meeting;* also in 15:29.   **15:15** Or *will make atonement for;* also in 15:30.   **15:16** Hebrew *until evening;* also in 15:18.

**15:19-30** Similar practices for handling impurity have appeared across many different cultures. For the ancient Israelites, periods of uncleanness—when a person was unable to touch something set apart as holy—could result from numerous scenarios. Such impurity often related to life and death—including the birth of a child or contact with a dead body. Blood represented life (Deuteronomy 12:23), a principle that probably informed the instructions here regarding menstruation. The types of offerings given after abnormal bleeding and childbirth were the same (Leviticus 12:6; 15:29). The so-called sin offering in 15:30

is better understood as a purification offering, as in 12:6; it was morally neutral.
**16:1-34** The Israelite Day of Atonement (Yom Kippur) involved fasting, resting from work, and performing a sacrificial rite that cleansed both the sacred space and the people. This ritual ceremony provides the background for understanding Jesus' sacrificial death. Hebrews 9:11-28 describes Jesus as the ultimate high priest who entered the heavenly temple and made a one-time sacrifice of his own life, making all those who follow him right with God (see also 1 John 2:1-2).

⁵Aaron must take from the community of Israel two male goats for a sin offering and a ram for a burnt offering.

⁶"Aaron will present his own bull as a sin offering to purify himself and his family, making them right with the LORD.* ⁷Then he must take the two male goats and present them to the LORD at the entrance of the Tabernacle.* ⁸He is to cast sacred lots to determine which goat will be reserved as an offering to the LORD and which will carry the sins of the people to the wilderness of Azazel. ⁹Aaron will then present as a sin offering the goat chosen by lot for the LORD. ¹⁰The other goat, the scapegoat chosen by lot to be sent away, will be kept alive, standing before the LORD. When it is sent away to Azazel in the wilderness, the people will be purified and made right with the LORD.*

¹¹"Aaron will present his own bull as a sin offering to purify himself and his family, making them right with the LORD. After he has slaughtered the bull as a sin offering, ¹²he will fill an incense burner with burning coals from the altar that stands before the LORD. Then he will take two handfuls of fragrant powdered incense and will carry the burner and the incense behind the inner curtain. ¹³There in the LORD's presence he will put the incense on the burning coals so that a cloud of incense will rise over the Ark's cover—the place of atonement—that rests on the Ark of the Covenant.* If he follows these instructions, he will not die. ¹⁴Then he must take some of the blood of the bull, dip his finger in it, and sprinkle it on the east side of the atonement cover. He must sprinkle blood seven times with his finger in front of the atonement cover.

¹⁵"Then Aaron must slaughter the first goat as a sin offering for the people and carry its blood behind the inner curtain. There he will sprinkle the goat's blood over the atonement cover and in front of it, just as he did with the bull's blood. ¹⁶Through this process, he will purify* the Most Holy Place, and he will do the same for the entire Tabernacle, because of the defiling sin and rebellion of the Israelites. ¹⁷No one else is allowed inside the Tabernacle when Aaron enters it for the purification ceremony in the Most Holy Place. No one may enter until he comes out again after purifying himself, his family, and all the congregation of Israel, making them right with the LORD. ¹⁸"Then Aaron will come out to purify the altar that stands before the LORD. He will do this by taking some of the blood from the bull and the goat and

putting it on each of the horns of the altar. ¹⁹Then he must sprinkle the blood with his finger seven times over the altar. In this way, he will cleanse it from Israel's defilement and make it holy.

²⁰"When Aaron has finished purifying the Most Holy Place and the Tabernacle and the altar, he must present the live goat. ²¹He will lay both of his hands on the goat's head and confess over it all the wickedness, rebellion, and sins of the people of Israel. In this way, he will transfer the people's sins to the head of the goat. Then a man specially chosen for the task will drive the goat into the wilderness. ²²As the goat goes into the wilderness, it will carry all the people's sins upon itself into a desolate land.

²³"When Aaron goes back into the Tabernacle, he must take off the linen garments he was wearing when he entered the Most Holy Place, and he must leave the garments there. ²⁴Then he must bathe himself with water in a sacred place, put on his regular garments, and go out to sacrifice a burnt offering for himself and a burnt offering for the people. Through this process, he will purify himself and the people, making them right with the LORD. ²⁵He must then burn all the fat of the sin offering on the altar.

²⁶"The man chosen to drive the scapegoat into the wilderness of Azazel must wash his clothes and bathe himself in water. Then he may return to the camp.

²⁷"The bull and the goat presented as sin offerings, whose blood Aaron takes into the Most Holy Place for the purification ceremony, will be carried outside the camp. The animals' hides, internal organs, and dung are all to be burned. ²⁸The man who burns them must wash his clothes and bathe himself in water before returning to the camp.

²⁹"On the tenth day of the appointed month in early autumn,* you must deny yourselves.* Neither native-born Israelites nor foreigners living among you may do any kind of work. This is a permanent law for you. ³⁰On that day offerings of purification will be made for you,* and you will be purified in the LORD's presence from all your sins. ³¹It will be a Sabbath day of complete rest for you, and you must deny yourselves. This is a permanent law for you. ³²In future generations, the purification* ceremony will be performed by the priest who has been anointed and ordained to serve as high priest in place of his ancestor Aaron. He will put on the holy linen garments ³³and purify the Most Holy Place, the Tabernacle, the

16:6 Or *to make atonement for himself and his family;* similarly in 16:11, 17b, 24, 34. 16:7 Hebrew *Tent of Meeting;* also in 16:16, 17, 20, 23, 33. 16:10 Or *wilderness, it will make atonement for the people.* 16:13 Hebrew *that is above the Testimony.* The Hebrew word for "testimony" refers to the terms of the LORD's covenant with Israel as written on stone tablets, which were kept in the Ark, and also to the covenant itself. 16:16 Or *make atonement for;* similarly in 16:17a, 18, 20, 27, 33. 16:29a Hebrew *On the tenth day of the seventh month.* This day in the ancient Hebrew lunar calendar occurred in September or October. 16:29b Or *must fast;* also in 16:31. 16:30 Or *atonement will be made for you, to purify you.* 16:32 Or *atonement.*

17:1–26:46 This section deals with how the community of Israel was to observe holiness. Holiness does not describe one attribute of God among many. Rather, it is the sum of all the attributes of his perfect person, nature, and character.

His "glory" is the manifestation of these attributes (see 9:6). God's covenant with Israel meant that the people and the nation participated in God's holiness. This holiness depended on Israel's right relationship with God, which brought certain ethical and ritual expectations for Israel to uphold.